CH00658936

ISBN: 9781313498784

Published by:
HardPress Publishing
8345 NW 66TH ST #2561
MIAMI FL 33166-2626

Email: info@hardpress.net
Web: http://www.hardpress.net

Cornell University Library

Ithaca, New York

BOUGHT WITH THE INCOME OF THE

SAGE ENDOWMENT FUND

THE GIFT OF

HENRY W. SAGE

1891

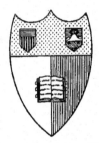

Date Due

AUG 31 1945

JAN 4 1946

~~NOV 25 1960 H S~~

~~MAR 21 1961~~

~~INTERLIBRARY LOAN~~

SEP 2003

Cornell University Library
PK 6415.B88
Press and poetry of modern Pe
3 1924 026 905 7(

THE PRESS AND POETRY OF MODERN PERSIA

CAMBRIDGE UNIVERSITY PRESS
C. F. CLAY, MANAGER
London: FETTER LANE, E.C.
Edinburgh: 100 PRINCES STREET

Berlin: A. ASHER AND CO.
Leipzig: F. A. BROCKHAUS
New York: G. P. PUTNAM'S SONS
Bombay and Calcutta: MACMILLAN AND CO., LTD.
Toronto: J. M. DENT AND SONS, LTD.
Tokyo: THE MARUZEN-KABUSHIKI-KAISHA

All rights reserved

Superstitious veneration of a *Mullá*

(From *Mullá Naṣru'd-Dín*, No. 36, Oct. 7, 1907, a Caucasian Turkish illustrated comic weekly, published at Tiflís)

THE

PRESS AND POETRY

OF

MODERN PERSIA

PARTLY BASED ON THE MANUSCRIPT WORK

OF

MÍRZÁ MUḤAMMAD ʿALÍ KHÁN "TARBIYAT"
OF TABRÍZ

by

EDWARD G. BROWNE

M.A., M.B., F.B.A., F.R.C.P.

Sir Thomas Adams' Professor of Arabic
and Fellow of Pembroke College in the
University of Cambridge

Cambridge:
at the University Press
1914

A.50075

Cambridge:
PRINTED BY JOHN CLAY, M.A.
AT THE UNIVERSITY PRESS

TABLE OF CONTENTS

تمنّای مخصوص از قارئین ایرانی *At end*

LIST OF ILLUSTRATIONS

ERRATUM

On p. 294, l. 20, second half, read :—

وزیرِ محتشم عنوان پرستد،

THE TRANSLATOR'S PREFACE

THIS book treats of two different though kindred subjects, the Persian Press, more particularly Persian Journalism, and the political and patriotic poetry of Modern Persia; in other words, with two aspects of Persian literary activity in recent years, especially since the Proclamation of the Constitution in 1906. It falls, therefore, into two distinct parts, of the first of which I am the translator, and of the second the compiler. Of each of these two parts something must now be said.

Part I (pp. 1–166) contains as complete a list of Persian newspapers, with particulars concerning each, as it has been possible to compile, preceded by a Preface and Introduction (pp. 1–6 and 7–26), and followed by a brief essay on some of the more important products of the Persian Press other than newspapers, especially such as conduced, directly or indirectly, to the "Awakening of Persia" (pp. 154–166). The whole of this portion is translated from a Persian treatise, at present unpublished, entitled, for reasons explained by the Author, Mírzá Muḥammad 'Alí Khán "Tarbiyat," at p. 5 of his Preface, "A Page from the History of the products of the Persian Press[1]"; and all that I have done besides translating it is to add a few explanatory foot-notes (the majority of which, however, are the Author's) and to append to the description of each newspaper in smaller type some additional particulars concerning its size, price, etc., derived from the inspection of copies in my own possession, of which, thanks to the generosity of Mr H. L. Rabino, whereof I shall shortly speak, I have a fairly extensive collection. It is important that the reader should bear in mind that these

[1] ورقی از دفتر تأریخ مطبوعات ایرانی و فارسی

paragraphs in smaller type are added by myself to the original articles, in order that he may not be puzzled by occasional discrepancies which appear between them and the paragraphs in larger type which precede them; for on the one hand I have not thought it right to modify (save in a few cases of evident inadvertence) the sense of the Author's statements, and on the other I have indicated, whenever reference to a copy of the paper in question was possible, the result of my own observations, inasmuch as the Author wrote in exile, for the most part from memory and scanty notes, and, as he has explained in his Preface (pp. 1–3), was unable to refer to the rich material which he had collected for the compilation of this work, and which is now, unhappily, lost beyond recall.

The Author's work, as he has explained in his Preface, was prior in conception, though subsequent in execution, to that of Mr H. L. Rabino, who was, until about two years ago, British Vice-Consul at Rasht in Persia, and is now at Saffi in Morocco. Mr Rabino, whom I have never had the pleasure of meeting, is one of those consular officers who take delight in devoting the time which they can spare from their official duties to the careful study of the language, history, literature, antiquities, customs and resources of the country in which they find themselves, and it is a matter of profound regret rather than of surprise that one so well acquainted with and so sympathetic to the Persians, and so well instructed in all that concerns them and their country, should have been removed thence to a distant and (I imagine) uncongenial post. At all events he made the best use of his time in Rasht, which has in many ways been fruitful of valuable results, especially in the domains of history, geography and geology, and not least in this hitherto almost unexplored field of Persian Journalism. In 1911 he published at Rasht what is, so far as I know, the first systematic treatise on this subject, a Persian pamphlet of 29 large pages (measuring 35 × 22·5 centimetres), printed at the *'Urwatu'l-Wuthqá* Press, of which the full title, both in Persian and English, and some description are given at pp. 2–3 of the Author's Preface and in the foot-notes thereto. In a short Preface of two pages he sketches the history of Persian Journalism from its beginnings (in or about 1848) down to the time of writing (August 29, 1911). This Preface is followed (pp. 6–25) by a list of 243 papers, arranged alphabetically, published in Persian or in Persia[1]. Each page is divided into ten columns, of which the first contains the ordinal number of the paper in the list, the second the title of the paper, the third the place of publication, the fourth the intervals of publication (daily, weekly, fortnightly, monthly, etc.), the fifth the method of production (print, lithography, or "jelly-graphy"), the sixth the date of inception, the seventh the date of conclusion, the eighth the political tendency, the ninth the name of the proprietor or editor, and the tenth and last any additional observations. Of the papers enumerated Nos. 1–226 are Persian, Turkish or Arabic, Nos. 227–230 French, and Nos. 231–236 Armenian, while Nos. 237–243 are additional Persian papers omitted in their proper place. Blank spaces are left, numbered 244–269, for additional entries, while the last two pages (28–29) contain a list of *errata*.

A French translation of Mr Rabino's Persian pamphlet by M. L. Buvat appeared in the *Revue du Monde Musulman* for 1913 (pp. 287–315). It was made, I believe, without Mr Rabino's knowledge or concurrence, and, by reason of mistranslations and omissions, is regarded by him as not wholly satisfactory. I possess a copy of these pages with numerous annotations and corrections in Mr Rabino's hand. One distinctive merit, however, it possesses, for foot-notes are added which give "*les principales indications bibliographiques, les comptes rendus et les Traductions* in extenso *donnés par la* Revue *des journaux persans.*"

In English, so far as I know, little has hitherto appeared on the Persian Press, except a small brochure of my own, originally delivered as a lecture to and afterwards published by the Persia Society under the title of *the Persian Press and Persian Journalism*[2], which was practically a very brief *résumé* of this present work, and, like it, owes whatever value it possesses to

[1] As in the present treatise, mention is made of all Persian newspapers, whether published in Persia or abroad, and of all papers, whether in Persian or in some other language (Armenian, Syriac, Turkish, French, etc.), published in Persia. This is what is meant in the title of this work by *Írání* (*i.e.* published in the Persian Kingdom) and *Fársí* (published in the Persian language).

[2] The lecture was delivered on May 23, 1913, and was afterwards published for the Society by John Hogg, 13, Paternoster Row, London, at the price of one shilling. It contains 28 pages.

the work of Mr Rabino and Mírzá Muḥammad 'Alí Khán "Tarbiyat." The *Times*, which, in pursuance of the reactionary and obscurantist policy which generally characterizes its views on Eastern politics, made some disparaging remarks on the "mischievous and dangerous" character of "the free Press of Persia" and "other Oriental lands" in its issue of July 2, 1908, published a short article on the subject on October 29, 1909[1]; while the *Standard* of November 15, 1909, contained a good and sympathetic account of Sayyid Ḥasan, the editor of the daily Ṭihrán *Ḥablu'l-Matín*, who had recently been imprisoned on the charge of speaking disrespectfully of the religion of Islám. Towards the end of May, 1910, the English daily press also contained some account of the protests evoked amongst Persian journalists by the suppression of the *Sharq*, and the violent scenes to which this high-handed measure gave rise in the National Assembly. The *Times* of June 28, 1910, again, contained some account of the printers' strike at Ṭihrán. The *Manchester Guardian* of September 28, 1910, contained an article on "Persian newspapers and their work." Lastly, the almost complete suppression of the Press on December 26, 1911, two days after the forcible closure of the National Assembly, was chronicled in several English papers. A certain amount of information about Persian newspapers, together with several translations of articles from some of them, is also contained in my *History of the Persian Revolution*, published in October, 1910.

As one would expect, the fortunes of the Press in Persia follow very closely those of the Constitutional Movement. Before the granting of the Constitution by Muẓaffaru'd-Dín Sháh in August, 1906, but few newspapers were published in Persia, and these were politically of no account, and only valuable, when they had any value at all, from the literary

[1] The disparaging article appeared ten days after the now deposed Sháh, Muḥammad 'Alí, had succeeded, with the aid of Colonel Liakhoff and the other Russian officers in his service, in destroying the First National Assembly, and when his cause appeared to have triumphed. The second article, which, though far from sympathetic, at least takes the Persian Press more or less seriously and gives a few more or less accurate facts about it, was written shortly after the Nationalist triumph and the deposition of the ex-Sháh. No one has ever accused Printing House Square of being "the home of lost causes."

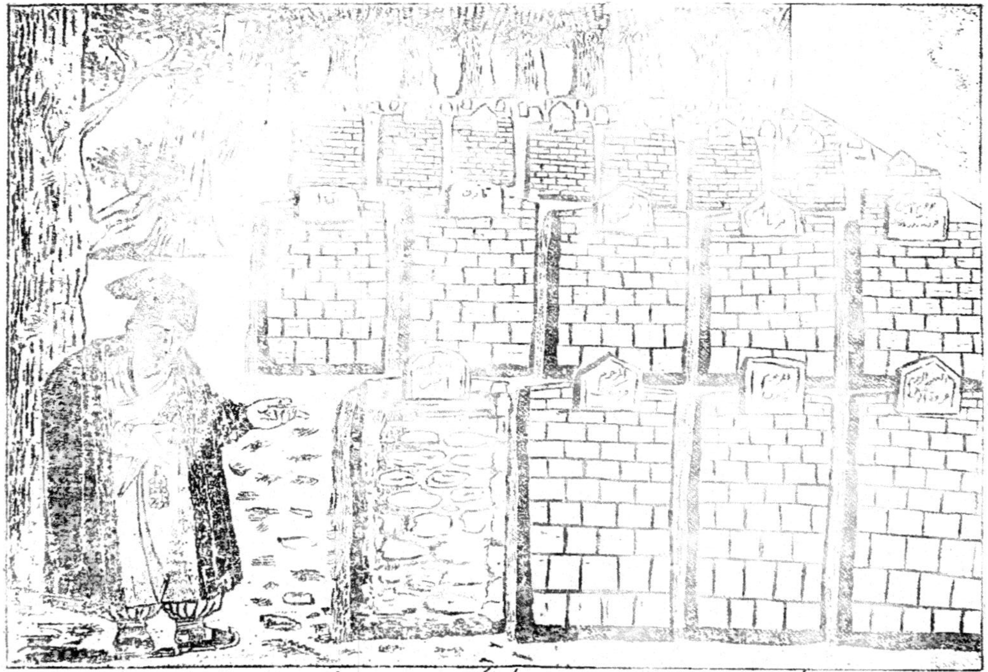

آفرین بر همت مسلمانان عجب سعی کرده و این قبرستان را آباد نموده اند با این ترقی بعضیها می گویند که مسلمانها خوابیده اند لا اله الا الله !!! افترا افترا تهمت !!!

The Cemetery of deceased Newspapers

(From the illustrated comic weekly *Ázarbáyján*, No. 6, March 30, 1907)

point of view, on account of the poems and critical articles which they occasionally contained. In the latter part of 1906 several important newspapers, printed with moveable types, began to appear, such as the *Majlis* (on November 25, 1906) and the *Nidá-yi-Waṭan* a month later. During the following year (1907) many more appeared, and the number continued to increase until the *Coup d'État* of June 23, 1908, which marked the beginning of the period known to the Persians as "the Minor Despotism" or "Lesser Autocracy" (*Istibdád-i-Ṣaghír*), when the free Press was practically destroyed for the time being. As the Constitutional forces began to rally and make headway in Gílán and Iṣfahán, the Press also began to revive in these localities, until, on the triumphant entry of the victorious Nationalists into Ṭihrán and the deposition of Muḥammad 'Alí in July, 1909, it speedily attained a luxuriance even greater than during the "First Constitutional Period," and (save for a brief period in August, 1910, after the fighting which attended the disarmament of the *fidá'ís* in Ṭihrán, when for some days the *Istiqlál-i-Írán* was the only paper appearing in the capital) continued in this flourishing condition until the forcible closure of the Second National Assembly and the violent aggressions of Russia during the last days of 1911. Since that time it has again been in abeyance: the only notable papers published in Ṭihrán since the beginning of 1912 are, so far as I know, the official or semi-official *Áftáb* ("Sun"), and the rather more independent *Írán-i-Kunúní* ("Present Persia")[1]; while at Tabríz, Rasht and Mashhad Russian brutality has effectually extinguished not only the Press, but every other manifestation of Liberalism and national life. Two infamous reactionary and anti-patriotic papers, the *Fikr* ("Thought") and the *Tawfíq* ("Divine Favour"), were successively promoted and subsidized by the Russians in Tabríz, but to describe them as worthless would be to pay them too high a compliment.

Of the Persian newspapers published outside Persia, which are naturally much more independent of political events in that

[1] The *Barq* ("Lightning") has since reappeared, No. 1 "of the Fifth Year" being dated October 12, 1913. Since November 27, 1913, it has changed its name to *Ra'd* ("Thunder").

country than those published within its borders, the most important have been or are the *Akhtar* ("Star"), printed at Constantinople (1875–1895); the *Qánún* (1889–1890) in London; the *Ḥablu'l-Matín* (Calcutta) founded in 1893 and still continuing; the *Thurayyá* (1898–9) and *Parwarish* (1900), printed in Cairo; the *Ḥikmat* and *Chihra-numá*, founded in Egypt in 1892–3 and 1904–5 respectively, and still continuing; and the *Shams* ("Sun") of Constantinople, founded in 1909 and still continuing.

During the greater part of the Constitutional Period I regularly received a certain number of the principal papers, such as the *Majlis*, *Nidá-yi-Waṭan*, *Tamaddun*, *Ṣúr-i-Isráfíl*, *Musáwát*, *Ḥablu'l-Matín* and *Ṣubḥ-i-Ṣádiq* during the First Constitutional Period; and the *Írán-i-Naw*, *Barq*, *Sharq*, *'Aṣr*, *Waqt*, etc. during the Second. I also inherited a number of papers left by Shaykh Ḥasan of Tabríz, formerly teacher of Persian in this University, on his return to Persia. Yet my collection would have been very imperfect had it not been for the extraordinary generosity of Mr H. L. Rabino, who, on his transference from Rasht to Morocco, presented me with the whole of his extensive and valuable collection, which contained complete or almost complete sets of several papers, especially of those published in Rasht, such as the *Nasím-i-Shimál*, *Kinkásh*, *Ṣadá-yi-Rasht*, *Gílán* and *Khayru'l-Kalám*, and some specimens at least of nearly all the papers mentioned in his pamphlet. Thanks to this act of generosity, I believe that I possess the most complete and extensive collection of Persian newspapers which exists outside Persia, and this has been of enormous help to me in the preparation of the present work.

One notable feature of the modern Persian Press is the large amount of excellent verse which is to be found in it, especially in the Rasht papers enumerated at the end of the preceding paragraph, in the *Bahár* of Mashhad, and in the *Ṣúr-i-Isráfíl*, *Írán-i-Naw* and other organs of the Ṭihrán Press. Much of this verse is "topical," referring to the stirring events of the recent Revolution and the principal *dramatis personæ*; or patriotic, inciting the youth of Persia to deeds of heroism and self-sacrifice; or satirical. It is, in my opinion, of great interest both from the historical and the literary points of view, and is often equally remarkable for its merit and its originality. As it has hitherto remained almost unnoticed in Europe, I have thought it desirable to include in this volume a selection of these recent patriotic and political poems, chosen more or less at random out of a great number contained in the bound volumes of newspapers in my possession, or supplied to me by some of my Persian friends and correspondents, to whom I here desire to tender my sincere thanks.

Part II of this book (pp. 167–308), which is devoted to these poems, is, therefore, an addition made by myself to the original book of which the translation constitutes Part I. Certain European students of Persian whose researches stop short at the period which, four hundred years ago, produced Jámí, the most celebrated of the later "classical" poets, and his contemporary Dawlatsháh, the most widely-read and one of the least trustworthy of their biographers, constantly assert that there is no modern Persian poetry worth reading, a statement which I can only account for by supposing that they have not taken the trouble to look for it or read it, but which is nevertheless widely credited. In a lecture on *the Literature of Persia* which I delivered before the Persia Society on April 26, 1912[1], I spoke briefly of this modern poetry, and gave some specimens of it, and after the lecture several of those present expressed surprise at learning that there was any modern poetry to speak of. This determined me to devote some attention to the refutation of a pernicious error chiefly attributable to the rarity of intimate relations between the literary worlds of Europe and Asia, but fostered and encouraged to some extent by those who desire for political reasons to represent such Asiatic peoples as the Persians as entirely decadent and degenerate, whereas in fact they have during the last eight years shown a vitality which, under happier circumstances, had it been unimpeded by malignant external forces entirely beyond the control of the Persian people, would, I am firmly convinced, have ultimately effected the moral and material regeneration of the country.

[1] Published for the Society by John Hogg, 13, Paternoster Row, London, E.C., price one shilling.

Of this renewed vitality the modern Press and Poetry are a reflection and manifestation, and I venture to think that neither the originality nor the merit of the literary products of the Persian Revolution, whether in prose or verse, will be denied by any competent and unprejudiced observer. True literature is the mirror of contemporary thought and sentiment, and the alternating phases of hope and despair of the Persians during the last eight years (1905–1913) are well reflected in the ephemeral literature of that period. It is for this reason that I have, as far as possible, arranged the poetical selections which conclude this volume in chronological order, and have chosen specimens representative of all the principal types, ranging from the classical *musammaṭ*, *mustazád* and *mathnawí* to the popular ballad (*taṣníf*) often abounding in slang and dialect.

At this point it may not be out of place to insert a few particulars concerning some half-dozen contemporary Persian poets, most of whom are represented in Part II of this book, which were supplied to me in January, 1913, by Mírzá Ḥusayn Káẓim-záda, to whose help the latter portion of this book owes much.

1. *Bahár Maliku'sh-Shu'ará* ("the King of Poets").

"He is a native of Mashhad, and is one of the attendants of the Shrine of the Imám Riẓá. He is about thirty-five years of age. During the latter period of the Constitution he founded the newspaper *Bahár* ('Spring') at Mashhad. In No. 18 of the Calcutta *Ḥablu'l-Matín* of the present year was inserted a poem of his entitled 'A critical offering to His Excellency Sir Edward Grey[1].'

2. *'Árif of Qazwín.*

"He is a man of dervish-like disposition, and often sings his poems to the accompaniment of music at public and patriotic meetings, where he is warmly applauded by all. On the occasion of a representation given in Ṭihrán a month before[2] the heart-rending catastrophe of Tabríz by the Literary Circle of the Democratic Party under the title of 'the National Festival to commemorate the Victory of the supporters of the Constitution

[1] This poem is No. 34 of the collection at the end of this volume, and will be found, with a versified translation, at pp. 253–257 *infra*.

[2] *i.e.* about the end of November, 1911.

and the defeat of Muḥammad 'Alí,' 'Árif undertook the *rôle* of minstrel, and, in a most charming and affecting manner, sung the poem which he had composed for this occasion, and which begins as follows:

پیام دوشم ز پیر میفروش آمد، بنوش باده که یك ملّتی بهوش آمد،
هزار پرده ز ایران درید استبداد، هزار شکر که مشروطه پرده پوش آمد،

'Last night a message reached me from the old Wine-seller:
'Drink wine, for a whole Nation has come to its senses!
'Despotism tore away from Persia a thousand veils:
'A thousand thanks that the Constitution has come to replace these veils[1]!'

"Most of 'Árif's poems, which consist of *ghazals* (odes), have been printed[2], and are sung in public and private assemblies. In consequence of a verse[3] offensive to the Regent he was imprisoned with other Democrats early in 1913, but shortly afterwards escaped to Iṣfahán.

3. *Mírzá Murtaẓá 'Farhang.'*

"He is a young man about twenty-eight years of age, who founded the newspaper *Kháwaristán* ('the Eastern Land') in Ṭihrán during the first Period of the Constitution. During the second Period he was Chief of Police, first at Samnán and afterwards at Qum. He is at present studying in Paris.

4. *Sayyid Ashraf of Gílán.*

"He is about forty years of age. During the Second Period of the Constitution he founded the paper *Nasím-i-Shimál* ('Breeze of the North') at Rasht[4]. After the tragic occurrences

[1] "To tear away veils" here means to expose the nakedness or defects, and "to replace the veils" to restore self-respect.

[2] I possess a printed pamphlet of 13 pp. containing six of these poems, arranged for the use of singers. It is dated the 26th of Shawwál, A.H. 1329 (= Oct. 20, 1911), and is described as "offered to the Literary Society in memory of the glorious Festival of the Victors," *i.e.* the Nationalists who captured Ṭihrán in July, 1909.

[3] This is the verse in question:—

کسی‌را که درین ملك سلیمان کردند، ملّت امروز بفهمید که او اهرمن

[4] See No. 354 (pp. 148–9 *infra*), from which it will be seen that this paper first appeared on Sept. 10, 1907, nine months before the destruction of the First National Assembly, and therefore during the First Period of the Constitution.

which took place there [in December, 1911, and January, 1912] he was compelled to leave that city, and his printing-press was destroyed [by the Russians]. The poems which he wrote criticizing the *Mullás* are much appreciated.

5. *Púr-i-Dáwúd.*

"He is a young man about twenty-five years of age. He studied French in Beyrout (Syria) and is now studying Law in Paris, where he has helped to found, and actively supports, the 'Literary and Scientific Society of the Persians in Paris.' He is especially skilful in the employment [in his poems] of old Persian words.

6. *Ja'far-i-Khámna'í.*

"He learned French surreptitiously in Tabríz, his father, a fanatical and old-fashioned merchant, having forbidden him to study foreign languages, or to write poetry, for which he shewed a natural aptitude. Hence his poems are, as a rule, unsigned."

Some twenty poems accompanied these brief biographies, of which the best are included in Part II (pp. 260–299). Other notable contemporary poets, of whose work I have not been able to give specimens here, are Malik-i-Sásání, Shúrída and Badí'u'z-Zamán of Shíráz, Adíb of Níshápúr, Ḥusámu'l-Islám "Dánish," Ahmad Suhaylí of Tabríz (hanged by the Russians in January 1912), Ḥusayn Khán Dánish, etc.

It seems natural at this point, for the sake of comparison, to say a few words about modern Arabic and Turkish patriotic poetry.

The best modern Arabic verse with which I am acquainted has been produced in Egypt. Of contemporary poets in that country Shawqí Bey and Ḥáfiẓ Ibráhím are two of the most famous. The former is essentially a Court poet, who writes graceful but insincere verses in praise of the Khedive or in description of State Balls and other Court functions. Ḥáfiẓ Ibráhím is a much more sincere and therefore effective poet, and his verses deal with a much wider range of subjects. Thus, to take at random a few of the poems contained in the second part of his *Díwán* (published at Cairo in 1907) we find two in praise of the Japanese; another addressed to the Empress Eugenie; another appealing for greater recognition of the Arabic language; another in praise of Victor Hugo; another on the victims of a fire at Mít Ghamr; another on the dearness of food; a threnody (*marthiya*) on the late Muftí of Egypt, Shaykh Muḥammad 'Abduh; another threnody on Maḥmúd Sámí Pasha al-Bárúdí; another addressed to the late King Edward the Seventh on the occasion of his Coronation, etc. The two finest of his poems, however, were called forth by the lamentable tragedy of Denshawi (or Deneshwáy) in the summer of 1906, of which, both on account of the celebrity which it attained, and of the painful and humiliating reflections which it evokes, I shall say nothing more in this place[1]. The first of these two poems (pp. 44–47 of the edition above mentioned) begins:

أيّها القائمون بٱلامر فينا،   هل نسيتم ولاءنا و ٱلودادا،

The second (pp. 102–104), which is the finer of the two, is addressed to Lord Cromer on his return to Egypt in the autumn of the same year, and begins:

قَصْرَ ٱلدوبارة هل أتاك حديثُنا،   فالشَّرْقُ ريع له و ضَجَّ ٱلمغربُ،
أهلاً بساكنك ٱلكريم و مرحبًا،   بعد ٱلتّحيّة إنّنى أتعتّبُ،

A line or two further on the poet finely says, addressing Lord Cromer:

علّمتَنا معنى الحياة فما لنا،   لا نشرئبّ لها و ما لكَ تغضبُ،
أنقمْتَ منّا أن نُحسّ و إنّما،   هٰذا الّذى تدعو إليه و تندبُ،

"*Thou didst teach us the meaning of Life, and why should we not aspire to it, and wherefore shouldst thou be angry?*
"*Art thou wrath with us because we have feelings* [*of patriotism*]*? It is even unto this that thou art wont to urge and incite us!*"

[1] The circumstances of this affair are ruthlessly exposed by Mr Wilfrid Scawen Blunt in a little pamphlet published by T. Fisher Unwin in August, 1906, and entitled *Atrocities of Justice under British Rule in Egypt*. See also Mr Bernard Shaw's *Preface for Politicians* (pp. xliv–lix: "the Denshawai Horror") prefixed to *John Bull's other Island* (London: Constable & Co., 1907).

This poem, which is written with equal power and restraint, undoubtedly expressed the deepest feelings of the Egyptian people, but it is to be feared that it was never read by him to whom it was addressed.

Another book of Arabic verse which created a great stir in Egypt, leading to the flight of the author to Constantinople, the prosecution and imprisonment of the Nationalist leaders, Muḥammad Feríd Bey and Shaykh 'Abdu'l-'Azíz Shawísh, and the confiscation of the book, was a collection of patriotic poems entitled *Waṭaniyyatí* ("My Patriotism"), by Shaykh 'Alí al-Gháyátí. Most of these poems are topical, referring to such events as Lord Cromer's departure from Egypt on May 6, 1907; the revival of the Press Law by Buṭrus Pasha on March 25, 1909; the assassination of Buṭrus Pasha by Ibráhím Efendi Náṣif al-Wardání on February 20, 1910; the execution of al-Wardání on June 28, 1910; Roosevelt's speech of March 29, 1910, at Cairo, and his Guildhall speech of May 31, 1910, both of which caused intense annoyance to the Egyptians, etc. Some of the earlier poems, composed in 1907, originally appeared in the paper *al-Mu'ayyad,* but most of the later ones were first published in the celebrated Nationalist organ *al-Liwá* ("the Standard"). Proceedings were instituted against the poet and against Feríd Bey and Shaykh 'Abdu'l-'Azíz Shawísh (each of whom had contributed a preface to the little volume) on July 14, 1910. Feríd Bey was at the time in Europe, and the poet Shaykh 'Alí al-Gháyátí[1] succeeded, as mentioned above, in escaping to Constantinople, so that Shaykh 'Abdu'l-'Azíz Shawísh was left for the moment to bear the brunt of the prosecution. He was sent for trial on July 26, and on August 6, 1910, was sentenced to three months' imprisonment, and Feríd Bey on his subsequent return to Egypt suffered a similar fate.

So effective was the suppression of this little book *Waṭaniyyatí* that it cost me an infinity of trouble to obtain even the loan of a

[1] I have recently learned that the poet al-Ghāyátí has renounced his Nationalist opinions and reconciled himself to the Khedive, in whose honour he composed a panegyric on the occasion of his anniversary, January 8, 1912, and from whom he now receives a pension on which he lives at Geneva, shunned by his former comrades, who call him "the Egyptian Gapon."

copy, and its rarity and inaccessibility may therefore excuse me for briefly describing it. It comprises 129 pages of 18 × 13 centimetres, and contains: (1) the Author's Preface (pp. 2–3); (2) his dedication of the work to the dead Nationalist leader, Muṣṭafá Kámil Pasha, and his living successors, Feríd Bey and Shaykh 'Abdu'l-'Azíz Shawísh (pp. 4–5); (3) Feríd Bey's Preface (pp. 6–8) on "the influence of Poetry in the education of Nations"; (4) Shaykh Shawísh's Preface (pp. 9–11) on "Poetry and the Poet"; (5) an Introduction (pp. 12–32), apparently by the poet, dealing chiefly with the dearth of patriotic verse in Egypt at the time of writing, the history and influence of the *Marseillaise*, and a panegyric on the French Revolution. This concludes the preliminary prose portion of the book, which also contains signed portraits of the three collaborators. It is followed by the poems, forty-six in number (pp. 33–128), which are fully annotated to explain the circumstances under which each was written.

I have not at hand an account of the trial, but, so far as my recollection serves me, the prosecution was chiefly based on three poems (Nos. 15, 27 and 30), of which the first (published in the *Liwá* on August 19, 1909) was addressed to Dingra (the murderer of Sir Curzon Wylie) who had been executed two days previously; the second dealt with the assassination of the Coptic Premier Buṭrus Pasha, who was shot by al-Wardání on February 20, 1910; and the third (a short poem of four verses) described the condemnation to death of al-Wardání, who was executed on June 28, 1910. The Prefaces contributed by Feríd Bey and Shaykh Shawísh contained nothing which would appear to justify a prosecution for sedition according to English ideas, but the writers seem to have been held responsible for the utterances of the poet whose work they thus in some measure endorsed, in spite of their contention that they had not read all the poems contained in the volume to which they placed themselves in the position of sponsors. In order to enable the reader to judge for himself how far the utterances of Feríd Bey and Shaykh Shawísh merited such draconic reprisals, and also because their remarks are of interest in connection with the general development of patriotic poetry in the East (a quite recent though widely-spread phenomenon), a complete translation of their two Prefaces is here given. Feríd Bey's Preface is as follows:

"*The Influence of Poetry in the Education of Nations.*

"Poetry is one of the most active agents in awakening nations from their lethargy and in inspiring them with the spirit of vitality, even as it is one of the chief incentives to battle and inspirers of heroic endeavour and risking of life in war. Hence from ancient times we find such heroic poetry prevalent amongst the Arabs and other noble nations, such as the Romans, the Greeks, and so forth.

"No one will deny that the French song composed by the French officer, Rouget de l'Isle, and entitled 'the Marseillaise,' was one of the most potent causes of the victory of France over the kings of Europe, who had combined to extinguish the Spirit of Freedom on its first appearance.

"Hence some writers amongst us have written much on the necessity of composing patriotic elegies and songs, so that our children may learn them by heart and sing them in their leisure hours or recite them in their play-time, instead of the songs and verses which the street-children repeat, especially during the nights of Ramaẓán the Blessed. So likewise they have written on the necessity of changing the songs which are sung on festive occasions, all of which revolve round one point, to wit Love and the attribution to the Beloved of qualities '*which God hath not revealed anything to authorize*[1].'

"One of the results of the autocratic government of an individual, equally in the West or in the East, is the destruction of heroic poetry, and the inducing of poets, by the means of gifts and favours, to compose insipid panegyrics and futile encomiums on kings, nobles and ministers, and to withdraw themselves from everything which can educate men's minds and implant in them the love of Liberty and Independence. So likewise another result of this despotism is the complete absence from the sermons delivered in places of worship of anything which might profit the hearer, since all of them revolve round the subject of withdrawal

[1] These words are a quotation from the *Súratu'n-Najm*, or "Chapter of the Star," in the *Qur'án* (liii, 23).

from the world, mingled with incitements to idleness and the patient expectation of daily bread without any effort or work.

"Hence those nations which have undergone political subjugation, becoming apprized of this fact, make the production of patriotic poems and heroic verses (in the classical language for the educated class and in the common language for peasants, artizans and others of the uneducated classes) one of the first of their principles; and this becomes one of the most potent factors in inspiring all classes with a spirit of patriotism. And I rejoice that this auspicious *Risorgimento* has permeated our country, and that most of the poets have left off composing panegyrics on nobles and governors, and have turned their attention to, and used their gifts for, the production of patriotic poetry, and the employment of it to describe the political circumstances which engage public attention. The present work, *Waṭaniyyati*, has appeared in the vanguard of this auspicious and righteous revival.

"My joy is increased by the fact that village poets have composed verses and songs about the Denshawi affair and what grew out of it; about the late Muṣṭafá Kámil Pasha and his patriotic efforts; and about the Suez Canal question and the repudiation of its legality by the General Assembly[1]; and that they have begun to sing them around their camp-fires and at their festivals to the accompaniment of their simple instruments of music. This, please God, is a movement full of promise, proving that the efforts of the patriotic party have borne fruit, and that their efforts have reached the depths of men's hearts in all classes of the people, promising a speedy deliverance, by God's permission, from the occupation and from the despotism of an individual.

"It therefore behoves the poets to abandon the habit of composing laudatory poems and panegyrics on the occasion of notable anniversaries and recognized festivals, and to employ their lofty and God-given talents for the service and education of the people, instead of devoting them to the service of the rich

[1] The deliberations of the General Assembly as to the proposed prolongation of the Suez Canal concession lasted from February 9 until April 9, 1910, when it was unanimously rejected by all the members of the Assembly with the exception of the Copt Marqus Bey Sumayka.

and the flattery of nobles, or using them as a means to gain the favour of Ministers; seeing that the rulers pass away, while the Nation remains.

"Peace be upon him who heareth and remembereth, and who succeeds in serving his country and striving for it: '*Verily his striving shall be regarded, and God will reward him with an abundant recompense*[1].'"

Here follows Shaykh 'Abdu'l-'Azíz Shawísh's Preface:

"*Poetry and Poets.*

"Some poetasters are wont to imagine that poetry consists merely in metrical sentences in which due regard is paid to the proper rhyme. Hence you see them as bold as can be in composing *qaṣídas* (panegyrics) and in laying claim to poetic talent, relying herein on the ignorance of the majority as to the real nature of poetry, its essential qualities, and the conditions on which depend its correctness and perfection, and well aware of the rarity of persons of sufficient culture to discriminate between the bad and the good, or to comprehend the subtle differences which distinguish fruitful from barren verses. Especially is this the case at this time, when the faculty of properly wielding the Arabic language has grown weak, in consequence of the growth of foreign influences over the Arabs and the bad taste which accompanies this, so that the very construction of its phrases is in the utmost need of rectification.

"If you wish to know what good poetry is, put away from yourself metrical feet and undue regard for rhyming letters and elaborate verbiage, and pay heed only to the effect which it leaves in your spirit. For indeed the best poetry is that which possesses your heart until you put it aside, even as the finest pictures are those which hold your vision until they are hidden from it. If, therefore, you would know the difference between natural and artificial poetry, if you perceive when you hear it that the ideas which it expresses are, as it were, spirits which whisper to you, while its words come forth almost

[1] This quotation is also from the *Súratu'n-Najm* (*Qur'án*, liii, 41–2). In the original text a facsimile of Feríd Bey's signature is subjoined.

spontaneously from your mouth, that is natural poetry; while if its motives enter your heart in diverse ways, and its exordium and arrangement do not harmonize when heard, that is artificial poetry[1], of the shallow outpourings of which none will drink the dregs save the ignorant poetaster or the hireling poet. For how can poetry be beautiful or sweet to hear when it issues forth from a heart unmoved and a soul unaffected? Or is poetry aught else than a mirror wherein are seen the effects of psychical influences controlling the spirit of the composer?

"'Abdu'l-Malik once said to Arṭát ibn Suhayya[2], 'How is it now with thy poetry?' 'By Alláh,' he replied, 'O Commander of the Faithful, I neither rejoice, nor am angry, nor desire, nor fear; and poetry is not produced save as the result of one of these four emotions!'

"That is not poetry which results from the poet's contemplation of fantastic forms which transcend realities, or from his pursuing the path of exaggeration in praise and blame. Poetry is naught else than the depicting of the images which circulate in the mind; and just as the most skilful painter is not he who combines incompatible elements or who pourtrays on his canvas something which does not correspond with any existing eternal reality, but rather he who turns his attention to something which does exist and pourtrays it with so fine a shading that it seems to him who gazes on it as though he were looking at its subject as something endowed with external existence, so likewise the most skilful poet is he who attains to true conceptions and judgements and sets them forth to the hearer in sentences which captivate his intelligence and impel him to act in conformity with their requirements.

"All that the poet has to do, therefore, after he has fully endowed his poetry with its due measure of sincerity and discriminating insight, is to clothe it in well-conceived sentences

[1] The writer's meaning is, I think, that the artificial poetry of the panegyrists which he is denouncing is generally a mere display of rhetorical figures not bound together by any strong underlying motive, so that such emotions as it evokes are disconnected and incoherent.

[2] 'Abdu'l-Malik, the fifth Umayyad Caliph, reigned A.D. 685–705 (A.H. 65–86). Arṭát was one of the most eminent poets who belong exclusively to the Umayyad period.

and emphasize the harmony of the ideas one with another. For the composition of poetry is only like setting words to music and adapting them to song; and just as melody is not pleasing to the ear except when its component parts harmonize, so also poetry, when its sentences do not harmonize and its ideas do not accord, is a mere deafening of the ears and a grief to the spirit of man.

"If anyone would see a specimen of poetry which combines grace of words with wealth of ideas, and strength of structure with sincerity of diction, let him read a little of this book *Waṭaniyyatí*; and let him who will enquire of its effects from these growing energies, and these ardent souls, and these loyal resolutions, for they are of its planting and of the fairest of its fruits."

As regards the poems of Shaykh 'Alí al-Gháyátí, while it is impossible to ignore their spirit and vigour, or to deny that many of them contain only legitimate though sometimes caustic criticisms of men and measures obnoxious to the author's political creed, several of them are quite indefensible, especially the poem on Dingra, which, in spite of certain qualifications made by the author in his notes, does undoubtedly convey the impression that he condoned to a certain extent the terrible and tragic crime with which this man's name is associated. It may be questioned whether any murder in recent times has produced results so evil and so far reaching. The assassin had no grudge, personal or political, against his victim Sir Curzon Wylie, who, indeed, was known as a friend and benefactor of Indian students of a kind greatly needed and too rarely found in this country in the present day. This fact greatly increased the indignation aroused by a crime which seemed almost insane in its purposelessness, and this indignation manifested itself, illogically enough, in a widespread and undiscriminating alienation of sympathy from the whole body of Indian students, most of them hard-working, peaceable, intelligent and deserving men, who visit this country, and even tended to increase that unhappy antipathy which has grown up in recent years between the West and the East. The more one loves the East, appreciates its virtues, and sympathizes with its aspirations, the more must one deplore this unhappy event, and desire that it should be buried in oblivion rather than enshrined in verse.

How far, in English law, the writer of a preface is held responsible for the contents of the book to which it is prefixed is another question; but neither of these prefaces, especially that of Shaykh Shawísh, would appear to the unprejudiced reader to contain in itself any matter so seditious or objectionable as to deserve so harsh a punishment as was meted out to its author. There is moreover a certain irony in the general attitude assumed by the most powerful "Liberal" Government of modern England towards freedom of speech and freedom of the Press in its Eastern dependencies which constantly recalls to my mind the following anecdote concerning the above-mentioned Umayyad Caliph 'Abdu'l-Malik related in that delightful history of the Caliphate the *Kitábu'l-Fakhrí*[1]:

"'Abdu'l-Malik before he succeeded to the Caliphate, was one of the pietists of al-Madína, so that he was nicknamed 'the Mosque Dove,' because of his indefatigable reading of the Scripture. But when his father died, and he was acclaimed Caliph, he closed the Sacred Volume and said, '*This is a separation between me and thee*[2]!'"

When I read or recall this passage there rises before my mind's eye the form of a veteran "Liberal" statesman on the eve of the "Seven fat years" reading, marking, learning, and inwardly digesting John Stuart Mill's *Liberty*. To him enter his enthusiastic followers and admirers to announce the triumph of "Liberalism" and his elevation to the rank of Secretary of State and Cabinet Minister; whereupon he lays aside the treatise on *Liberty*[3], saying, as 'Abdu'l-Malik said more than twelve hundred years ago, "*This is a separation between me and thee!*"

1 There are three editions of this book (composed in the thirteenth century of our era), that of Ahlwardt (Gotha, 1860), that of Derenbourg (Paris, 1895), and the cheap but excellent Egyptian reprint (A.H. 1317). The anecdote here quoted occurs on p. 110 of the latter. A French translation of the text by Émile Amar has recently been published by Leroux of Paris.

2 This is a quotation from the *Súratu'l-Kahf* (*Qur'án*, xviii, 77).

3 Not only in Egypt but also in India the Press Law is now (November, 1913) excessively stringent. A pamphlet entitled "Come over into Macedonia and help us,"

It would be out of place here to speak at length of the contents of *Waṭaniyyatí*, though most of the forty-six poems which it contains are interesting both on account of their intrinsic merit and because of their connection with recent political events. I will only mention two excellent ones (Nos. 33 and 34, pp. 108–112) addressed to Mr Roosevelt in remonstrance against the speeches he delivered at the Egyptian University in Cairo on Monday, March 29, 1910, and at the Guildhall in London on May 31 of the same year. I subjoin a score of verses from the first, which is at once the more spirited and the more graceful.

لعمرك لسْتَ بالرّجل الهُمام، اذا عُدّ الهُمامُ من الكرام،

كرام النّاس أصدقهم حديثًا، و أبعد عن أكاذيب اللّئام،

فما لك لم تَقُمْ فى النّيل إلّا، لتُسْمِعَنا أباطيلَ الكلام،

أراك ترى البلاد بغيرِ عين، رأيْتَ بها بلادك مُنْذُ عام،

كأنّا دون قومك فى المعالى، و دونك فى اليراعة و الحسام،

رُوَيْدًا يا فتى التّأريخ إنّا، لنا خطرٌ على الأيّام نام،

جَمَعْنا الدّين و الدّنيا وكُنّا، أساتذة الورى من عهد سام،

فمن أنتم اذا افْتَخَرَتْ شعوبٌ، بمجدٍ فى ذُرَا الأهرامِ سام،

appealing for help for the Turkish victims of the Balkan Crusaders, and published by Moḥammed 'Alí, the editor of the Indian *Comrade*, was confiscated; and the same fate has, I understand, overtaken my pamphlet entitled "*The Reign of Terror in Tabríz*," describing the cruelties perpetrated by the Russians at the beginning of 1912 in that unhappy city. The law is so stringent that it can, apparently, be employed to suppress historical statements of facts, even if unaccompanied by unfavourable comments and criticisms, as appears from the following paragraph from the Delhi *Comrade* of November 13, 1912: "Again, there is the question of the liberty of the Press, which has of late been rising in the scale of public notice. The Press Act of 1910 has given a rude check to the progress of what is known in the West as the Fourth Estate, and has almost choked the mouth of the Indian Journalist, who gasps at the freedom of writing which is practically enjoyed by the Anglo-Indian section of the Press in spite of the dreaded Act. The worst features of the Act have been signally brought to light by the judgment on the application of Mr Moḥammed 'Alí, by a Special Bench of the Calcutta High Court, against an order of the Bengal Government declaring, under Section 12 of the said Act, a perfectly harmless pamphlet entitled *Come over into Macedonia and help us* forfeited to His Majesty. In the course of the judgment we have seen how the learned Judges have exposed the absurdity of Section 4, which condemns the printing and publishing of 'any newspaper, book or other document containing any words, signs or visible representations which are likely or may have a tendency, directly or indirectly, whether by reference, suggestion, allusion, metaphor, implication or *otherwise* (the italics are ours) to bring into hatred or contempt any class or section of His Majesty's subjects in British India.'"

لنا ما كان من مجدٍ تليد‘ و ما كنتم هنالك فى الأنام‘ ،
فإن شئتم سلوا التأريخ انّا‘ أضاناه و أنتم فى ظلام‘

* * * * * *

أراك و قد جهلْتَ فَلَيْتَ شعرى‘ أباغى الحرب أنت أم السّلام
تهبّ فتُرْسِل ٱلبهتان فينا‘ و ترمينا بطائشة السّهام‘
فهل أعداك طبع الوحش حتّى‘ عبسْتَ وأنت فى دار ٱبتسام‘
خطبْتَ و لقبّوا من غير علمٍ‘ فكانت رميةً من غير رام‘
لعمرك انّ كوكًا منك أولى‘ بألقاب الدّكاتره ٱلفخام‘
نراهم كذّبوه و لا نراه‘ روى ما قال عن حزب الخصام‘
و لكنّا نراك و أنت تُلْقِى‘ علينا ما رويتَ عن الطغام‘
كِلا الرّجلَيْن مختلق و لكن‘ أرى روزفلت اخلق بٱلملام‘
فلا تنقم علينا بعد هذا‘ و أكبر ما نروم من المرامى‘
و دونك من بنات ٱلشّعر بيتًا‘ رواه النيل عن ربّ ٱلكلام‘
خطبْتَ فكنْتَ خطبًا لا خطيبًا”‘ أُضيف الى مصائبنا الجسام‘

(*Translation*)

"*By thy life, thou art not a magnanimous man, if the magnanimous man is reckoned amongst the noble!*
The noble ones of mankind are the most truthful in their speech, and the furthest removed from the falsehoods of meaner men.
What ails thee that thou didst not stand up by the Nile save to cause us to listen to vain words?
I perceive that thou regardest [other] countries with a different eye from that wherewith thou didst regard thine own country a year ago!
As though we were inferior to thy people in lofty qualities, and inferior to thee in the [use of] the pen and the sword!
Gently, O champion of history! For we hold a position which waxes with the days;
We combine [preeminence in] this world and in the Faith, and have been lords of creation since the days of Shem!

c 2

Who are ye, what time the nations boast of glory high enthroned on the pinnacles of the pyramids?
We had what we have of ancient glory when you were not there amongst mankind.
If you will, ask history concerning us, for verily we illuminated it when you were still in darkness.

* * * * *

I see thee ignorant, and would that I knew whether thou seekest war or peace!
Thou breathest forth and sendeth calumny amongst us, shooting at us with arrows which miss the mark.
Hath the nature of the wild beasts[1] *passed over into thee, until thou frownest when thou art in a place where thou should'st smile?*
Thou didst make a speech, and they gave thee a title without [thy having] any knowledge, and it was [a case of] 'a bow drawn at a venture.'
By thy life, verily Cook[2] *hath a better claim than thee to the title of 'Honorary Doctor'!*
We see men calling him a liar, but we do not see him relating what he says on the authority of a hostile faction[3].
But we see thee casting up against us what is reported by ignoble persons.
Both men were fabricators of falsehood, but I consider Roosevelt the more deserving of blame.
Henceforth do not cast reproach on us, nor on the greatest of the objects at which we aim!
Enough for thee is one verse of the daughters of song which the Nile hands down from that Master of Words:
'Thou didst speak, and thou wast not an orator, but rather a burden which was added to our other great calamities[4]*!'"*

[1] *i.e.* the wild beasts which Mr Roosevelt went to Africa to hunt, and by the slaughter of which he earned the *soubriquet* of "the Butcher of Africa" (*Jazzáru Ifríqiyya*).

[2] *i.e.* the American Cook, who claimed to have reached the North Pole, and was at first received with great honour, but afterwards became the laughing-stock of all.

[3] *i.e.* even if he told lies, they were not inspired by malice, nor did he injure his fellow-men.

[4] The last verse is a quotation or "insertion" (*taḍmín*) from one of Shawqí Bey's poems.

Lord Cromer's work, *Modern Egypt*, called forth some angry verses, and although the poet exaggerates when, in a footnote on p. 36, he describes this book as "crammed with vituperation and calumny of Egypt and the Egyptians and Islám and the Muslims," it undoubtedly contains statements and expressions which are unnecessarily wounding to Egyptian and Muslim sentiment, and in some cases quite unjustifiable. One specimen of each kind may be given. In vol. ii, pp. 228–9, Lord Cromer says: "It should never be forgotten that Islám cannot be reformed; that is to say, reformed Islám is Islám no longer; it is something else; we cannot as yet tell what it will eventually be"; and he quotes the opinion of Sir William Muir in support of this view, which I believe to be incorrect, and which, thus baldly phrased, is certainly calculated to wound Muslim sentiment. This point, however, is susceptible of argument and discussion; but it is otherwise when Lord Cromer speaks (vol. i. p. 324) of "some illiterate Egyptian of the type of Arábi or Mahmoud Sami." 'Arábí Pasha, a simple soldier, had no pretensions to literary culture, though he was far from illiterate in his own language; but Maḥmúd Sámí Pasha was not only a great bibliophile but one of the most notable poets of modern Egypt, some of whose verses are included in every anthology of modern Arabic poetry[1]. No doubt Lord Cromer spoke in perfect good faith, being obsessed by the idea "that there was only one true civilization in the world, and that was the civilization of Europe[2]"; but the very fact that he did not even know, after spending nearly a quarter of a century in Egypt, that so famous a man as Maḥmúd Sámí Pasha was a great poet amongst his own people shews better than anything else can do how far removed he was from any real sympathy with or interest in the higher manifestations of the intellectual life of that people concerning whose material circumstances he writes with such unquestioned authority.

Waṭaniyyatí is undoubtedly a remarkable book, deserving a

[1] See, for example, the anthology of Arabic verse published in A.H. 1322 (A.D. 1904) at Cairo by Amín 'Umar al-Bájúrí and Muḥammad Ḥasan Maḥmúd, pp. 248–252. Maḥmúd Sámí himself compiled an extensive anthology of Arabic verse, which has been published since his death (in A.H. 1322=A.D. 1904–5) in four volumes comprising 1803 pages.

[2] *Op. cit.*, vol. ii, p. 343.

fuller notice than can here be accorded it. If, on the one hand, it contained, as already admitted, certain things which had better have remained unwritten and unpublished, it also contained genuine poetry inspired by a fervent though indiscreet patriotism —poetry of the kind so well described by Shaykh Shawísh as "that which possesses your heart until you put it aside," and the ideas embodied in which "are, as it were, spirits which whisper to you, while its words come forth almost spontaneously from the mouth"; or which, in the words of a much older Oriental critic, the twelfth century Persian poet Niẓámí-i-'Arúḍí of Samarqand, "by acting on the imagination excites the faculties of anger and desire in such a way that by its suggestion men's temperaments become affected with exultation or depression, whereby it conduces to the accomplishment of great deeds in the order of the world[1]."

Patriotic poetry, as we understand it, hardly existed in the Muhammadan East until the most recent times. The nearest approach to it is to be found in such old Arabic poems as the *Mu'allaqa* of 'Amr b. Kulthúm, who, writing in the "Days of Ignorance" or "Barbarism" (*Ayyámu'l-Jáhiliyyat*) before the advent of the Prophet Muḥammad, boasted of the prowess of his tribe in words which, *mutatis mutandis*, might, as my old friend the late Sayyid 'Alí Bilgrámí used to say, have been written by Rudyard Kipling about the English, as where he says (to quote one verse only):

مَلَأْنَا ٱلْأَرضَ حتّى ضاق عنّا،   و نحن ٱلْبَحْرَ نَمْلَؤُهُ سفينا،

"*We have filled the earth until it hath become too narrow for us,*
And the sea likewise we have filled with our ships."

In Persia some four centuries later (early eleventh century of the Christian era) the great Firdawsí displays in the "Epic of the Kings" or *Sháh-náma* something of the same spirit of pride in his nation and race and that love of heroic deeds and high achievements which the Arabs call *Ḥamása*. Such poetry in

[1] See my translation of the *Chahár Maqála* ("Four Discourses") of this poet, published by the *J. R. A. S.* (pp. 42–43 of the *tirage-à-part*), and the text of the same, published in the Gibb Memorial Series, vol. xi, p. 26.

ancient times is, however, so far as my studies go, always of the triumphant, victorious and imperialistic type; while of the more subtle and moving patriotic verse of the conquered and helpless nation (that verse wherein Ireland stands supreme[1]), which can only strive to maintain its spiritual life under the more or less galling yoke of the foreign invader, and must sustain its sense of nationhood by memories of a glorious past and hopes of a happier future, there is hardly a trace in Persian or Arabic until this present century.

In this connection I may with advantage insert a translation of the Preface prefixed by Mírzá Áqá Khán of Kirmán, one of the first "Martyrs of the Constitution,"[2] to his *Sálár-náma*, a poem written in imitation of the *Sháh-náma*, of which the suppressed portions have been lately rendered accessible in the Introductory volume of the *Náẓimu'l-Islám's* "History of the Persian Awakening" (pp. 242—4):

"Having regard to the fact that I have made use in the compilation of this brief history of ancient monuments, old writings, and the substantial discoveries of contemporary historians, I have concluded the book also with an epic ending, after the fashion and method of the poets of Europe. Possibly some of the accomplished scholars and fortune-favoured men of letters of Persia may make me the object of attack on account of this, and may say, 'What sort of versification is this, and what kind of poetical composition, wherein, setting thyself in opposition to all the poets of Persia, thou hast come out from the circle of good manners and good sense, which it behoves all good tail-wagging trencher-lickers to observe, and, abandoning the straight and safe high-road of flattery and servility, takest upon thyself to speak words of so true and serious an import? "*Travel the road as previous travellers have travelled.*"'

"To this I answer, trees must be known by their fruits, and

[1] I need hardly allude to the once proscribed but now justly admired "Spirit of the Nation"; but I should like to call attention to Alice Milligan's *Hero Lays*, a most charming little volume of verses which should be more widely known. Amongst the plays of the Irish players, Mr W. B. Yeats's *Kathleen ni Houlihan* seems to me the most beautiful and delicate expression of Irish Nationalist sentiment.

[2] Concerning Mírzá Áqá Khán and his *Sálár-nama*, see my *Persian Revolution*, pp. 93-96 and 409-415.

deeds must be judged by their results. No one disputes the effectiveness or originality of the old poets and orators of Persia, nor does anyone contest the brilliancy and grace of their verses, while the insolent charm inherent in the poetry of many of the moderns is a matter on which all are agreed. But he must consider what sort of effect has hitherto been produced by the writings of our poets and men of letters, what kind of fruit has been borne by the tree which they have planted in the garden of song, and what results have been given by the seed which they have sown.

"The result of their exaggerations and hyperboles has been to concentrate falsehood in the simple natures of the people.

"The result of their praise and flattery has been to stimulate kings and ministers to the commission of all manner of vile and foolish actions.

"The result of their metaphysics and mysticism has been nothing but a crop of brutish idleness and sloth, and the production of religious mendicants and beggars.

"The result of their odes to roses and nightingales has been nothing but the corruption of our young men's morals, and the impelling of them towards smooth cheeks and red wine.

"The result of their satires and *facetiae* has been nothing but the diffusion of vice and immorality and the promotion of sinful and reprehensible practices.

"If we examine the history of the poets of Islám and the patrons whom they flattered we shall say:

"It was the poems and panegyrics of Abú Nuwás and others like him which plunged the 'Abbásid Caliphs into the folly of wine-drinking, mid-day slumbers, and other mischiefs.

"It was the *qaṣídas* of 'Unṣurí, Rúdagí, Farrukhí and others like them which destroyed and undermined the Royal Houses of Sámán and Ghazna.

"It was the 'Divine Metaphysics' and Mysticism of 'Iráqí and Maghribí and such as they which begot all these thriftless mendicants and worthless idlers.

"It was the flatteries of Anwarí, Ẓahír [-i-Fáryábí], Rashíd [-i-Waṭwáṭ] and Kamál [-i-Iṣfahání] which produced such tyrannical, worthless and arrogant Kings.

"It was the erotic verses of Sa'dí, Humám, and such as they which utterly corrupted the morals of the youth of Persia.

"It was the satires and *facetiae* of Súzaní, Saná'í (*sic*!) and others which gave such currency to immorality and sin.

"It was the detestable obscurities of Kháqání and such as he which involved Mírzá Mahdí Khán [the historian of Nádir Sháh], and the Sáḥib ['Alá'u'd-Dín 'Aṭá Malik-i-Juwayní, the historian of the Mongols], and 'the Court Panegyrist' [*Waṣṣáf-i-Ḥaẓrat*] in their senseless inanities of verbiage.

"It was the long-winded rodomontades of Ṣabá, the hair-splittings of Shiháb, and the Kuláh-julís and 'Alí-qulís of Qa'ání which have to-day entirely obliterated love of virtue and hatred of vice from the natures of the Persian nobles, plunging them into extraordinary vices and vilenesses: even as God Most High says [*Qur'án*, xxvi, 224], '*As for the poets, the erring follow them.*'

"The poets of Europe have composed and do compose every variety of these poems, but they have brought poetry and the poetic art under so sound a scheme of arrangement, and have made their verses so conformable to the laws of Logic that they have no other effect than to illuminate men's ideas, dispel vain legends, endow their minds with insight, admonish the careless, educate the foolish, castigate the ignorant, incite men's souls to virtuous deeds, reprove and turn aside their hearts from vicious actions, admonish them and inspire them with zeal, patriotism and devotion to their people. This is the true meaning of '*Verily in poetry there is somewhat of wisdom.*'

"Yes, the proper effect of poetry is the stirring of men's hearts, the moving of their compassion, and the quickening of their understandings and thoughts; but it must impel them to virtues, piety and moderation, not to vile, evil and mean deeds, and the like. Of the Persian poets the only one whom European men of letters praise is that same Firdawsí of Ṭús, the verses of whose *Sháh-náma*, although in some places they are not free from hyperbole, do nevertheless in some degree inspire in the hearts of Persians patriotism, love of their race, energy and courage; while here and there they also strive to reform their characters.

"I trust that the result of my own worthless verses may also shortly become evident and apparent in the world of humanity, and may hereafter be, alike to the eloquent and effective writer, a model and exemplar leading them to imitate the poets of Europe, so that they may realize that such poetry as does not convey some moral or lead to some philosophical conclusion is merely of the nature of empty phrases and idle tales and vapourings."

The views here advanced by Mírzá Áqá Khán are, of course, a monstrous exaggeration of the real facts, and I have only quoted them to illustrate the development amongst Persians also of a demand for patriotic poetry and for a note of greater sincerity and higher purpose in verse. His disparagement of the great classical poets is, in my opinion, ill-considered and unjustifiable: the noble mysticism of Jalálu'd-Dín Rúmí, the tender passion of Ḥáfiẓ, and the practical wisdom of Sa'dí will never be superseded so long as the Persian language is spoken and studied. But this passion for the Fatherland is a new thing in Asia, or at any rate in Western and Central Asia, and it is perhaps natural and inevitable that its votaries should be impatient of the centuries of poetical talent devoted to other, and, in their eyes, less worthy objects.

Curiously enough it was the Ottoman Turks, a people far less original and talented than either the Persians or the Arabs, who, so far as the Near East is concerned, introduced the hitherto unknown ideas of "the Fatherland" (*Waṭan*), "the Nation" or "People" (*Millat*), and "Liberty" (*Ḥurriyyat*), and who succeeded in giving to these old words this new and potent significance. The origin of that movement, half literary and half political, associated with the "New Turks" (*Yeñi Turkler*), or, as they are absurdly called, in phraseology which they themselves have now unfortunately accepted, "Young Turks," has been well sketched by my friend the late Mr E. J. W. Gibb in the fifth volume of his monumental *History of Ottoman Poetry*, and is elaborated in much fuller detail in a supplement to that work compiled by the learned and ingenious Dr Riẓá Tevfíq, formerly Deputy for

Adrianople in the Turkish Parliament, which I am now translating into English and hope to publish before long. The pioneers of this movement, as is well known, were Shinásí Efendi (died in 1871), Ẓiyá Pasha (died in 1880), and Kemál Bey (died in 1888), who was the greatest of the three. All these drew their ideas, both political and literary, from France, and the period of their greatest activity may be placed between 1863, when Kemál, then only twenty-three years of age, joined forces with Shinásí, and 1873, when he published his great patriotic play *Waṭan, yakhod Silistra* ("Silistria, or the Fatherland") of which the production at the theatre at Gedik Pasha caused so extraordinary an ebullition of feeling. These three eminent writers represent what Gibb calls the "Period of Preparation" (1859–1879) of Modern Turkish Poetry, the succeeding period, inaugurated in 1879 by the publication of 'Abdu'l-Ḥaqq Ḥámid Bey's *Ṣaḥrá* ("the Country"), being what he terms the "Period of Achievement." Apart from his merits as a poet and dramatist, to Kemál Bey undoubtedly belongs the credit of giving to the three old Arabic words mentioned above the new meanings of "Fatherland," "People" and "Freedom," not only in Turkey, but throughout the Muhammadan East[1]. In classical Arabic *waṭan* means merely the place of birth or domicile; *millat* a religious community; and *ḥurriyyat* the state of a free man or one nobly born as opposed to that of a slave or plebeian; and Kemál's great and enduring achievement was that he succeeded in giving to these words, not only in literary circles but in the mouths of the people, and not only in Turkey but in Persia and the Arabic-speaking lands as well, the full and exact significance of *Patrie*, *Peuple* or *Nation*, and *Liberté*; so that the humblest patriots who died on the Russian gallows at Tabríz in January 1912 cried with their last breath "*Yashasun Waṭan*" or "*Zinda bád Waṭan*" in the full sense of "*Vive la Patrie!*"

Turkish patriotic poetry, as has been already suggested, is rather of the "Rule Britannia" than of the "God save Ireland" type, and contemplates death on the field of battle as the alternative to a glorious victory, rather than death on the gallows

[1] See Gibb's *History of Ottoman Poetry*, vol. v, p. 19.

as the alternative to the renunciation of National aspirations. Of recent Turkish patriotic poetry a very interesting example is afforded by a little book entitled *Turkja Shi'r-ler* ("Turkish poems") by Emín Bey, published in A.H. 1316 (A.D. 1898–9), the proceeds of the sale of which were assigned to the relief of the widows and orphans of Turkish soldiers killed in the war with the Greeks. This book, beautifully printed and illustrated, was produced at the celebrated printing-press of the late Ebu'-ẓ Ẓiyá Tevfíq Bey, is prefaced by laudatory letters from Rijá'í-zádé Ekrem Bey, 'Abdu'l-Ḥaqq Ḥamid Bey, Dr Riẓá Tevfíq Bey, and other eminent contemporary Turkish poets and thinkers, and is remarkable for the extraordinarily Turkish quality of its vocabulary, from which every endeavour has been made to banish the Arabic and Persian elements prevalent in the older Turkish literary idiom. The author may be most briefly described as a Turkish Rudyard Kipling, and his poems as *Barrack Room Ballads* of the Imperial Ottoman Army. They bear such titles as "A Voice from Anatolia: or, Going to the War"; "Crossing the Greek frontier"; "After planting the Flag on Trikhála (Tirḥála) Castle"; "the Martyr; or the Heart of 'Osmán"; "the Orphan Child; or Aḥmed's Anxiety"; "O, Fatherhood! or, Zeynab's Prayer," and the like. The illustrations are of Turkish privates, filled with the rage of battle, flushed with victory, or charging with the bayonet; and the volume concludes with a martial song, set to music, of which the opening words are as follows:

بن بر تُركم دينم جنسم اولودر:
سينهم اوزوم آتشيله طولودر:
انسان اولان وطننڭ قولودر.
ترك اولادى اوده طورماز—آه گيدرم!

"*I am a Turk; my religion, my race are high;*
My breast, my soul, are filled with fire!
Whosoever is a man is the servant of his Country!
The sons of the Turk stay not at home: O! I go!"[1]

[1] In spite of the poet's desire to employ, as far as possible, a purely Turkish vocabulary, this one verse contains five Arabic and two Persian words.

Amongst the many bizarre developments of the most modern Turkish schools of poetry, including the "Coming Dawn" (*Fejr-i-Átí*) and "New Literature" (*Edebiyyát-i-jedídé*), with their "Symbolists," "Parnassians," "Pre-Raphaelites," and imitators of Mallarmé, Verlaine and the like, one known as the "New Túránian" (*Yeñi Túrán*), which has a magazine called *Turk Yurdu* ("the Turkish Folk" or "Hearth") as its special organ and counts Muḥammed Emín, the poet just mentioned, amongst its chief supporters, merits a few words in this place, not so much on account of its literary as of its political peculiarities. This "New Túránian" school, of course, affects in its writings an excessively Turkish style, and endeavours as far as possible to eliminate the Arabic and Persian elements from its vocabulary, but, not content with this natural, and, to a certain extent, laudable desire to nationalize the language, it displays the most violent hatred of Arabic and Persian influences in all their forms, and even of the Arabs and Persians, especially the latter. It demands a federation of all the Turkish, Tartar, Mongolian and other allied peoples (including even the Bulgarians!) with a view to the ultimate creation of a new "Empire of Chingíz Khán." So far, indeed, does it go in its admiration for even the most barbarous forms of "Túránianism" that it idolizes the bloodthirsty Tamerlane (*Tímúr-i-Lang*, or "Limping Tímúr"), the scourge of Asia in the fifteenth century, and blames the Ottoman Sultan Báyezíd "the Thunderbolt" (*Yildirim Báyezíd*) as a "rebellious vassal" who vainly strove to check the victorious advance of his Túránian overlord, whose advent he should rather have hailed with joy as the incarnate all-conquering martial spirit of the Tartar or Túránian race. This insane vandalism of the "New Túránian School" in Turkey may best be likened to the literary and artistic vagaries of Marinetti and the Italian Futurists.

Here I will conclude this brief review of certain aspects (not, in my opinion, devoid of significance and interest) of the literary activities which have accompanied the strange political movements witnessed in recent years in the Near and Middle East, of which the Persian manifestations are not the least interesting or the least significant. To Mr H. L. Rabino and Mírzá Muḥammad

'Alí Khán I have already expressed the measure of my indebtedness, and it only remains for me to thank Sir Albert Houtum Schindler, Mírzá Muḥammad of Qazwín, Dr Aḥmad Khán, Mírzá Káẓim-záda, and other friends for help in correcting the proofs and solving doubtful points arising out of the text, as well as for aiding me to obtain some of the portraits which illustrate these pages. Of the other illustrations a few have already appeared in my *Persian Revolution*, but the majority are new, and represent cartoons, caricatures or title-pages of some of the more interesting newspapers mentioned in this book. The illustrated comic paper *Mullá Naṣru'd-Dín*, being written in Turkish and published at Tiflis, is not included in the *Alphabetical List of Newspapers*, but its influence in Persia was so great, and the artistic merit of its cartoons is so considerable, that I have included six typical specimens of the latter in these pages.

EDWARD G. BROWNE,

Feb. 7, 1914.

PART I

List of Persian Newspapers, arranged in Alphabetical Order.

Compiled by Mírzá Muḥammad 'Alí Khán "Tarbiyat,"

and translated into English

by

EDWARD G. BROWNE.

AUTHOR'S PREFACE

FOR the last fourteen years, during which first the *Tarbiyat* Library and then the office of the magazine entitled *Ganjína-i-Funún* ("the Treasury of Arts") have served as centres of distribution and interchange for most of the Persian, Arabic and Turkish papers published in Persia, and have maintained epistolary and other relations with the chief educational centres, it has been my hobby to collect specimen copies of Persian newspapers, and I have exerted myself to make this collection as complete as possible[1].

In the year A.H. 1317 (= A.D. 1899–1900) the Arabic magazine *al-Hilál*, published in Cairo, then in its ninth year, printed an account of the history and enumerated the results of the new civilization in Persia, especially the printing-presses, newspapers and colleges[2]. Most of the information contained in this article was derived from Mírzá Mahdí Khán, the editor of the Persian periodical *Ḥikmat* ("Wisdom"), also resident in Cairo. Delighted as I was at the publication of such information, partial though it was, I found it to be very defective, not only in relation to the facts, but even to such particulars as I myself had acquired. From that time onwards, accordingly, I resolved to publish a tabular summary of Persian periodicals, and devoted myself with still greater assiduity to acquiring the necessary information on this subject, and to completing my collection of newspapers. The political Revolution in Persia, however, left me no leisure for such work; and finally all the documents, books, and files of newspapers, magazines and papers which I possess were left in

[1] The *Tarbiyat* Library lasted from A.H. 1316 to 1326 (= A.D. 1898–1908). The *Ganjína-i-Funún* was founded in A.H. 1320 (= A.D. 1902).

[2] The article in question appeared in February, 1900 (*al-Hilál*, vol. IX, pp. 257–263). The account of the Press, which is very short, is on pp. 262–263.

Tabríz and Ṭihrán, where they are at present beyond my reach[1], else I should have been able to make this little pamphlet fuller and more complete.

At the beginning of this year (A.H. 1330 = January, 1912) I learned through some of my friends of the publication at Rasht of a treatise identical in aim with that which I had in view, entitled *A table of the newspapers of Persia, and of newspapers in the Persian language published outside Persia*, compiled in Persian by the learned and accomplished Mr H. L. Rabino, British Vice-Consul at Rasht[2]. Although I was thus anticipated in the execution of a design which I had long cherished, and for the fulfilment of which I had long sought opportunity, I was nevertheless greatly delighted at the appearance of so valuable a work, and felt myself deeply indebted to the respected author, to whom I at once wrote asking for a copy. This he was kind enough to send me, together with a letter informing me that copies had become scarce.

Having perused the above-mentioned treatise, which constitutes, indeed, one of the greatest services yet rendered by any foreigner to the literary history of Persia, and is a veritable treasury of information, arousing our admiration and amazement as to how all these particulars could be collected in one corner of Persia, I hesitated at first as to the publication of the data which I had myself collected and which I had with me in the form of scattered notes and memoranda. Indeed I almost decided to abandon my original intention; but after a little consideration, and a comparison of the facts collected on either side, I resolved not to neglect or cast aside this information, of part of which I have personal cognizance, but at least to publish

[1] Unhappily they are now for ever beyond human reach, for, as I recently learned from the author, who is now at Constantinople, these and all other papers were destroyed by his family when the Russians entered Tabríz in December, 1911, and inaugurated a Reign of Terror under which no one suspected of sympathy with Liberal ideas was safe.

[2] The Persian title of this admirable pamphlet is as follows:

صورت جرايد ايران و جرايدى كه‌درخارج ايران بزبان فارسى طبع شده‌است

It was printed at the '*Urwatu'l-Wuthqá* Press at Rasht in A.H. 1329 (= A.D. 1911), and comprises 30 pp. of $14'' \times 8\frac{3}{4}''$. A brief "Foreword" is contributed by Muḥammad Riẓá son of Isma'íl of Rasht. Mr Rabino has now been transferred to Morocco.

it in some way, even in the form of disjointed notes, that perchance it may be of some little use to subsequent students who may be eager to collect details as to the preliminary signs of the Persian awakening, which will be my sufficient reward.

In comparing my own memoranda with the contents of the above-mentioned treatise, I discovered certain divergences and differences in the way of defect and excess on both sides. Chief amongst these differences were the names of 29 newspapers overlooked by me and of nearly a hundred overlooked by Mr Rabino, the remainder being included in both lists. And although it was not necessary that I should include in this compendium those with which I was unacquainted before I had read the above-mentioned treatise, yet, with a view to the completeness and comprehensiveness of this table of Persian newspapers, I supplemented my omissions and shortcomings from Mr Rabino's treatise, confident in the permission and approval of the respected author, whose sole object was the dissemination of the actual facts, but indicating in each case under the name of the newspaper in question the source of my information by means of the abbreviation "*Ṣ. J. I.*" (ص. ج. ا), standing for صورت جرائد ایران, "*Ṣúrat-i-Jará'id-i-Írán*" ("List of Persian Newspapers"), which is the title of Mr Rabino's pamphlet. Yet withal the rule maintains that "the superiority is to the pioneer, and the first in order are the first in merit."

As has been already explained, the greater part of the material collected by me was left in Persia amongst my other papers, and though I hope in another edition to complete, revise and supplement the particulars here set forth, yet for the moment I publish this abstract so that at least some small basis for further researches may be available.

I further deem it necessary to mention here several points in connection with the subjoined text, which points are as follows:

First, what is meant by the "date of publication of newspapers," so far as it is mentioned in this treatise, is the date of their foundation and inception.

Secondly, since a division of periods is historically necessary in the recent history of Persia to indicate the successive revolutions and the sequence of momentous and continual changes and great public events whereby it is characterized, and since a special title and fixed designation is required for each cycle and period, and for each one of the great historical events which may be reckoned as stages and landmarks, and which serve as the starting-points of yet other events wherewith they are correlated and by which they must be judged, and since such division of periods and appropriate nomenclature has not hitherto been established, therefore many names and expressions occur in the course of these pages which need to be explained to anyone who has not carefully followed the successive events of recent years in Persia. Thus the term "Period of Autocracy" (*Dawr-i-Istibdád*) is applied to the period preceding the proclamation of the Constitution (14th of Jumáda ii, A.H. 1324=August 5, 1906); the "Reactionary Triumph" (*Waq'a-i-Irtijá'iyya*), "Coup d'État" (*Ẓarba-i-Ḥukúmat*), or "Bombardment of the *Majlis*" (*Ṭúpbandi-i-Majlis*: 23rd of Jumáda i, A.H. 1326=June 23, 1908) to the destruction of the First National Assembly by command of Muḥammad 'Alí Sháh and at the hands of Colonel Liakhoff; and the "Minor Autocracy" (*Istibdád-i-Ṣaghír*), or "Cycle of General Revolution" (*Dawr-i-Inqiláb-i-'Umúmí*), or "Great Revolution" (*Inqiláb-i-Kabír*), or "Revolution of Tabríz" (*Inqiláb-i-Tabríz*) to the period extending from the above-mentioned Bombardment to the second proclamation of the Constitution by Muḥammad 'Alí Sháh after the intervention of the Russian and British Governments, which synchronized with the fall of Tabríz and the entry into it of the Russian troops, and the formation of the Cabinet of Sa'du'd-Dawla (Rabí' ii, A.H. 1327=April–May, 1909). The conquest of Ṭihrán and deposition of Muḥammad 'Alí Mírzá (28th of Jumáda ii, A.H. 1327=July 17, 1909) is termed "the Restoration of the Second Constitution" (*I'áda-i-Mashrúṭiyyat-i-thání*). Other important events are the "Revolution of Gílán" (Rasht) on Muḥarram 16, A.H. 1327 (=Feb. 7, 1909); the "Revolution of Iṣfahán" (Dhu'l-Ḥijjá, A.H. 1326 (=beginning of January, 1909); the last Russian Ultimatums; the sanguinary acts of aggression perpetrated by the Russians in Tabríz, Rasht and Anzalí; the dissolution of the Second *Majlis* (beginning of Muḥarram, A.H. 1330=December 21, 22, etc., 1911); the Bombardment of Mashhad (11th of

Rabí' ii, A.H. 1330 = March 30, 1912), *et caetera*. Thus the "first period of the Constitution" is the term applied to the period of freedom preceding the Bombardment of the First *Majlis*, and the "second period of the Constitution" to that succeeding the capture of Ṭihrán.

Thirdly, the list of newspapers mentioned in this treatise is not confined to those published in Persian, but includes, besides the Persian newspapers published throughout the world, all newspapers published in Persia in whatever language (French, Armenian, Syriac, Turkish, etc.).

Fourthly, in the accounts given of the different newspapers, various details and notes, apparently foreign to the subject, have sometimes been included, which, though not directly connected with the account of the publication of the journal in question, have not been withheld because they may perhaps be of use for the history of the Persian Revolution, and because such information, including biographical particulars concerning their respective editors and their adventures, might otherwise be lost.

Fifthly, since, in addition to the account of the newspapers and magazines which fills the greater part of this compendium, something has been said of the general history of printing in Persia, and of the more useful books which had some effect on the progress, revival and awakening of that country, therefore I have entitled my treatise not "A List of Persian Newspapers," but "A Page from the History of the products of the Persian Press."

Sixthly, since, in spite of my endeavours to include in the following index as far as possible all newspapers published in Persian, and all newspapers published in Persia in some language other than Persian, it is probable that some may have escaped my notice (since many of them endured but a little while, like the *Sitára-i-Saḥarí*, or "Morning Star," which came into being and disappeared in Tabríz in A.H. 1325 = A.D. 1907–8, and were soon completely forgotten), I hope that should any of my readers know of any Persian newspaper omitted from this list, or detect any error in its contents, or be acquainted with any fresh materials or particulars concerning any one of them, or the biographies of their editors, publishers or staff, or the names of their editors (where they are omitted), or the dates and intervals of their publication, and other like matters of every kind which have been omitted from my List, he will communicate such information to me as a service to knowledge and history, and to preserve such memorials of the Nation's life from destruction and loss. The same request applies in a still greater degree to the list of titles of useful books contained in the concluding portion of this treatise, since, so far as I know, this sample is the first small foundation in this subject.

Before concluding my remarks I must discharge the debt of gratitude and thanksgiving incumbent on me to......my friend Edward Browne,......Professor of Oriental Languages in the University of Cambridge, to whom all Persians and those who use the Persian language, the whole community of Islám, and all lovers of Justice throughout the world owe a deep debt of gratitude, both on account of his fruitful services in rendering accessible to the public and reviving the memory of the works, literatures and histories of the Muhammadan nations, especially the Persians, and of his great and continued efforts, inspired by a love of Justice, in defending, both by speech and writing, in England particularly and in Europe generally, the rights of the down-trodden peoples of Islám against their cruel oppressors. In addition to all the claims which he has on the Persians generally and on me in particular, it is he who has encouraged and enabled me to publish these pages. With prayers for the endurance of his help and that the world of Islám may long continue to profit by his services, I conclude this Preface.

MUḤAMMAD 'ALÍ "*TARBIYAT.*"

CONSTANTINOPLE,
15th of Jumáda ii, A.H. 1330
June 1, 1912.

INTRODUCTION

(I)

THE date of the introduction of the printing-press into Persia nearly a century ago, during the reign of Fatḥ-'Alí Sháh Qájár and when 'Abbás Mírzá *Ná'ibu's-Salṭana* was Crown Prince, was about A.H. 1232 (A.D. 1816–17). It was introduced into Tabríz by the efforts of the above-mentioned *Ná'ibu's-Salṭana*, while about the same time another printing-press was established at Ṭihrán under the supervision of Mírzá 'Abdu'l-Wahháb *Mu'tamadu'd-Dawla*. In the latter were printed such books as the Holy Qur'án, the *Jalá'u'l-'Uyún*, the *Ḥayátu'l-Qulúb*, Practical Treatises on Jurisprudence, etc., each known as the "edition of *Mu'tamadu'd-Dawla*."

Amongst the first books printed in Persia were the *Ma'áthír-i-Sulṭání* ("Royal Monuments") of 'Abdu'r-Razzáq Beg Dunbulí, a history of the reign of Fatḥ-'Alí Sháh dedicated to the *Ná'ibu's-Salṭana* and printed at Tabríz in A.H. 1241 (= A.D. 1825–6), and a Treatise on Inoculation for Small-pox (*Risála-i-Ábila-kúbí*), also printed at Tabríz[1]. Neither from my own personal investigations nor from the perusal of Persian books can I find any indication of the existence of printing-presses in Persia prior to this date. And although I have seen it stated in some foreign scientific magazine that printing was first introduced into Persia in the year A.D. 1784 (= A.H. 1198–9) at Bushire, I have met with no trustworthy evidence in support of this assertion.

After this, according to the statement transmitted by certain persons, the *Ná'ibu's-Salṭana*, about A.H. 1240 (= A.D. 1824–5), sent one Mírzá Ja'far of Tabríz to Moscow to learn the art of lithography and to bring to Tabríz the necessary apparatus, which

[1] Throughout these pages "printed" means printed with moveable types, lithographed books and papers being explicitly described as such. The word *cháp* in Persian includes both, the former being called *cháp-i-surbí* ("lead-printed") and the latter *cháp-i-sangí* ("stone-printed").

he accordingly introduced and employed there. The well-known Mashhadí Asad Áqá "*Básma-chí*" ("the Printer") of Tabríz (whose father and elder brother were amongst the founders of and partners in the first lithographic press, and who is still living and whose old press is still at work in Tabríz), also relates that Mírzá Ṣáliḥ of Shíráz, the *Wazír* of Ṭihrán, sent at great expense one Mírzá Asadu'lláh, of the province of Fárs, to St Petersburg to learn the art of printing, and that on his return thence he founded at Tabríz, with the assistance of the late Áqá Riẓá, father of the above-mentioned Mashhadí Asad Áqá, a lithographic press, the first book lithographed at which was the Holy Qur'án in the hand-writing of Mírzá Ḥusayn the famous calligraphist. Five years later, at the Sháh's command, this press and its appurtenances were transferred to Ṭihrán, where the first book printed was the *Díwán* of Nisháṭí Khán the poet. As Tabríz was the first Persian town into which the press was introduced, it became known by its Turkish name of *Báṣma-khána*[1]. After Tabríz and Ṭihrán it was introduced to the following towns of Persia in chronological order: Shíráz, Iṣfahán, Mashhad, Anzalí, Rasht, Ardabíl, Hamadán, Khúy, Yazd, Qazwín, Kirmánsháh, Kirmán, Garrús and Káshán. In the remaining towns and villages of Persia the art of printing neither is nor ever has been practised, save at Urmiya, where it was introduced at an earlier date than in most of the towns above-mentioned[2].

Amongst the older lithographed books are a good many military, mathematical and astronomical works printed at Ṭihrán, such as the *Khuláṣa* ("Compendium") of Mírzá Ja'far Khán, the *Jám-i-Jam* ("Goblet of Jamshíd") printed in A.H. 1272 (= A.D.

[1] The word *cháp*, now most commonly used in Persia for printing, is connected by the author with the word *cháw* (of Mongolian or Chinese origin) applied to the paper money introduced for a short and disastrous period into Persia by the Mongol ruler Gay-Khátú (A.D. 1291–5). The author's note on this will be found in the Appendix.

[2] Various Christian missions began to arrive at Urmiya in Ázarbáyján nearly eighty years ago: first the English and American Protestant missionaries, then the French Catholics, and latterly missionaries of the Russian Orthodox Church, all of whom, for the better diffusion of their respective doctrines, founded numerous religious institutions, such as colleges, hospitals, and printing-presses in the district, where there exist some 30,000 Chaldean or Syrian Nestorian Christians. The Americans in particular have for long possessed an important printing-press for the publication of English, Syriac and Persian works.

1855–6), etc., and some works of history and literature at Tabríz, such as the Histories of Peter the Great, publ A.H. 1262 (= A.D. 1846), Charles the Twelfth (A.H. 1263 = A.D. 1847) and Alexander the Great, all three of which were translated by order of 'Abbás Mírzá *Ná'ibu's-Salṭana*; the geography entitled *Jahán-numá* ("the World-shower"), compiled by Mírzá Rafá'íl; the *Burhán-i-Jámi'* ("Compendious Proof," a Persian dictionary explained in Persian, compacted from the older *Burhán-i-Qáṭi'*, or "Decisive Proof"), compiled by Mírzá 'Abdu'l-Karím b. Muḥammad Mahdí of Tabríz, lithographed in A.H. 1260 (= A.D. 1844); the *Kulliyyát*, or Complete Works, of Sa'dí in A.H. 1264 (= A.D. 1848); the *Sháhnáma*, or Book of Kings, of Firdawsí in A.H. 1275 (= A.D. 1858–9); the *Díwán* of Náṣir-i-Khusraw in A.H. 1280 (= A.D. 1863–4), the three books last mentioned being all in the hand-writing of the celebrated calligraphist 'Askar Khán Urdúbádí; and the *Díwán* of Anwarí in A.H. 1266 (= A.D. 1849–50). Another class of old lithographs which are not devoid of importance consists of Persian almanacs and calendars in cypher published in various towns, such as the cypher almanac of Muḥammad Taqí Aharí, "printed in A.H. 1261 (= A.D. 1845) under the supervision of Mírzá Riẓá at the Press of Mullá Najaf 'Alí at Tabríz"; the cypher almanac of Mírzá Báqir of Mázandarán, lithographed in A.H. 1265 (= A.D. 1848–9); the cypher almanac of Mírzá Asadu'lláh of Mázandarán in A.H. 1266 (= A.D. 1849–50), *et caetera*. One of the strangest things connected with the history of the art of printing in Persia from the time of its first introduction until the present day is that notwithstanding the chronological priority of the introduction of typography into Persia, it entirely went out of fashion in a short while, and that for a long time (more than fifty years) the presses of Persia confined themselves exclusively to lithography, until typography again became current and popular after the enthronement of Muẓaffaru'd-Dín Sháh (A.D. 1896–1907).

The earliest newspapers in Persia, before the foundation of the newspapers of the present period which resemble those of other countries and kingdoms, consisted of brief news-sheets confined to the personal doings of the King. The writers of these were known as *Waqáyi'-nigár* ("chroniclers of events"), a post which now no longer exists, although its style and title has not yet disappeared. The foundation of the first newspaper of the present form and arrangement took place in the third year of the reign of Náṣiru'd-Dín Sháh (who came to the throne in A.D. 1848) by the command and at the direction of Mírzá Taqí Khán *Amír-Niẓám*. The first Persian newspaper which circulated in Ṭihrán in the above-mentioned year was entitled *Rúznáma-i-Waqáyi'-i-Ittifáqiyya* ("Diary of Casual Events"), and was a weekly publication. In size it resembled the usual smaller newspapers, like the daily *Ḥablu'l-Matín* of Ṭihrán, and generally comprised four, but sometimes eight pages. The writer possesses a collection extending from No. 7 to No. 444, the former number being dated Friday the 17th of Jumáda i, A.H. 1267, corresponding with the last day of the Year of the Pig (= March 20, 1851)[1], and the latter Thursday, the 17th of Ṣafar, A.H. 1276 (= Sept. 15, 1859). This was the first Persian lithographed newspaper published in Ṭihrán[2]. In the year A.H. 1277 (=A.D. 1860–1),

[1] It was a weekly newspaper, and was published pretty regularly on Thursdays. The author of the *Muntaẓam-i-Náṣirí* states that the first number appeared in the month of Rabí' ii, A.H. 1267 (=February, 1851). After No. 456 the paper appeared irregularly, until, about No. 480, it changed its title (while keeping the serial numbers) to the *Rúznáma-i-Dawlat-i-'Aliyya-i-Írán* next mentioned in the text, and became an illustrated paper.

[2] From the recorded fact that in A.H. 1277 (=A.D. 1860–1) "the publication of *newspapers* was conferred on Mírzá Abu'l-Ḥasan Khán *Naqqásh-báshí*" (*i.e.* "Chief Artist") it may be deduced that at that date and even before it there existed another official paper or papers besides the *Rúznáma-i-Waqáyi'-i-Ittifáqiyya* and the *Rúznáma-i-Dawlat-i-'Aliyya-i-Írán*, though as to the nature and titles of these I have been unable to ascertain anything definite. H. E. the *I'timádu's-Salṭana* writes: "the above-mentioned Mírzá Abu'l-Ḥasan Khán *Ṣaní'u'l-Mulk* was not really a newspaper-editor but an artist, who was chiefly engaged in making designs of "the Lion and the Sun," and in drawing portraits of State notables. He was connected with the paper from its inception until the control of the Press passed to the late *I'timádu's-Salṭana*, and, being an artist and directly connected with the Press, he started several illustrated papers, single numbers of which I possess." In another place he writes: "from the first the newspapers were associated with the Ministry of Sciences, until, in A.H. 1288 (=A.D. 1871–2), while the *I'tiẓádu's-Salṭana* was Minister of Sciences, several newspapers were printed at the *Dáru'l-Funún*. These Government papers never had a regular editor who signed his name to articles, but, while their publication continued, the editors were continually changed. Several were always chosen to write these papers, the choice of persons depending on the caprice of the Minister." H. E. the *Zaká'u'l-Mulk* writes: "the late Mírzá Ḥasan Khán *Ṣaní'u'l-Mulk*, called *Naqqásh-báshí*, was at one time connected with the editing of the Government newspapers, and contributed illustrations to some of them. This was before the late *I'tiẓádu's-Salṭana*

when the superintendence of the Government Press and the printing of newspapers was conferred upon Mírzá Abu'l-Ḥasan Khán Naqqásh-báshí-i-Ghifárí, entitled *Ṣaní'u'l-Mulk*, the *Rúz-náma-i-Dawlat-i-'Aliyya-i-Írán* ("Gazette of the Sublime State of Persia"), which was an illustrated continuation of that previously mentioned, was published with portraits of the leading men and notables of the Empire, and is accounted the first illustrated Persian newspaper. Afterwards, as it would appear, the name and title of this same newspaper was changed to *Rúznáma-i-Dawlatí* ("State Gazette"). The writer has seen No. 622 of this paper, which is dated the 7th of Jumáda ii, A.H. 1285 (= Sept. 25, 1868), and is described as "printed in the workshops of the

undertook editorial duties." It must also be noted that the title of "Ministry of Sciences" came into use long after the introduction of the newspaper. From a consideration of the dates of No. 444 (the last in the author's possession), No. 456 (the last preserved in the British Museum), and No. 474 (the last in the possession of *Zaká'u'l-Mulk*) of the *Rúznáma-i-Waqáyi'-i-Ittifáqiyya*, which dates are respectively Ṣafar 17, A.H. 1276 (=Sept. 15, 1859), Jumáda i, 19, A.H. 1276 (=Dec. 14, 1859), and Rabí' ii, 18, A.H. 1277 (=Nov. 3, 1860), and from Rabino's statements that No. 471 of this paper was dated Muḥarram 28, A.H. 1277 (=Aug. 16, 1860), that No. 482 was entitled *Rúznáma-i-Dawlat-i-'Aliyya-i-Írán* and was illustrated, and that in A.H. 1277 (=A.D. 1860–1) "the superintendence of the State Press and the publication of newspapers was conferred on the *Naqqásh-báshí-i-Ghifárí*, and the *Rúznáma-i-Dawlatí* became an illustrated paper" (what is intended by this last being the above-mentioned *Rúznáma-i-Dawlat-i-'Aliyya-i-Írán*), it results that the *Rúznáma-i-Waqáyi'-i-Ittifáqiyya* appeared pretty regularly every Thursday until No. 456, after which it was published irregularly and often delayed; and that about No. 480, under the *régime* of the *Ṣaní'u'l-Mulk* it changed its name and form, and appeared under the title of *Rúznáma-i-Dawlat-i-'Aliyya-i-Írán*, while preserving a serial numeration continuous with its predecessor, of which it was in part a continuation, No. 565 of the latter paper being dated, according to Rabino, Jumáda ii, 17, A.H. 1281 (=Nov. 17, 1864), and still preserving the same name. Perhaps it was still the same paper which afterwards became entitled *Rúznáma-i-Dawlatí*, which, according to the official Year-books (*Sál-náma*), together with the *Rúznáma-i-'Ilmí*, was placed under the charge of 'Alí-qulí Mírzá *I'tiḍádu's-Salṭana*. Of this I have seen a copy of No. 622, bearing this very title, dated Jumáda ii, 7, A.H. 1285 (=Sept. 25, A.D. 1868). In the early days of the Ministry of Mírzá Muḥammad Ḥusayn Khán *Sipahsálár*, in A.H. 1288 (=A.D. 1871–2), when the control of the Government newspapers passed out of the hands of the Minister of Sciences, and the Press Department (afterwards elevated into a Ministry) was founded and conferred on Muḥammad Ḥasan Khán *Ṣaní'u'd-Dawla* (afterwards *I'timádu's-Salṭana*), it again changed its name, and was entitled *Rúznáma-i-Írán*. In A.H. 1321 (=A.D. 1903–4), when the Ministry of the Press was conferred on Mullá Muḥammad *Nadímu's-Sulṭán*, its name was once more changed to *Rúznáma-i-Írán-i-Sulṭání* ("the Royal Gazette of Persia"). Finally, a year and a half later, the Ministry of the Press was again conferred on Muḥammad Báqir Khán *I'timádu's-Salṭana*.

State Printing-press in the auspicious College of the *Dáru'l-Funún*." Even so in later days this same newspaper continued to be published, from A.H. 1288 (= A.D. 1871–2) until the period of the Constitution, *i.e.* A.H. 1324 (= A.D. 1906), under the name of *Írán* ("Persia"), and again, in even later times (*i.e.* in A.H. 1329 = A.D. 1911) it was revived under the name of *Rúznáma-i-Rasmí-yi-Dawlat-i-Írán* ("the Official Gazette of the Persian Empire"), and used to report the deliberations of the National Consultative Assembly of Persia. The production of the first newspaper in Persia synchronizes with the foundation of the *Dáru'l-Funún*, or École Polytechnique, of Ṭihrán, the establishment of the Post to Ázarbáyján and Fárs, and the institution of passports for Persian subjects travelling abroad[1].

In the year A.H. 1283 (= A.D. 1866–7) another newspaper, entitled *Rúznáma-i-Millatí* ("the National Gazette"), so-called to distinguish it from the *Rúznáma-i-Dawlatí*, was published in Ṭihrán.

After Ṭihrán, the priority of which in the possession of newspapers is incontestable, the first and foremost of Persian towns in respect to the publication of newspapers is Shíráz, where the newspaper *Fárs* was published in A.H. 1289 (= A.D. 1872–3)[2], and after it come Iṣfahán and Tabríz, which were the respective capitals of Náṣiru'd-Dín Sháh's two eldest sons, rivals of long standing, Sulṭán Mas'úd Mírzá *Ẓillu's-Sulṭán* and the Crown Prince [afterwards Sháh] Muẓaffaru'd-Dín Mírzá. Thus in the year A.H. 1296 (= A.D. 1879), at the instigation of the *Ẓillu's-Sulṭán* and under the care and editorship of Mírzá Taqí Khán of Káshán[3], was founded the *Farhang* ("Culture") at Iṣfahán,

[1] A full statement of the establishment of passports and the regulations affecting them is inserted in No. 10 of the *Rúznáma-i-Waqáyi'-i-Ittifáqiyya*.

[2] In the *Rúznáma-i-Waqáyi'-i-Ittifáqiyya* of A.H. 1275 (= A.D. 1858–9) there occur allusions to a paper printed in Tabríz, which would suggest that this city had the priority over Shíráz.

[3] Mírzá Taqí Khán was conspicuous amongst the older generation of those who were learned in the new arts and European sciences, and was in his day a profound and accomplished scholar, especially devoted to the astronomical and natural sciences, on which he composed many treatises, which, having regard to the time when they were written, contain a mass of valuable information. His style and method of explanation are especially plain and simple. Of these works only two, so far as I am aware, the *Ḥadá'iqu'ṭ-Ṭabí'iyya* ("Gardens of Nature") on Natural Science and Astronomy, and the *Tarbiyat-i-Aṭfál* ("Education of Children"), have been

and in the same year the newspaper entitled *Tabríz* at Tabríz. Both of these papers continued to be published and to circulate for a considerable time, and I have seen numbers of the *Tabríz* up to the third year of issue.

The first daily Persian newspaper was the *Khuláṣatu'l-Ḥawádith* ("Summary of Events"), printed and published in Ṭihrán in A.H. 1316 (= A.D. 1898–9), a small quarto sheet, printed with type on one side, and containing foreign telegraphic news, derived from the telegraphic summaries of current events transmitted from Europe to India by Reuter's Agency, under the title of "Public News," by the Indo-European Telegraph for publication in the Indian and other newspapers, of which a copy was furnished to the British Legation in Ṭihrán and to the Sháh.

After the proclamation of the Constitution four daily newspapers began to appear under the names of the *Majlis*, *Nidá-yi-Waṭan*, *Ḥablu'l-Matín* and *Ṣubḥ-i-Ṣádiq*, some of which at first appeared once a week, until by degrees they developed into daily papers. Of these the *Majlis* ("Assembly") was the first to publish the deliberations of the National Assembly. It was founded by Mírzá Muḥammad Ṣádiq-i-Ṭabáṭabá'í (son of Sayyid Muḥammad-i-Ṭabáṭabá'í, the *Mujtahid*, one of the chief founders and supporters of the Persian Constitution) on the 8th of Shawwál, A.H. 1324 (= Nov. 21, 1906). Again, after the deposition of Muḥammad 'Alí Mírzá, several new daily papers appeared,

printed. In order fully to set forth the Author's position in the learned and social world, it may not be out of place to quote *verbatim* the long list of his titles and qualifications as given by himself on the title-page of the above-mentioned *Ḥadá'iq*. This is as follows:—"General Mírzá Taqí Khán of Káshán, possessor of the Order and Red Ribbon of the Second Degree of the rank of Colonel; the Gold Medal of the Military College; the Order of St Anne of the Second Class, and the Order of St Stanislas of the Second Degree, both conferred by the Imperial Russian Government; editor and chief writer of the former newspaper *Fárs* and the present newspaper *Farhang*; President of the Medical Society and Member of the Council of Notables (Section of Public Utility) of Iṣfahán; Honorary President of the Académie d'Ethnographie of Bordeaux (Gironde); Honorary President of the Académie Byzantine of Constantinople; Corresponding Member of the Society of Oriental Arts and Scientific Treatises of St Barthélémy; Honorary Member of the Surgical, Medical and Pharmaceutical Societies, etc." Exactly the same list of titles is found on the first page, that is the wrapper, of the *Ḥadá'iqu'ṭ-Ṭabí'iyya*, printed in the *Farhang* Press at Iṣfahán, A.H. 1300 (= A.D. 1882–3).

amongst these being the *Írán-i-Naw* ("New Persia"), of the large folio size usual in foreign newspapers, which, in form and style, it resembled. Its first number was published on Saturday, the 7th of Sha'bán, A.H. 1327 (= August 24, 1909).

The appearance of scientific periodicals in Persia in the Persian language began with the publication of the *Rúznáma-i-'Ilmiyya-i-Dawlat-i-'Aliyya-i-Írán* ("Scientific Gazette of the Sublime State of Persia"), which from A.H. 1280 (= A.D. 1863–4) was published for the administration of the *Dáru'l-Funún* (or École Polytechnique of Ṭihrán) under the superintendence of 'Alí-qulí Mírzá *I'tiẓádu's-Salṭana.* Another newspaper entitled *Rúznáma-i-'Ilmí* ("the Scientific Gazette") was in circulation in A.H. 1293 (= A.D. 1876)[1].

The first scientific magazine (*jung*)[2] published in Persia was the periodical entitled *Ganjína-i-Funún* ("Treasury of Arts"), founded in Tabríz in the year A.H. 1320 (= A.D. 1902–3). The first number of it is dated the first of Dhu'l-Qa'da in that year (= Jan. 30, 1903), and it was published with the utmost regularity for a whole year. It was carried on by four friends of learning and culture in Tabríz, one of whom was the present writer, and

[1] As regards the foundation of the *Rúznáma-i-'Ilmiyya-i-Dawlat-i-'Aliyya-i-Írán*, Mr Rabino ascribes it to Mírzá Muḥammad Ḥusayn Khán *Mushíru'd-Dawla*, better known as *Sipahsálár-i-A'ẓam.* This is very improbable, since he returned to Persia and was made *Sipahsálár* (Commander-in-Chief) in A.H. 1287 (= A.D. 1870–1) while Náṣiru'd-Dín Sháh was visiting the Holy Thresholds (*i.e.* Karbalá and Najaf), and although, by permission, he paid a brief visit to Ṭihrán from Constantinople in the very year wherein this paper first appeared, *i.e.* A.H. 1280 (= A.D. 1863–4), was made a Member of the Council of the Empire, and remained for some months in Ṭihrán ere he returned to Constantinople, at that time he did not bear the title of *Sipahsálár*, which was held by Mírzá Muḥammad Khán Qájár. It is therefore possible that the paper ascribed to Mírzá Ḥusayn Khán was the *Rúznáma-i-'Ilmí*, which began to be published during the time when he was actually *Sipahsálár*; or else the *Rúznáma-i-Niẓámí* ("Military Gazette"), both of which papers are mentioned in this compendium. Perhaps the founder of the *Rúznáma-i-'Ilmiyya-i-Dawlat-i-'Aliyya-i-Írán* was the *I'tiẓádu's-Salṭana* himself, under whose management it continued until the end.

[2] The title of "Review" (*dawr*) is applied in Europe to papers which contain lengthy scientific, literary, political or historical articles rather than news of current events, which are generally provided with a cover, and which are not published daily, but at regular intervals of time, in the form and size of a tract or of the sheets of a book. In contemporary Arabic they are called *Majalla* and in Turkey *Majmú'a*, but in my opinion the best name for them in Persian is *Jung* or *Safína*, by which titles we have designated them, for in old books the same kind of records and note-books were called *Jung*, just as *Jarída* is the name of another kind of note-book.

the three others Sayyid Ḥasan Taqí-záda, Member of the First and Second National Assemblies; Mírzá Sayyid Ḥusayn Khán, editor of the newspapers *Ḥadíd*, *'Adálat*, *Ṣuḥbat* and *Khabar*; Mírzá Yúsuf Khán *I'tiṣám-i-Daftar*, originally of Áshtiyán, who here made use of the signature "Y. Y.", and who afterwards became *I'tiṣámu'l-Mulk*, editor of the magazine *Bahár* ("Spring"), and Member of the Second National Assembly; and it soon achieved popularity. Although some papers of a scientific character, as has been already mentioned, existed before it, such as those enumerated above, and the *Miftáḥu'ẓ-Ẓafar* ("Key of Victory"), printed at Calcutta and owned by the *Ḥablu'l-Matín* office, yet these in form and size were like newspapers, news-sheets and journals, and were not arranged like what are known in the terminology of Europe as reviews and magazines. After this scientific magazine, the periodicals known as *Faláḥat-i-Muẓaffarí* (scientific), *Majmú'a-i-Akhláq* (ethical), *Da'watu'l-Ḥaqq* (religious), *Bahár* (literary), and *Áftáb* (literary and scientific) are each worthy of esteem and praise in their respective spheres, on which account their appearance is recorded in the List of newspapers and magazines contained in this brief history.

The first satirical, comic, or derisive Persian paper was the *Ṭulú'*, published at Bushire in A.H. 1318 (= A.D. 1900–1), founded and edited by 'Abdu'l-Ḥamíd Khán *Matínu's-Salṭana*, who was subsequently a Member of the Second National Assembly. After this came the *Ázarbáyján*, published by 'Alí-qulí Khán, known as Ṣafaroff, formerly editor of the *Iḥtiyáj* ("Need"), at Tabríz in A.H. 1325 (= A.D. 1907–8), and printed with moveable types and coloured pictures and caricatures[1].

[1] The editor of this paper published in A.H. 1316 (= A.D. 1898–9) another paper entitled *Iḥtiyáj*, which, after the publication of seven numbers, was suppressed by order of Ḥasan 'Alí Khán Garrúsí *Amír-Niẓám* (agent and governor of Ázarbáyján during the time when Muḥammad 'Alí Mírzá was Crown Prince) on account of an article in which he had criticized in a ridiculous manner the need of the Persian people in every branch of life of foreign goods, such as tea-pots and the like. In addition to this, the above-mentioned editor was submitted to the degrading punishment of the bastinado; but after a little while he changed the name of his newspaper to *Iqbál* ("Progress") and began to publish it again, but it did not last long, and only a few numbers were issued. Wonderful to state, the above-mentioned 'Alí-qulí Khán, after the suspension of his newspaper, accepted a most detestable service, and became

During the Constitutional Period satirical and comic papers became numerous and varied. Such were the *Kashkúl, Tanbíh, Ḥasharátu'l-Arẓ, Buhlúl, Shaydá, Shaykh Chughundar*, etc. Of these the first, third and fourth were elegantly got up, pleasing and worthy of perusal. Of this class the satirical portion of the *Ṣúr-i-Isráfíl* ("Trumpet-call of Isráfíl"), which appeared under the heading *Charand-Parand* ("Charivari"), held the first place in this category, and may usefully be mentioned here, for the paper entitled *Mullá Naṣru'd-Dín*, which began to be published at Tiflís in A.H. 1324 (= A.D. 1906–7) in the Ázarbáyjání Turkish dialect, under the editorship of Mírzá Jalíl Muḥammad-qulí-záda of Nakhjuwán, a man well acquainted with Persian customs, and which was one of the best and most entertaining papers of this sort, and, indeed, unrivalled in the Oriental world, inasmuch as it used to discuss Persian matters also, had a very important historical influence in those parts of Persia bordering on the Caucasus and even in Ṭihrán itself, and the *Charand-Parand* column in the *Ṣúr-i-Isráfíl* was wholly indebted to and inspired by it in its form and style, the writer, Mírzá 'Alí Akbar Khán of Qazwín, known as "*Dakhaw*" or "*Dih-Khudá*," being acquainted with the Ázarbáyjání dialect.

The appearance of illustrated newspapers in Persia dates from the year A.H. 1277 (= A.D. 1860–1), when, as has been already mentioned, the official Gazette became illustrated under the editorship of the *Naqqásh-báshí*. The illustrations of the illustrated papers *Sharaf* and *Sharáfat* deserve mention on account of the excellence of the drawing and beauty of the typography, and the *Ázarbáyján* and *Ḥasharátu'l-Arẓ* ("Reptiles of the Earth") on account of their polychromatic printing.

The first paper published in Persia in a foreign language was the French paper *La Patrie* (*Waṭan*), of which one single number was issued on the 5th of February, 1876 (= A.H. 1293).

the chief and director of the spies or secret police of the tyrannical Crown Prince (Muḥammad 'Alí Mírzá), which organization was one of the primary causes of the disgust and dissatisfaction of the people of Tabríz at the institutions of the old, or autocratic, *régime*, and was an important factor in determining the strength of the Revolution at Tabríz. After the establishment of the Constitution, however, 'Alí-qulí Khán repented of his deeds, and died early in A.H. 1326 (Feb. 1908) while actively employed in the National Service.

هله تو تاخ که بو چکرتکه لری من قیروب قورتاردیم پس بو سارېخلی چکرتکه لره من نه چاره قیلیم ؟ ...

"How shall I deal with the turbaned locusts?"

(From *Mullá Naṣru'd-Dín*, No. 19, May 25, 1907)

The editor of this paper, Baron Louis de Norman, a Belgian, was brought to Ṭihrán in 1875 by Náṣiru'd-Dín Sháh, but the inkling of freedom perceptible in the first number proved displeasing to that monarch, and the paper was therefore suspended and its editor dismissed. After this the *Echo de Perse* (*Ṣadá-yi-Írán*) was published for some time, under the editorship of a Frenchman, Dr Morel. It lasted from March 21, 1885 (= A.H. 1302) to February 15, 1888[1].

Amongst other noteworthy newspapers one which is worthy of mention and not devoid of importance was a woman's paper entitled *Dánish* ("Knowledge") founded in Ṭihrán in A.H. 1328 (= A.D. 1910) by the wife of Mírzá Ḥusayn Khán *Kaḥḥál* ("the Oculist").

The freedom of the Press for papers published in Persia did not exist until the end of the reign of Náṣiru'd-Dín Sháh, but outside Persia several papers were in circulation each of which strove for a while to awaken and arouse men's thoughts. Their editors had to endure all kinds of losses and troubles. Some of these papers were from time to time prohibited from entering Persia, yet notwithstanding this they continued to be sent enclosed in books or envelopes. The *Akhtar* ("Star") was the first Persian newspaper printed outside Persia. Its founder and editor was Áqá Muḥammad Ṭáhir of Tabríz, who is still living, and who inaugurated it at Constantinople in A.H. 1292 (= A.D. 1875) at the instigation of Mírzá Najaf-qulí Khán, one of the officials of the Persian Government in that city, and author of the book entitled *Mízánu'l-Mawázín* ("the Measure of Measures"). It was published for more than twenty years, and was ultimately suspended in A.H. 1313 (= A.D. 1895–6) by the Ottoman Government. This newspaper attained such importance in Persia that the term *Akhtar* came to be applied to the purveyors of newspapers, and that news of current events was discussed in assemblies and meetings on its authority. The light of civilization shone from its pages on the people's hearts, and the taste for reading newspapers was derived from it. Wonderful to relate, this newspaper

[1] The above-mentioned Dr Morel subsequently passed his life in the service of the Government at Ṭihrán and in teaching in the Colleges, and finally died on his way home to France, at the age of about 55, in 1910.

in course of time acquired such fame in the Caucasus, Persia, Turkistán, India, 'Iráq (Mesopotamia), etc., that in some districts of the Caucasus the common people, who regard the reading of newspapers as improper and culpable, were wont to call those of better quality who habitually read them *Akhtari-maz-hab* ("Sectaries of the 'Star'"), regarding "*Akhtar*" as the designation of a sect.

The *Akhtar* was always in each period of its existence the lamp of all assemblies of cultivated men and the centre round which rallied the most accomplished and enlightened of the Persian exiles, and was maintained by the literary co-operation of patriotic scholars. Thus amongst others who worked on this paper were the late Mírzá Áqá Khán of Kirmán, author of many works; and Shaykh Aḥmad-i-Rúḥí[1], also of Kirmán, two of the earlier martyrs of the cause of Freedom; Mírzá Mahdí of Tabríz (now editor of the *Ḥikmat*—"Wisdom"—at Cairo)[2]; Mírzá 'Alí Muḥammad Khán of Káshán, editor of the *Thurayyá* ("Pleiades") and *Parwarish* ("Education"); and Ḥájji Mírzá Mahdí of Tabríz, who was subsequently the principal writer and acting editor of the paper until it came to an end.

After the *Akhtar*, Prince Mírzá Malkom Khán *Náẓimu'd-Dawla*, son of Mírzá Ya'qúb Khán, an Armenian of Julfá of Iṣfahán[3], who had lately been dismissed from the office of Persian envoy at the Court of St James's, founded and put in circulation a newspaper called the *Qánún* ("Law") in London in A.H. 1307 (= A.D. 1890)[4]. It was written by himself, and produced an important revolution in men's opinions, while its simple style of writing and peculiar form made people eager and desirous to read it. Several new terms, such as *Qánún* ("Law"), *Tanẓímát* ("Reforms"), *Uṣúl-i-Idára* ("Principles of Administration"), etc.,

[1] Some account of these two talented and unfortunate men will be found on pp. 93–95 of my *Persian Revolution*, 1905–1909. They were both put to death at Tabríz, together with Mírzá Ḥasan Khán *Khabíru'l-Mulk*, on July 17, 1896.

[2] His title is *Za'ímu'd-Dawla*, and he has written in Arabic a history and refutation of the Bábís entitled *Miftáḥu Bábi'l-Abwáb* ("the Key of the Gate of Gates").

[3] "Julfá of Iṣfahán" is so called to distinguish it from Julfá on the Araxes, on the Russo-Persian frontier.

[4] See pp. 35–42 of my *Persian Revolution of* 1905–1909. The first number of the *Qánún* was published on Feb. 20, 1890, and it continued to appear about once a month until No. 41.

Prince Malkom Khán *Náẓimu'd-Dawla*

Born at Iṣfahán in A.H. 1249 (A.D. 1833–4), died at Rome in A.H. 1326 (A.D. 1908)

passed from this newspaper into the current Persian language, and came into general use. By reason of the incomparable style and expression of Mírzá Malkom Khán in Persian, this became the best newspaper in the Persian language, and, by reason of its effects, has an important historical position in the Persian awakening. In short, the writings of Mírzá Malkom Khán have, generally speaking, a great twofold historical importance in the political and literary revolution of the latest Persian Renaissance. Politically they were one of the chief supports of the promoters of the Revolution and the renovation of Persia, and the founders of the movement of the *Risorgimento*; while from the literary point of view they were the sole originator of a peculiar style at once easy and agreeable.

After these two newspapers, the *Ḥablu'l-Matín* (" Firm Cord ") began to be printed in Calcutta in A.H. 1311 (=A.D. 1893–4), and the *Ḥikmat* (" Wisdom ") in Cairo in A.H. 1310 (=A.D. 1892–3). Both of these papers still continue to be published.

(II)

Some of the older publications, tracts and books and more especially certain newspapers, apart from other aspects, possess also a special historical importance deserving of closer investigation, because of their influence in bringing about the Persian Revolution and their connection with this matter. For in examining the causes and means which produced the prodromata of this Revolution it will be established that these publications also were an important agent, and hold a conspicuous place amongst numerous other influences.

It is evident that we must seek the causes and antecedents of the great historical Revolution of A.H. 1324 (= A.D. 1906) and the succeeding period in conditions which preceded it, and those who have investigated this matter have detected and discovered the germs of the embryo which was born at that date in a period twenty years earlier. Now as regards this class of revolutionary agencies and influences, that is to say publications designed to awaken the people and stir their thoughts, one may say that the earliest go back to a period antecedent to the Revolution by at least thirty years. In this category we include in particular those publications which contained criticisms, mild or vituperative, of the principles of administration; complaints of the current methods of government; and a revolt against the prevalent soul-destroying autocracy. Of these the first place, alike by reason of their influence, eloquence and lofty attitude, and in virtue of their chronological priority, belongs to the tracts of Prince Malkom Khán, which were first circulated in Ṭihrán in manuscript copies amongst Court circles and the notables of the kingdom, and afterwards passed from hand to hand throughout the whole of Persia[1]; but of these numerous treatises, which may perhaps exceed thirty in number (most of which the writer has seen) only a few, such as the *Uṣúl-i-Maz-hab-i-Díwániyán* ("Principles of Conduct of Officials"), *Ḥubbu'l-Waṭan mina'l-Ímán* ("Patriotism is a part of Faith"), and his Introduction to the *Gulistán* of Sa'dí printed with the new types invented by him and advocating the necessity of a reform in the alphabet, etc., were printed in Europe and published[2].

After the writings of Prince Malkom Khán; the newspaper *Akhtar* ("Star"); the writings of the late Mírzá Yúsuf Khán *Mustasháru'd-Dawla* of Tabríz, martyred in Qazwín; and the

[1] Were it not beyond the scope of this treatise, which deals only with printed publications, we should like to glance at some of the manuscript tracts and writings of the earlier Persian reformers which circulated amongst the people, and inspired the older progressives, since these also were in their way not devoid of historical importance. Of such were the Epistles of Kamálu'd-Dawla; the critical observations on the *Rawżatu'ṣ-Ṣafá-yi-Náṣirí* of Mírzá Fatḥ-'Alí Ákhundoff of Tiflís, author of several Turkish plays translated into Persian; other little-known tracts of Prince Malkom Khán; certain tracts in manuscript by Mírzá Áqá Khán, such as the *Sad Khiṭába* ("A hundred Addresses"), *Riżwán*, etc.; the *Siyáḥat-náma* ("Book of Travels") of Farrukh Khán *Amínu'd-Dawla*; *Maḥbúb and Háshim*, a pleasant treatise, written in the form of a comedy by Mírzá 'Abdu'l-Ḥusayn Khán *Mu'allifu'd-Dawla*, and the like, which considerations of space prevent us from discussing more fully.

[2] Prince Malkom Khán composed numerous treatises concerning the reform of the alphabet, such as the *Mabda-i-Taraqqí* ("Source of Progress") and the *Shaykh u Wazír*, which were never printed, and also, in order to familiarize men with the alphabet which he had invented, he printed several books in that alphabet, such as the above-mentioned *Gulistán*, the "Sayings of 'Alí," the "Writings of Humanity" (*Khuṭúṭ-i-Ádamiyyat*), etc. After the inauguration of the Constitution a collection of these manuscript writings was printed at Ṭihrán, but it is very badly edited and contains many errors.

A typical *Shab-náma*, or "Nocturnal Letter,"
"jelly-graphed" in purple ink, in November, 1906

paper *Qánún* ("Law"), mention must be made of certain "jelly-graph" publications which first became known at Tabríz, under the name of *Shab-náma* ("Night-books"), and which were issued by 'Alí-qulí Khán, editor of the *Iḥtiyáj* and some others, and the *Talqín-náma-i-Írán* issued in Tabríz during the reign of Náṣiru'd-Dín Sháh in the form of the admonition addressed to the dying (*talqín*), of which a garbled copy was subsequently published in the paper *Irshád* at Bákú during the period of Liberty, and which begins thus:—

"*O servant of God, and son of the servant of God, hear and understand! When there come to thee the proximate envoys from the Russians, the English and the House of 'Othmán* (*i.e.* the Ottoman Turks), *and ask thee concerning thy colleges, thine army, thy roads, thine arts, thy commerce and thy sciences...fear not, be not grieved, and say in answer to them...*" etc. There was also another "jelly-graphed" newspaper printed at Constantinople under the name *Shah-seven* ("King-lover," the name of a well-known group of tribes in N.W. Persia), under the title of which was written, "one number is published every forty years," and which used to criticize the old methods and principles of administration in a very entertaining and laughable manner. There were also the secret "jelly-graphed" newspaper-like publications produced in Ṭihrán under the names *Lisánu'l-Ghayb* ("Tongue of the Unseen") and *Ghayrat* ("Zeal")[1], etc., and the *Rúznáma-i-Ghaybí*, written in Iṣfahán and printed in St Petersburgh. This last was ascribed to the late *Maliku'l-Mutakallimín* (one of the most eminent victims of the *Coup d'État* of June 23, 1908) and was chiefly

[1] These publications were issued during the years A.H. 1319–20 (=A.D. 1901-2) on the part of a secret committee consisting of Mírzá Muḥammad 'Alí Khán, who died a martyr to the cause, Shaykh 'Abdu'l-'Alí "Múbad," Ḥájji Mírza Ḥasan "Rushdiyya," Shaykh Yaḥyá of Káshán, etc. They consisted chiefly of attacks on the *Amínu's-Sulṭán* (or *Atábak-i-A'ẓam*) and his administration, and exposures of the way in which he was selling the country to the Russians. In one of the later numbers there appeared a fragment of poetry, after the manner of, and containing quotations from, an ode of Ḥáfiẓ, which is worthy of notice. Considerations of space do not permit us to quote it here in its entirety, but we give one verse which forecasts in a manner almost prophetic the end of this Minister (who was assassinated by 'Abbás Áqá on August 31, 1907, the day on which the Anglo-Russian Convention was signed):—

"*O man of base appetites, why wilt thou drain the dregs of the Russians' cup?*
For this dark cup in the end kills the guest."

directed against the tyrannies of the *Ẓillu's-Sulṭán.* Mention must also be made amongst others of the *Ḥammám-i-Jinniyán* ("Genies' Bath"), which was "jelly-graphed" in Ṭihrán during the last days of the autocracy. Since we shall consider briefly in the Conclusion of this treatise the printed books and treatises which, from the earliest times until the present day, whether by peaceful methods of progress and evolution, like scientific books or political pamphlets moderate in tone, or in a revolutionary manner, by attacks on the Government and other classes, had an effect in awakening the people's minds, therefore we shall here only mention and indicate those publications which were directly and obviously connected with the last *risorgimento* and the course of that freedom-loving revival and revolution, especially such as explicitly blamed and criticized the prevalent methods of government.

In this category the books of Ḥájji Mírzá 'Abdu'r-Raḥím Ṭáliboff of Tabríz, and especially the *Kitáb-i-Aḥmad*, or *Safína-i-Ṭálibí*, in two volumes, had a specially great effect which cannot be denied. So also the *Siyáḥat-náma* ("Book of Travels") of Ibráhím Beg, especially by reason of its approximate coincidence in time with the outburst of the matter of disaffection, and its suitability to the occasion as regards the general disgust and aversion of the people of Persia to the ruinous and scandalous procedures which characterized the reign of Muẓaffaru'd-Dín Sháh, had a great effect and won a wide popularity. We must also mention amongst the books which had an effect in bringing about the National Awakening the translation into Persian by Mírzá Ḥabíb of Iṣfahán and Shaykh Aḥmad Rúḥí of Kirmán of Sir John Morier's *Ḥájjí Bábá*; the Memoirs of Mademoiselle de Montpensier, which were translated and added as a supplement to the Year-book, or *Sál-náma*, of A.H. 1313 (= A.D. 1895–6), and which, on their publication, aroused the extreme anger of Náṣiru'd-Dín Sháh, who caused all copies of them to be confiscated and destroyed; the stories of Alexandre Dumas translated into Persian; and a few other books translated and published during the later days of Muẓaffaru'd-Dín Sháh. But the most important factors in the Revolutionary movement, as voicing the public complaints and dissatisfaction and the disgust of the people at the principles on which the administration was conducted, were undoubtedly the newspapers, amongst which (leaving aside the *Akhtar*, which was relatively mild) the *Qánún* holds the first place. After it the greatest influence on public opinion was exerted by the newspapers *Thurayyá* and *Parwarish*, written by Mírzá 'Alí Muḥammad Khán-i-Shaybání of Káshán, which produced results much wider and more conclusive than even the *Qánún*, and in the years A.H. 1316–18 (= A.D. 1898–1901) effected a great intellectual revolution amongst young Persians, stirring up public opinion and filling the creatures of the Court with consternation. The coincidence of the publication of these newspapers with the Anglo-Boer War is also an important point. At this date the *Ḥablu'l-Matín* and the *Ḥikmat* held the next place to the *Thurayyá*, and exercised a considerable influence. Besides these Persian newspapers, four papers written in Caucasian Turkish, the *Sharq-i-Rús* ("Eastern Russia") and *Mullá Naṣru'd-Dín*, published at Tiflís, and the *Irshád* ("Direction") and *Ḥayát* ("Life") published at Bákú, were not without effect on the more enlightened classes in Ázarbáyján.

During the period of the Constitution the awakening of thought increased both in speed and extent, and the newspapers had a great influence and an important share in the renovation of public opinion, especially the reports of the debates in the *Majlis* (National Assembly), which were published in the newspaper entitled *Majlis* and other organs of the Press. The *Ṣúr-i-Isráfíl* and *Írán-i-Naw* also did good work in enlarging men's minds, and the *Sharáfat*, *al-Jamál*, and the *Chanta-i-Pá-barahna*, etc., in awakening the common people.

In a general survey of the newspapers and magazines, and a critical estimate of their respective values, we must state it as our opinion that, in point of literary style and expression the best of the older ones (that is, of those antecedent to the Revolution of A.H. 1324 = A.D. 1906) were the *Qánún* of Mírzá Malkom Khán, and the *Thurayyá* and *Parwarish* of Mírzá 'Alí Muḥammad Khán, and among the later ones (that is, those subsequent to the Revolution) the *Ṣúr-i-Isráfíl*, *Tamaddun*, daily *Ḥablu'l-Matín* of Ṭihrán, *Írán-i-Naw*, and *Tiyátr*. The boldest in their language were the *Rúḥu'l-Qudus*, *Musáwát*, *Jihád-i-Akbar*, *Naw-Bahár*, *Sharq*, *Barq*, *Ṣúr-i-Isráfíl* and *Ṣuḥbat*, while amongst these the moral courage of the *Ṣúr-i-Isráfíl* in criticizing the spiritual authorities, and the *Ṣuḥbat* in condemning prevailing customs are specially noteworthy.

The most amusing of the comic or satirical papers was the *Charand-parand* column of the *Ṣúr-i-Isráfíl*, the *Zisht u Zíbá* ("Foul and Fair") of the *Náqúr*, the literary column of the *Sharq* and *Nasím-i-Shimál*, and the newspapers *Ázarbáyján*, *Ḥasharátu'l-Arẓ*, *Kashkúl* and *Buhlúl*.

The simplest of the Persian newspapers in style were the *Qánún* of Malkom Khán, *al-Jamál*, the *Sharáfat*, the *Ḥikáyat-i-Ján-gudáz*, and the *Chanta-i-Pá-barahna*, the last of which was specially important in another way by reason of its diffusion of liberal ideas amongst the villagers and common people, and its success in awakening their minds by means of language easily understood by them.

The most firmly established and prosperous of the Persian newspapers, with the exception of the *Mufarriḥu'l-Qulúb*, were the *Akhtar* and the *Ḥablu'l-Matín* of Calcutta, whose great services in later times cannot be compared with those rendered by any other paper.

Amongst the illustrated newspapers the finest in point of illustration were the *Sharáfat* and *Sharaf*, and after them the *Adab* and the *Ázarbáyján*.

The *Tarbiyat*, *Adab* and *Bahár* must be reckoned first amongst the Persian literary papers.

Of all these newspapers only three openly championed the cause of autocracy, namely the *Uqyánús*, *Áy Mullá 'Amú* and the *Fikr* ("Thought"), while the broadsides published by Shaykh Faẓlu'lláh and his followers at Sháh 'Abdu'l-'Aẓím, where they had assembled and taken sanctuary in A.H. 1325 (= A.D. 1907), against the National Assembly, if these be reckoned as newspapers, were the most important of the reactionary organs, and have a special significance in the history of the Persian Revolution.

There exist also amongst these newspapers two which, unlike the others, though written in Persian had no particular concern with Persia nor any special reference to its affairs, namely, the *Siráju'l-Akhbár* ("Lamp of News") published at Kábul in Afghánistán, and *Bukhárá-yi-Sharíf* ("Bukhárá the Holy"), published at New Bukhárá in Turkistán, besides some of the Persian newspapers published in India, etc.

Before the Constitution the circulation of newspapers in Persia and the number of those who read them were very restricted. Those which enjoyed the largest circulation at that time were perhaps the *Thurayyá*, *Ḥablu'l-Matín* and *Náṣirí*, of which the last had a circulation of something over a thousand.

During the Constitutional Period the circulation of the newspapers went up, each of them enjoying a circulation of from two to three thousand copies. Thus the *Musáwát* had a circulation of 3000, the *Ṣúr-i-Isráfíl* from 5000 to 5500; the *Majlis* gradually rose from 7000 to 10,000, the *Anjuman* in Tabríz 5000. During the Second Period of the Constitution (July 1909—latter part of 1911), when the daily newspapers increased in size, their circulation diminished. Thus the *Istiqlál-i-Írán* ("Independence of Persia") had a circulation of from 800 to 1000 copies, and the *Írán-i-Naw* ("New Persia"), which enjoyed the largest circulation, from 2000 to 2500, very rarely reaching 3000. This diminution in the number of readers is chiefly to be ascribed to the general increase of poverty resulting from the disturbances, in consequence of which it often happened that several readers combined to buy and share one copy. One point worthy of mention is that in the latter days of the period of Autocracy the wealthy and well-known Ḥájji Zaynu'l-'Ábidín Taqioff of Bákú, an eminent philanthropist, subscribed yearly for nearly 500 copies of the Calcutta *Ḥablu'l-Matín*, paying the subscription himself, and arranging that they should be sent gratuitously to the Shí'ite doctors of theology and students residing at Karbalá, Najaf and others of the Holy Shrines, regularly and directly from the chief office. This great service rendered by him to the enlightenment of the *'ulamá* and their political awakening greatly conduced to the circulation of newspapers in spiritual circles and societies.

The older Persian newspapers, and broadly speaking the greater part of the newspapers in general, were published in the *nasta'líq* writing, and the publication of newspapers in the *naskh* writing is to be reckoned a step forward in the perfecting of them. As is well known, the number of lithographed papers exceeded that of papers printed with moveable types, of which latter the *Akhtar* was the first[1].

[1] During the Constitutional period "jelly-graphed" publications of various forms and shapes were countless and beyond computation, but in this treatise we have only

Until the foundation of the *Írán-i-Naw* in A.H. 1327 (=A.I 1909) the *format* of the Persian newspapers has generally, wit the exception of the *Sayyidu'l-Akhbár*, printed in India, and th Persian Supplement of the *Irshád* of Bákú, been small; generall of the size of the smaller sheets of Russian paper used in Persi: more rarely somewhat larger. The *Írán-i-Naw* was the first c the large-sized Persian newspapers, resembling in every way i its arrangement the newspapers of Europe. After it the *Sharq Barq*, *Istiqlál-i-Írán*, *Waqt*, *Majlis*, *Surúsh*, and finally the *Áftá* came out in the same *format*.

Amongst recent years that wherein the circulation of news papers reached its maximum was A.H. 1325 (= A.D. 1907), during which 84 newspapers were founded. Next comes the year A.H 1328 (=A.D. 1910), when 36 newspapers were in circulation then the year A.H. 1329 (=A.D. 1911) with 33 newspapers, anc the years A.H. 1326 (=A.D. 1908) and 1327 (1909), each witl 31 newspapers. The city in Persia where the greatest numbe of newspapers was published was Ṭihrán (148 newspapers), anc next to it Tabríz (51), Rasht (25), Iṣfahán (20), and Mashhad (10)

It is worth calling attention to one small point deserving o notice, and that is that the official political parties, such as the Democrats, Union and Progress, Moderates, etc., only came into being in the Second Period of the Constitution, and were generally recognized only after the opening of the Second *Majlis* (Nov. 15, 1909). It is, therefore, not correct to ascribe to any one of the above-mentioned parties any newspaper antecedent to that date. During the First Period of the Constitution the only organized party was that of the Social Democrats (*Ijtimá'iyyún-i-'Ámmiyyún*), whose organ was the *Mujáhid*, published at Tabríz.

After these brief general observations follows the detailed List or Catalogue, arranged in alphabetical order, of all the papers of every sort and in every language, whether Persian or otherwise, published in Persia, and in addition the Persian papers published abroad, which have come under the writer's notice.

noticed such as resembled newspapers in arrangement, form and title. Some of the others also appeared repeatedly under the same title, but they were for the most part unsigned and circulated secretly.

The late *Amínu's-Sulṭán* meditating the sale of the province of Ázarbáyján

(From the illustrated comic weekly *Ázarbáyján*, No. 4, March 16, 1907)

LIST OF NEWSPAPERS PUBLISHED IN PERSIA OR IN PERSIAN, ARRANGED IN ALPHABETICAL ORDER

(1)

Ádamiyyat (*Humanity*). آدمیّت

A weekly newspaper printed in Ṭihrán in A.H. 1325 (= A.D. 1907) under the editorship of Mírzá 'Abdu'l-Muṭṭalib of Yazd, who, from the beginning of the Constitution, was an object of suspicion to the Constitutionalists and was in league with the Reactionaries. After the Reaction of the 23rd of Jumáda i, A.H. 1326 (= June 23, 1908), he was one of the Members of that unrighteous tribunal of the Bágh-i-Sháh which interrogated, tormented and slew the Liberals. After the restoration of the Constitution and the conquest of Ṭihrán (July, 1909) he was arrested and imprisoned for a year with other political offenders.

According to Rabino, No. 12, the third number of this paper was dated 28 Jumáda ii, A.H. 1325 (= August 8, 1907), and the eleventh number Ramaẓán 13 (October 20) of the same year. I possess Nos. 3, 8 and 11. Bi-weekly; 4—8 pp.; 12″ or 13″ × 7″ or 7½″; 15 *qráns* yearly in Ṭihrán, 18 in provinces, 12 francs abroad.

(2)

Ázarbáyján. آذربایجان

A weekly comic newspaper printed in Tabríz with coloured caricatures in the beginning of A.H. 1325 (= A.D. 1907) under the editorship of 'Alí-qulí Khán, known as Ṣafaroff, also editor of the *Iḥtiyáj* ("Need") and the *Iqbál* ("Progress")[1]. This newspaper was published in Persian and Ázarí Turkish. In politics it was thoroughly Liberal and Constitutional.

According to Rabino, No. 13, the first number was published on Muḥarram 2, A.H. 1325 (= Feb. 15, 1907), but my copy of No. 1, which bears on the outer sheet the dates "1324–1906," is dated on p. 2 Muḥarram 6, 1325, so that Mr Rabino's "2" appears to be an error for "6." Weekly; 8 pp.; 14 *sháhís* each number, or four *túmáns* a year in Tabríz; 12″ × 7⅜″. I possess Nos. 1–22, with some omissions.

[1] See p. 15 and note *ad calc.*, *supra*.

(3)

Áráwôd (*Morning*, Armenian). առաւօտ

A weekly newspaper printed in Tabríz in the Armenian language and serving as the organ of the Armenian Dáshnáksútiyún. It was founded in A.H. 1327 (= A.D. 1909), and continued until the Russian massacre in Tabríz in Muḥarram, 1330 (= Jan. 1912). This paper, by reason of its Liberal opinions, had a considerable influence in the Caucasus, and its entry into Russia was consequently prohibited ; and subsequently it gave rise to complaint on the part of the Russians, who continually exerted themselves to secure its suppression. It was well known both on account of the important telegraphic news which it obtained from Ṭihrán and from abroad, and also in consequence of its polemics with the Persian newspaper *Shafaq* (" Dawn "), also printed at Tabríz.

See Rabino, No. 232. According to him No. 119 of this paper, which I have never seen, bore the date October 18, 1911.

(4)

Ázád (*Free*). آزاد

A newspaper published in India at Delhi in A.D. 1885 (= A.H. 1302–3), known to us only through the *Sayyidu'l-Akhbár* (published at Ḥaydarábád in the Deccan), in consequence of a literary duel which took place between these two papers.

(5)

Ázád (*Free*). آزاد

A weekly newspaper published at Calcutta (India) by lithography, early in A.H. 1317 (= A.D. 1899), under the editorship of Mírzá Sayyid Ḥasan of Káshán (brother of Sayyid Jalálu'd-Dín *Mu'ayyidu'l-Islám*, better known as the editor of the *Ḥablu'l-Matín* of Calcutta), subsequently editor of the daily *Ḥablu'l-Matín* of Ṭihrán. The above-mentioned Mírzá Sayyid Ḥasan, in consequence of his being the agent in Ṭihrán for the Calcutta *Ḥablu'l-Matín* during the second Ministry of the *Amínu's-Sulṭán* (or *Atábak-i-A'ẓam*), and the attacks made by it on this Minister after the Russian loans (of 1900 and 1902) and his suppression of the newspapers *Parwarish*, *Ḥikmat* and *Ḥablu'l-Matín*, was exposed to the vengeance of this powerful minister, and, after remaining for some time in prison and chains, was banished, and went by way of Egypt to his brother at Calcutta. During his stay there he started the newspapers *Miftáḥu'ẓ-Ẓafar* ("Key of Victory") and *Ázád* ("Free").

See Rabino, No. 15. According to him it began publication on the 8th of Rabí' ii, A.H. 1317 (=August 15, 1899). I possess No. 1. The yearly subscription was 10 rupees for India, Burma, and the Persian Gulf; 25 *qráns* for Persia and Afghánistán, 25 francs for China, Japan, Russia and Europe; and 5 mejidiyyés for Turkey, Turkish Arabia and Egypt. It is very well lithographed, the written page measuring 12″ × 7″, and each number containing 8 pp.

(6)

Ázád (*Free*). آزاد

A weekly paper lithographed in Tabríz and containing portraits of notable patriots of older and more recent times, founded towards the end of A.H. 1324 (= beginning of A.D. 1907) under the control of the *Kitáb-khána-i-Tarbiyat* ("Tarbiyat" Library) and the immediate editorship of Mírzá Riẓá Khán "Tarbiyat," brother of the writer, and manager of the above-mentioned Library, and Mírzá Maḥmúd Khán Ashraf-záda. The "Tarbiyat" Library, founded in A.H. 1316 (= A.D. 1898–9) by the present writer and two or three friends, has a specially great importance in the history of the awakening of Ázarbáyján, and played a considerable part in the last Revolution. The above-mentioned Library, which in the beginning was the first specimen of a book-shop on modern lines in Ázarbáyján, but in a very small and humble way, continued day by day, by persistent efforts and endeavours, to increase its scope and prestige, importing useful books in every language from every part of the world, and circulating and making them known in Tabríz, so that it eventually became the best, most important and most comprehensive of all book-shops without exception throughout the whole of Persia, publishing every year a printed catalogue in the European fashion. In addition to this it became one of the centres of Liberal political action in Ázarbáyján, until during the Reaction (23 Jumáda i, A.H. 1326 = June 23, 1908) it was looted and burned by the Reactionaries and the scoundrels who followed

Raḥím Khán of Qará-dágh. In politics this paper was thoroughly Liberal and Constitutional.

See Rabino, No. 14. I possess Nos. 2, 3 and 4. The first is dated 24 Dhu'l-Ḥijja, A.H. 1324 (=Feb. 8, 1907). No. 2 contains a portrait of Muḥammad 'Alí (at that time Sháh), and No. 3 one of Sayyid Jamálu'd-Dín, the latter drawn by Sayyid 'Abbás al-Ḥusayni. Each number cost 3 *sháhís* in Tabríz, where the yearly subscription was 7 *qráns*, and 15 in the provinces and abroad. The pages (four in number) measure 13" × 6½". The writing and lithography are good.

(7)

Ázád (*Free*). آزاد

A weekly newspaper published in Ṭihrán in A.H. 1327 (= A.D. 1909).

Not mentioned by Rabino, and no copy seen.

(8)

Ázádí (*Freedom*). آزادی

A fortnightly newspaper published in Constantinople in A.H. 1327 (= A.D. 1909) under the editorship of Ḥasan Nájí of Khúy. Only one number was published, on Muḥarram 8 (= Jan. 30, 1909).

Not mentioned by Rabino, and no copy seen.

(9)

Ázádí (*Freedom*). آزادی

A newspaper published at Ṭihrán, mentioned without any particulars by Mr Rabino (No. 16), but otherwise unknown to the writer.

(10)

Ázádí chi chíz-ast? (*What is Freedom?*). آزادی چه چیز است

A newspaper printed in Ṭihrán in A.H. 1326 (= A.D. 1908).

See Rabino, No. 17. The second issue was dated the 15th of Rabí' ii, A.H. 1326 (=May 17, 1908).

(11)

Azd-arar (*The Advertiser*, Armenian). ազդ-արար

A weekly Armenian newspaper printed at Tabríz, mentioned without further particulars by Mr Rabino (No. 236), but otherwise unknown to the writer.

(12)

Astgh Arevelean (*The Star of the East*). աստղ արեւելեան

A weekly Armenian newspaper printed at Ṭihrán in A.D. 1893 (= A.H. 1310–11).

See Rabino, No. 231, which gives no further details.

(13)

Áfáq (*The Horizons*). آفاق

A newspaper published in Shíráz in A.H. 1327 (= A.D. 1909), mentioned (No. 24) by Mr Rabino, but otherwise unknown to the writer.

(14)

Áftáb (*The Sun*). آفتاب

A scientific and literary magazine printed at Iṣfahán under the editorship of Mírzá "Maḥmúd Khán S." of Ṭihrán. This magazine, of which the first issue appeared on the 20th of Rabí' i, A.H. 1329 (= March 21, 1911), was encouraged and inspired by Shaykh Muḥammad Báqir (son of Ḥájji Shaykh Muḥammad Taqí of Iṣfahán, better known as Áqá-yi-Najafí), one of the most enlightened theologians of the time. It is democratic in politics, and is still issued.

See Rabino, No. 25. I possess the first two numbers. No. 1 is bound in a red paper cover and contains 56 pp. of 6½" × 3¾". Price of each number 1 *qrán* in Iṣfahán and 1½ *qráns* elsewhere. Yearly subscription 10 *qráns* in Iṣfahán, 12 elsewhere in Persia, and 14 abroad.

(15)

Áftáb (*The Sun*). آفتاب

A large-sized paper printed every other day at Ṭihrán in A.H. 1330 (= A.D. 1912) under the editorship of Mírzá 'Abdu'l-Ḥusayn, son of 'Abdu'l-Wahháb. This paper was established at the cost and with the support of the Government after the *Coup d'État* of Muḥarram 1, A.H. 1330 (= Dec. 22, 1911), and the suppression of all the free papers of Ṭihrán, and became the semi-official organ of the Government. It defends the conduct and actions of the Government, criticizes its opponents, and endeavours to win the approval of the Russian and English

Legations. Its more important leading articles are ascribed to the Minister for Foreign Affairs himself, *Wuthúqu'd-Dawla*. Its editor was formerly one of the correspondents of the *Írán-i-Naw*. In politics it is Moderate.

Not included in Rabino's list, which was published before it came into existence.

(16)

Ágáhí (*Information*). آگاهی

A weekly newspaper lithographed in Ṭihrán in A.H. 1325 (= A.D. 1907).

Not mentioned by Rabino, and no copy seen.

(17)

Ámúzgár (*The Teacher*). آموزگار

A fortnightly newspaper printed in Ṭihrán in A.H. 1326 (= A.D. 1908) under the editorship of Shaykh 'Alí 'Iráqí.

See Rabino, No. 31. I possess No. 3, dated 19 Rabí' i, A.H. 1326, and April 21, 1908. Subscription, 4 *qráns* a year in Persia, 5 francs abroad. Page, $11\frac{1}{4}'' \times 6\frac{3}{4}''$.

(18)

Ámúzgár (*The Teacher*). آموزگار

A weekly newspaper printed in Rasht in A.H. 1329 (=A.D. 1911) under the editorship of Mírzá Muḥammad Taqí of Shíráz.

See Rabino, No. 30, according to whom it was founded on the 7th of Jumáda ii, A.H. 1329 (=June 5, 1911), and was Democratic in politics. I possess Nos. 1—24. Each comprises 4 pp. of $12'' \times 7''$ Yearly subscription, 6 *qráns* in Rasht, 8 elsewhere in Persia, and 12 abroad.

(19)

Ana dili (*The Mother Tongue*). انا دیلی

A newspaper published in Tabríz in the Ázarbáyjání Turkí language as part of the paper *'Adálat* ("Justice," *q.v.*) to which it formed a supplement and by the office of which it was published.

Not mentioned by Rabino.

(20)

Á'ína-i-Ghayb-numá (*Mirror shewing the Unseen*). آئینهٔ غیب نما

A fortnightly illustrated newspaper lithographed at Ṭihrán in A.H. 1325 (= A.D. 1907) under the editorship of Sayyid

'Abdu'r-Raḥím of Káshán. It renewed publication in the second Constitutional Period in Rajab, A.H. 1329 (= July, 1911).

See Rabino, No. 42. I possess Nos. 7, 12, 20, 21 and 31-33, of the First Year; and No. 6 of the Second Year. The first is dated 22 Jumáda i, A.H. 1325, and July 4, 1907. The yearly subscription was 25 *qráns* in Ṭihrán, 30 in the provinces, and 17 francs abroad, and each number comprised 4 pp. of 12" × 7¼". The date of the last number in my possession is Rajab 26, A.H. 1329 = July 23, 1911. The illustrations, which are somewhat crude, include portraits of notable patriots and caricatures.

(21)

Áy Mullá 'Amú! آی ملّا عمو

A newspaper lithographed in Tabríz in the Ázarbáyjání Turkish language, in quarto size as I have heard, edited and written by Mírzá Aḥmad, director of the *Baṣírat* College, and editor of the newspapers *Ukhuwwat* ("Fraternity"), *Ittiḥád* ("Union") and *Islámiyya*. According to another account, it was edited by Mírzá Ḥasan and the *Sa'ídu's-Sulṭán*. It was published in the year A.H. 1326 (= A.D. 1908) by the Reactionaries and members of the *Anjuman-i-Islámiyya* of the Devechi (or Shuturbán) quarter of Tabríz in order to excite the people against the Constitution.

See Rabino, No. 43.

(22)

Iblágh (*Conveyance*). ابلاغ

A weekly lithographed paper published at Tabríz in A.H. 1324 (= A.D. 1906) under the editorship of Mashhadí Maḥmúd Iskandání, writer of the paper *Naẓmiyya* in Tabríz.

See Rabino, No. 1, according to whom the first and sixth issues (the only ones seen) bore no date. I possess No. 1, which comprises 4 pp. of 11½" × 6¾", written in a fine bold *naskh*. Seven *qráns* a year in Tabríz, ten elsewhere in Persia.

(23)

Ittiḥád (*Union*). اتّحاد

A lithographed newspaper published at Tabríz in A.H. 1324 (= A.D. 1906) under the editorship of Mírzá Aḥmad the scribe of Tabríz, known as *Baṣírat* after the College of that name of which he was formerly director. Only a few numbers were published.

Not mentioned by Rabino.

(24)

Ittiḥád (*Union*). اتّحاد

A fortnightly newspaper printed in Ṭihrán in A.H. 1325 (= A.D. 1907) under the editorship of the Mu'tamadu'l-Islám of Rasht.

See Rabino, No. 3. I possess Nos. 2—20, of which the first is dated 5 Rabí' ii, A.H. 1325 (=May 18, 1907). Contains as a rule 4 pp. of 11″ × 6¾″. Yearly subscription, 15 *qráns* in Ṭihrán, 20 in provinces, 5 roubles in Russia, 8 rupees in India.

(25)

Ittiḥád (*Union*). اتّحاد

A fortnightly newspaper printed at Tabríz in A.H. 1326 (= A.D. 1908) under the management of the *Anjuman-i-Ittiḥád* ("Society of Union"), which was one of the unofficial *anjumans* of the Constitutionalists. Such *anjumans* were numerous in most towns of Persia during the First Period of the Constitution. They were first formed in Ṭihrán, whence they spread to other parts of the country. Of these unofficial provincial *anjumans* the above-mentioned *Anjuman-i-Ittiḥád*, founded by the present writer on his return from Ṭihrán towards the end of the year A.H. 1325 (=winter of 1907–8), was the first. Its organ, the *Ittiḥád*, was inaugurated at the beginning of Ṣafar, A.H. 1326 (= March, 1908). After the Minor Disturbance of Tabríz (by which is meant the strife and struggle of the Reactionaries, collected in the Devechi quarter of the city, and the Constitutionalists of the other quarters, in Dhu'l-Ḥijja, 1325 = January, 1908) it strove to defend the latter and oppose the former, who on their side, aided by the *Anjuman-i-Islámiyya* which they had founded, published in Ázarbáyjání Turkish the paper *Áy Mullá 'Amú* (see No. 21 *supra*) in the Devechi quarter. In a supplement or *feuilleton* the *Ittiḥád* published a dramatic sketch written by Mírzá Malkom Khán under the title of "Ashraf Khán, Governor of 'Arabistán," which pourtrayed in four Acts, in a most amazing and attractive manner, the governors of the old autocratic *régime*. This paper continued to be published until the beginning of the Great Revolution in Tabríz. In politics it was Liberal or Radical, and Constitutional.

See Rabino, No. 2. I possess Nos. 1, 2, 5, 7 and 8. It contains 4 pages of 11¼″ × 7½″. The yearly subscription was 12 *qráns* in Tabríz, 16 in other parts of Persia, and 20 abroad.

(26)

Ittiḥád (*Union*). اتّحاد

A lithographed newspaper published in Yazd in A.H. 1328 (= A.D. 1910).

See Rabino, No. 4. He states that only two or three numbers appeared.

(27)

Ittiḥadiyya-i-Sa'ádat. اتّحاديّهٔ سعادت

A weekly newspaper published in Ṭihrán in A.H. 1325 (= A.D. 1907).

Not mentioned by Rabino.

(28)

Ittifáq (*Concord*). اتّفاق

A weekly newspaper published at Urmiya in Ázarbáyján in A.H. 1328 (= A.D. 1910) under the editorship of Ḥájji Mírzá Ibráhím of Ṭihrán.

Not mentioned by Rabino.

(29)

Ittifáq (*Concord*). اتّفاق

A fortnightly newspaper printed in Rasht in A.H. 1329 (= A.D. 1911) under the editorship of Ma'ṣúm-záda Shukúrí and Ḥ. Jamshíd-záda. It was an organ of the "Union and Progress" Party.

See Rabino, No. 5, according to whom the first number was dated 16 Jumáda ii, A.H. 1329 = June 14, 1911. I also possess one number (No. 1) of a weekly *lithographed* newspaper of this name, also published at Rasht, dated the 21st of Rabí' i, A.H. 1327, and April 12, 1909, edited by Mír 'Abdu'l-Báqí and 'Alí Áqá Náẓim, founders of the Ittifáq College. It contains rather a fine poem addressed to Muḥammad 'Alí, who was at that time still Sháh.

(30)

Ittifáq-i-Kárgarán (*Union of Workers*). اتّفاق کارگران

A newspaper published in Ṭihrán by the United Association of Printers, who, in consequence of the strike to which they had recourse in order to further their aims and obtain from their employers and the owners of the printing-presses their nine demands, brought it out during their strike in A.H. 1328 (= A.D.

1910). This strike and this newspaper have both a special historical importance, inasmuch as they were the first manifestations in Persia of a collectivist or socialistic movement; for although other strikes had taken place before this, yet these had not the form and character of European strikes. This newspaper did not run to more than four or five numbers. In politics it was Socialistic (*Ijtimá'í*).

Not mentioned by Rabino, and not seen.

(31)

Iḥtiyáj (*Need*). احتياج

A weekly newspaper lithographed in Tabríz in A.H. 1316 (= A.D. 1898–9) under the editorship of 'Alí-qulí Khán, known as Ṣafaroff, some account of whom and his paper has been already given in the Introduction (p. 15 and note 1 *ad calc., supra*).

See Rabino, No. 6, according to whom only 7 numbers (the first dated Muḥarram 16, A.H. 1316=June 6, 1898) were published. At the request of the Amír Niẓám the name of the paper was then changed to *Iqbál* ("Good Fortune"), under which title the eighth number appeared.

(32)

Iḥyá (*Revivification*). احيا

A weekly newspaper printed at Shíráz in A.H. 1329 (= A.D. 1911) under the editorship of Ḥájji Mírzá 'Abdu'l-Ḥusayn.

See Rabino, No. 7. I possess No. 4, dated Monday the 3rd of Rabí' ii, A.H. 1329 (=April 3, 1911). It contains 4 pp. of 13" × 7¼". Yearly subscription in Shíráz, 6 *qráns*.

(33)

Akhbár-i-Imrúz (*To-day's News*). اخبار امروز

A newspaper printed in Ṭihrán in the month of Shawwál, A.H. 1329 (= Sept.–Oct. 1911). The editor's name appeared only as 'Alí at the bottom of the sheet.

Not mentioned by Rabino, and not seen.

(34)

Akhtar (*Star*). اختر

A weekly newspaper printed at Constantinople. It began to be published in A.H. 1292 (= A.D. 1875) under the editorship of Áqá Muḥammad Ṭáhir of Tabríz, who is still living.

See Rabino, No. 8. I possess a considerable collection of numbers belonging to the fourteenth to the seventeenth years (May, 1888–Feb. 1891). The paper came to an end about 1895 or 1896. The yearly subscription was 5 mejidiyyés in Turkey, 25 *qráns* in Persia, 25 francs in Europe, etc. Each issue, as a rule, comprised 8 pp. of 13″ × 8½″.

(35)

Ukhuwwat (*Fraternity*). اخوّت

A weekly newspaper lithographed at Tabríz in A.H. 1324 (= A.D. 1906) under the editorship of Mírzá Aḥmad, known as "Baṣírat," who was also editor of the *Ittiḥád* (see No. 23, *supra*).

Not mentioned by Rabino, and not seen.

(36)

Ukhuwwat (*Fraternity*). اخوّت

A weekly newspaper printed at Rasht (not Yazd, as stated in the original MS.) in A.H. 1328 (= A.D. 1910).

See Rabino, No. 10, according to whom only 13 numbers were published, at irregular intervals, the first on the 8th of Sha'bán, A.H. 1328 (= August 15, 1910), the last on the 24th of Jumáda ii, A.H. 1329 (= June 22, 1911), the editor being first "Mu'ayyid" and then "Mawlawí." I possess all thirteen numbers. Nos. 2 and 3 were entitled *Ukhuwwat-i-'Álí*. The paper was chiefly ethical and literary, and contained a good deal of poetry. It consisted of pp. 4—6 of 12″ × 7¼″. Yearly subscription, 10 *qráns* a year in Rasht, 12 elsewhere in Persia.

(37)

Ukhuwwat (*Fraternity*). اخوّت

A weekly newspaper printed at Baghdad in A.H. 1328 (= A.D. 1910) under the editorship of Muḥammad Taqí of Yazd. In politics this paper was Liberal and Constitutional.

See Rabino, No. 9, according to whom the fifth issue was dated the 6th of Rabí' ii, A.H. 1328 (= April 27, 1910). I possess No. 18, which is dated the 4th of Sha'bán, A.H. 1328 (= August 11, 1910), and comprises 8 pp. of 9¼″ × 6½″. The yearly subscription was 30 piastres in Baghdad and 40 elsewhere in Turkey; 20 *qráns* in Persia; 5 roubles in Russia; 10 francs in Europe; and 6 rupees in India.

(38)

Adab (*Culture*). ادب

A weekly newspaper lithographed in the *ta'líq* writing in Tabríz in A.H. 1316 (= A.D. 1898–9). The owner and editor of this paper was Mírzá Ṣádiq Khán *Adíbu'l-Mamálik*, one of the

"*Qá'im-maqámí*" Sayyids, a descendant of Mírzá Abu'l-Qásim of Faráhán, the celebrated *Qá'im-maqám*, who was Prime Minister to Muḥammad Sháh Qájár. This paper was illustrated with portraits of the celebrated sages and great men of the world, and contained some scientific articles written or translated by Mírzá Najaf-qulí Khán-i-*Qá'im-maqámí*, the physician. After the publication of the seventeenth number it was suspended for some time, until the College known as *Luqmániyya* was founded and opened under the direction of the *Adíbu'l-Mamálik*, when it again appeared under the management and at the cost of the above-mentioned College. Only three or four numbers appeared, lithographed in *naskh* handwriting and illustrated with portraits of the *Qá'im-maqám*, Mírzá Taqí Khán *Amír-Niẓám*, etc., when the editor resigned the direction of the College. He published one more number (the last) at Tabríz, and a little while after the second suspension of the paper set out for Mashhad. Some poetical fragments and *qaṣídas* of the *Adíbu'l-Mamálik* himself, who was one of the most eminent contemporary poets of Persia, were generally included in the paper. Of his many excellent poems only one—a threnody in fourteen stanzas—has been printed at Tabríz.

See Rabino's supplementary list, No. 237, where the date of first publication is given as the 15th of Sha'bán, A.H. 1317 (=Dec. 28, 1898), and it is stated that only three numbers were published. I have no copy of the Tabríz *Adab*.

(39)

Adab (*Culture*). ادب

A weekly newspaper lithographed at Mashhad in A.H. 1318 (= A.D. 1900–1). Its editor was the same *Adíbu'l-Mamálik* mentioned above, and it continued at Mashhad until A.H. 1320 (= A.D. 1902–3).

See Rabino, No. 11, according to whom this paper continued from the 4th of Ramaẓán, A.H. 1318 (=Dec. 26, 1900) until the 28th of Shawwál, A.H. 1320 (=Jan. 28, 1903). The *Adíbu'l-Mamálik's* proper name was Mírzá Ṣádiq Khán of Faráhán. I possess Nos. 1 and 9. Each comprises 8 pp. of 12" × 8½" well lithographed in large, clear *naskh*. Yearly subscription, 20 *qráns* in Mashhad, 25 elsewhere in Persia, 6 roubles in the Caucasus and Russia, 3 mejidiyyés in Turkey, 10 rupees in India, and 12 francs in Europe.

(40)

Adab (*Culture*). ادب

A weekly newspaper lithographed and subsequently printed in Ṭihrán in A.H. 1322 (= A.D. 1904–5), at first edited and written by the same *Adíbu'l-Mamálik* who founded the two papers of the same name (*Adab*) published at Tabríz and Mashhad respectively, and afterwards by *Majdu'l-Islám* of Kirmán, editor of the *Nidá-yi-Waṭan*, *Kashkúl* and *Muḥákamát* (*q.v.*). The *Adíbu'l-Mamálik*, who edited it at first, after a while transferred it to *Majdu'l-Islám*, and himself went to Bákú, where he edited the Persian supplement of Aḥmed Bey Aghayeff's Turkish paper *Irshád*. After the issue of eleven numbers of this he returned to Ṭihrán in the [first] Constitutional Period, when so many *anjumans* (committees) were formed by the Constitutionalists, and founded a paper entitled *'Iráq-i-'Ajam*, which was the organ of the *anjuman* of that name.

See Rabino, No. 11, according to whom the third issue was dated the 8th of Ṣafar, A.H. 1322 (=April 24, 1904), and the 189th issue the 14th of Rabí' ii, A.H. 1324 (=June 7, 1906). I possess Nos. 40, 146 and 188 (all lithographed). These comprise pp. 4—8 of $12\frac{1}{2}'' \times 8\frac{1}{2}''$ and generally contain a portrait on the first and a caricature on the last page. Yearly subscription, 24 *qráns* in Ṭihrán; 20 *qráns* to students in Ṭihrán and Mashhad; 30 *qráns* in other parts of Persia; 8 roubles in Russia and the Caucasus; 4 mejidiyyés in Turkey and Egypt; 15 rupees in India and China; and 20 francs in Europe and America. I also possess three of the printed numbers, No. 161 (fourth year) dated the 18th of Rajab, A.H. 1323 = Sept. 13, 1905; No. 184 (fifth year) dated the 2nd of Rabí' ii, A.H. 1324 = May 26, 1906; and No. 189, dated sixteen days later. These were printed at the Khurshíd ("Sun") printing-press at Ṭihrán, but bear no editor's name. The subscription price is somewhat higher than the homonymous lithograph.

(41)

Irshád (*Direction*). ارشاد

A half-page Persian supplement to the daily Turkish newspaper *Irshád* printed at Bákú in the year A.H. 1323 (= A.D. 1905–6), written by the above-mentioned *Adíbu'l-Mamálik* under the editorship of Aḥmed Bey Aghayeff of Qarábágh.

(42)

Urmiye Orthodoxyáitá. ܐܘܪܡܝܗ ܐܘܪܬܕܘܟܣܝܬܐ

A newspaper published at Urúmí (Urmiya) in the Chaldaean (Syriac) language for the promotion of the "Orthodox" faith.

(43)

Istiqlál (*Independence*). استقلال

A newspaper printed at Tabríz, and appearing every alternate day, in the year A.H. 1327 (= A.D. 1909) under the editorship of Mírzá Áqá of Tabríz, known as *Nála-i-Millat* ("Cry of the Nation"), because he edited another paper of this name, and was called after it, according to a custom prevalent in Persia. This newspaper was the result of the assembling under the protection of the Ottoman Consulate at Tabríz of the Constitutionalists and defenders of Tabríz, headed by Sattár Khán and Báqir Khán, in consequence of the continued aggressions of the then newly arrived Russian troops in Jumáda i of that year (= May 21–June 20, 1909), when a committee was formed amongst the refugees consisting of certain men of education who used to take counsel as to the conduct of its affairs. Amongst its members were Sayyid Muḥammad Riẓá of Shíráz, editor of the *Musáwát* ("Equality"), who was at that time in Tabríz, and Mírzá Aḥmad of Qazwín, both of whom were afterwards deputies for Tabríz in the [second] National Assembly. This newspaper continued to be published until A.H. 1328 (= A.D. 1910). In politics it was Liberal and Constitutional, not Democratic, as stated by Mr Rabino.

See Rabino, No. 18, according to whom the seventh issue was dated the 22nd of Rajab, A.H. 1327 (=Aug. 9, 1909), and the forty-seventh number the 5th of Rabí' ii, A.H. 1328 (=April 16, 1910). I possess Nos. 7, 39, 45–54. Each number comprised 4 pp. of 12" × 8¼". The yearly subscription was 16 *qráns* in Tabríz, 20 *qráns* elsewhere in Persia, and 15 francs abroad.

(44)

Istiqlál-i-Írán (*Independence of Persia*). استقلال ایران

A large-sized daily newspaper printed in Ṭihrán in the month of Jumáda i, A.H. 1328 (= May–June, 1910). It was the organ of the party of Union and Progress, and was at first edited by Dr Ḥusayn Khán *Kaḥḥál* ("the Oculist"), then by Sayyid Muḥammad Khán *Muhandis-i-Humáyún*, and lastly by Dr Abu'l-Ḥasan Khán of Tabríz. It continued publication until the month of Sha'bán, A.H. 1329 (August, 1911).

See Rabino, No. 19. I possess Nos. 8, 12, 19, 39, 40, 72, 86, 88, 99, 183, 19?, 208, 212–216, and 234. Each number comprises 4 pp. of 20" × 14½". The yearly subscription was 50 *qráns* in Ṭihrán, 55 in the provinces, and 75 abroad.

(45)

Al-Islám. الاسلام

A monthly religious paper lithographed at Iṣfahán in A.H. 1320 (= A.D. 1902–3), and more generally known as *Guftagúy-i-Ṣafá-Khána-i-Iṣfahán* ("Talk of the House of Purity of Iṣfahán"). Its editor was Sayyid Muḥammad 'Alí entitled *Dá'i'l-Islám* ("the Propagandist of Islám") of Iṣfahán, who also edited another paper called *Da'watu'l-Islám* ("the Preaching of Islám"), published at Bombay.

See Rabino, No. 20. I do not possess the paper.

(46)

Islámiyya. اسلاميّه

A weekly newspaper lithographed in Tabríz in A.H. 1324 (= A.D. 1906–7), edited by Mírzá Abu'l-Qásim *Ẓiyá'u'l-'Ulamá* of Tabríz, son of the *Shamsu'l-'Ulamá.* He belonged to one of the great families of learned men in Tabríz, was one of the first Constitutionalists of that city, and was amongst those who assembled in the British Consulate on the 29th of Rajab, A.H. 1324 (= Sept. 19, 1906) to demand the proclamation of the Constitution and the signature of the Crown Prince (or *Walí-'ahd, i.e.* Muḥammad 'Alí Mírzá). He had studied with success the old and new learning, knew French and Russian, and was one of the truest patriots and Constitutionalists, and an intimate friend of the writer. The idea of founding this newspaper first arose during the days when we were together in the British Consulate and were discussing the publication of a newspaper. The late *Ẓiyá'u'l-'Ulamá* during the whole six years of the Constitutional Period devoted himself entirely to the service of the Nation, was for a long time a member of the Council of Education (*Anjuman-i-Ma'árif*) of Tabríz, was Head of the department of Justice during the Revolution, and later Chief of the Court of Appeal. He also participated in person with great valour in the National struggles and wars with the Reactionaries. Unhappily during the last cruel catastrophe and slaughter of the Liberals in which the Russian aggressions in Tabríz culminated (in Muḥarram, A.H. 1330 = January, 1912) the Russians hanged him with seven others on the day of the *'Áshúrá* (Muḥarram 10, 1330 = Jan. 1, 1912) without any fault on his part.

Not mentioned by Rabino, and not seen.

(47)

Islámiyya. اسلاميّه

A weekly newspaper lithographed in small *format* in Tabríz in A.H. 1324 (= A.D. 1906–7) under the editorship of Mírzá Aḥmad "*Baṣírat*," editor of the newspapers *Ukhuwwat* ("Fraternity") and *Ittiḥád* ("Union").

Not mentioned by Rabino, and not seen.

(48)

Ishráq (*Dawn*). اشراق

A weekly newspaper lithographed in Ṭihrán in A.H. 1326 (= A.D. 1908–9).

Not mentioned by Rabino, and not seen.

(49)

Iṣfahán. اصفهان

A weekly newspaper lithographed in Iṣfahán in A.H. 1325 (= A.D. 1907–8).

See Rabino, No. 21.

(50)

Iṣláḥ (*Reform*). اصلاح

A newspaper mimeographed in Paris in the *nasta'líq* handwriting in the early part of A.H. 1326 (= early spring of A.D. 1908), edited by Dr Jalíl Khán. Its contents consisted for the most part of translations of articles concerning Persia which had appeared in the European Press.

According to Rabino, No. 22, it appeared fortnightly. I possess Nos. 1, 2, 6 and 7. It was edited from No. 82, Boulevard St. Marcel, Paris, and comprised 4–8 pp. of 11½" × 8¼".

(51)

Iṣláḥ (*Reform*). اصلاح

A weekly newspaper lithographed in the *naskh* handwriting in Bombay in A.H. 1327 (= A.D. 1909).

Not mentioned by Rabino. I possess Nos. 31 of the second and 1, 6 and 8 of the third year of issue, the first dated the 3rd of Muḥarram, A.H. 1329 (=Jan. 4, 1911). Each issue contains as a rule 8 pp. of 9½″ × 8½″. The editor was Muḥammad Riẓá of Bushire. Yearly subscription, 10 *qráns* in Persia, 5 rupees in India, and 6½ rupees elsewhere.

(52)

Iṣláḥ (*Reform*). اصلاح

A weekly newspaper printed in Khúy in A.H. 1329 (= A.D. 1911) under the editorship of 'Alí Ḥusayn-Záda. The first number was dated the 29th of Sha'bán of that year (= August 25, 1911).

Not mentioned by Rabino.

(53)

Iṭṭilá' (*Information*). اطّلاع

A fortnightly paper first printed and afterwards lithographed in Ṭihrán in A.H. 1295 (= A.D. 1878). This was the semi-official organ of the Persian Government, twin-brother to the official *Írán* ("Persia"), and issued under the control of the Ministry of the Press and the supervision of Muḥammad Ḥasan Khán *I'timádu's-Salṭana*, son of Ḥájji 'Alí Khán *Ḥájibu'd-Dawla* of the Muqaddam family of Marágha, and afterwards of his nephew Muḥammad Báqir Khán *I'timádu's-Salṭana*. It continued publication until A.H. 1325 (= A.D. 1907–8). This paper, on account of its connection with the Government, was devoid of useful political articles or such as might awaken thought, and was therefore always the object of severe criticism on the part of Persian Liberals and men of letters. Its only importance lay in the fact that it sometimes contained the textual agreements connected with certain State concessions and the like. This paper and its companion-paper the *Írán* were for some time the only papers published within Persian territory, yet notwithstanding this they enjoyed no popularity, but were only forced upon Government employés, land-owners and officers of the State, from whose salaries the subscription was deducted.

See Rabino, No. 23. I possess Nos. 15–19 of the 29th year (Nov. 29, 1906–April 11, 1907). Each issue comprises 4 pp. of 14½″ × 8¾″. The yearly subscription was 18 *qráns* in Ṭihrán, 20 *qráns* elsewhere in Persia, 4 roubles in Russia and the Caucasus, 40 piastres in Turkey, and 7 rupees in India and China.

(54)

Iṭṭilá'át-i-Muhimma (*Important Information*). اطّلاعات مهمّه

A daily paper printed in Ṭihrán in A.H. 1329 (= A.D. 1911) under the editorship of Ḥasan al-Ḥusayní and Riẓá son of Aḥmad of Núr (in Mázandarán).

Not mentioned by Rabino.

(55)

Iṭṭilá'át-i-Rúzána (*Daily Information*). اطّلاعات روزانه

See pp. 63–64 *infra*, under No. 106, *Tamaddun* ("Civilization").

(56)

Aflátún (*Plato*). افلاطون

A paper printed in Rasht with coloured illustrations, of which one number only was published on the 26th of Rajab, A.H. 1328 (= August 3, 1910).

See Rabino, No. 26. I possess a copy. It comprises 8 pp. of 12½″ × 7¼″, 4 of which contain coloured cartoons. Yearly subscription, 25 *qráns* in Rasht, 27 elsewhere in Persia, and 6 roubles abroad.

(57)

Iqbál (*Progress*). اقبال

A weekly paper lithographed in Tabríz in A.H. 1316 (= A.D. 1898–9) under the editorship of 'Alí-qulí Khán, known as Ṣafaroff, who was also editor of the newspapers *Iḥtiyáj* and *Ázarbáyján* (*q.v.*).

See Rabino, No. 27, who says that the first issue of the paper under this new name was the eighth of the older *Iḥtiyáj* which it replaced, and that it was dated the 29th of Rabí' i, A.H. 1316 (= August 17, 1898).

(58)

Uqyánús (*The Ocean*). اقیانوس

A weekly paper printed in Ṭihrán in A.H. 1326 (= A.D. 1908–9) under the editorship of Sayyid Faraju'lláh of Káshán, the former editor of the *Thurayyá* in Egypt and Ṭihrán. The real founder, owner and writer of the paper was Mírzá 'Abdu'r-Raḥím of Qarájadágh, known as *Ḥakím-i-Iláhí* ("the Philosopher"). This is the only Persian newspaper which openly defended the autocratic methods of the ex-Sháh and his creatures and championed the cause of the Reaction, and which accordingly continued after the Reactionary *Coup d'État* of the 23rd of Jumáda ii, A.H. 1326 (= June 23, 1908). After the capture of Ṭihrán by the Constitutionalists (July, 1909), its editor Mírzá 'Abdu'r-Raḥím was arrested and imprisoned for a year amongst other political offenders.

See Rabino, No. 28.

(59)

Ekbátán (*Ecbatana*). اکباتان

A paper published in Hamadán in A.H. 1325 (= A.D. 1907–8), of which the writer has never seen a copy. It succeeded the *'Adl-i-Muẓaffar* (*q.v.*), was under the same management, and continued publication until recently.

Not mentioned by Rabino.

(60)

Echo de Perse.

A paper published in Ṭihrán in A.D. 1885 (= A.H. 1302–3).

See Rabino, No. 228, and p. 17 *supra*.

(61)

Ulfat (*Friendship*). الفت

A weekly paper printed in Hamadán in A.H. 1325 (= A.D. 1907–8) under the editorship of Mírzá Sayyid Muḥammad Hamadání.

See Rabino, No. 29. I possess No. 6, dated the 26th of Rabí' i, A.H. 1325 (= May 9, 1907). It contains 4 pp. of 11¾" × 7". The yearly subscription was 10 *qráns* in Hamadán and 15 elsewhere in Persia.

(62)

Ummíd (*Hope*). امید

An illustrated weekly newspaper lithographed at Tabríz in A.H. 1324 (= A.D. 1906–7). This was one of the first papers to appear after the granting of the Constitution, and was founded by five or six students of the Luqmániyya College. It continued publication for about 8 months.

See Rabino, No. 32. I possess Nos. 7 and 14, the former dated the 28th of Shawwál, A.H. 1324 (=December 15, 1906). It contains 4 pp. of $12\frac{3}{4}'' \times 7''$.

(63)

Ummíd-i-Taraqqí (*Hope of Progress*). امید ترقّی

A paper printed in Rasht in A.H. 1329 (= A.D. 1911), giving particulars as to the receipts and expenses of certain theatrical performances.

See Rabino, No. 33. No. 1, which I possess, is dated 29 Jumáda i, A.H. 1329 (=May 28, 1911) and comprises 6 pp. of $12\frac{1}{2}'' \times 6\frac{1}{2}''$. Price of each number, 1 *sháhí*.

(64)

Anjuman (*the Assembly* or *Club*). انجمن

A paper first lithographed and later printed in Tabríz from two to four times a week, in the early part of A.H. 1325 (= Feb.–March, A.D. 1907). See under *Rúznáma-i-Millí*.

See Rabino, No. 34. I possess a good many numbers, both of the lithographed and printed issues. The former begin with No. 44 of the First Year, dated the 4th of Muḥarram, A.H. 1325 (=Feb. 7, 1907), and end with No. 3 of the Third Year, dated the 5th of Sha'bán, A.H. 1326 (=Sept. 2, 1908), and each contains 4 pp. of $12'' \times 6\frac{3}{4}''$, written in a large, clear *naskh*. The yearly subscription was 10 *qráns* (for 100 issues) in Tabríz; 15 *qráns* elsewhere in Persia; 4 roubles in Russia; 15 *qráns* in Europe and Turkey. Of the printed issues the first is No. 1 of the Second Year, dated the 4th of Ṣafar, A.H. 1326 (=March 8, 1908), and the last No. 31 of the same year, dated the 12th of Jumáda i, A.H. 1326 (=June 12, 1908). The pages (4) measure $12'' \times 6\frac{1}{2}''$, and the yearly subscription differed little from that of the lithographed issues. There seems to have been some confusion and overlapping in the printed and lithographed issues.

(65)

Anjuman-i-Aṣnáf (*the Trades' Guild*). انجمن اصناف

A weekly newspaper printed in Ṭihrán in A.H. 1325 (= A.D. 1907–8) under the editorship of Sayyid Muṣṭafá of Ṭihrán, under the management of the Trades' Guild.

See Rabino, No. 35, according to whom the third issue was dated the 8th of Ramaẓán, A.H. 1325 (=Oct. 15, 1907). The issue next or next but one to this appeared under the title *Bámdád* ("Morning"), *q.v.* I possess a copy of No. 3, which comprises 4 pp. of $14\frac{1}{2}'' \times 8\frac{3}{4}''$. Yearly subscription, 10 *qráns* in Ṭihrán, 5 francs abroad.

(66)

Anjuman-i-Iṣfahán. انجمن اصفهان

A weekly paper lithographed in Iṣfahán in A.H. 1325 (= A.D. 1907–8) under the editorship of Sayyid Siráju'd-Dín. This paper was the official organ of the Provincial Council, or *Anjuman*, of Iṣfahán, whose deliberations it used to publish.

See Rabino, No. 36. I possess a good many numbers, ranging in dates from the 13th of Rabí' ii, A.H. 1325 (= May 26, 1907), which is No. 21 of the First Year, to No. 38 of the Fourth Year, which is dated the 7th of Rabí' ii, A.H. 1329 (= April 7, 1911). Each number contains 8 pp. of 12½" × 8½". The earlier ones are in *nasta'líq*, the later ones in *naskh*, with some lines in *nasta'líq* at the foot. Yearly subscription, 18 *qráns* in Iṣfahán, 20 elsewhere in Persia, 22 abroad.

(67)

Anjuman-i-Ukhuwwat (*Society of Brotherhood*). انجمن اخوّت

A weekly newspaper lithographed at Shíráz in A.H. 1326 (= A.D. 1908–9).

Not in Rabino, and not seen.

(68)

Anjuman-i-Baladiyya (*The Municipal Council*). انجمن بلديّه

A paper published in Iṣfahán on the 5th of Shawwál, A.H. 1325 (= Nov. 11, 1907), which continued publication for five months.

See Rabino, No. 238, on whose authority it is inserted.

(69)

Anjuman-i-Millí-i-Wiláyatí-i-Gílán انجمن ملّى ولايتى گيلان
(*The National Provincial Council of Gílán*).

A paper printed in Rasht in A.H. 1325 (= A.D. 1907–8) under the editorship of *Dabíru'l-Mamálik*. Four numbers of this paper were to be published weekly, but apparently only four numbers were published altogether.

See Rabino, No. 37. I possess four numbers (1–4), the first dated the 22nd of Rajab, A.H. 1325 (= August 31, 1907), and the last the 22nd of Sha'bán (September 30) of the same year. Each consists of 4 pp. of 11½" × 7". Yearly subscription (200 issues), 30 *qráns* in Rasht and Gílán, 45 *qráns* in other parts of Persia, 9 roubles in Russia and the Caucasus.

(70)

Anjuman-i-Wiláyatí-i-Yazd انجمن ولایتی یزد

(*The Provincial Council of Yazd*).

A weekly paper published in Yazd in the early part of A.H. 1328 (= Jan.–Feb., 1910) under the editorship of Mírzá Muḥammad Ṣádiq of Qum.

See Rabino, No. 38, according to whom No. 2 was dated the 5th of Muḥarram, A.H. 1328 (=Jan. 17, 1910). I possess Nos. 2 and 4. The former consists of 8 pp. of small size, 8″ × 5″; the latter of 4 pp. of 12″ × 6″. Yearly subscription, 12 *qráns* in Yazd, 14 elsewhere in Persia.

(71)

Indépendance Perse.

A French weekly newspaper printed in Ṭihrán in A.D. 1910 (= A.H. 1328) under the editorship of Dr Ḥusayn Khán *Kaḥḥál* ("the Oculist") in connection with the *Istiqlál-i-Írán* (No. 44, *supra*).

See Rabino, No. 230, according to whom only three numbers were issued, the first on June 4 and the third on June 17, 1910.

(72)

Insániyyat (*Humanity*). انسانیّت

A paper published in Ṭihrán in A.H. 1325 (= A.D. 1907–8). It appears to have been the organ of the *Anjuman* of the same name, which consisted chiefly of natives of Áshtiyán and Tafrísh, and was under the presidency of the *Mustawfi'l-Mamálik*.

Not in Rabino, and not seen.

(73)

Anṣár (*Helpers*). انصار

A paper of small *format* lithographed in *naskh* handwriting at Iṣfahán in A.H. 1325 (= A.D. 1907–8). The second number appeared under the title of *Ganjína-i-Anṣár* ("Treasury of the Helpers").

Not in Rabino, and not seen.

(74)

Inṣáf (*Equity*). انصاف

A paper printed in Ṭihrán in A.H. 1326 (= A.D. 1908–9) under the editorship of Ḥájji Sayyid Isma'íl, called *Sulṭánu'l-Maddáḥín* ("the King of Eulogists") of Kirmánsháh.

See Rabino, No. 39, according to whom No. 2 was dated the 26th of Rabí' i, A.H.

نمره ۸۳۳ — نمره هشتصد و سی و سیم — صفحه اول

سه‌شنبه پنجم ماه صفر المظفر سنه ۱۳۱۲ هجری
یونت ئیل
ادای قیمت در هر قسط
سالیانه در طهران سه تومان و شش هزار دینار
در خارج سه تومان و شش هزار و [illegible]

۸۳۳
ایران

هفتم ماه اوت فرانسه سنه ۱۸۹۴ مسیحی
اداره وزارت انطباعات در ارک همایون
محل فروش در دار الطباعه دولتی
قیمت اعلانات سطری یکهزار دینار است

اخبار رسمی
اردوی همایون

چنانکه در نمره قبل اشارت یافت روز
دوشنبه دوازدهم شهر محرم الحرام موکب
با احتشام بندگان اعلیحضرت اقدس
همایون صاحبقرانی خلد الله تعالی سلطنته
از صاحبقرانیه شمیران بناصرخوانی
فرموده تشریف فرمای قریه اوشان شدند
دو شب در آنجا اقامت فرموده از آنجا به
شهرستانک و قصر سلطنتی آنجا تشریف
قدوم ارزانی داشتند پس از چهار شب
توقف در شهرستانک عزیمت گچسر فرمودند
دو شب نیز در قریه گچسر مضرب خیام موکب
فیروزی اثر بود از گچسر عزیمت آزادبر
فرمودند سه شب هم ساحت این قریه
بشرف نزول موکب مسعود مشرف بود
از آنجا بپای گردنه (کندوان) کوچ دادند
و پس از دو شب اتراق در این منزل روز
یکشنبه بیست و پنجم تشریف فرمای [illegible]
کلاردشت شدند
حمد خدا را ذات ملکی صفات اقدس همایون
شاهنشاهی ابد الله ایام دولته همواره
قرین کمال خرمی و سلامت و سرور و خاطر
خورشید مظاهر مبارک غالباً بمعظمات
مهام و جلایل امور سلطنتی مشغول است
و از قرار معلوم پس از یک دو هفته اقامت
خسروانی در کلاردشت عزیمت معاودت
بشهرستانک خواهند فرمود
جناب مستطاب اشرف امجد صدر اعظم
نیز در این سفر میمنت اثر ملتزم رکاب
همایون اعلی و پیوسته بجلایل خدمات و
فیصل مهمات دولتی مشغول هستند

سواد قانون تابعیت دولت علیه ایران

(بند اول) هر کسی که در خاک دولت
علیه ایران متولد شده باشد تبعه ایران محسوب
میشود مگر اینکه معلوم شود که در حین ولادت
والدین یا والد او تبعه خارجه بوده‌اند آنوقت
مولود نیز اجنبی شمرده خواهد شد
(بند دویم) اولاد تبعه خارجه که در خاک
ایران متولد شده باشند بعد از بلوغ بسن
رشد خود تحصیل تابعیت ایران را
خواهند داشت و استدعای آنها قبول
خواهد شد
(بند سیم) هر کس از تبعه خارجه بخواهد
داخل تابعیت دولت علیه ایران بشود اولاً
باید بسن رشد رسیده باشد ثانیاً پنج سال
متوالیاً در یک نقطه از خاک ایران اقامت
کرده باشد ثالثاً در تابعیت اصلیه خود
محکوم بجنایت یا فراری از نظام نباشد
در اینصورت استدعانامه بجای لازم تقدیم
کرده تحصیل اجازه و تابعیت ایران را
میتواند بکند
(بند چهارم) از تبعه خارجه آنانکه
شرط اقامت در خاک ایران را بطوریکه
در ماده فوق درج است بعمل نیاورده
استدعای تابعیت دولت علیه ایران بکنند
در صورتیکه دولت علیه شایستگی
آنان را ملاحظه نماید باستثناء بتابعیت
دولت علیه ایران قبول خواهند شد
(بند پنجم) کسانیکه از تبعه ایران
خواه خودشان و خواه پدرانشان
تبدیل تابعیت کرده باشند بخواهند
بتابعیت اصلیه خود رجوع نمایند
بدون ایفای شروط مقرره بمجرد استدعا
قبول خواهند شد
(بند ششم) از تبعه ایران آنان که
با زنان خارجه ازدواج کرده باشند
زنهای آنها طبعاً بتابعیت ایرانیت
شوهر تابع خواهند بود و بعد از تطلیق
یا فوت شوهر اگر زنها بخواهند بتابعیت
اصلیه رجوع نمایند مجاز خواهند بود
(بند هفتم) زنانیکه در تابعیت خارجه
و در قید زوجیت تبعه دول خارجه
هستند در خاک آنها بتابعیت ایران
قبول نمیشود مگر آنکه باتفاق شوهر
خودشان با شرایط مقرره بتابعیت
دولت علیه ایران داخل شوند
(بند هشتم) از تبعه ایران کسی که

First page of No. 833 of the old lithographed *Írán*,
dated Tuesday, Ṣafar 5, A.H. 1312 (Aug. 8, 1894)

1326 (=April 28, 1908). I possess Nos. 2–4. Each comprises 4 pp. of 11½" × 6¾". Yearly subscription, 8 *qráns* in Ṭihrán; 10 *qráns* in the provinces; 30 piastres in Turkey; 2 roubles in Russia and the Caucasus; 5 francs in other foreign countries.

(75)

Úrdú-yi-Humáyún (*The Royal Camp*). اوردوی همایون

A paper published during the march to Khurásán at the time of Náṣiru'd-Dín Sháh's second journey to Mashhad in A.H. 1300 (= A.D. 1882–3), written in the course of the journey at the different halting places on the road, and circulated amongst the members of the Royal Suite, commonly called "the Royal Camp." The first number was printed at Damáwand on Sha'bán 11 (A.H. 1300 = June 17, 1883), and the last at Ṭihrán when the Sháh reached the capital on his return on Dhu'l-Ḥijja 12 of that year (= Oct. 14, 1883). In all twelve numbers were published. The editor was Muḥammad Ḥasan Khán *I'timádu's-Salṭana*, aided by his secretary Mírzá Muḥammad Ḥusayn *Zaká'u'l-Mulk*, editor of the newspaper *Tarbiyat*, and the writer was the calligraphist Mírzá Muḥammad Riẓá of Kalhur.

Omitted by Rabino, but mentioned in the *Kitábu'l-Ma'áthir Wa'l-Áthár* ("Book of Institutions and Monuments") amongst the newspapers published during the reign of Náṣiru'd-Dín Sháh. The details concerning it given above were obtained by the author from H.E. *Zaká'u'l-Mulk*.

(76)

Írán (*Persia*). ایران

A newspaper lithographed, and subsequently printed, in Ṭihrán, at first every alternate day and afterwards once a fortnight, in A.H. 1288 (= A.D. 1871–2). It was at first edited by Muḥammad Ḥasan Khán *I'timádu's-Salṭana*, Minister of Publications, and afterwards by Muḥammad Báqir Khán *I'timádu's-Salṭana*, also Minister of Publications, until the beginning of the Constitutional Epoch. Some brief account of its history has been given at the beginning of this treatise. Its first number was dated Sunday, Muḥarram 11 of the above-mentioned year (A.H. 1288 = April 2, 1871), and the paper at first appeared regularly thrice a week. At the beginning of the first number was an announcement, signed by Muḥammad Ḥasan, referring to the suspension of the *Rúznámas* entitled respectively *Dawlatí*,

Millatí and *'Ilmí*, and their replacement by this paper, which would publish three numbers a week instead of the single weekly number published by each of them. In the department of the British Museum Library assigned to Periodical Publications are preserved (under the class-mark 757. I. 11) Nos. 1–10, 90–92 and 94–125 of this paper, which I have examined.

This paper was an official Government organ, containing Court news, Imperial Rescripts (*farmáns*), appointments and dismissals, the assignment of posts and titles, and especially such personal doings of the Sháh as levées, hunting-expeditions, religious mournings (in the month of Muḥarram), excursions, and the like, as well as other State functions. Its business was to praise the Royal performances and the doings of the Courtiers, and to enlarge on the security of the country and the progress of the Government; so that this paper, more than all others, was the object of criticism on the part of Persian Liberals and Persian newspapers published abroad. In its early days it contained a scientific part, which treated of the modern sciences, while at the foot of the page appeared in instalments a translation by Muḥammad Ḥasan of Jules Verne's *Les Anglais au Pole Nord: Aventures du Captaine Hatteras.*

The *I'timádu's-Salṭana* writes: "The newspaper *Írán* ('Persia') was first published in the year A.H. 1288 (= 1871–2) when the superintendence of the Printing-press was entrusted to my uncle, the old *I'timádu's-Salṭana*, and Mírzá Ḥusayn Khán *Sipahsálár* was Prime Minister."

Zaká'u'l-Mulk writes: "In the beginning of A.H. 1288 (March–April, 1871) the newspapers generally were placed under the charge of Muḥammad Ḥasan Khán, Page in waiting (*píshkhidmat*), who subsequently received the title of *Ṣaní'u'd-Dawla*, and finally that of *I'timádu's-Salṭana.* He converted the three *Rúznámas* entitled *Dawlatí*, *'Ilmí* and *Millatí* (which had hitherto been published under the management of the Ministry of Sciences and the *Dáru'l-Funún* College, and the supervision of the *I'tiẓádu's-Salṭana*) into one newspaper entitled *Írán*, which originally appeared three times a week, but gradually ceased to appear so regularly. This paper was first written by a certain Mírzá 'Alí Khán of Ná'in; afterwards, until about the year A.H. 1300 (= A.D. 1882–3), by my late father; and after that by Mírzá 'Alí Muḥammad Khán, who lately received the title *Mujíru'd-Dawla*[1]."

See Rabino, No. 40. I possess one number (No. 934) of the lithographed issue, dated the 15th of Dhu'l-Ḥijja, A.H. 1315 and the 7th of May, 1898. It is written in a fine bold *naskh* and consists of 4 pp. of 16" × 10" Yearly subscription in Ṭihrán, 36 *qráns*, abroad 38½ *qráns*. Of the printed issue I possess Nos. 10, 17, 18, 22, 23, 24, 25 and 26 of the 59th year of publication, ranging from July 26, 1906, to Feb. 7, 1907. These numbers consist of 4 pp. of 15¼" × 8½". The subscription price remained nearly the same, with equivalents added for Europe, Turkey and Russia. No. 22, dated Jan. 10, 1906, appeared in mourning, and contains the announcement of Muẓaffaru'd-Dín Sháh's death, and the *Niẓám-náma*, or Constitution, of the newly-established National Assembly in 51 articles, dated the 14th of Dhu'l-Qa'da, A.H. 1324 (= December 30, 1906).

[**Írán-i-Sulṭání** (*Royal Persia*). ایران سلطانی

See below under *Rúznáma-i-Írán-i-Sulṭání*, which is the correct title of the paper in question.]

[1] The founder and editor of this paper was the late Muḥammad Ḥasan Khán *I'timádu's-Salṭana*, son of Ḥájji 'Alí Khán *Ḥájibu'd-Dawla*, of the Muqaddam family of Marágha, and founder of the newspaper *Iṭṭilá'* (*q.v.*), which on his death was made over to his nephew Muḥammad Báqir Khán, the present *I'timádu's-Salṭana*, who for a long while held the post of Minister of Publications. Its chief writer was Mírzá Muḥammad Ḥusayn of Iṣfahán, poetically surnamed *Furúghí*, and entitled *Zaká'u'l-Mulk*, father of the present *Zaká'u'l-Mulk*.

Since certain doubtful and difficult points arose in connection with the earlier official and scientific newspapers published by the Persian Government, after the completion of the original draft of this treatise, and while it was still in the hands of the translator, I wrote a letter to H.E. the *I'timádu's-Salṭana*, another to H.E. *Zaká'u'l-Mulk* (Mírzá Muḥammad 'Alí Khán, President of the Second National Assembly), and a third to Mírzá Riẓá-qulí Khán, Principal of the *Dáru'l-Funún*, these three persons being the present successors of those who were concerned with the earliest newspapers published in Persia, and the leaders in all scientific and educational matters, and addressed to them certain enquiries. The *I'timádu's-Salṭana* was kind enough to send me, besides solutions of some of my difficulties, three or four copies of some of the rarer newspapers, both old and new. From *Zaká'u'l-Mulk* also, on the eve of publication, I received a still fuller reply, written after much careful investigation. To both these eminent men I owe a deep debt of gratitude. I regret that hitherto no answer has been received from Mírzá Riẓá-qulí Khán, who might perhaps have given fuller information on certain points specially connected with his administration. From the communications above mentioned such quotations and corrections as the progress of this work allowed have been made, these emendations being in all cases duly acknowledged. In some cases also, even when no important addition was made by them to the information already collected and recorded, I have quoted *verbatim* from their observations, merely in order still further to support and confirm matters recorded on other authority, such as those included in this article.

(77)

Írán-i-Naw (*New Persia*). ایران نو

A daily full-sized paper printed in Ṭihrán in A.H. 1327 (= A.D. 1909), of which the first number was published on Sha'bán 7th of that year (= Aug. 24, 1909). The proprietor and (nominal) editor was Sayyid Muḥammad Shabistarí of Ázarbáyján, known as Abu'ẓ-Ẓiyá, formerly editor of *al-Ḥadíd* and the *Mujáhid*. The real and actual editor, as well as the principal writer, was, however, Muḥammad Amín Rasúl-záda of Bákú, while the editor, who also financed the paper, was Basil the Armenian of Ṭihrán. This paper was the greatest, most important and best known of all the Persian newspapers, and the first to appear in the large size usual in Europe. It began to appear regularly during the Second Constitutional Period, after the conquest of Ṭihrán (July, 1909), introduced into Persia the journalistic methods of Europe, and became a model for other papers. Some of its leading articles were from the pen of Amír Ḥájibí or Ghulám Riẓá, a Georgian who pretended to be a Muslim, who used to write in French, from which language they were translated into Persian. Some of the lighter facetious articles, signed *Nísh* ("Sting") were from the pen of Rasúl-záda. The *Írán-i-Naw* had the most extraordinary adventures in defending its Liberal policy, and during the period of its publication was frequently the object of vehement attacks on the part of the journals which opposed it, so that most of its time was spent in polemics, and it became both the agent and victim of important political events. Amongst these was the publication of one of the allegorical stories of the well-known Russian writer I. A. Kriloff about the Concert of the Animals, and how they interchanged places when they noticed its disorderly character; for it used occasionally to insert in one of its issues one of Kriloff's allegories which had some bearing on current events in the country. So it published this allegory of the Concert at the time when the Sipahdár's Cabinet was continually tendering its resignation, or when an interchange of portfolios took place amongst the Ministers composing it. This caused a great commotion amongst the supporters of the Government, which resulted first in the temporary suppression of the paper, and afterwards in the resignation of the Ministers. Since the *Írán-i-Naw* was in opposition, that is to say was the partisan and organ of the minority (*i.e.* the Democrats), it was always liable to repression or suppression, and was the constant object of the anger, vengeance and recriminations of the supporters of the Government. It continued publication, supported by the above-mentioned Basil the Armenian, until the month of Jumáda ii, A.H. 1328 (= June–July, 1910), when it finally suspended publication in consequence of financial embarrassments. Some months later, however, it resumed publication on the 21st of Shawwál of the same year (= Oct. 26, 1910) as the official organ of the Democratic Party, by whom it was managed and financed, under the editorship of Sayyid Mahdí, the son of Sayyid Jamál of Afcha. This time it was even more exposed than before to the attacks of its opponents, the Government, and their organs in the press, and finally Rasúl-záda, its chief writer, was exiled from Ṭihrán at the instance of the Russian Legation in the latter part of Jumáda i [A.H. 1329] (= end of May, 1911). After his departure the paper still continued to be published by the Party until it was suppressed by the Government on the 22nd of Sha'bán, A.H. 1329 (= Aug. 18, 1911). It reappeared on the 18th of Dhu'l-Ḥijjá (= Dec. 21, 1911), but was again suppressed ten days later, the last issue being No. 121 of the Third Year. It then reappeared under the name of *Írán-i-Nawín*, and was again suppressed after the publication of a single number. Once more it appeared under the name of *Rahbar-i-Írán-i-Naw* ("the Guide of New Persia"), but was again suppressed after the publication of two numbers. The *Írán-i-Naw's* special importance lay in its publication of the Russian aggressions, its fiery denunciation of them, and its exposure of foreign intrigues, for which reason it was the object of special enmity on the part of the Russians.

See Rabino, No. 41. I possess a fairly extensive collection of numbers of this paper, viz. Nos. 1–230 (with a few lacunae) of the First Year, extending from August 24, 1909, to June 14, 1910; Nos. 41–121 of the Second Year, extending from December 8, 1910, to March 21, 1911; and Nos. 1–110 of the Third Year, extending from March 26 to August 16, 1911. Each issue comprised 4 pp. of 20½" × 14½". The yearly subscription was 50 *qráns* in Ṭihrán, 55 *qráns* in the provinces, and 75 *qráns* abroad.

(78)

Írán-i-Nawín (*Newest Persia*). ایران نوین

A daily paper printed in Ṭihrán in A.H. 1329 (= A.D. 1911). The first and only number was dated the 29th of Dhu'l-Ḥijja of that year (= Dec. 21, 1911). It took the place of the *Írán-i-Naw* (see immediately above). Editor, Sayyid Mahdí of Afcha.

Not mentioned by Rabino, and not seen.

(79)

Bámdád (*Morning*). بامداد

A weekly newspaper printed in Ṭihrán in A.H. 1325 (= A.D. 1907–8), edited by Ghulám 'Alí Khán Qájár on behalf of the United Guilds' Society (*Anjuman-i-Ittiḥádiyya-i-Aṣnáf*). Most of the leading articles were written by Ḥájji Mírzá Yaḥyá of Dawlatábád.

See Rabino, No. 44. No. 20 of this paper is dated the 12th of Rabí' ii, A.H. 1326 (= May 14, 1908). It comprises 4 pp. of 14¼" × 8". Yearly subscription, 10 *qráns* in Ṭihrán, 5 francs abroad. See p. 46 *supra*, No. 65.

(80)

Bukhárá-yi-Sharíf (*Bukhárá the Holy*). بخارای شریف

A large-sized daily paper printed in New Bukhárá (Turkistán) in A.H. 1330 (= A.D. 1912), the first number being dated the 4th of Rabí' ii of that year (= March 23, 1912). The proprietor of this paper is K. L. Livine, the editor Mír Ḥaydar son of Khwája Qásim Muridloff, and the chief writer M. T. Jalál Yúsuf-záda, a Caucasian by origin.

Not in Rabino, and not seen.

(81)

Barq (*Lightning*). برق

A daily paper printed in Ṭihrán in Shawwál, A.H. 1328 (= October, 1910). The proprietor and editor was Sayyid Ẓiyá'-u'd-Dín son of Sayyid 'Alí Yazdí, also editor of the *Nidá-yi-Islám* and the *Sharq*. On the suspension of the last-named paper, this was published in its place. (See under *Sharq.*) In politics the paper was revolutionary.

See Rabino, No. 45, according to whom about 20 numbers were published. I possess Nos. 3–6 and 8, the first dated Oct. 20, the last Nov. 23, 1910. Each number comprises 4 pp., the last being in French, of 20″ × 14¼″. Yearly subscription, 45 *qráns* in Ṭihrán, 50 in the provinces, 65 abroad.

(82)

Barg-i-Sabz (*The Green Leaf*). برگ سبز

A fortnightly paper lithographed in Ardabíl (Ázarbáyján) in A.H. 1326 (= A.D. 1908) under the editorship of Áqá Mír Aḥmad.

See Rabino, No. 46. I possess Nos. 4, 7, 9, 10 and 12, the first dated the 27th of Rabí' ii, A.H. 1326 (= May 29, 1908). Each number comprises 4 pp. of 11″ × 8½″, lithographed in a fine, large *naskh*. Yearly subscription, 10 *qráns* in Ardabíl, 15 elsewhere in Persia, 4 roubles in Russia, 40 piastres in Turkey, 10 francs in Europe.

(83)

Bishárat (*Good Tidings*). بشارت

A paper printed in Mashhad (Khurásán) in A.H. 1324 (= A.D. 1906–7) under the editorship of Shaykh Muḥammad 'Alí, which continued publication for more than two years.

See Rabino, No. 47, according to whom it was a weekly. No. 4 was dated the 20th of Dhu'l-Qa'da, A.H. 1324 (= Feb. 4, 1907), and publication appears to have ended in A.H. 1326 (1908). I possess Nos. 4, 13, 14, 18, 22. Each number contains 4 pp. of 13″ × 6½″. Yearly subscription, in Mashhad 12 *qráns*, elsewhere in Persia 15 *qráns*, Russia and Turkistán 4 roubles, India and China 24 *qráns*, Afghanistán 20 *qráns*, Turkey and Egypt 20 *qráns*.

(84)

Baṣírat (*Insight*). بصيرت

A weekly newspaper published in Ṭihrán in A.H. 1325 (= A.D. 1907).

Not in Rabino, nor do I possess a copy.

(85)

Baladu'l-Amín (*The Secure Land*). بلد الامين

A weekly paper lithographed in Mashhad early in A.H. 1328 (= Jan.–Feb. 1910) under the editorship of Mírzá Muḥammad Ṣádiq.

See Rabino, No. 48. I possess Nos. 2, 6, 12, 15, 17. No. 2 is dated the 28th of Muḥarram, A.H. 1328 (= Feb. 9, 1910). According to Rabino the paper was published for the *Baladiyya* or Municipal Council of Mashhad, and ceased publication on the 24th of Jumáda ii, A.H. 1328 (=July 3, 1910). Each number consists of 4 pp. of 13″ × 7½″ and is lithographed in a large, clear *naskh*. Yearly subscription, 10 *qráns* in Mashhad, 12 *qráns* elsewhere in Persia, 15 *qráns* abroad.

(86)

Baladiyya (*Municipality*). بلديّه

A paper printed in Ṭihrán in A.H. 1325 (= A.D. 1907).

See Rabino, No. 49, according to whom it appeared irregularly, under various editors. I possess Nos. 7, 10, 16, 21, 43, 46, 47. No. 7 is dated the 3rd of Rabí' ii, A.H. 1325 (=May 16, 1907), and comprises 4 pp. of 11½″ × 6¾″. Yearly subscription, 18 *qráns* in Ṭihrán, 23 *qráns* elsewhere in Persia, 5 roubles in Russia and the Caucasus, 9 rupees in India, 3 mejidiyyés in Turkey and Egypt, and 21 francs in Europe.

(87)

Baladiyya (*Municipality*). بلديّه

A weekly newspaper lithographed in Tabríz in A.H. 1327 (= A.D. 1909) under the editorship of Aḥmad Mírzá, which published the deliberations of that Municipality, under whose management it was produced.

Not in Rabino, nor do I possess a copy.

(88)

Baladiyya-i-Iṣfahán (*The Municipality of Isfahán*). بلديّهٔ اصفهان

A weekly newspaper lithographed in Iṣfahán in the latter part of A.H. 1325 (= January, 1908).

See Rabino, No. 50, who describes it as bi-weekly, and states that it was first published on the 4th of Dhu'l-Ḥijja, A.H. 1325 (=Jan. 8, 1908). This is in fact the date borne by No. 1, which I possess. It comprises 4 pp. of 12½″ × 7″, and is lithographed in a large, clear *naskh*. Yearly subscription, 25 *qráns* in Iṣfahán, 30 *qráns* elsewhere in Persia, and 32 *qráns* abroad.

(89)

Bú Qalamún (*The Chameleon*, or *Turkey*). بو قلمون

A small-sized paper printed in Tabríz in A.H. 1327 (= A.D. 1909) under the editorship of Mírzá Maḥmúd Ghaní-záda of Salmás, who was also editor of the *Anjuman*, *Faryád* and *Shafaq*.

See Rabino, No. 51, according to whom the second issue was dated the 24th of Rajab, A.H. 1327 (=August 11, 1909). I do not possess a copy.

8

England surreptitiously by guile and Russia openly by force combine to expel Mr W. Morgan Shuster from Persia and prevent his financial reforms

From No. 34 of the *Buhlúl*, Dec. 22, 1911

(90)

Buhlúl. بهلول

A weekly illustrated comic paper lithographed in Ṭihrán in the early part of A.H. 1329 (=A.D. 1911) under the editorship first of Shaykh 'Alí 'Iráqí, and afterwards of Asadu'lláh Khán called "Pársí." This paper defended the methods of the Democratic Party and attacked and criticized the antagonistic parties and the Government, just as in like manner the paper *Tanbíh* (*q.v.*) supported the Moderates (*I'tidáliyyún*), and finally the paper *Shaykh Chughundur* (*q.v.*) was similarly connected with the Party of Union and Progress and defended them.

See Rabino, No. 52. I possess Nos. 6, 10, 13, 29 and 34. The first is dated the 21st of Jumáda i, A.H. 1329 (=May 20, 1911). Each number comprises 4 pp. of $12\frac{1}{2}'' \times 6\frac{1}{2}''$, the first and last pages being occupied by illustrations. Each number, 100 *dínárs* ($\frac{1}{10}$ *qrán*).

(91)

Bídárí (*Wakefulness*). بیداری

A paper lithographed in Ṭihrán every other day in A.H. 1325 (=A.D. 1907) under the editorship of *Fatḥu'l-Mamálik.*

See Rabino, No. 53, according to whom it began on the 23rd of Jumáda ii, A.H. 1325 (=August 3, 1907). I possess Nos. 1 and 3. Each number comprises 4 pp. of $12'' \times 7''$, and is lithographed in *ta'líq*. Yearly subscription, 30 *qráns*.

(92)

Páy-i-Takht (*The Capital*). پای تخت

A weekly newspaper lithographed in Ṭihrán in A.H. 1329 (=A.D. 1911).

Not mentioned by Rabino, and not seen.

(93)

Parwána (*The Moth*). پروانه

A paper printed in Iṣfahán in A.H. 1328 (=A.D. 1910) under the editorship of Sayyid Ḥasan Mú'min-záda. Forty numbers a year were published, the first on the 7th of Shawwál, A.H. 1328 (=Oct. 12, 1910).

See Rabino, No. 55, who adds that in politics the paper was Democratic. I possess Nos. 8, 10, 18 and 21, the first dated the 10th of Dhu'l-Ḥijja, A.H. 1328 (=Dec. 11, 1910). Each number comprises 8 pp. of $13'' \times 6\frac{1}{2}''$. Yearly subscription 12 *qráns* in Iṣfahán.

(94)

Parwarish (*Education*). پرورش

A weekly newspaper printed in Cairo (Egypt) in the early part of A.H. 1318 (= A.D. 1900–1), the first number dated the 10th of Ṣafar of that year (= June 9, 1900). The owner, editor and writer was Mírzá 'Alí Muḥammad Khán of Káshán, the brother of [Mírzá 'Abdu'l-Ḥusayn Khán] *Waḥídu'l-Mulk*, who was a Member of the Second *Majlis*. This was one of the best Persian newspapers, and as regards influence amongst the young Persians held the first place, both exciting the emotions and compelling the affections of the Persian public. In style and tone, moreover, it had a peculiar quality of beauty. It took the place of the *Thurayyá* ("Pleiades") after the dissolution of the partnership which previously existed between Mírzá 'Alí Muḥammad Khán and Sayyid Faraju'lláh of Káshán. The fiery utterances and sweet eloquence of this paper had an extraordinary effect on public opinion, and in truth effected an intellectual revolution. Some of its special articles, such as "the Daughter of Ḥájji Felt-maker" (*Dukhtar-i-Ḥájji Namad-mál*), "Fancy's Dream" (*Khwáb-i-Khayál*), "A Topic of Conversation" (*Maqála-i-Muṣáḥaba*), "Arguing in a circle" (*Dawr u Tasalsul*), and "the Court of Judgement, or, before the Judge of Conscience" (*Majlis-i-Muḥákama, yá Maḥẓar-i-Qáẓi-yi-Wijdán*) may be taken as literary models in the Persian language. After the *Qánún*, it was the freest in its language of all the Persian papers during the period of Autocracy; and by reason of the vehemence of its utterances, and its violent attacks on the methods of administration of the Government of Persia, particularly its criticisms on the unpatriotic actions and policy of the *Amínu's-Sulṭán*, it became an object of hatred to the Court and of affection to the people. In consequence of an article comparing the merits of the *Amínu'd-Dawla* and *Amínu's-Sulṭán* which was published in No. 23 of the paper, it was prohibited from entering Persia, but it still continued publication until the 33rd number, and by secret channels continued to find entrance into Persia. In the last number appeared a famous article, entitled "Lament for the Broken Pen: '*for what crime was it slain?*'" (*Zárí bar shikastagi-yi-qalam: 'bi-ayyi dhanb*^{in} *qutilat?*'), which had a special importance. After the suppression of the paper, Mírzá 'Alí Muḥammad Khán was for some time ill with consumption, of which he finally died in A.H. 1320 (= A.D. 1902–3) at Ḥalwán near Cairo. See also under *Thurayyá*.

See Rabino, No. 55. I possess Nos. 11–19 of this paper. Each number comprises 16 pp. of 9½″ × 6″. Yearly subscription, 40 *qráns* in Persia, 10 roubles in the Caucasus, 4 mejidiyyés in Turkey, 25 francs in Europe, and 12 rupees in India and China. Of the articles specially mentioned above, *Dawr u Tasalsul* occurs in No. 19 and deals with the exactions practised by the Persian Consuls on the Persian pilgrims to Mecca; and the *Majlis-i-Muḥákama* occurs in No. 18.

(95)

Pulís-i-Írán (*The Police of Persia*). پلیس ایران

A daily newspaper printed in Ṭihrán in A.H. 1327 (=A.D. 1909), edited by Sayyid Jawád of Tabríz and owned by Murtaḍá-qulí Khán *Mu'ayyidu'l-Mamálik* the Qájár. This was one of the papers connected with the party who were in the majority, and defended the policy of the Government, that is of the "Moderates" (*I'tidáliyyún*).

See Rabino, No. 56. I possess a good many numbers, the first being No. 1, dated the 4th of Dhu'l-Qa'da, A.H. 1327 (=November 18, 1909), and the last No. 480, dated the 20th of Muḥarram, A.H. 1329 (=Jan. 21, 1911). The size of the paper was originally 14⅓″ × 11″, but it was afterwards enlarged to 18″ × 12¼″. Yearly subscription, 35 *qráns* in Ṭihrán, 40 *qráns* elsewhere in Persia, 10 roubles in Russia, 25 francs in Europe, and £T1 in Turkey; but the price was subsequently raised.

(96)

Payámbar-i-Bákhtar (*The Prophet of the West*). پیامبر باختر

A small-sized magazine published in Washington (U.S.A.) once every 19 days by the Bahá'ís of America for the propagation of the Bahá'í religion. Its name was afterwards changed to the "Star of the West" (*Najm-i-Bákhtar*).

See Rabino, No. 57. I possess the "Star of the West," Vol. ii, Nos. 1–4, 7–8, and 14–16, the first dated March 21, 1911, the last Dec. 31 of the same year. The magazine is bilingual, the greater part (about two-thirds) being printed in English, and the remainder lithographed in Persian. In connection with the same "Persian-American Educational Society" was published in October, 1911, the first number of another monthly magazine (entirely in English) entitled the "Illustrated Monthly Bulletin of the Persian-American Educational Society," of which I possess Nos. 1, 5 and 8, the last dated May–June, 1912.

(97)

Paykár (*Strife*). پیکار

A paper published in Ṭihrán in A.H. 1329 (= A.D. 1911) under the editorship of Mírzá Ḥaydar 'Alí Kamálí. It was the organ of the then recently formed party of the *Ijtimá'iyyún-i-Ittiḥádiyyún*.

Not mentioned by Rabino, and not seen.

(98)

Táza Bahár (*Early Spring*). تازه بهار

A weekly paper printed in Mashhad in A.H. 1329 (= A.D. 1911) under the editorship of the Poet Laureate (*Maliku'sh-Shu'ará*), or "M. Bahár," which replaced the *Naw Bahár* (*q.v.*) on its suppression. In politics it was Democrat.

Not in Rabino. I possess No. 3, dated the 22nd of Dhu'l-Ḥijja, A.H. 1329 (= December, 14, 1911). It comprises 4 pp. of 16″ × 10¼″. Yearly subscription, 25 *qráns* in Mashhad, 30 *qráns* elsewhere in Persia, and 6 roubles abroad.

(99)

Tabríz. تبریز

A weekly paper published in Tabríz in A.H. 1296 (= A.D. 1879) under the editorship of a certain Kamál. No. 3, which I possess, is dated Thursday, Muḥarram 25, A.H. 1297 (= Jan. 8, 1880), corresponding with the Year of the Hare. Numbers belonging to the third year of publication have been seen. Mention has been made of it in the Introduction. (See p. 13, *supra*.)

Not in Rabino.

(100)

Tabríz. تبریز

A paper printed three times a week in Tabríz towards the end of A.H. 1328 (= A.D. 1910) under the editorship of Mírzá Isma'íl Yakání, and subsequently of Mírzá Ḥusayn *Ṭabíb-záda*, known as "Kamál," formerly editor of the paper *Kamál* ("Perfection"). The publisher of this paper was Karbalá'í Ḥusayn, known as *Fishangchí* ("the Cartridge-seller"), a Member of the Tabríz Provincial Council. This paper was suppressed with all the other papers published in Tabríz at the time of the Russian aggression of Muḥarram, A.H. 1330 (= Christmas, 1911), and its

تصدیق مباشر مالیهٔ خوی

بندهٔ درگاه حاجی میرزا علی خان که عمل خوی مداخله کرده‌ام حساب مالیاترا منتقل هستم ماروسو برده حضرت آقای حاجی محتشم السلطنه حکمران کل ردکرده بوصول اسناد خرج هم بست گرفته آورده بحناب آقای سالار اسعد تسلیم کنم احتمالاً تشخیص امر حساب ماندهٔ است شهر ذیقعدة الحرام ۱۳۲۷ (علی)

وحال اینکه بنده مسئول حساب مالیات نبودم ودیناری هم برای خود حقوق حکومتی برداشت نکرده‌ام بطوریکه محض رسیدگی در مشروطیت مبلغ یکصد وبیست تومان بجناب آقای میرزا سید محمد خان مأمور دفتر مالیه پول داده قبض رسید هم گرفتم که سواد حکم باخط خود میرزا سید محمد خان را مستدعیم بعد ازملاحظه درج فرمائید

تصدیق مأموریت میرزا سید محمد خان

ازریاست مالیهٔ آذربایجان

جناب میرزا سید محمد خان چون عمل مالیه ولایات خوی وسلماس وخالصجات آنجا درسوات ماضیه قوی ئیل وییجی ئیل وتحاقوی ئیل بواسطهٔ انقلابات ازهرجهة مهمل ومعطل مانده بوده و تسویه وتفکیک محاسبات سنواة ماضیه لازم است وشمارا که از ادارهٔ اجرای مالیه برای تحقیق وتعیین محاسبات سنواتی ولایتی وخالصگی آنجا منتخب نموده‌اند لهذا من هم مأموریت شمارا تصویب نموده مینویسم که باهمراهی حاجی میرزا علی خان مباشر سابق خوی عاجلاً بمحل مأموریت رفته ودر تشخیص سنواتی ولایتی وخالصگی اقدامات لازمه نموده وفلوس ماخوذی آنجارا اعم ازدولتی وملتی هرچه باشد جمع کرده تااوایل شوال نتیجهٔ مأموریت خودرا باداره محاسبات بیاورید

(معتمد السلطنه)

قبض الوصول حق الزحمهٔ میرزا محمد خان

مبلغ یکصد وبیست تومان موافق قرار داد حضرت آقای معتمد السلطنه وزیر مالیه ... از بابت حق الزحمهٔ اقل السادات در حین مأموریت خوی بتوسط جناب اجل آقای سالار اسعد واصل و عاید اقل گردید شهر شوال المکرم تحاقوی ئیل ۱۳۲۸ (محمد الحسینی)

بنده مراتب را بحضرت ایالت جلیله ... عرض کردم ایشان مرقومهٔ ذیل را بریاست مالیه مرقوم فرموده‌اند مستدعی است عیناً درج فرمائید

ازایالت جلیلهٔ سابق بریاست مالیه

ادارهٔ جلیلهٔ مالیه سالار اسعد اظهار میکند که درمشروطیت چه روا است یکصد وبیست تومان بیدرسیدگی ازجاکر پول بگیرند بمأمور دفتر بدهند درصورتیکه مأمور رفته رسیدگی کرده جاکر سند نوشته داده است که عدوی دیناری ماخوذ نکرده ومالیات را حیف ومیل نکرده‌ام) دراین باب چه میگویند راپورت کنید ملاحظه شود (مجیر السلطنه)

آقا میرزا محمد خان مدتی در خوی مانده ماخوذی مردم را جمع کرده بدفتر مالیه آورده سند هم سند داده و در حضور سرکار والا آقای ضیاء الدوله نایب الایاله روبرو نمود که سالار اسعد دست بمالیات خوی نزده دیناری ماخوذ نکرده مستدعی است مرقومهٔ آقای ضیاء الدوله را هم عیناً درج فرمائید

ازنیابت ایالت جلیله بریاست مالیه

سالار اسعد سابقاً که حکومت خوی را موجب سند آقای محتشم السلطنه قرارداده اید ماهی دویست تومان ازبابت شهریه برداشت نامه سواد نوشتهٔ آقای محتشم السلطنه را امضا فرستادم دراین صورت اگر ایرادی هم باشد لازم است از خود آقای محتشم السلطنه سوال نمود درهرحال سالار اسعد اظهار اینکه حق است (ضیاء الدوله) بعد دارد

تلگراف از طهران به تبریز

جواد انجمن ایالتی آذربایجان دامت تائیدا تهم تلگرافات جنابعالی واصل گردید درباب تنخواه برای تدارکات قشونی وسایر مخارجات بوزارت جلیلهٔ مالیه تاکید شد که بیست هزار تومان فوری حواله بدهند البته خواهد رسید باز هم درموقع ضرورت حواله میشود درباب عدم حرکت قزاق ساخلو هم بوزارت جنگ نوشته شد که اقدامات لازمه نمایند و تلگراف عدم حرکت انهارا مخابره نمایند نمره ۶۷۸ ریاست وزرا

سواد راپورت ادارهٔ تفتیش

تقریرات اشخاص ذیل اینکه امروز چهار نفر سالدات ازدکان علی اکبر بقال پنج چارک خیار گرفته براه افتاده پول ندادند ازآنجا رد شده بدکان کربلائی حسن بقال رسیدند دو عدد هندوانه برداشته براه افتادند کربلائی حسن مزبور خواست ممانعت کند بابانچه کشیده بیچاره بقال عاجز شده بعد ایشان نادر باغ رفت سالداتها بباغ رفته ... را باغ شدند

تحریر بمطبعهٔ ...

U NOM DE LA LIBERTE DE LA PRESSE

LES RUSSES en PERSE

La diplomatie russe, très peu scrupuleuse dans le choix des moyens qu'elle met en œuvre pour arriver à ses fins, emploie tout l'art qu'on lui connaît à enflammer la Perse de tous les côtés, afin d'avoir un motif plausible pour ne pas retirer ses troupes, afin de pouvoir mieux pêcher en eau trouble.

Chaque fois que le pays s'apaise et va entrer dans sa voie normale, une nouvelle émeute éclate, comme par enchantement, sur un point quelconque du territoire et tout le monde sait que ces troubles sont dûs tous aux provocations étrangères.

Presque toujours c'est un provocateur quelconque, recruté parmi les Persans servant la politique russe qui est mis en jeu; mais les Russes ne craignent pas d'agir quelquefois directement sans l'intermédiaire de leurs serviteurs zélés,

Ils nous en donnent récemment une bonne preuve

Le 27 juillet, une patrouille de soldats russes fait irruption dans le palais du gouvernement à Tauris. Elle le cerne et en retire et emmène, tambour battant, l'ancien gouverneur d'Ardébil, Rachidul-Mulk, un type de traître-tyran qui avait été arrêté, il y a cinq ou six mois, dans un appartement particulier du Palais et que maintenant les Russes appellent leur "protégé".

Il y a eu par suite quelques meetings contre cet acte de pure violence; mais, bien entendu, dans le seul but de protester, dernier remède des faibles opprimés

Le 28, à 8 heures du soir, nouvelle apparition de soldats russes dans une rue très-fréquentée de la ville

Les cosaques font mine d'attaquer les passants en braquant sur eux leurs fusils chargés; puis, ils les dispersent à coups de crosse. Au milieu d'une panique générale des femmes et des enfants se blessent en se laissant piétiner par la foule en fuite,

Après quoi Messieurs les "pacificateurs" rentrent tranquillement chez eux, c'est-à-dire au Jardin Baghé-Chémal

⁂

Le fait de cette provocation est tellement criant et il montre avec tant de clarté le rôle joué par les Russes en Perse que tout commentaire nous semble superflu

Et on ne prévoit pas de fin à cette ignoble tragi-comédie qui bouleverse le pays!

Il y aura, peut être, quelque chose de plus nouveau, de plus tragique et de plus horrible encore à voir et à raconter, nous devons bien l'attendre

Voilà comment les Russes, apôtres de la paix, prêchent l'humanité chez les Persans

Et voilà la signification, dans le langage diplomatique, du verbe "pacifier",

A. E.

P. S. Nous prions tous nos confrères de vouloir bien faire reproduire le texte ci-dessus ou sa traduction dans leurs journaux respectifs

مدیر مسئول : حسین

Last page, with column in French, of No. 89 of the newspaper *Tabríz*, dated August 2, 1911

editor was arrested. The politics of the paper were Conservative and Moderate Constitutionalist.

See Rabino, No. 58. I possess Nos. 72 and 89, the former dated the 23rd of Jumáda ii, A.H. 1329 (=June 21, 1911), and the latter the 7th of Sha'bán (August 4) of the same year. Each number comprises 4 pp. of 15½″ × 9¼″. Yearly subscription, in Tabríz 21 *qráns*, elsewhere in Persia 30 *qráns*, abroad 42 *qráns*.

(101)

Tadayyun (*Religiousness*). تديّن

A weekly religious paper printed in Ṭihrán in A.H. 1325 (= A.D. 1907) under the editorship of Mullá Ṣádiq, entitled *Fakhru'l-Islám* ("the Pride of Islám"), originally a Chaldaean or Syrian Christian of Urmiya, who was converted to Islám (*Jadídu'l-Islám*).

See Rabino, No. 59. I possess No. 11 of the first year, dated the 1st of Sha'bán, A.H. 1325 (=Sept. 9, 1907), and No. 2 of the third year, dated the 16th of Rajab, A.H. 1327 (=August 3, 1909). Each number comprises 4 pp. of 12″ × 6¾″. Yearly subscription, 12 *qráns* in Ṭihrán, 15 *qráns* elsewhere in Persia, 4 roubles in Russia and the Caucasus, and 7 rupees in India.

(102)

Tarbiyat (*Education*). تربيت

A weekly paper lithographed in very fine *nasta'líq* in Ṭihrán in A.H. 1314 (= A.D. 1896–7). Its owner, editor and chief writer was Mírzá Muḥammad Ḥusayn of Iṣfahán, entitled *Zaká'u'l-Mulk* and poetically surnamed *Furúghí*, author of numerous works on history and literature, father of the present Mírzá Muḥammad 'Alí Khán *Zaká'u'l-Mulk*, who was a member of the Second National Assembly. This paper had a special literary importance in regard to its style, composition, and quality of eloquence, for the late *Zaká'u'l-Mulk*, who was in his time one of the first men of letters and poets of Persia, used frequently to publish his poems in it, for which reason amongst others it held a high and distinguished place amongst the papers of the period of Autocracy, and enjoyed a considerable influence, though its practice of flattering and praising contemporary notables detracted from its literary value. Its celebrity was chiefly due to its controversy with the paper *Thurayyá* ("Pleiades," *q.v.*) about the Persian Calendar of Ḥájji Najmu'd-Dawla. In consequence of the well-founded criticisms levelled by Mírzá 'Alí Muḥammad Khán of Káshán the editor of the *Thurayyá*, against the absurdities of the Persian Calendar, the *Tarbiyat* devoted two of its issues from beginning to end to a defence of Ḥájji Najmu'd-Dawla and an attack on the *Thurayyá*. This attack gave occasion to the admirers of the *Thurayyá* to express their feelings and to pour forth their objections, and many articles in refutation of the *Tarbiyat* from all parts of Persia and from abroad appeared in the *Thurayyá* and other papers. Translations of useful treatises [composed in other languages] often appeared as *feuilletons* (*pá waraqí*) at the foot of the pages of the *Tarbiyat*. Amongst these were "*la Chaumière indienne*" (*Kulba-i-Hindí*) of Bernardin de Saint-Pierre, "Love and Virtue" (*'Ishq u 'Iffat*), a translation of Chateaubriand's *Aventures du dernier des Abencérages*, etc. The *Tarbiyat* continued publication until the end of the period of Autocracy and almost until the Constitutional Period.

See Rabino, No. 16, according to whom this paper began on the 11th of Rajab, A.H. 1314 (=Dec. 16, 1896). It was still going on (No. 424) on the 4th of Dhu'l-Qa'da, A.H. 1324 (=Dec. 20, 1906). I possess a good many numbers, of which the first is No. 58 (second year), dated the 26th of Sha'bán, A.H. 1315 (=Jan. 20, 1898), and the last No. 433, dated the 22nd of Muḥarram, A.H. 1325 (=March 7, 1907). Each number comprises 8 pp. of 12″ × 6¾″, the pages being numbered continuously with a view to binding. Yearly subscription, 20 *qráns* in Ṭihrán, 25 *qráns* elsewhere in Persia, 5 roubles in Russia, 10 rupees in India, and 12 francs in Europe, Turkey and Egypt.

(103)

Taraqqí (*Progress*). ترقّی

A fortnightly paper printed in Ṭihrán in A.H. 1325 (= A.D. 1907) under the editorship of Mírzá Muḥammad 'Alí Khán of Ṭihrán, known as "Islámbúlí" ("the Constantinopolitan"), who was one of those imprisoned in the Bágh-i-Sháh after the Reactionary *Coup d'État* of the 23rd of Jumáda i, A.H. 1326 (= June 23, 1908).

See Rabino, No. 61, according to whom the publication of the paper began on the 17th of Ṣafar, A.H. 1325 (=April 1, 1907). I possess Nos. 16, 21 and 22. Each number comprises 4 pp. of 12″ × 6¾″. The yearly subscription was 12 *qráns* for Ṭihrán, 15 for other parts of Persia, 5 roubles for Russia and the Caucasus, 3 mejidiyyés for Turkey, and 10 rupees for India.

(104)

Tashwíq (*Encouragement*). تشویق

A weekly paper printed in Ṭihrán in A.H. 1325 (= A.D. 1907) under the editorship of Mírzá Sayyid 'Alí Ṭabáṭabá'í. This paper, like many others, used to attempt a feeble imitation of the *Charand-Parand* ("Charivari") of the *Súr-i-Isráfíl*, and published a comic or satiric section under the title of *Shirr-Wirr*.

See Rabino, No. 62, according to whom only 8 issues of the paper were published, the first on the 19th of Sha'bán, A.H. 1325 (=Sept. 27, 1907), and the last on the 26th of Shawwál (=Dec. 2) of the same year. I possess Nos. 2-8. Each number comprises 8 pp. of 12½" × 6¾". Yearly subscription, 15 *qráns* in Ṭihrán, 20 *qráns* in other parts of Persia, and 25 *qráns* abroad.

(105)

Tafakkur (*Thought*). تفكّر

A weekly paper printed in Ṭihrán in A.H. 1325 (=A.D. 1907) under the editorship of *Náẓimu'z-Zákirín*.

See Rabino, No. 63, according to whom only one number was issued on the 3rd of Rabí' i, A.H. 1325 (=April 16, 1907). I possess this number, which comprises 4 pp. of 11¼" × 6¾". Yearly subscription, 30 *qráns* in Ṭihrán, 35 *qráns* elsewhere in Persia, and 25 francs in Europe.

(106)

Tamaddun (*Civilization*). تمدّن

A weekly paper printed in Ṭihrán in A.H. 1324 (=A.D. 1906–7). The proprietor and principal writer was the *Mudabbiru'l-Mamálik* of Hirand, who originally belonged to the class of doctors of theology and divinity students in Iṣfahán, and afterwards applied himself to journalism in Ṭihrán. This was one of the best newspapers of the Constitutional Period, and was conspicuous alike for its literary style and for its boldness and steadfastness for the Constitution. After the Reactionary *Coup d'État* and bombardment of the Majlis (June 23, 1908) the *Mudabbiru'l-Mamálik* was able to save his life from the revengeful claws of the partisans of Autocracy, and fled by way of Bushire to India, where he again began to publish the *Tamaddun* in Bombay. He also spent some time at Calcutta, where he published several articles in the *Ḥablu'l-Matín*. He subsequently went to Constantinople, but returned to Persia during the Revolution (of 1909), and again started his paper at Rasht. After the conquest of Ṭihrán [by the Nationalists] in A.H. 1327 (July, 1909) he returned thither and again started his paper, which continued publication until A.H. 1330 (=A.D. 1912). During its final appearance in Ṭihrán the *Tamaddun* stood aside from the strife of the other conflicting parties, and described itself as the partisan of the policy of fundamental reforms (Radical). During its first publication the *Tamaddun* published eighty numbers a year, but afterwards appeared once a week. During the latter part of A.H. 1329 (=A.D. 1911) it became a daily, and was published in small quarto form under the title of *Iṭṭilá'át-i-rúzána-i-Tamaddun* ("Daily information of the *Tamaddun*"). This paper epitomized in a very pleasing form the weekly happenings and news of Persia and foreign countries, and in this respect it occupied a unique position amongst Persian newspapers.

See Rabino, No. 64. I possess a good many numbers of the First and Second Years of publication, of which the first is No. 1 of the First Year, dated the 17th of Dhu'l-Ḥijja, A.H. 1324 (=Feb. 1, 1907), and the last No. 14 of the Second Year, dated the 11th of Jumáda i, A.H. 1326 (=June 11, 1908). Each number comprises 4 pp. of $11\frac{1}{2}'' \times 6\frac{3}{4}''$. Yearly subscription, 24 *qráns* in Ṭihrán, 30 *qráns* elsewhere in Persia, 7 roubles in Russia and the Caucasus, and 14 rupees in India. A supplementary number dated the 1st of Ramaẓán, A.H. 1326 (=Sept. 27, 1908), bears over the title the words "*Nála-i-Millat*" ("the Nation's Lament"), and above this the verse from the Qur'án: "*Deem not them who were slain in the Way of God as dead, but rather as living, cared for by their Lord.*" Instead of the usual price stand the words: "a grain of activity," and readers in Persia are requested to pass the paper on to others. It contains a proclamation from the *Mujtahids* of Karbalá against Muḥammad 'Alí Sháh and in favour of the Constitution, and was printed at the *Ḥablu'l-Matín* Press at Calcutta.

(107)

Tamaddun (*Civilization*). تمدّن

A paper published in Bombay in A.H. 1327 (=A.D. 1909) by the above-mentioned *Mudabbiru'l-Mamálik* during his stay in India. Only one number appeared.

Not in Rabino, and not seen.

(108)

Tamaddun (*Civilization*). تمدّن

A paper published in Rasht in A.H. 1327 (=A.D. 1909), edited and written by the above-mentioned *Mudabbiru'l-Mamálik*, during his return from India to Ṭihrán. Only one number appeared, dated 29 Rabí' ii, A.H. 1327 (May 19, 1909).

See Rabino, No. 64, according to whom the single Rasht issue was No. 15 of the Second Year. We have seen above that No. 14 of the Second Year was published on June 11, 1908, 12 days before the *Coup d'État*, while the next (Rasht) issue, No. 15, must have been published about 13 months later, in July, 1909, just before the capture of Ṭihrán by the Nationalists.

(109)

Tanbíh (*Admonition*). تنبیه

A comic paper, partly lithographed and partly printed, published in Ṭihrán, and illustrated with coloured caricatures, in A.H. 1325 (= A.D. 1907), under the editorship of *Mu'taẓidu'l-Aṭibbá*. After the restoration of the Constitution (in July, 1909) this paper was again published, and continued until these last times (end of 1911). In politics it belonged to the Moderate Party.

See Rabino, No. 65, according to whom No. 7 was dated the 14th of Jumáda ii, A.H. 1325 (= July 25, 1907). I possess No. 1 of the Third Year, which, however, is undated. It comprises 4 pp. of 12½" × 6¾". Pp. 1 and 4 each contain a caricature (not coloured) and are lithographed: pp. 2 and 3 are printed.

(110)

Tahdhíb (*Purification*). تهذیب

A weekly newspaper printed in Ṭihrán in A.H. 1328 (= A.D. 1910).

Not in Rabino, and not seen.

(111)

at-Tawaddud (*Affection*). التّودّد

A paper published in Paris in A.D. 1891 (= A.H. 1308–9) under the editorship of Shaykh Abú Naẓẓára (-*Nadhdhára*). This paper was published in four languages, Arabic, Persian, Turkish and French, and was illustrated. As it contained a Persian section it has been recorded amongst the Persian newspapers. Some of its Persian articles were written by Shaykh Muḥammad Ḥasan of Sírján (near Kirmán), entitled *Shaykhu'l-Mulk*.

Not in Rabino, and not seen. Shaykh Abú Naḍḍára (a vulgar form of the name given above), one of the Egyptian political exiles in Paris, was better known as the editor of the Arabic comic lithographed paper called by the same name ("the Father of Spectacles") which he had assumed. His real name was James Sanna.

(112)

Tiyátr (*The Theatre*). تیاتر

A bi-weekly paper printed in Ṭihrán in A.H. 1326 (=A.D. 1908), edited and written by Mírzá Riẓá Khán-i-Ṭabáṭabá'í of Ná'in, afterwards a member of the Second National Assembly. Its contents consisted of scenes cast in dramatic form referring to the conditions of administration under the Autocracy, and the methods of government adopted by princes and governors under the ancient *régime*. It may be reckoned one of the best newspapers in Persian.

See Rabino, No. 66, according to whom the paper first appeared on the 4th of Rabí' i, A.H. 1326 (=April 6, 1908). He adds that he had seen No. 1 of the Third Year, which bore no date. I possess Nos. 1–4, which contain each 4 pp. of 11″ × 7″. Yearly subscription, 12 *qráns* in Ṭihrán, 16 *qráns* elsewhere in Persia, 4 roubles in Russia and the Caucasus, and 8 francs in Europe.

(113)

Thurayyá (*The Pleiades*). ثریّا

A weekly newspaper printed in Cairo (Egypt) in A.H. 1316 (=A.D. 1898–9). The first number was dated the 14th of Jumáda ii of that year (=Oct. 30, 1898), and it was at first edited by Mírzá 'Alí Muḥammad Khán of Káshán and afterwards by Sayyid Faraju'lláh of Káshán. So long as it was edited and written by the former it was much sought after and attained a great renown, so much so that during the Period of Autocracy no Persian newspaper was so much appreciated. It participated in most of those qualities which have been already mentioned in our eulogy of the *Parwarish*, than which it was even better known in consequence of the longer duration of its publication. One of its well-known articles was the "Topic of Conversation" (*Maqála-i-Muṣáḥaba*), and one of the most important episodes in its career was the prolonged controversy concerning Ḥájji Najmu'd-Dawla's Calendar (see pp. 61–2, *supra*) which took place between it and the *Tarbiyat* newspaper. Another was its defence of the *Tarbiyat* College established in Tabríz by the present writer and others, and its continued attacks on Ḥájji Sayyid Muḥammad of Yazd, the notorious intriguer who had been instrumental in bringing about the closure of that College. The violent attacks on this man published in Nos. 36 and 37 of the First Year of this paper led to his banishment from Tabríz. In the middle of the Second Year of its publication, Mírzá 'Alí Muḥammad Khán handed over the paper to Sayyid Faraju'lláh, and himself founded the *Parwarish* (*q.v.*). Thereafter the *Thurayyá* entirely lost its former importance, and no longer retained its popularity. It continued to be published in Egypt under the editorship of Sayyid Faraju'lláh for some time, but was finally suspended, and the editor went to Ṭihrán and there resumed its publication.

See Rabino, No. 67. I possess an almost complete set of the paper comprising Nos. 1–51 of the First Year, the date of No. 1 being the 14th of Jumáda ii, A.H. 1316 (=Oct. 30, 1898), and Nos. 1–36 of the Second Year, the date of the last number being the 20th of Jumáda i, A.H. 1318 (=Oct. 15, 1900). The first number of the *Parwarish* is dated the 10th of Ṣafar, A.H. 1318 (=June 8, 1900). Each number of the *Thurayyá* comprises from 16 to 18 pp. of 9″ × 5¾″. Yearly subscription, 36 *qráns* in Persia, 4 mejidiyyés in Turkey, 10 roubles in Russia and tbe Caucasus, 25 francs in Europe, and 12 rupees in India.

(114)

Thurayyá (*The Pleiades*). ثريّا

A weekly newspaper printed in Ṭihrán in A.H. 1321 (=A.D. 1903–4) under the editorship of the above-mentioned Sayyid Faraju'lláh of Káshán.

See Rabino, No. 67, according to whom No. 21 of the Sixth Year (dating from the foundation of the paper at Cairo) was dated the 22nd of Rajab, A.H. 1321 (=Oct. 14, 1903).

(115)

Thurayyá (*The Pleiades*). ثريّا

A paper published at Káshán in A.H. 1328 (=A.D. 1910) by the same Sayyid Faraju'lláh.

Not mentioned by Rabino, and not seen.

(116)

Járchi-yi-Millat (*The People's Herald*). جارچی ملّت

A weekly paper lithographed in Ṭihrán towards the end of A.H. 1328 (=A.D. 1910), under the editorship of Áqá Sayyid Ḥusayn, and illustrated with comic caricatures.

See Rabino, No. 68, according to whom No. 5 was dated the 5th of Muḥarram, A.H. 1329 (=Jan. 6, 1911). I possess Nos. 5–8. No. 6 is dated the 23rd of

Muḥarram, A.H. 1329, and has on the first page a portrait of M. Panoff, the celebrated Bulgarian revolutionary who was expelled from Ṭihrán by the Russians and afterwards took part in the fighting near Astarábád. See my *History of the Persian Revolution*, pp. 214–228 and 418. Each number comprises 4 pp. of 12½″ × 6½″. Yearly subscription, 8 *qráns* in Ṭihrán, 10 *qráns* elsewhere in Persia, and 6 francs abroad.

(117)

Járchi-yi-Waṭan (*The Country's Herald*). جارچی وطن

A weekly paper published in Ṭihrán in A.H. 1328 (= A.D. 1910).

Not in Rabino, and not seen.

(118)

Jám-i-Jam (*The Goblet of Jamshíd*). جام جم

A weekly newspaper lithographed in Ṭihrán in A.H. 1325 (= A.D. 1907) under the editorship of Ḥájji Sayyid Riẓá (the nephew of Ḥájji Sayyid Muḥammad the banker), one of the registrars of the National Assembly, and illustrated with portraits of former kings of Persia.

See Rabino, No. 69, according to whom this paper first appeared on the 14th of Jumáda ii, A.H. 1325 (=July 25, 1907). I possess Nos. 1–10, 12–18, 20–23, 26–27. Each number comprises as a rule 4 pp. of 12″ × 6¾″, and has on the first page a picture of one of the ancient Persian kings of the Kayání or Sásání dynasty, the first being Kayúmarth and the last Bahrám II. Yearly subscription, 12 *qráns* in Ṭihrán, 15 *qráns* elsewhere in Persia, 3 roubles in Russia and the Caucasus, one mejidiyyé and a half in Turkey, and 7 francs in Europe.

(119)

Jám-i-Jamshíd (*The Goblet of Jamshíd*). جام جمشید

A weekly newspaper published at Bombay every Monday in A.H. 1262 (= A.D. 1846).

This paper, together with some other Persian newspapers, is mentioned in Zenker's *Bibliotheca Orientalis* (Leipzig, 1846), under article No. 1831. According to this statement, the papers mentioned by name as published in India were earlier by at least five years than even the *Rúznáma-i-Waqáyi'-i-Ittifáqiyya*, which was the earliest Persian newspaper, since they were in circulation in A.H. 1262, which was the date, according to the Muhammadan computation, of Zenker's work, and some of them may have been founded years before that date. This paper is not mentioned by Rabino, nor have I seen it.

(120)

Jám-i-Jahán-numá (*The World-shewing Goblet*). جام جهان نما

A weekly newspaper published in Calcutta, appearing on Thursdays in A.H. 1262 (= A.D. 1846).

Mentioned by Zenker, *op. cit.*, under article No. 1833. Not mentioned by Rabino, and not seen.

(121)

Jarída-i-Tijárat (*The Mercantile Magazine*). جریدهٔ تجارت

A weekly paper lithographed in the *naskh* handwriting in Ṭihrán in A.H. 1297 (= A.D. 1880).

Not in Rabino, and not seen.

(122)

Jarída-i-Kirmán (*The Kirmán Magazine*). جریدهٔ کرمان

A paper lithographed in the *naskh* handwriting, and appearing once in every ten days, under the editorship of Mírzá Ghulám-Ḥusayn of Kirmán, in A.H. 1329 (= A.D. 1911). The first number was dated the 17th of Rabí' i (= March 18) of that year.

Not in Rabino. I possess No. 1, which comprises 8 pp. of 12¼" × 6¾". Yearly subscription, 20 *qráns* in Kirmán, 24 *qráns* elsewhere in Persia, and 15 francs abroad.

(123)

Jarída-i-Millí (*The National Magazine*). جریدهٔ ملّی

A bi-weekly paper lithographed at Tabríz in A.H. 1324 (= A.D. 1906) under the editorship of Mírzá 'Alí Akbar Khán. See *infra*, under *Rúznáma-i-Millí*.

See Rabino, No. 70. I possess Nos. 32–37, the first of which is dated the 4th of Dhu'l-Ḥijja, A.H. 1324 (= Jan. 9, 1907), comprises 4 pp. of 12" × 6½", and is lithographed in a large, clear *naskh*. The yearly subscription (100 copies) was 10 *qráns* in Tabríz, 15 *qráns* elsewhere in Persia, and 3½ roubles in Russia.

(124)

al-Jamál (*Beauty*). الجمال

A weekly paper printed in Ṭihrán in A.H. 1325 (= A.D. 1907) under the editorship of Mírzá Muḥammad Ḥusayn of Iṣfahán, in which were published the homilies and harangues of the celebrated orator Sayyid Jamálu'd-Dín of Iṣfahán, the Martyr[1].

See Rabino, No. 71. I possess Nos. 3, 10, 12, 14 and 17–26. The first is dated the 13th of Ṣafar, A.H. 1325 (=March 28, 1907), and the last the 15th of Shawwál (=Nov. 21) of the same year. Each number comprises 4 pp. of 11″ × 6¾″. Yearly subscription, 8 *qráns* in Ṭihrán, 10 *qráns* elsewhere in Persia, 1½ mejidiyyés in Turkey and Egypt, 2 roubles in Russia and the Caucasus, and 6 francs in Europe and America.

(125)

Jamáliyya. جماليّه

A weekly newspaper printed in Hamadán in A.H. 1328 (= A.D. 1910) under the editorship of Ḥájji Muḥammad Ḥusayn and written by the *Mu'ayyid-i-Ḥuẓúr* in connection with the arrest of the late Áqá Sayyid Jamálu'd-Dín in Hamadán as a preliminary to his martyrdom in A.H. 1326 (June–July, 1908). It was founded to perpetuate his name.

See Rabino, No. 72. I have no copy of this paper.

(126)

Al-Janáb. الجناب

A weekly newspaper lithographed at Iṣfahán towards the end of A.H. 1324 (= Dec. 1906) under the editorship of Mír Sayyid 'Alí Janáb.

See Rabino, No. 73, who describes it as "printed," but it is in fact lithographed. I possess Nos. 1–11, of which the first is dated the 20th of Shawwál, A.H. 1324 (=Dec. 9, 1906). Each number comprises 8 pp. of 13½″ × 7½″ Yearly subscription, 25 *qráns* in Iṣfahán. The first number is very badly lithographed in a very bad *ta'líq* hand, but the subsequent numbers are much better.

(127)

Jangal-i-Mawlá (*The Lord's Jungle*). جنگل مولا

A weekly comic paper published in Ṭihrán in A.H. 1329 (= A.D. 1911) under the editorship of Ḥusayn. The first number is dated the 20th of Rajab of that year (= July 17, 1911).

Not mentioned by Rabino, and not seen.

[1] For an account of his life and death, see my *Persian Revolution*, pp. 113, 116, 117, 137, 164, 165, 167, 199, 204 (with portrait) and 208. He was captured and put to death near Hamadán shortly after the *Coup d'État* of June 23, 1908.

Áqá Sayyid Jamálu'd-Dín of Iṣfahán,

Killed at Hamadán in the summer of 1908

(128)

Janúb (*The South*). جنوب

A weekly newspaper printed in Ṭihrán in A.H. 1328 (= A.D. 1910) under the editorship of "Tangistání," with Sayyid Ya'qúb-i-Shírází as the chief writer. This newspaper was the organ of the party called "Progressives" (*Taraqqí-khwáhán*), who championed the development of the Southern provinces of Persia, and was promoted and managed by a group of deputies representing the South in the Second National Assembly. Its most important contents consisted in criticisms of the Bakhtiyárís.

See Rabino, No. 74. I possess Nos. 3, 5, 10 and 11, of which the first is dated the 5th of Muḥarram, A.H. 1329 (=Jan. 6, 1911). Each number comprises 8 pp. of $14\frac{1}{2}'' \times 8\frac{1}{2}''$. Yearly subscription, Ṭihrán, 18 *qráns*, elsewhere in Persia, 20 *qráns*, abroad, 22 *qráns*.

(129)

Jihád-i-Akbar (*The Greater Warfare*). جهاد اكبر

A weekly paper lithographed in Iṣfahán early in A.H. 1325 (= A.D. 1907) under the editorship of Mírzá 'Alí Áqá of Khurásán. The first number appeared on Muḥarram 6 of that year (= Feb. 19, 1907). It was one of the most violent newspapers, and its extreme boldness and fiery utterances were an especial cause of complaint to Muḥammad 'Alí Sháh. Endeavours were made from Ṭihrán to suppress it, but notwithstanding this it lasted for more than a year. Its policy was to promote liberal ideas and a thorough-going Constitutionalism.

See Rabino, No. 75, according to whom it continued publication from the 6th of Muḥarram, A.H. 1325 (=Feb. 19, 1907), until the 4th of Rabí' ii, A.H. 1326 (=May 6, 1908). I do not possess a copy.

(130)

Jahán-árá (*The World-adorning*). جهان آرا

A weekly paper lithographed in Ṭihrán in A.H. 1325 (=A.D. 1907) under the editorship of Mírzá 'Abbás Khán and Mírzá Sulaymán Khán.

See Rabino, No. 76, according to whom the paper first appeared on the 20th of Rajab, A.H. 1325 (=August 29, 1907). I do not possess a copy.

(131)

Júgháyí Lráber (*The Julfá Intelligencer*). Ջուղայի լրաբեր

An Armenian newspaper published in Julfá of Iṣfahán under the editorship of Bákir Adwár Tázáryáns, deputy agent of the Armenians.

See Rabino, No. 235. I do not possess a copy.

(132)

Chápuk (*The Rapid*). چاپك

A weekly newspaper published on Thursdays in Bombay in A.H. 1262 (= A.D. 1846).

Mentioned by Zenker under article No. 1832, but not by Rabino, and not seen.

(133)

Chanta-i-Pá-barahna (*The Beggar's Wallet*). چنتهٔ پا برهنه

An illustrated weekly paper lithographed in Ṭihrán in A.H. 1329 (= A.D. 1911) under the editorship of Mírzá Maḥmúd Afshár the Druggist. This paper wrote in very simple and popular language about the advantages of Constitutionalism and the conditions of labourers and peasants, and had a good effect amongst the common people and villagers. It defended the policy of the Democrats.

See Rabino, No. 77. I possess a copy of No. 11, which is undated. It comprises 4 pp. of 13″ × 7¾″. Yearly subscription, 5 *qráns* in Ṭihrán. The writing is a large and clear but ungraceful *ta'líq*. It contains a poetical section entitled *Adabiyyát-i-Bábá Aḥmad.*

(134)

Chihra-numá (*The Face-shower*). چهره نما

An illustrated paper printed in Alexandria, and published once every ten days, in A.H. 1322 (= A.D. 1904–5), under the editorship of Mírzá 'Abdu'l-Muḥammad of Iṣfahán. After a while it became a weekly paper, and was transferred to Cairo.

See Rabino, No. 78, who only mentions the Cairo edition. I have no copy of any of the Alexandria issues.

(135)

Chihra-numá (*The Face-shower*). چهره نما

A weekly illustrated newspaper printed in Cairo (Egypt), which still continues publication.

See Rabino, No. 78. I have a fairly complete set from the second to the ninth year (August 1906 until Dec. 1912). Each number comprises 16 pp. of 9¼″ × 6¼″. Yearly subscription in Egypt, 3 dollars, Persia, 30 *qráns*, Turkey, 4 mejidiyyés, England and India, 10 rupees, Turkistán and the Caucasus, 8 roubles, Europe and China, 20 francs.

(136)

Ḥablu'l-Matín (*The Firm Cord*). حبل المتين

A weekly newspaper published in Calcutta, originally lithographed and subsequently printed, in A.H. 1311 (= A.D. 1893–4), which has continued to appear regularly down to the present time, edited and written by Sayyid Jalálu'd-Dín of Káshán, entitled *Mu'ayyidu'l-Islám*. It is the oldest regular Persian newspaper which still survives, and holds an important position, especially amongst men of learning and in religious circles, in which it has a special weight and influence. Some portion of it is always devoted to religious matters, and it is the champion of Pan-Islamism. One of the most important events connected with its history was the continuation of its publication after the suppression by the *Amínu's-Sulṭán* in A.H. 1318 (= A.D. 1900–1) of the Persian newspapers published abroad, and the influence exerted by its efforts in bringing about his dismissal, especially by the publication in all countries of a photographic facsimile of the *takfír-náma*, or declaration of infidelity, of the *Amínu's-Sulṭán* signed by the chief *mujtahids* (divines) of Najaf, which *takfír-náma* the Transcaspian Gazette (*Majmú'a-i-Má-wará-yi-Baḥr-i-Khazar*: see *infra, sub voce*) vainly endeavoured to discredit and prove fictitious. Mention must also be made of its fruitful efforts during the Reactionary Period known as "the Short Tyranny" (*Istibdád-i-Ṣaghír*) to secure the renewal of the Constitution and to incite the *'ulamá* to take action. The office of this newspaper, by reason of its old-established and steadily progressive character, produced many other publications and institutions, amongst which we may mention sundry useful

Persian books printed in and published by its Press, and also the foundation of the Persian newspapers *Miftáḥu'z-Ẓafar* ("Key of Victory") and *Ázád* ("Freeman") and the *Mulk u Millat* ("Kingdom and Nation") in English, all in Calcutta; also the daily *Ḥablu'l-Matín* in Ṭihrán; and numerous printing-presses established under its name in Ṭihrán, Najaf, Iṣfahán, etc.

See Rabino, No. 80. I possess a fairly complete set for the last seven or eight years (July 1905–December 1912) and a few of the older numbers, including No. 9 of the Seventh Year, which is lithographed, and bears the date 28 Sha'bán, A.H. 1317 (=Jan. 1, 1900). I do not know when the paper began to be printed instead of lithographed, but by A.D. 1905 the change had been effected. The lithographed copies are of larger size, comprising 12 pp. of $15\frac{1}{2}'' \times 9\frac{1}{2}''$. The yearly subscription was then 10 rupees for India, 35 *qráns* for Persia and Afghánistán, 5 mejidiyyés for Turkey and Egypt, 25 francs for Europe and China, and 10 roubles for Russia. The later printed numbers comprise 16 pp. of $12\frac{3}{4}'' \times 6\frac{1}{2}''$, and the subscription price is slightly higher.

(137)

Ḥablu'l-Matín (*The Firm Cord*). حبل المتين

A daily paper printed in Ṭihrán in the early part of A.H. 1325 (= A.D. 1907) under the editorship of Sayyid Ḥasan of Káshán, brother of the *Mu'ayyidu'l-Islám*. Its publication was interrupted by the Reactionary *Coup d'État* and Bombardment of the *Majlis* (June 23, 1908), but after the restoration of the Constitution and the conquest of Ṭihrán by the Nationalists it again issued several numbers. It was, however, suspended and its editor tried and condemned to two years imprisonment for printing an article *à propos* of the execution of Shaykh Faẓlu'lláh of Núr[1] which was considered to contain an attack on religion. This was the most important daily newspaper of the Constitutional Period, and in particular its political articles on Foreign Affairs, especially its criticisms on the Anglo-Russian Entente of A.D. 1907, were of a noteworthy character[2].

(138)

Ḥablu'l-Matín (*The Firm Cord*). حبل المتين

A daily paper printed at Rasht early in A.H. 1327 (=A.D. 1909) under the editorship of Mírzá Sayyid Ḥasan of Káshán, editor

[1] See my *Persian Revolution*, pp. 329–30 and 444–5. He was hanged on July 31, 1909.

[2] Some of the most important of these articles, published in September, 1907, are translated on pp. 175–92 of my *Persian Revolution*.

of the above-mentioned Ṭihrán *Ḥablu'l-Matín*, who was exiled after the *Coup d'État* of June 23, 1908, and withdrew to the Caucasus, until, after the successful revolution at Rasht in Muḥarram, A.H. 1327 (=Jan.–Feb., 1909), he hastened thither and resumed the publication of his paper, which was continued there for four months and a half.

See Rabino, No. 79, who conveniently brackets this and the above-mentioned paper, which are in fact identical in all save place of publication, while the Calcutta *Ḥablu'l-Matín* differs by being a weekly, not a daily paper, and by being under different editorship. I possess an almost complete set of the Ṭihrán and Rasht *Ḥablu'l-Matín*. No. 1 is dated the 15th of Rabí' i, A.H. 1325 (=April 29, 1907), and the First Year ends with No. 274 (April 16, 1908). Of the Second Year I possess Nos. 1–51, the last dated June 18, 1908, only five days before the *Coup d'État* and Bombardment of the *Majlis*. The next number in my possession, dated March 15, 1909, belongs to the Rasht issue, and is entitled No. 56 of the Second Year, so that presumably four numbers appeared during the nine preceding months. It contains an article headed "the Time of Parting is ended," so that it may be the first number published at Rasht. No. 71 (April 5, 1909) is the last of the Second Year. Nos. 1–58 of the Third Year were published at Rasht, the latter bearing the date July 21, 1909. The next number (No. 1 of the Third Year of the revived Ṭihrán issue) is dated July 25, 1909, and No. 5 of the same issue, dated July 29, 1909, is the last which I possess. The article which led to the suppression of the paper and the imprisonment of the editor probably appeared three or four days later. Each number comprises 4 pp. of $11\frac{1}{2}'' \times 7''$. Yearly subscription, 40 *qráns* in Ṭihrán, 45 elsewhere in Persia, 12 roubles in Russia and the Caucasus, and 30 francs in other countries.

(139)

al-Ḥadíd (*Iron* or *The Keen One*). الحديد

A weekly paper lithographed in Tabríz in A.H. 1315 (= A.D. 1897–8), founded and edited by Mírzá Sayyid Ḥusayn Khán, editor of the newspapers *Ṣuḥbat* ("Conversation"), *'Adálat* ("Justice") and *Khabar* ("News"). After three numbers of this paper had been published, the Russian Consulate at Tabríz took the above-mentioned editor into its service in the Passport department, and this led to the suspension of the paper. After a while, however, in A.H. 1323 (=A.D. 1905–6) the paper was revived under the editorship of Áqá Sayyid Muḥammad of Shabistar, editor of the papers *Mujáhid* ("Volunteer") and *Írán-i-Naw* ("New Persia"), and continued to be published until the first general rising in Tabríz and the Proclamation of the Constitution, after which it changed its name to *'Adálat* ("Justice"). Some numbers of this paper were published under the title *Ḥadíd* without the article.

See Rabino, No. 81, who describes it as "printed," not lithographed, and only mentions its second appearance in A.H. 1323–4. I possess a good many numbers of *al-Ḥadíd*, extending from No. 2 of the Second Year, dated the 8th of Jumáda i, A.H. 1324 (=June 30, 1906), to No. 49 of the same year, dated the 2nd of Jumáda i, A.H. 1325 (1324 is erroneously printed on the paper)=June 13, 1907. The numbering of the *'Adálat* seems to have been continuous with *al-Ḥadíd*, for No. 15 of the former paper, Sha'bán 11, A.H. 1325 (printed "1324")=Sept. 19, 1907, begins with an announcement of the change of title. Each number comprises 8 pp. of 12" × 6¾". Yearly subscription, 17 *qráns* in Tabríz, 20 *qráns* elsewhere in Persia, 4 roubles in Russia, and 10 francs in Europe.

(140)

Ḥurriyyat (*Liberty*). حرّيّت

Mentioned by Rabino (No. 82), on whose authority it is here inserted, without any particulars. It is not otherwise known to me.

(141)

Ḥarf-i-Ḥaqq (*Straight Talk*). حرف حقّ

A weekly paper printed in Tabríz in the latter part of A.H. 1325 (= Winter of 1907–8) by the former administration of the newspaper *'Adálat*, edited and written by Sayyid Ni'matu'lláh of Iṣfahán. In politics it was Conservative and moderate Constitutionalist.

See Rabino, No. 83, according to whom No. 2 was dated the 5th of Dhu'l-Ḥijja, A.H. 1325 (=Jan. 9, 1908). I possess a copy of this number, which comprises 4 pp. of 11½" × 6½" Yearly subscription, 10 *qráns* in Tabríz, 15 elsewhere in Persia, 20 abroad. The printing is particularly good.

(142)

Ḥasharátu'l-Arẓ (*Reptiles of the Earth*). حشرات الأرض

A comic weekly paper printed in Tabríz with coloured lithographed caricatures in the early part of A.H. 1326 (= A.D. 1908). It was founded and published by Ḥájji Mírzá Áqá Billúrí, and edited by Mírzá Áqá, known as *Nála-i-Millat* ("The Nation's Lament"), and was one of the best produced comic papers. In the Second Constitutional Period (end of July, 1909) it again appeared, but not more than one number had been published

The Myrmidons of the ex-Sháh Muḥammad 'Alí attend and report on a Constitutional Meeting

From No. 12 of the *Hasharátu'l-Arż*, June 8, 1908

when it was suppressed by the Government. In politics this paper was Liberal and thorough-going Constitutionalist.

See Rabino, No. 84, according to whom the first number was published on the 14th Ṣafar, A.H. 1326 (=March 18, 1908). I possess several numbers of the earlier issue. Each contains 4 pp. of 13″×7″, of which pp. 1 and 4 chiefly consist of caricatures. Yearly subscription, 12 *qráns* in Tabríz, 16 *qráns* elsewhere in Persia, and 10 francs abroad.

(143)

Ḥifẓu'ṣ-Ṣiḥḥat (*The Preservation of Health*). حفظ الصحّة

A paper published in Ṭihrán, mentioned by Rabino (No. 85), but not otherwise known.

Dr Aḥmad Khán says that it was founded about A.H. 1319 (A.D. 1901–2) in connection with the Council of Health established four or five years earlier.

(144)

Ḥaqá'iq (*Verities*). حقايق

A weekly illustrated magazine printed at Bákú in the early part of the year A.H. 1325 (= A.D. 1907), edited and written by Mírzá 'Alí Muḥammad Khán Uwaysí, Persian Vice-Consul at Bákú. Seven numbers were published.

See Rabino, No. 86, according to whom the first number was published on the 7th of Ṣafar, A.H. 1325 (=March 22, 1907). I have no copy in my possession.

(145)

Ḥuqúq (*Rights*). حقوق

A weekly paper printed in Ṭihrán in the early part of the year A.H. 1325 (= A.D. 1908) under the editorship of Sulaymán Mírzá, Yaḥyá Mírzá, and Mírzá Muḥammad of Khurásán, editor of the paper *Naját* ("Deliverance"), all three of whom were members of the Second National Assembly. It was first founded by the two brothers Sulaymán Mírzá and Yaḥyá Mírzá, who subsequently included Mírzá Muḥammad of Khurásán in their partnership. In politics the paper was Liberal and thorough-going Constitutionalist, but not Democrat, as stated by Rabino.

See Rabino, No. 87, according to whom No. 2 was dated the 22nd of Rabí' i, A.H. 1326 (= April 24, 1908). I possess Nos. 4 and 5 of this paper. Each number comprises 8 pp. of $11\frac{1}{2}'' \times 6\frac{1}{2}''$. Yearly subscription, 12 *qráns* in Ṭihrán, 17 *qráns* elsewhere in Persia, and 15 francs abroad.

(146)

Ḥaqíqat (*The Truth*). حقیقت

A weekly paper published in Ṭihrán in A.H. 1325 (= A.D. 1907).

Not in Rabino, and not seen.

(147)

Ḥaqíqat (*The Truth*). حقیقت

A weekly paper lithographed in Iṣfahán early in the year A.H. 1325 (= A.D. 1907) under the editorship of Ḥájji Sayyid Aḥmad.

See Rabino, No. 89, from whom the above particulars are taken. He adds that the second issue appeared on the 22nd of Muḥarram, A.H. 1325 (= March 7, 1907). I do not possess a copy.

(148)

Ḥaqíqat (*The Truth*). حقیقت

A "jelly-graphed" newspaper published at Rasht in A.H. 1326 (= A.D. 1908) on the part of the Executive of the *Anjuman-i-Ḥaqíqat*.

See Rabino, No. 88, from whom the above particulars are taken. I do not possess a copy.

(149)

حکایت جان گداز وقایع از یزد الی شیراز

Ḥikáyat-i-Ján-gudáz-i-Waqáyi' az Yazd ila Shíráz
(*The Soul-melting Tale of Events from Yazd to Shíráz*).

A migratory newspaper lithographed in Shíráz and on the roads of Fárs in A.H. 1329 (= A.D. 1911). The following superscription stood at the top of the first page: "News-editor, Ḥájji Fatḥu'lláh, poetically surnamed *Maftún*, son of the late Áqá 'Abdu'r-Raḥím of Yazd, known as Najafí, resident in the province of 'Arabistán in Persia." This paper is deserving of attention on account of its originality.

Not in Rabino, and not seen.

(150)

Ḥikmat (*Wisdom*). حکمت

A weekly newspaper printed in Cairo in A.H. 1310 (= A.D. 1892–3) under the editorship of Mírzá Mahdí of Tabríz, entitled

Za'ímu'd-Dawla and *Ra'ísu'l-Ḥukamá*, which still appears in a somewhat irregular fashion, usually about three numbers a month being published. This paper also is one of the older papers which achieved a considerable celebrity in the earlier days, and especially promoted the use of pure Persian undiluted with Arabic. One of the most notable productions of this paper was the poem known as "The Lament of the Fatherland" (*Faryád-i-Waṭan*) in the metre known as *Ṭawíl* ("the Long").

See Rabino, No. 90. I possess a number of copies ranging from No. 246 (of the Seventh Year), dated Ṣafar 1, A.H. 1316 (=June 21, 1898), to No. 881 (of the Fifteenth Year) dated Ṣafar 1, A.H. 1325 (=March 15, 1907). The former is printed in a larger size than the succeeding numbers, and comprises 8 pp. of 14″ × 9″. The later numbers (at any rate from the Eighth Year onwards) comprise 16 pp. of 9½″ × 8″. Yearly subscription, 40 *qráns*; Russia and the Caucasus, 10 roubles; India, 15 rupees; Egypt and Europe, £1 E.

(151)

Ḥayát (*Life*). حیات

A weekly newspaper printed in Ṭihrán in A.H. 1328 (= A.D. 1910).

Not in Rabino, and not seen.

(152)

Ḥayát (*Life*). حیات

A paper lithographed in Shíráz in A.H. 1328 (= A.D. 1910). It was published there by a fugitive Liberal patriot from India called "Ṣúfí," who was presently again compelled to seek safety in flight by the harshness of the British Consul, and the newspaper was thereupon suspended, after only eight numbers of it had appeared. The editor's full name was Ṣúfí Ánbabárshá, a native of Murádábád in the Deccan.

See Rabino, No. 91. I possess the number described by him (No. 2, dated the 11th of Jumáda i, A.H. 1328 = May 21, 1910), but am not certain as to the identification with the paper described in the text, for though on the one hand there are evidences of Indian authorship (as in the form *Angrêz* for *Inglís*, English), the editor's name appears as Muḥammad Ḥusayn *Khádim-i-Sharí'at* ("Servant of the Holy Law"), and the place of publication as the *Maydán-i-Túpkhána*, or "Gun Square," which suggests Ṭihrán rather than Shíráz. (I am informed by Dr Aḥmad Khán, however, that *maydáns* of the same name exist at Shíráz and Mashhad, if not at Iṣfahán also.) In any case this paper comprises 4 pp. of 12″ × 6½″ and is lithographed in a good *ta'líq* hand. Yearly subscription, 10 *túmáns*.

(153)

Kháwaristán (*The Eastern Land*). خاورستان

A daily paper printed in Ṭihrán in A.H. 1327 (= A.D. 1909) under the editorship of Murtaẓá Khán *I'tiẓádu'l-Milla.*

See Rabino, No. 92. I possess Nos. 1 and 2, the first dated the 20th of Shawwál, A.H. 1327 (= November 4, 1909). Each number comprises 4 pp. of 11¼" × 6¾". Yearly subscription, 35 *qráns* in Ṭihrán, 40 *qráns* elsewhere in Persia, and 45 *qráns* abroad.

(154)

Khabar (*News*). خبر

A daily newspaper printed in Ṭihrán in A.H. 1328 (= A.D. 1910) under the editorship of Mírzá Sayyid Ḥusayn Khán, the former editor of the newspapers *al-Ḥadíd*, *'Adálat* and *Ṣuḥbat* (*q.v.*).

See Rabino, No. 93, according to whom No. 5 was published on the 5th of Shawwál, A.H. 1328 (= Oct. 10, 1910). I do not possess a copy.

(155)

Khurásán. خراسان

A weekly paper printed in Mashhad (Khurásán) in A.H. 1327 (= A.D. 1909).

See Rabino, No. 94, according to whom this paper first appeared on the 25th of Ṣafar, A.H. 1327 (= March 18, 1909). I possess several numbers ranging from No. 2 (dated the 3rd of Rabí' i, A.H. 1327 = March 25, 1909) to No. 24 (dated the 25th of Rajab, A.H. 1327 = August 12, 1909). Each number comprises 4 pp. of 13" × 6¼". Yearly subscription, 12 *qráns* in Mashhad, 15 *qráns* elsewhere in Persia, 18 *qráns* abroad. Editor M. S. Ḥusayn.

(156)

Khurram (*Gay*). خرّم

A fortnightly paper printed in Ṭihrán in A.H. 1325 (= A.D. 1907–8) under the editorship of Ḥájji Mír Ḥusayn.

See Rabino, No. 95. I possess No. 2, which is dated the 29th of Rabí' i, A.H. 1325 (= May 12, 1907), and comprises 4 pp. of 11½" × 6¾". Yearly subscription, 15 *qráns* in Ṭihrán and neighbourhood, 24 *qráns* elsewhere in Persia.

(157)

Khuláṣath'l-Ḥawádith (*Summary of News*). خلاصة الحوادث

A daily paper printed in Ṭihrán in A.H. 1316 (= A.D. 1898–9). This paper, which appeared as a single sheet or leaf, contained a summary of telegraphic news, was the first daily paper in

این روزنامهٔ یومیه سوای ایام یکشنبه
وجمعه همه روزه بطبع میرسد

محل فروش چاپخانهٔ (فرالکو پرسان)
(در خیابان علاء الدوله)

پنج شنبه دویم جمادی الاولی ۱۳۲۰
مطابق هفتم اوت ماه فرانسه
(۱۹۰۲ میلادی)

(قیمت ابونه در ماهی سه قران)

نمرهٔ هشتصد و هفتاد و چهارم

№ 874

خلاصة الحوادث

هرگونه مقالهٔ مفیده و إعلاناتیکه منافی مصلاح دولت و ملت نباشد باداره روزنامهٔ خلاصة الحوادث بفرستند بکمال امتنان طبع ونشر خواهد شد

افغانستان

روزنامه هـای انگلیس هندوستان چنین مینگارند
که نواب امیر جدید افغانستان در مواظبت
ومراقبت در انتظام امور عسکریه میکوشد قشون
حاضر رکاب افغانستان در زمان صلح مرکب از
هشتاد هزار نفر وامیر معظم مترصد است که
قشون حاضره را از تفنگهای پنج تیره مسلح
مسلح نماید

انتیل

یك رشته زلزله مجددا در حدود انتیل اتفاق
افتاده وآنچه از ابنیه وعمارات در جزیره سن
ونسن باقی مانده بود از این حادثه جدیده متلاشی
ومنهدم گردید
در حین یکی از حملات زلزله آب دریا خود را
از ساحل قریب یکصد ذرع کنار کشیده مانند
دیواری در میان دریا توقف نموده بعد از چند
لحظه بمحل خود مراجعت نموده وموافق حدس
علماء طبیعی چنین تصور میشود که وقوع این
حادثه بواسطهٔ ایجاد دهانه آتش فشان تحت
البحری میباشد زیراکه بعد از مشاهده حادثه
غریبه انقلاب و تغییری در آب دریا مشاهده شد
بدین طور که دفعة آب گل آلوده شده انواع
کثافات مختلفه در آن دیده شد و بسطح دریا
از اجساد ماهیهای مرده و نیم پخته پوشیده
گردید
بعد از مرور وقعه وحادثه چشمه های آب گرم
از جریان افتاده
عقیده علماء طبیعی بر آنست که جزیره سن
ونسن عنقریب معدوم ومنهدم خواهد گردید
زیرا که پایه آن بواسطه سخونت از هم گسسته و
بنیاد آن خالی گردیده
شکه بواسطه بروز حوادث متوالیا راه مهاجرت را
پیش گرفته بنقاط دیگر راه سپار شده اند

پاریس

بواسطه بستن مکاتب و مدارسیکه متعلق برؤساء
روحانیین بود جمعی بمحل عماره که بر ضد
دولت برخاسته اجتماع نموده بعضی تعرضات نمایند
در این هنگامه احتمال میرفت پارهٔ مخاطرات
اتفاق بیفتد ولی از حسن مراقبت پلیس و
مستحفظین بلدیه اغتشاشی در وضع امور رخ
نداد و انتظام شهر بر قرار بود

No. 874 of the *Khuláṣatu'l-Ḥawádith* (Aug. 7, 1902),
the oldest printed daily paper in Persia

Persia, and lasted more than five years. It was founded by Muḥammad Báqir Khán *I'timádu's-Salṭana* at the time when he was made Minister of the Press.

See Rabino, No. 96, according to whom it first appeared in Jumáda ii, A.H. 1316 (=Oct.-Nov., 1898), while the last issue seen (No. 1107) was dated the 18th of Rabí' ii, A.H. 1321 (=August 13, 1903). I possess Nos. 874 (Aug. 7, 1902) to 879. Each consists of one sheet (2 pp.) of 12¾" × 6½". Monthly subscription, 3 *qráns*.

(158)

Khiláfat (*Caliphate*). خلافت

A fortnightly paper printed in London in A.H. 1324 (= A.D. 1906) under the editorship of Ḥájji Shaykh Ḥasan of Tabríz. This newspaper was founded by the above-mentioned Shaykh Ḥasan in partnership and co-operation with a fugitive from Egypt [Najíb Hindiya, a Syrian, brother of the well-known Cairo printer Amín Hindiya], and successive numbers appeared, some in Persian, some in Arabic, and some in Turkish. The Persian numbers, most of which were devoted to attacks on "Prince" Arfa'u'd-Dawla, then Persian Ambassador at Constantinople, were written by the above-mentioned Shaykh Ḥasan.

See Rabino, No. 97, who gives the date of first appearance as the 9th of Jumáda i, A.H. 1324 (=July 1, 1906). I possess a good many copies of the Turkish, Arabic and Persian issues, for I was acquainted with both editors, and Shaykh Ḥasan was for some time (about 1907-9) Persian teacher at Cambridge. The oldest Turkish issue which I possess is No. 43 of the Second Year, dated April 5, 1901, and the oldest Arabic issue No. 163 of the Seventh Year, dated Nov. 1, 1906, so that the paper must have been started early in 1900. Of the Persian issue I possess Nos. 1-13, the first dated July 1, 1906, and the last Feb. 15, 1907. Each number comprises 4 pp. of 14" × 8½" Yearly subscription, England, 8*s*.; Persia, 20 *qráns*; Turkey and Egypt, 50 piastres; Russia, 4 roubles; Europe and China, 10 francs.

(159)

Khurshíd (*The Sun*). خورشيد

A newspaper published in Ṭihrán under the management of the Principal of the *Dáru'l-Funún*, or University.

Not in Rabino, and not seen.

(160)

Khurshíd (*The Sun*). خورشيد

A weekly paper printed and lithographed in Mashhad in A.H. 1325 (= A.D. 1907) under the editorship of Mírzá Muḥammad

Ṣádiq Khán of Tabríz. Subsequently four numbers of this paper were published weekly. In politics it was Moderate, not Democrat, as stated by Rabino.

See Rabino, No. 98, who says that the paper was started in Muḥarram, A.H. 1325 (=Feb.–March, 1907), and was still appearing when he wrote in A.H. 1329 (=A.D. 1911). I possess a good many copies, of which the first is No. 1 (dated Muḥarram 21, 1325=March 6, 1907). This as well as No. 3 is lithographed in a large, clear *naskh*, but No. 10 (dated the 29th of Rabí' i, A.H. 1325=May 12, 1907) is printed. No. 104 (dated the 25th of Dhu'l-Ḥijja, A.H. 1325=Jan. 29, 1908) is the last number of the First Year which I possess. No. 139 (Second Year) is dated the 13th of Rabí' i, A.H. 1326 (=April 15, 1908). No. 2 of the Third Year (the next in my possession) is again lithographed in a poor *ta'líq* hand, and is dated the 24th of Rajab, A.H. 1327 (=August 11, 1909). No. 33 of the same year is still lithographed, but once more in *naskh*. No. 36 of the Fourth Year, dated the 21st of Dhu'l-Ḥijja, A.H. 1328 (=Dec. 24, 1910), is again printed, while No. 68 of the same year, dated the 27th of Jumáda ii, A.H. 1329 (=June 25, 1911), is considerably enlarged in size, each page containing three instead of two columns. With this exception the pages (originally eight, later four) measure 12″ × 7″. Yearly subscription, 32 *qráns* in Mashhad, 36 *qráns* elsewhere in Persia, 8 roubles in Turkistán and the Caucasus, and 20 francs abroad.

(161)

Khayál (*Imagination*). خیال

Of this paper, not mentioned by Rabino or Mírzá Muḥammad 'Alí Khán "Tarbiyat," I possess one copy (No. 1), undated, which was lithographed at Rasht. On page 1 is a coloured portrait of Sulṭán Aḥmad Sháh (who succeeded his deposed father, Muḥammad 'Alí, on July 16, 1909), and on page 4 is a political cartoon. Yearly subscription, 12 *qráns* in Rasht, 17 *qráns* elsewhere in Persia, 20 *qráns* abroad. Size of page, 12″ × 7½″. Editor, *Afṣaḥu'l-Mutakallimín*.

(162)

Khayru'l-Kalám (*The Best of Discourses*). خیر الکلام

A paper published at Rasht, originally lithographed, afterwards printed, in A.H. 1325 (=A.D. 1907) under the editorship of *Afṣaḥu'l-Mutakallimín*. Of this paper 80 numbers a year were published, and in witty writing it was one of the most amusing of all the Persian newspapers. Its editor in A.H. 1325 (= A.D. 1907) incurred the displeasure of Amír Khán Sardár, entitled *Amír-i-A'ẓam*, then Governor of Gílán, who, from motives of revenge,

تازه گلینه احترام .

گلینه احترام (بر آیدان سوگرا)

Before and after the Honeymoon

(From *Mullá Naṣru'd-Dín*, Year iii, No. 5, Feb. 16, 1908)

caused him to be severely bastinadoed. On regaining his freedom he fled to Ṭihrán, and there renewed the publication of his paper, of which, however, only six numbers were published in the course of two months, when it was again transferred to Rasht. During its later days (A.H. 1328–9 = A.D. 1910–11) the paper was Democrat in politics.

See Rabino, No. 99, who gives the 24th of Jumáda ii, A.H. 1325 (= August 4, 1907), as the date of the first issue at Rasht, where the paper was still continued in A.H. 1329 (= A.D. 1911) when he wrote. He adds that Nos. 13–19 of the First Year were published at Ṭihrán, and that it was issued at Ṭihrán from the 25th of Dhu'l-Ḥijja, A.H. 1325, until the 23rd of Ṣafar, A.H. 1326 (= Jan. 29, 1908, until March 27, 1908).

(163)

Khayru'l-Kalám (*The Best of Discourses*). خير الكلام

A paper printed in Ṭihrán towards the end of A.H. 1325 (= A.D. 1907–8) under the editorship of *Afṣaḥu'l-Mutakallimín*. Only six numbers appeared in the course of six months at Ṭihrán, when it was again transferred to Rasht. Latterly the politics of the paper were Democrat.

See Rabino, No. 99. I possess a fairly complete set extending from No. 1 of the First Year (Aug. 4, 1907) to No. 5 of the Fourth Year (26th of Jumáda i, A.H. 1329 = May 25, 1911). The last two numbers only are lithographed, the rest printed. Each number comprises 4 pp. of 12″ × 7″. Yearly subscription, Rasht, 25 *qráns*; elsewhere in Persia, 30 *qráns*; Russia, 6 roubles.

(164)

Khayr-andísh (*Well-meaning*). خير انديش

A paper lithographed in Tabríz which first appeared on the 2nd of Rabí' i, A.H. 1327 (= March 24, 1909), in the Turkish language. This statement is quoted from Rabino, but the writer has great doubts as to the existence of such a paper at that date, which corresponded with the later days of the siege of Tabríz, a time of great distress and severe want; nor have I been able to trace it by enquiries of the leading personages of that period.

See Rabino, No. 100. I possess No. 1 of this paper, from which it appears that the year of publication was A.H. 1326, not 1327, so that the date of its first publication was April 4, 1908, and the difficulty raised above is solved. My copy consists of a single sheet (2 pp.) only of 12″ × 6¾″. Price, 1 *sháhí* in Tabríz, 1½ *sháhís* elsewhere.

(165)

Dáru'l-'Ilm (*Home of Learning = Shíráz*). دار العلم

A weekly paper lithographed in Shíráz in A.H. 1327 (= A.D. 1909) under the editorship of Mírzá 'Ináyatu'lláh *I'timádu't-Tawliya* of Shíráz, known as "The Hand from the Unseen" (*Dast-i-Ghayb*).

See Rabino, No. 101. I possess Nos. 9, 12, 14, 16, of which the first is dated the 22nd of Shawwál, A.H. 1327 (=Nov. 6, 1909). Each number comprises 8 pp. of 10" × 5¾". Yearly subscription, 17 *qráns* in Shíráz, 22 *qráns* elsewhere in Persia, 25 *qráns* in Europe and America, 5 mejidiyyés in Turkey and Egypt.

(166)

Dánish (*Knowledge*). دانش

A fortnightly newspaper lithographed in Ṭihrán in A.H. 1299 (= A.D. 1881–2). Concerning it the *I'timádu's-Salṭana* writes: "The late *Mukhbiru'd-Dawla* founded this paper in the *Dáru'l-Funún* when he was Director of that College and Minister of the Press out of rivalry with the late *I'timádu's-Salṭana*." *Zaká'u'l-Mulk* writes: "The newspaper *Dánish* was printed in the *Dáru'l-Funún*, and was written by the late Mírzá Káẓim, Professor of Chemistry. The first number of it was published on Rajab 23, 1299 (= June 10, 1882), and the last on Ṣafar 16, A.H. 1300 (= Dec. 27, 1882). Two numbers were published monthly, and in all fourteen numbers appeared."

Not in Rabino, and not seen.

(167)

Dánish (*Knowledge*). دانش

A weekly paper lithographed in Ṭihrán in A.H. 1299, the first number being dated the 22nd of Dhu'l-Ḥijja in that year (= Nov. 4, 1882).

Not mentioned by Rabino, and not seen.

(168)

Dánish (*Knowledge*). دانش

A weekly newspaper printed in Ṭihrán in A.H. 1328 (= A.D. 1910) under the editorship of the wife of Dr Ḥusayn

Khán the Oculist (*Kaḥḥál*). This is the only Persian newspaper written exclusively for women and discussing topics of special interest to women.

See Rabino, No. 102, according to whom No. 4 was issued on the 22nd of Shawwál, A.H. 1328 (=Oct. 27, 1910). I do not possess a copy.

(169)

Dabistán (*The School*). دبستان

A fortnightly paper lithographed in Tabríz in the earlier part of A.H. 1324 (= A.D. 1906) under the editorship of Mírzá Riẓá, Principal of the "Parwarish" College.

Not in Rabino, and not seen.

(170)

Dabíriyya. دبيريّه

A publication in the form of a newspaper produced at Rasht under the editorship of *Dabíru'l-Mamálik*, and containing poems and literary articles. Though not in the strict sense of the word a newspaper, but rather resembling a tract or irregular leaflets, yet, as it bore some resemblance to a newspaper, it is mentioned here amongst them.

See Rabino, No. 103. I possess two numbers, one dated only with the year (A.H. 1326), the other dated the 15th of Rabí' ii of that year (=May 17, 1908). Each consists of a single sheet of 12″ × 5¾″, printed on one side only, and each contains one single poem only.

(171)

Dastúr. دستور

A newspaper printed at Rasht twice a week in Rajab, A.H. 1328 (= July, 1910), of which three numbers only were published.

See Rabino, No. 104, from whom the above particulars are derived. He describes it as a religious paper. I possess No. 2, dated the 18th of Rajab, A.H. 1328 (=July 28, 1910). It comprises 4 pp. of 14½″ × 10″. Yearly subscription, 25 *qráns* in Rasht, 30 elsewhere in Persia. It describes itself as "a historical, political and ethical paper, supporting the independence of Persia."

(172)

Da'watu'l-Islám (*The Preaching of Islám*). دعوة الاسلام

A fortnightly religious paper lithographed in Bombay in A.H. 1324 (= A.D. 1906), under the editorship of Sayyid

Muḥammad 'Alí of Iṣfahán, called *Dá'i'l-Islám* ("The Missionary of Islám").

See Rabino, No. 105, who gives the date of the first and last issue as Ramaẓán 1, A.H. 1324 (=Oct. 19, 1906), and the 1st of Jumáda ii, A.H. 1325 (=July 12, 1907). I possess Nos. 1–19 (with a few lacunae), of which Nos. 15 and following are printed, not lithographed. Each number contains 8 pp. of 9½" × 6½". Yearly subscription, 3 rupees in India, 15 *qráns* in Persia, 1½ mejidiyyés in Turkey, 3 roubles in the Caucasus and Turkistán, and 7 francs in Europe, China and Egypt.

(173)

Da'watu'l-Ḥaqq (*The Preaching of the Truth*). دعوة الحقّ

A monthly religious magazine printed in Ṭihrán in A.H. 1321 (= A.D. 1903–4) under the editorship of Shaykh Muḥammad 'Alí of Dizfúl, known as *Bahjat*, a Member of the Second National Assembly, and proprietor of the *Ma'árif* Library and newspaper.

See Rabino, No. 106, according to whom this paper was first issued on the 1st of Sha'bán, A.H. 1321 (=Oct. 23, 1903). Only 10 numbers appeared in the First Year. Not seen.

(174)

Difá'iyya (*Defence*). دفاعيّه

A paper lithographed in A.H. 1329 (= A.D. 1911) under the editorship of Afṣaḥ-Záda, of which only one number appeared.

See Rabino, No. 107, from whom this information is derived.

(175)

Díwán-i-'Adálat (*The Court of Justice*). ديوان عدالت

A weekly paper printed in Ṭihrán in A.H. 1328 (= A.D. 1910) under the editorship of *Mudabbiru'l-Mamálik* of Hirand, editor of the *Tamaddun* ("Civilization": see *supra*, Nos. 106–108).

Not in Rabino, and not seen.

(176)

Ráh-i-Khayál (*Fancy's Way*). راه خيال

A weekly paper printed in Rasht in A.H. 1329 (= A.D. 1911) under the editorship of *Afṣaḥu'l-Mutakallimín*, the editor of the

Khayru'l-Kalám, who founded it when the last-named paper was suspended. In politics it was Democrat.

See Rabino, No. 108, who gives the first of Sha'bán, A.H. 1329 (=July 28, 1911), as the date of inception. I have no copy.

(177)

Ra'd (*Thunder*). رعد

A weekly newspaper printed in Qazwín in A.H. 1329 (= A.D. 1911) under the editorship of Sayyid 'Alí, written by Shaykh 'Abdu'l-'Alí of Ṭihrán, known as *Múbad*, editor of the paper *Madí* (*q.v.*). Democrat in politics.

See Rabino, No. 109, who gives Rabí' ii, A.H. 1329 (=April, 1911), as the date of inception. I possess Nos. 1, 2 and 4 (the first dated April 23, 1911). Each comprises 4 pp. of 12½″ × 6¾″ Yearly subscription, 6 *qráns* in Qazwín and 8 *qráns* elsewhere in Persia.

(178)

Rúḥu'l-Amín (*The Trusty Spirit*). روح الأمين

A weekly newspaper printed in Ṭihrán in A.H. 1326 (= A.D. 1908–9).

See Rabino, No. 110. I do not possess a copy of this paper.

(179)

Rúḥu'l-Qudus (*The Holy Spirit*). روح القدس

A paper printed in Ṭihrán in A.H. 1325 (= A.D. 1907–8) under the editorship of the *Sulṭánu'l-'Ulamá* of Khurásán. This paper achieved a special notoriety on account of its extraordinary boldness, and published in its thirteenth number a personal attack on Muḥammad 'Alí Sháh and his anti-constitutional actions, threatening him with the fate of Louis XVI, King of France, and recalling the Great French Revolution. In consequence of this article it was suppressed, but after a while resumed publication. The editor of this newspaper was a man of extraordinary convictions and zeal, and took a personal share in the National efforts to defend the Constitution. Thus he participated *vi et armis* in the struggle between the Nationalists and the troops of Muḥammad 'Alí Sháh on the occasion of the

Reactionary *Coup d'État* of June 23, 1908, and fought valorously in defence of the *Majlis*. Finally he was taken prisoner, was confined in chains in the Bágh-i-Sháh, and ultimately suffered a martyr's death, and was thrown into a well. The politics of the paper were Revolutionary.

See Rabino, No. 111, according to whom the paper first appeared on the 25th of Jumáda ii, A.H. 1325 (=August 5, 1907), while No. 26 appeared on the 18th of Rabí' ii, A.H. 1326 (=May 20, 1908). I possess tbe celebrated No. 13 (published on Nov. 5, 1907) alluded to above, and the article in question will be found translated on pp. 156–161 of my *Persian Revolution*. The paper comprises 4 pp. of 11" × 6½". Yearly subscription, 12 *qráns* in Ṭihrán, 17 *qráns* elsewhere in Persia, 5 roubles in Russia, and 10 francs in other foreign countries.

(180)

Rúznáma-i-Írán-i-Sulṭání روزنامهٔ ایران سلطانی
(*The Royal Gazette of Persia*).

An official fortnightly newspaper printed in Ṭihrán in A.H. 1321 (= A.D. 1903–4) under the management of Mullá Muḥammad *Nadímu's-Sulṭán* (formerly *Nadím-báshí*, or Chief Attendant at the Court), at that time Minister of Publications, and edited and written by *Afẓalu'l-Mulk*, "Deputy-Minister of Publications and Accountant of the Supreme Court." This paper was the original *Írán* (*q.v.*), thus renamed when it was placed in charge of the *Nadímu's-Sulṭán*. Its first number was published early in the month of Muḥarram in that year (April, 1903). At the top of the title-page it bore the following inscription: "This Royal paper, which appears by special command and enjoys the particular regards of His Most Sacred and Imperial Majesty, is entirely free from all control or limitation, and whatever it writes is truly written" (!). Of its more pleasing contents one portion was devoted to literary matters. Amongst these was the "*Niṣáb* of Abu'ẓ-Ẓafar Ṣádiq-i-Faráhání," an imitation of the well-known rhymed vocabulary of Abú Naṣr-i-Faráhí known as the *Niṣáb-i-Ṣibyán*, composed by Mírzá Ṣádiq Khán *Adíbu'l-Mamálik*, poetically named *Amírí*, editor of the newspaper *Adab*. This rhymed glossary of old Persian words began to appear in No. 4 of the paper, and was continued in the succeeding numbers, one *chakáma*, or canto, being published in each. I possess the whole in manuscript, and here subjoin as a specimen some verses from the beginning of the first *chakáma*, written in the metre called *Khafíf* ("The Light").

آن بُتِ شوخ چشمِ مه سیما، نظمِ فرهنگ فُرس جُست از ما،
فاعلاتن مفاعلن فعلن، شوِ ببحرِ خفیف چامه سرا،
پاك یزدان و ایزدست خدا، هُده حق زنده حیّ عیان پیدا،
دان نبی‌را پیمبر و وخشور، خاندان اهلِ بیت و جامه کسا،
شرع آئین نظام دهناد است، حکم پرمان روش بود یاسا،
گرزمان عرش و زیرگه کرسی، هست کِرْفَه بزه ثواب و خطا،
نار دوزخ صراط چینود است، باغ منو بهشت روح افزا،
کارِ بِه نافله چنب سُنّت، ناروا منع شد حلال روا،
سحر فرهست و معجزه فرهود، نیز فرجاد فاضل دانا،
کعبه آباد خوان نوی فرقان، گنگ دژهوخت مسجد الاقصی،

This *changáma* comprises more than forty couplets, and includes in its verses many unfamiliar and obsolete words to which it assigns definite scientific meanings.

The year A.H. 1321 (= A.D. 1903–4) in which the *Rúznáma-i-Írán-i-Sulṭání* first appeared under this title is described at the top of the page as the "fifty-sixth year of publication," and so is continued until it came to an end in A.H. 1324 (= A.D. 1906–7), which is described as the "fifty-ninth year of publication." Now the first foundation of a Government newspaper in Persia was in A.H. 1267 (= A.D. 1850–1), before which date we are unaware of the existence of any newspaper; and this is confirmed by the following passage in the third volume of the *Muntaẓam-i-Náṣirí* treating of the events of the year A.H. 1267: "It was also in this year that there was founded in this Empire of eternal duration, that is to say in the glorious metropolis thereof, a Government newspaper containing domestic and foreign news, commercial advertisements, etc." Now according to this computation, the year A.H. 1321 would be the fifty-fifth, not the fifty-sixth, of this foundation, and in order to solve this difficulty I wrote to H.E. the *I'timádu's-Salṭana*, who returned the following answer, which I give *verbatim*:

"The solution of this difficulty is as follows. During the period of the late lamented *I'timádu's-Salṭana* and the earlier period of my management of the paper, no allusion was ever made in the title of the newspaper to the year of its foundation. But when the management of the paper passed into the hands of the *Nadímu's-Sulṭán*, he changed the title of the old *Írán* to *Rúznáma-i-Írán-i-Sulṭání*, and added the words 'fifty-sixth year' at the top of the page. Afterwards when *Mujíru'd-Dawla*, the writer of the paper, withdrew for a while from it, and it was written by *Afẓalu'l-Mulk*, at this juncture an error of two years crept into the computation. When I again accepted this service, I repeatedly called the attention of *Mujíru'd-Dawla* to this error, but he always replied, 'There is no need to reverse this act or revise this date, for it is now a thing of the past.' It is, however, certain that there was an error here."

As a specimen of the manner in which the contents of the newspapers of that period were edited, I here append a paragraph of a few lines occurring in No. 4 of this paper, dated Tuesday, Ṣafar 21, A.H. 1321 (= May 19, 1903), under the heading of "Court News," which runs as follows.

"Praise be to God, the auspicious and fortunate person of His Most Sacred Majesty, the Shadow of God on this earth (may our lives be his sacrifice!), is in the extreme of health and happiness, and daily devotes attention to matters of importance conducive to the well-being of the community. On the ninth day of this month His Most Sacred Majesty, the Shadow of God, attended by the nobles of the Court and intimates of the Royal Threshold, set out for a stay of some days at the village of Kan, situated at a distance of two parasangs from Ṭihrán, in order to divert and refresh the mind, and to practise horsemanship and marksmanship. There they alighted in Royal state, with all due pomp and circumstance, and signal splendour and glory, and abode in that village several days and nights. Every day until after noon His Majesty busied himself with the perusal of the reports received from the different Ministries and Governors, and with reading telegrams from the home provinces and remoter districts of Persia, while in the afternoon he employed his auspicious time in marksmanship and the chase.

On the morning of Wednesday the fifteenth he returned from Kan to the capital of Ṭihrán, which is the Abode of the supreme Sovereignty, in order to deal with various domestic and foreign affairs."

It is worth noting that this specimen of journalistic style belongs to the latter period of Muẓaffaru'd-Dín Sháh's reign, only a short time before the Constitution was proclaimed!

Not in Rabino. I possess No. 4 of this paper, dated Ṣafar 21, A.H. 1321, and May 19, 1903. It comprises 8 pp. of 9" × 6½", and is very well printed in double columns.

(181)

Rúznáma-i-Tabríz (*The Tabríz Gazette*). روزنامهٔ تبریز

A newspaper published in Tabríz in A.H. 1275 (= A.D. 1858–9) of which mention is made in the *Rúznáma-i-Waqáyi'-i-Ittifáqiyya* (see footnote on the article dealing with that paper). As the correct title of this newspaper is unknown to us, we have placed it under the above title, but it is very probable that it is that same *Tabríz* which was afterwards revived when Muẓaffaru'd-Dín was Crown Prince.

(182)

Rúznáma-i-Ḥakímu'l-Mamálik روزنامهٔ حکیم الممالك
(*The Ḥakímu'l-Mamálik's Journal*)[1].

A paper printed in Ṭihrán under the editorship of Mírzá 'Alí Naqí the physician, son of Áqá Isma'íl, a Jew converted to Islám, entitled *Ḥakímu'l-Mamálik*, chief page-in-waiting (*Písh-khidmat-báshí*) of Náṣiru'd-Dín Sháh. This man, having completed his studies in Europe, returned to Persia in A.H. 1278 (= A.D. 1861–2), received the title of *Ḥakímu'l-Mamálik* during the Sháh's journey to Khurásán in A.H. 1284 (= A.D. 1867–8), and was made Governor of Burújird in A.H. 1293 (= A.D. 1876). Náṣiru'd-Dín Sháh was himself the writer of this newspaper, though he attributed it by way of a joke to the *Ḥakímu'l-Mamálik*, under whose signature it was published. In all, three numbers were published, all written by Náṣiru'd-Dín Sháh. Of these, one describes the emotions of a young man who comes forth

[1] The proper name of this paper is not certainly known, and it has been inserted under this title only for the sake of introducing it to the reader.

from his house on a Spring morning to enjoy the Spring season; another the emotions of an old man who likewise tastes the Spring; and the third the Ascension to Heaven (*mi'ráj*) of the *Ḥakímu'l-Mamálik*, which led to his being denounced as an infidel and to the paper being discontinued. These three sheets are very amusing. (The last particulars are taken from a letter from H.E. the *I'timádu's-Salṭana.*)

As is well known, Náṣiru'd-Dín Sháh used to "chaff" the *Ḥakímu'l-Mamálik* a great deal, especially on the journey to Khurásán, when the Sháh himself composed, in the form of a panegyric, some verses satirizing him. As these verses are not lacking in wit, some of them are here given.

ای حکیم الممالك سلطان ، که بشاگردیت سزد لقمان ،
ای فلاطون ترا کمینه غلام ، ای ارسطو بپیش تو نادان ،
لیکن اوصاف حکمتترا من ، نکنم بر جهانیان پنهان ،
نسخهاترا چو می برند بروم ، زیره گوئی برند در کرمان ،
گر بگیری تو نبض بیماری ، روز محشر بگیردت دامان ،
گر معالج شوی بمسکینی ، ندهی فرق گوش از دندان ،
زعفران گر دهی بگریه شود ، آنکه بودی بصبح وشب خندان ،
خواهی ار داروئی نمائی سحق ، جای هاون بیاوری سندان ،
اثر ملح خواهی از شکّر ، خشکی معده جوئی از ریحان ،

. . . .

هر دوائی که می دهی بمریض ، واجب است استخارهٔ قرآن ،
چون بعجز آئی از علاج کسی ، مدد و بخت جوئی از شیطان ،
گر شفا یافت از تو بیماری ، داد عمر دو باره اش یزدان ،
گر تو باشی طبیب یك دو سه سال ، کس نماند بخطّهٔ ایران ،
اینچنین بو العجب فلاطون را ، شاید ار شه نوازد از احسان ،

(183)

Rúznáma-i-Dawlat-i-'Aliyya-i-Írán روزنامهٔ دولت علیّهٔ ایران
(*Journal of the Sublime State of Persia*).

A paper lithographed in Ṭihrán early in A.H. 1277 (July–Aug. 1860), and containing accounts of happenings in the various provinces of Persia, and portraits of statesmen and persons of note, with narratives of their circumstances. Probability points to its having succeeded the *Waqáyi'-i-Ittifáqiyya* ("Fortuitous Events"), which assumed this new name in about the 470th issue.

See Rabino, No. 112, according to whom No. 471 (*i.e.* the first number of the *Waqáyi'* which appeared under the new name) was dated the 28th of Muḥarram, A.H. 1277 (=Aug. 11, 1860), while No. 565 was dated the 17th of Jumáda ii, A.H. 1281 (=Nov. 17, 1864).

(184)

Rúznáma-i-Dawlatí (*State Journal*). روزنامهٔ دولتی

A paper lithographed in Ṭihrán, containing domestic, foreign and Court news. I have seen No. 622 of this paper, which is dated Thursday the 7th of Jumáda ii, corresponding to the auspicious Year of the Leopard, A.H. 1285 (=Sept. 25, A.D. 1868). Above the title on the first page stand the Lion and the Sun, over which is written: "Printed in the Victorious Abode of the Caliphate" (*Dáru'l-Khiláfa, i.e.* Ṭihrán) "in the Blessed College of the *Dáru'l-Funún*, in the workshops of the State Printing-Press. Price of each copy, 14 sháhís; yearly subscription, in addition to the *Rúznáma-i-'Ilmí* ('Scientific Gazette') and the *Rúznáma-i-Millatí* ('National Gazette'), 36 *qráns*." This paper, according to the most probable conjecture, succeeded the previously-mentioned *Rúznáma-i-Dawlat-i-'Aliyya-i-Írán* (No. 183 *supra*). A brief account of both of these papers has been given in the Introduction (pp. 10 *et seqq.*).

I possess No. 622, mentioned above. It comprises 5 pp. of 11½" × 6", bears a large Lion and Sun on the top of p. 1, and is lithographed in good *ta'líq*.

Not mentioned by Rabino.

(185)

Rúznáma-i-Rasmí-i-Dawlat-i-Írán روزنامهٔ رسمی دولت ایران
(*Official Gazette of the Persian Government*).

A daily paper printed in Ṭihrán in A.H. 1329 (= A.D. 1911) under the editorship of the *Mu'ayyidu'l-Mamálik*, editor of the *Pulís-i-Írán* (*q.v.*). It used to publish full reports of the debates of the Second National Assembly, and its publication is still continued.

See Rabino, No. 113, who says that three numbers a week were published, and that the date of inception was the 18th of Rabí' ii, A.H. 1329 (=April 18, 1911). I possess No. 1, which, in fact, is so dated. It comprises 50 pp. of 10" × 7½" and is printed in three columns. Yearly subscription, 45 *qráns* in Ṭihrán, 55 elsewhere in Persia, 70 abroad.

(186)

Rúznáma-i-Shaykh Faẓlu'lláh روزنامهٔ شیخ فضل الله
(*Shaykh Faẓlu'lláh's Journal*).

A paper lithographed at Sháh 'Abdu'l-'Aẓím in A.H. 1325 (= A.D. 1907–8) on behalf of the Reactionaries (Shaykh Faẓlu'lláh-i-Núrí and his confederates) who had taken sanctuary in the above-mentioned shrine, and who remained there, at the instigation and by the encouragement of Muḥammad 'Alí Mírzá, the deposed Sháh, for nearly five months, endeavouring to subvert the Constitution. During this period they used to publish a paper for the propagation of their ideas amongst the common people, with the professed object of demanding the *Sharí'at* (or Religious Law of Islám, as opposed to any *Qánún*, or Civil Law), and denouncing as a blasphemous innovation the *Majlis* and the Constitution. Of this paper some 19 numbers appear to have been published, mostly under the name and title of "Objects of those now in sanctuary in the Holy Shrine," but sometimes under that of "Explanation of the pious objects of the Proof of Islám and the Muslims, and the other fugitives in sanctuary at the Holy Shrine," or under the heading of the verse from the *Qur'án* (viii, 48), "*And obey God and His Apostle, and be not refractory, lest ye be discouraged, and your success depart from you; but persevere with patience, for God is with those who persevere.*" Nearly all of the contents of these issues were quoted and refuted in the *Ḥablu'l-Matín.*

For lack of certainty as to the correct title, this paper is placed under the descriptive title given above.

(187)

Rúznáma-i-'Ilmí (*The Scientific Gazette*). روزنامهٔ علمی

A newspaper published in Ṭihrán in A.H. 1293 (= A.D. 1876–7), concerning which *Zaká'u'l-Mulk* writes: "This paper was founded by Muḥammad Ḥasan Khán *Saní'u'd-Dawla.* In all, sixty-four numbers of it were published, the first dated the 22nd of Dhu'l-Ḥijja, A.H. 1293 (= Jan. 8, 1877), and the last the 23rd of Jumáda ii, A.H. 1297 (= June 2, 1880).

Not in Rabino, and not seen.

(188)

روزنامهٔ علميّهٔ دولت عليّهٔ ايران

Rúznáma-i-'Ilmiyya-i-Dawlat-i-'Aliyya-i-Írán

(*Scientific Gazette of the Sublime State of Persia*).

A monthly newspaper lithographed in A.H. 1280 (= A.D. 1863–4) under the management of 'Alí-qulí Mírzá *I'tiẓádu's-Salṭana,* Minister of Sciences, of which the first number was published on Sha'bán 1 of the above year (= Jan. 11, 1864), and the last number on Shawwál 1, A.H. 1287 (= Dec. 25, 1870). In all, 53 numbers were published. This paper was sometimes spoken of by the abbreviated title of *Rúznáma-i-'Ilmí*, and was published under the same management as the *Rúznáma-i-Millatí* and *Rúznáma-i-Dawlatí*, the combined subscription for all three being 36 *qráns.* It was sometimes issued in three languages, Persian, Arabic and French, and sometimes only in the two last, as in the case of No. 52, which I possess, and which is dated "Tuesday the eleventh of Mihr-máh in the auspicious year 792 of the Jalálí era," or in the concurrent Arabic portion, Rajab 1, A.H. 1287 (= Sept. 27, 1870). The contents of this number consist for the most part of investigations into the nature of a certain form of literary composition used by modern writers and entitled "prose-verse" (*Shi'r-i-manthúr*), or, as the paper puts, "a kind of poetry which in truth one may consider as intermediate between verse and prose." On this subject it puts forward an explanation referring to the invention of this method by Abu'l-'Alá al-Ma'arrí (d. A.H. 449 = A.D. 1057–8); afterwards by Muẓaffar b. Ibráhím, the blind Egyptian (d. A.H. 623 = A.D. 1226); and still later by Khwája Mas'úd, known as *'Iṣmat*, of Bukhárá; and gives some specimens of discourses and anecdotes in this kind of poetry. The Arabic is an exact translation of the Persian portion of the paper, which is indeed a useful and admirable production. In this same number it refers to previous remarks on the same subject in the last issue of the *Rúznáma-i-Millatí*, where some mention is made of Sayyid 'Alí Mihrí of Jabal-'Ámil and of some of his verses of this sort; which indicates that both papers dealt with common topics.

The number of this paper alluded to above comprises one sheet of the size customary in Persia, folded into four pages, of which one is blank. On the top of the first page, under the title *Rúznáma-i-'Ilmiyya-i-Dawlat-i-'Aliyya-i-Írán*, stand the words "No. 52: yearly subscription, in conjunction with the *Rúznáma-i-Dawlatí* and the *Rúznáma-i-Millatí*, 36 *qráns*. Printed in the Victorious Capital, in the auspicious *Dáru'l-Funún* College, in the Government Printing-press." There is also an illustration, which appears to represent the *Shamsu'l-'Imára* and the *Maydán-i-Túp-i-Marwáríd.*

Rabino (No. 114) mentions No. 2 of this paper, dated the 26th of Bahman-máh in the year 785 of the Jalálí era; and No. 4, dated the 9th of Farwardín-máh in the year 786 of the same era. Although nominally the paper was published monthly, yet it is evident that it appeared at irregular intervals. The total number of issues and the dates of the first and last numbers are given on the authority of H.E. *Zaká'u'l-Mulk*. I possess the above-mentioned No. 52, which comprises 4 pp. (one blank) of 12" × 7½". The Persian portion is lithographed in *ta'líq* and the Arabic in *naskh*.

(189)

Rúznáma-i-Millatí (*The National Journal*). روزنامهٔ ملّتی

A paper lithographed in Ṭihrán in A.H. 1283 (= A.D. 1866–7). At the top of the page it bore the figure of a mosque, a conventional sign of its National character. Mírzá Fatḥ-'Alí Ákhúndoff of Tiflís wrote a long and laughable criticism of this paper, analyzing one of its numbers which had come under his notice, and of which more than half was taken up with an account of the genealogy and circumstances of a poet who bore the *nom de guerre* (*takhalluṣ*) of *Surúsh* and the title of *Shamsu'sh-Shu'ará* ("Sun of the Poets"), and with two of his poems, a *qaṣída* and a *ghazal*. The criticism in question begins as follows: "On Friday the 14th of the month of Rabí'u'l-Awwal A.H. 1283 (= July 27, 1866) I happened to see in Tiflís a copy of the *Rúznáma-i-Millat-i-Írán* under circumstances which will be mentioned below. First of all I read this sentence: 'It has been ordered and determined on the Illustrious part of His Imperial Majesty (may God immortalize his Kingdom and Sovereignty !) that the *Rúznáma-i-Millí* shall be written in the freest fashion, so that gentle and simple may share alike in its advantages.' The meaning of this sentence is..." etc.

Zaká'u'l-Mulk writes: "The *Rúznáma-i-Millatí* used to be published, together with the *Rúznáma-i-Dawlatí* and the *Rúznáma-i-'Ilmí*, under the superintendence of the late *I'tiẓádu's-Salṭana.* Its first number was dated Friday, the 14th of Rabí' i, A.H. 1283 (=July 27, 1866), and its last number the 20th of Jumáda ii, A.H. 1287 (=Sept. 17, 1870). It was published monthly, and in all 33 numbers appeared. Its contents consisted chiefly of the biographies of eminent poets."

I'timádu's-Salṭana writes: "Another paper was the *Rúznáma-i-Millat-i-Írán* [of which the first number was] dated Wednesday, Muḥarram 15, A.H. 1283 (=May 30, 1866). This paper appeared while Mírzá Muḥammad Khán *Sipahsálár* was Prime Minister, and was under the management of the Ministry of Sciences."

As may be seen from the above, there exists a certain discrepancy and contradiction as to the date of this paper's first appearance, unless, indeed the *Rúznáma-i-Millat-i-Írán* is a different paper from the *Rúznáma-i-Millatí*, which seems somewhat improbable.

Not in Rabino, and not seen.

(190)

Rúznáma-i-Millí (*The National Journal*). روزنامهٔ ملّی

A quarto-sized weekly paper lithographed in Tabríz in A.H. 1324 (= A.D. 1906–7), the first number of which appeared on Ramaẓán 1st (= Oct. 19, 1906) of that year. This was the first newspaper published in Tabríz after the Revolution and the Proclamation of the Constitution. Its founder and editor was Mírzá 'Alí Akbar Khán, son of the well-known Sayyid Háshim of Charandáb, who used at first to sign under the *nom de guerre* of *Surúsh-i-Ghaybí* ("The Angel from the Unseen World"), but who afterwards wrote under his own name when, in the latter part of the same year, the paper changed its title to *Jarída-i-Millí* (see No. 123, *supra*). A little later, namely in the early part of A.H. 1325 (=Feb.–March, 1907), it again changed its name, and was published under the title of *Anjuman* (see No. 64, *supra*). This paper, and likewise its successors, *i.e.* the *Jarída-i-Millí* and the *Anjuman*, were produced under the supervision and at the expense of the *Anjuman-i-Millí*, or National Council, of Tabríz.

See Rabino, No. 115. I do not possess a copy.

(191)

Rúznáma-i-Niẓámí (*The Military Newspaper*). روزنامهٔ نظامی

A paper published in Ṭihrán, of which Mírzá Ḥusayn Khán *Sipahsálár* was probably the founder. In any case it was founded before A.H. 1296 (=A.D. 1879), for, as *Zaká'u'l-Mulk* states in a letter, its place was taken in that year by the *Mirríkh* (*q.v.*).

Not in Rabino, and not seen.

(192)

Rúznáma-i-Waqáyi'-i-Ittifaqiyya روزنامهٔ وقایع اتّفاقیّه
(*Journal of Current Events*).

A weekly newspaper lithographed in Ṭihrán in A.H. 1267 (=A.D. 1850–1), concerning which something has been already said in the Introduction. This was the first Persian newspaper published in Persia, and was started while Mírzá Taqí Khán *Amír-i-Niẓám* was Prime Minister. At first, *i.e.* until the appearance of No. 16, dated Rajab 21, A.H. 1267 (=May 22, 1851), it was published every Friday, but afterwards until the end of its career on Thursdays. The yearly subscription was 24 *qráns*, while a single copy cost 10 sháhís. It was published very regularly and punctually, without any delay, sometimes comprising one sheet of the size usual in Persia (4 pp.), like Nos. 1 to 9; sometimes 6 pp., like Nos. 17, 23, 24 and 25–40; sometimes 8 pp., as was generally the case in its middle and later period, occasionally regularly for some considerable time, though still numbers comprising 4 or 6 pp. would appear occasionally.

This paper continued publication until A.H. 1277 (=A.D. 1860–1), after which period it apparently received the title of

Rúznáma-i-Dawlat-i-'Aliyya-i-Írán (*q.v.*). There exists a complete set of this paper in the State Library at Ṭihrán, while Nos. 409–456 inclusive are preserved in the British Museum under the class-mark 757.1.12 amongst the Periodical Publications. I myself possess Nos. 7–444.

"The first number of this paper," writes the *I'timádu's-Salṭana*, "appeared on Friday the 5th of Rabí' ii, A.H. 1267 (=Feb. 7, 1851), and bore only the superscription 'O Victorious Lion of God!' ('*Yá Asada'lláhi'l-Ghálib!*'), but subsequently it bore the title *Waqáyi'-i-Ittifáqiyya* with the Lion and the Sun."

Zaká'u'l-Mulk writes: "Originally, that is in the time of Mírzá Taqí Khán *Atábak*, when the paper was first founded, Ḥájji Mírzá Jabbár *Tazkira-chí* and the father of the present *Sa'du'd-Dawla*, who owned a printing-press, were instrumental in producing and circulating the paper, which was written by a certain Mírzá 'Abdu'lláh. No. 474 of this paper, which I have seen and possess, is dated the 18th of Rabí' ii, A.H. 1277 (= Nov. 3, 1860)."

See Rabino, No. 116, who states that it was published by the Ministry of the Press, that No. 261 was dated the 22nd of Jumáda i, A.H. 1273 (=Jan. 18, 1857), and that it "appears to be the same newspaper which Mírzá Taqí Khán *Amír-Niẓám* founded about A.H. 1265 (=A.D. 1848–9) in the early part of the reign of Náṣiru'd-Dín Sháh." I do not possess an original copy, but have a transcript of No. 8.

(193)

Rahbar-i-Írán-i-Naw (*The Guide of the New Persia*). رهبر ایران نو

A daily paper printed in Ṭihrán in the latter part of A.H. 1329 (= A.D. 1911). It was the successor of the *Írán-i-Naw*, which, after its suppression, appeared under this name, but only one number was published. See above under No. 77.

Not in Rabino, and not seen.

(194)

Rahnumá (*The Guide*). رهنما

A weekly paper printed in Ṭihrán in A.H. 1325 (= A.D. 1907) under the editorship of 'Abdu'lláh Qájár.

See Rabino, No. 117, who gives the date of inception as the 26th of Jumáda ii, A.H. 1325 (=August 6, 1907). I possess Nos. 1, 3, 5–10, 12, 14 and 23, the first dated as above, the last the 21st of Rabí' i, A.H. 1326 (=April 23, 1908). Each number comprises 8 pp. of 12½" × 7¾", with a large coloured title (the colour varying in each number) illustrating the idea of Progress with a railway-train, a steamer, a lighthouse and factories. Yearly subscription, 15 *qráns* in Ṭihrán, 20 *qráns* elsewhere in Persia, and 25 *qráns* abroad.

(195)

Zarárit Bahrá (*The Ray of Light*). ܙܪܪܝܬ ܒܗܪܐ

A religious paper published in the Chaldaean (Syriac) tongue by the Protestants in Urmiya. It is under American direction.

Not in Rabino, and not seen.

(196)

Záng (*The Bell*). զանգ

A weekly paper printed in Tabríz in A.H. 1328 (= A.D. 1910) in the Armenian language. This paper was the organ of the Armenian Hanchákists.

See Rabino, No. 233. Not seen by the translator.

(197)

Záyanda-rúd. زاینده رود

An illustrated weekly newspaper lithographed in Iṣfahán in A.H. 1327 (= A.D. 1909) under the editorship of the *Mu'ínu'l-Islám* of Khwánsár. In politics it was Democrat.

See Rabino, No. 118. I possess Nos. 10, 37 and 39 of the Second Year, and Nos. 3, 7, 9 and 13 of the Third Year, the first dated the 19th of Rabí' i, A.H. 1328 (= March 31, 1910), and the last the 27th of Rabí' ii, A.H. 1329 (= April 27, 1911). All these numbers are printed except the first, which is lithographed, and a rather rude lithographed caricature or cartoon occupies the last page of each printed number. Each number comprises 8 pp. of 12" × 6½". Yearly subscription, in Iṣfahán 16 *qráns*, elsewhere in Persia and abroad, 24 *qráns*.

(198)

Zabán-i-Millat (*The Tongue of the Nation*). زبان ملّت

A paper printed in Ṭihrán twice a week in A.H. 1325 (= A.D. 1907).

See Rabino, No. 119. I possess No. 3, which is dated the 28th of Ramaẓán, A.H. 1325 (= Nov. 4, 1907), and comprises 4 pp. of 11½" × 6¾". Yearly subscription, 15 *qráns* in Ṭihrán, 18 *qráns* elsewhere in Persia, and 12 francs abroad.

(199)

Zisht u Zíbá (*Foul and Fair*). زشت و زیبا

An illustrated weekly paper lithographed in Ṭihrán in A.H. 1325 (= A.D. 1907) under the editorship of *Fatḥu'l-Mamálik.*

See Rabino, No. 120, where the date of inception is given as the 2nd of Jumáda ii, A.H. 1325 (=July 13, 1907). I possess Nos. 1, 2 and 3. Each comprises 8 pp. of 12" × 7¼". Yearly subscription, 30 *qráns* in Ṭihrán, and the same plus postage elsewhere in Persia.

(200)

Zamán-i-Wiṣál (*The Time of Union*). زمان وصال

A weekly paper printed in Rasht in A.H. 1329 (= A.D. 1911) under the editorship of Mírzá 'Alí Aṣghar of Shíráz entitled *Náṣiru'sh-Shu'ará.*

See Rabino, No. 121, who states that only eight numbers appeared, the first on the 19th of Jumáda i, A.H. 1329 (=May 18, 1911), and the last on the 22nd of Rajab (=July 19) of the same year. I possess Nos. 1, 2, 3, 5, 7 and 8. Each comprises 4 pp. of 12½" × 6½". Yearly subscription, 10 *qráns.*

(201)

Sáḥil-i-Naját (*The Shore of Safety*). ساحل نجات

A paper printed in Anzalí twice a week in A.H. 1325 (= A.D. 1907) under the editorship of *Afṣaḥu'l-Mutakallimín*, the editor of the *Khayru'l-Kalám* (*q.v.*).

See Rabino, No. 122, who states that only eight numbers were published, the first on the 26th of Rajab, A.H. 1325 (=Sept. 4, 1907). I possess Nos. 1–5, but No. 1 is dated not as above but the 7th of Sha'bán (=Sept. 22) of the same year. Each number comprises 4 pp. of 12" × 7". Yearly subscription, 18 *qráns* in Gílán, 20 *qráns* elsewhere in Persia, 5 roubles in Russia and the Caucasus, and 14 francs in Europe.

(202)

Sáḥil-i-Naját (*The Shore of Safety*). ساحل نجات

A daily paper printed in Rasht in A.H. 1328 (= A.D. 1910) under the editorship of *Afṣaḥu'l-Mutakallimín.*

See Rabino, No. 122. I possess Nos. 8–13, the former dated the last day of Shawwál, A.H. 1328 (=Nov. 3, 1910). Each number comprises 4 pp. of 12" × 7" Yearly subscription, 25 *qráns* in Rasht, 30 *qráns* elsewhere in Persia, 6 roubles in Russia.

(203)

Siráju'l-Akhbár (*The Lamp of News*). سراج الأخبار

A fortnightly paper lithographed in the *nasta'líq* hand in Kábul (Afghánistán) in A.H. 1329 (=A.D. 1911). Its editor and chief writer was Maḥmúd Ṭarzí, and it was under the supervision of 'Alí Aḥmad the Chief Chamberlain (*Ishik-ághásí*) of His Majesty the Amír. The first number was dated the 5th of Shawwál (= Oct. 10) of the above year.

Not in Rabino, and not seen.

(204)

Surúsh. سروش

A paper published in Rasht in A.H. 1325 (=A.D. 1907). Given on the authority of Rabino.

See Rabino, Nos. 123 and 124, where mention is made of the Constantinople and Ṭihrán papers of this name, but no mention of such a paper at Rasht.

(205)

Surúsh. سروش

A weekly newspaper printed in Constantinople in A.H. 1327 (=A.D. 1909–1910) under the editorship of Sayyid Muḥammad Tawfíq. It was founded during the time of the Persian Revolution or the "Lesser Autocracy" (June, 1908–July, 1909) by the *Anjuman-i-Sa'ádat-i-Íráníyán*, and received contributions from the pens of Mírzá 'Alí Akbar Khán (formerly a regular contributor to the *Ṣúr-i-Isráfíl*, *q.v.*), Aḥmad Bey Aghayeff, and Ḥájji Mírzá Yaḥyá of Dawlatábád.

See Rabino, No. 123, who erroneously describes it as lithographed. According to him it first appeared on the 12th of Jumáda ii, A.H. 1327 (=July 1, 1909).

(206)

Surúsh. سروش

A paper printed in Ṭihrán in the latter part of A.H. 1328 (= A.D. 1910) under the editorship of 'Aẓudu'l-Islám of Láhíján. It was written by Mírzá 'Ísá Khán (the Sardár-i-Manṣúr's man) of Rasht, who signed under the letter *'ayn* (ع), and enjoyed the support of the Sardár-i-Manṣúr and his followers. In politics it was Moderate.

See Rabino, No. 124, according to whom it first appeared on the 23rd of Dhu'l-Qa'da, A.H. 1328 (=Nov. 26, 1910).

(207)

Sa'ádat (*Felicity*). سعادت

A weekly paper printed (*not* lithographed) in Hamadán in A.H. 1325 (=A.D. 1907)—not 1326—under the editorship of Muḥammad Taqí Niráqí.

See Rabino, No. 126. I possess Nos. 43, 46 and 47. Each comprises 4 pp. of 11⅓″ × 7″. Yearly subscription, 10 *qráns* in Hamadán, 15 *qráns* elsewhere in Persia, 4 roubles in Russia and the Caucasus. No. 43 is dated the 10th of Ṣafar, A.H. 1326 (=March 14, 1908).

(208)

Sa'ádat (*Felicity*). سعادت

A fortnightly paper printed (*not* lithographed) in Tabríz in A.H. 1329 (=A.D. 1911). The first number was dated the 23rd of Rabí' ii (=April 23) of that year. It was edited by Sa'íd-záda, the Superintendent of the Madrasa-i-Sa'ádat, and founded by Mírzá Ibráhím, the Director of the above-mentioned College. Its contents were purely academical and literary.

See Rabino, No. 125. I possess No. 4, dated the 8th of Jumáda ii, A.H. 1329 (=June 6, 1911). It comprises 4 pp. of 11½″ × 9½″. Yearly subscription, 5 *qráns* in Tabríz, 10 abroad.

(209)

Safína-i-Naját (*The Ark of Deliverance*). سفینهٔ نجات

A weekly paper first "jelly-graphed" and then lithographed at Yazd in A.H. 1325 (=A.D. 1907) under the editorship of Muḥammad Ṣádiq.

See Rabino, No. 127, according to whom the paper was first issued on the 22nd of Shawwál, A.H. 1329 (=Nov. 28, 1907). He adds that on the arrival of the Bakhtiyárí chief Sardár-i-Jang as governor at Yazd this paper was suppressed, on account of the publication of a caricature of the Sardár, and his Deputy Mudíru'd-Dawla, and his Treasurer Mushíru'l-Mamálik. The latter was represented in the form of a dog, while a dog's tail was visible under the Mudíru'd-Dawla's coat, and both of them were urging the Sardár to take money from the people. As it was supposed that this caricature had been produced by lithography on the gelatine process in the workshops of the *Safína-i-Naját*, the paper was suppressed. I possess Nos. 3, 6, 16, 20 and 21 of the First Year, and No. 10 of the Second Year. The first is dated the 22nd of Shawwál, A.H. 1325 (as stated above by Rabino), and the last the 22nd of Dhu'l-Qa'da, A.H. 1328 (=Nov. 25, 1910). Of the six numbers which I possess, the first three are "jelly-graphed" and the last three lithographed. Each contains 4 pp. of 10½" × 6" (later enlarged to 12¾" × 6½"), and is written in a large, clear *naskh* hand. Yearly subscription, 20 *qráns* in Yazd, 25 *qráns* elsewhere in Persia, and 30 *qráns* abroad.

(210)

Sikandar (*Alexander*). سکندر

A weekly newspaper published every Sunday in Calcutta in A.H. 1262 (=A.D. 1846).

Mentioned in Zenker's *Bibliotheca Orientalis*, No. 1829, but not by Rabino. Zenker gives the title in Roman characters only. Not seen.

(211)

Salám 'alaykum! (*Peace be upon you!*). سلام علیکم

A paper published in Ṭihrán in A.H. 1325 (=A.D. 1907).

Not in Rabino, and not seen.

(212)

Salsabíl. سلسبیل

A paper "jelly-graphed" in Ṭihrán in A.H. 1328 (=A.D. 1910).

See Rabino, No. 128, on whose authority the paper is given.

(213)

Sulṭánu'l-Akbar (*The Greatest King*). سلطان الاکبر (? الاخبار)

A weekly newspaper published every Sunday in Calcutta in A.H. 1262 (=A.D. 1846).

Mentioned in Zenker's *Bibliotheca Orientalis*, No. 1830, but not in Rabino, and not otherwise known. It appears probable that there may be a mistake in the name of this paper, and that Zenker never saw it, but only its title written in Roman characters, in which what was probably its real title *Sulṭánu'l-Akhbár* ("The King of News") might easily be corrupted into the obviously incorrect title *Sulṭánu'l-Akbar*.

(214)

Sayyidu'l-Akhbár (*The Lord of News*). سیّد الاخبار

A large-sized weekly newspaper lithographed at Ḥaydarábád in the Deccan in A.H. 1306 (=A.D. 1888–9) under the editorship of Áqá Sayyid Áqá Shírází. It was published regularly on

Saturdays, and comprised eight large-sized pages. Amongst the Periodical Publications in the British Museum, under the class-mark 757. m. 1, are preserved 35 numbers of this paper, of which No. 1 is dated the 4th of Rabí' ii, A.H. 1306 (= Dec. 8, 1888), and No. 35 the 5th of Dhu'l-Ḥijja, A.H. 1306 (= August 2, 1889). At the top of each title-page stands the Lion and the Sun, beneath which are placed some Arabic and Persian verses in praise of the newspaper, of knowledge, etc., which verses are textually repeated in each number. Beneath these in turn the name of the newspaper is contained and inscribed in the following hemistich:

جیّدِ اخبارِ عالم سیّد الاخبار شد '

(The *Sayyidu'l-Akhbár* is the best newspaper in the world.)

This paper (like the present day papers in Persia) was very instructive, containing full information, foreign news and telegraphic despatches. It translated from the English papers important political articles about Persia and Russia, and generally wrote against Russia and its designs in Persia. Some of its numbers contain particulars as to the third and last journey of Náṣiru'd-Dín Sháh in Europe, which corresponded in time with those issues. In No. 35 there appears an announcement concerning the reduction in size of the newspaper in the forthcoming number.

One rather comic incident is that in the later numbers the editor complains much about the non-payment of subscriptions, and in one of them he writes in praise of Tabríz, its leading men, and the progress of science and education there. Finally, after giving a most brilliant and glowing account of Mírzá Yúsuf Khán *Mustasháru'd-Dawla* of Tabríz, he observes that the above-mentioned personage has been "graciously pleased" to remit the full amount of his subscription to the newspaper. In the first number he complains very much of obtaining permission in Ḥaydarábád to publish the paper, and describes the editor's protracted wanderings in pursuit of this object. At the end of each copy is the signature "Sayyid Áqá-yi-Shírází, owner and editor of the paper."

In some numbers he reproduces matter from the newspaper *Farhang* published at Iṣfahán, while in the tenth number he publishes an attack on and refutation of the Persian paper *Ázád* (apparently published in Delhi), which, in the fourth number of the fifth volume, published on Friday, Feb. 1, 1889, attacks and reviles the higher circles of Ḥaydarábád in the Deccan, and the newspapers of that place, which do not enjoy freedom. From this it appears that a paper named *Ázád*, otherwise unknown to us, was published in India in A.D. 1885 (= A.H. 1302–3).

I possess No. 34 of the second volume, dated Ramaẓán 21, A.H. 1307 (= May 11, 1890). It comprises 12 pp. of 12″ × 7¾″, and is lithographed in a fairly good *ta'líq*.

(215)

Sháhseven (*The King-lover*:—name of well-known tribe). شاهسون

A "jelly-graphed" paper produced in Constantinople about A.H. 1306 (= A.D. 1888–9) or perhaps a little earlier, which vehemently criticized in a comical and sarcastic vein the autocratic Government of Persia. The production and publication of this paper was attributed to Ḥájji Mírzá 'Abdu'r-Raḥím Ṭáliboff and some of his associates, who were aided in its publication by Sayyid Muḥammad Shabistarí Abu'ẓ-Ẓiyá, afterwards editor of the *Írán-i-Naw*, who was at that time in Constantinople and shared in this enterprise; indeed it appears to have been reproduced from his handwriting. It was published secretly, and the issue was limited to 300 copies, which were placed in envelopes like letters and sent with various precautions to statesmen, theologians, merchants and others in Persia. Often, in order to conceal the place of publication, they were first sent to Paris, London, etc. to be forwarded thence to Persia. At the top of one copy which I possess stands the inscription, "Published once in forty years." In the portion devoted to "telegraphic news" occurs the following passage:

"The British Consul at Hamadán has sent an official communication to the Government in which he complains that there is a public bath in the neighbourhood of the Consulate, and that the Consulate is sorely troubled by the filth thereof, and by the infection which emanates from it, by reason of which two of its employés have died; and requesting that the Government will either close the bath, or provide a more suitable place for the Consulate."

Another runs as follows:

"Our correspondent of the Foreign Telegraphic Agency in Ṭihrán observed a great activity, accompanied by much haste and bustle, in the principal avenues, where most of the notables, ministers and leading personages of the kingdom, mounted in their carriages, were rapidly driving one after another in a particular direction. Before he had succeeded in ascertaining the true state of the case, he telegraphed to London stating that on that day a serious political crisis had arisen in Ṭihrán, and that an important movement was visible in official circles. After having despatched this telegram, he applied himself to the investigation of this matter and its real nature, and after a while was compelled, with the utmost shame, to send another telegram contradicting his first conjecture, and stating that it now appeared that all these gentlemen were merely going to attend a commemorative religious function (*majlis-i-rawẓa-khwání*) given by one of the great ecclesiastics (*mujtahidín*) of Ṭihrán."

There are many telegrams of this sort, whereof the above (of which only the substance, not the exact phraseology, is given) will suffice to serve as a sample.

I have only seen one copy of this paper.

(216)

Sháhinsháhí (*The Imperial*). شاهنشاهی

A weekly illustrated paper lithographed in Ṭihrán in A.H. 1323 (= A.D. 1905–6) under the editorship of Mírzá 'Abdu'l-Ḥusayn Khán, entitled *Maliku'l-Mu'arrikhín* ("The King of Historians").

See Rabino, No. 134, who gives the date of inception as the 9th of Shawwál, A.H. 1323 (= Nov. 7, 1905). I possess Nos. 18, 21, 26, 43, 44, 45, 46 and 47. The first is dated the 13th of Rabí' i, A.H. 1324 (= May 7, 1906), and the last the 13th of Muḥarram, A.H. 1325 (= Feb. 26, 1907). Each number has on p. 1 the portrait of some notable Persian or foreign statesman, and comprises 4 pp. of 12" × 6½". Yearly subscription, 20 *qráns*. Similar in form and character to the *Sharaf* and *Sharáfat*. (See *infra*.)

(217)

Shab-náma (*Nocturnal*). شب نامه

A publication which appeared in Tabríz about A.H. 1310 (= A.D. 1892–3) and circulated for some time, but not in any regular or journalistic fashion, but only amongst a number of those who were inspired by the new ideas in a very secret manner. These publications were sarcastic and very amusing, and were written by 'Alí-qulí Khán, editor of the *Iḥtiyáj* and the *Ázarbayján* (*q.v.*), who was at that time known as Áqá-qulí. The name *Shab-náma* was, however, subsequently applied in a general way to all secret "jelly-graphed" publications. One or two specimens may be given of the contents of the *Shab-námas*, though it is difficult to give the preference to one over another. Concerning the deplorable condition of bread and the detestable confusion of the bread-market it wrote:

"Yesterday I sent the servant to get a loaf of bread for luncheon from the bazaar. He went early in the morning, and returned three hours after dusk, his clothes torn to rags, his face scratched, and his body wounded and bruised, bringing one cake of 'pebble bread' (*nán-i-sangak*), on which, by reason of our extreme hunger, we incontinently fell and tore it in pieces. Out of it fell the objects enumerated below: one night-shirt; one ewer and basin; one head of...; one bundle of...; one..., etc."

Concerning the mud in the streets he writes:

"A string of camels sunk in the mud in the main street in front of the Royal Gynaecium, and disappeared from sight. They afterwards reappeared in the bed of the Ájí River (distant about one parasang)." And so on.

Not in Rabino. I possess one *Shab-náma* of Nov. 1906, written in Turkish. It consists of a single sheet of 14″ × 8¾″, "jelly-graphed" in violet ink. A caricature occupies the upper half of the page, and below it are thirteen lines of letter-press. There is no date, title, or indication of author or place of publication.

(218)

Shajara-i-khabítha-i-Kufr: Shajara-i-ṭayyiba-i-Ímán شجرهٔ خبیثهٔ کفر شجرهٔ طیّبهٔ ایمان

(*The foul Tree of Infidelity: the good Tree of Faith*).

A lithographed publication which appeared in Ṭihrán in A.H. 1325 (= A.D. 1907–8).

Not in Rabino, and not seen.

Portrait of Mírzá 'Alí Aṣghar Khán
Amínu's-Sulṭán by *Muṣawwiru'l-Mulk*
From No. 51 of the illustrated monthly *Sharáfat* of Oct.-Nov. 1900

(219)

Sharáfat (*Nobility*). شرافت

A monthly illustrated paper lithographed in Ṭihrán in A.H. 1314 (= A.D. 1896–7) under the management of the Ministry of the Press. It was a continuation of the newspaper *Sharaf* (see *infra*), and was founded by Muḥammad Báqir Khán, the present *I'timádu's-Salṭana*, early in the reign of Muẓaffaru'd-Dín Sháh.

See Rabino, No. 129, who says that No. 3 was issued in Rabí' ii, A.H. 1314 (=August–Sept. 1896). I possess No. 51, dated Rajab, A.H. 1318 (=Oct.–Nov. 1900). It comprises 4 pp. of 13″ × 7½″, and the front page is adorned with a portrait of the Atábak-i-A'ẓam (*Amínu's-Sulṭán*). Yearly subscription, 12 *qráns*.

(220)

Sharáfat (*Nobility*). شرافت

A monthly paper lithographed in Ṭihrán in A.H. 1326 (= A.D. 1908) under the editorship of Áqá Sayyid Ḥusayn, Director of the *Sharáfat* Library. This paper has a special importance inasmuch as it was written in very popular language, in the idiom of the Ṭihrán "Mashhadís" (common people), and was sold at a very low price, so that it had a considerable influence on the humbler classes. It was instructive as regards subject-matter, and strongly supported the fullest form of Constitutional Government.

See Rabino, No. 130, who describes this paper as bi-weekly, and gives the date of No. 2 as the 4th of Ṣafar, A.H. 1326 (=March 8, 1908). I possess Nos. 8, 22, 23, 24, 25 and 26. Each number comprises 4 pp. (with continuous pagination throughout the "set," or *dawra*, of 40 numbers) of 12½″ × 6¾″. Subscription for the "set" of 40 numbers, 3 *qráns* in Ṭihrán, 5 *qráns* elsewhere in Persia, and 6 *qráns* abroad.

(221)

Sharaf (*Honour*). شرف

A monthly illustrated paper lithographed in Ṭihrán, of which the first issue was published on the first of Muḥarram, A.H. 1300 (=Nov. 12, 1882). This paper and its successor the *Sharáfat* (see *supra*, No. 219) used to publish portraits of nobles and statesmen, accompanied by explanatory and biographical matter, and enjoyed a certain distinction and value by reason of the excellence of these portraits, which were executed by *Kamálu'l-Mulk*, the well-known Persian artist. Muḥammad Ḥasan Khán

I'timádu's-Salṭana founded this paper, of which in all 78 numbers were published.

See Rabino, No. 131, according to whom this paper lasted until A.H. 1309 (=A.D. 1891) and published in all 87 numbers. I do not possess a copy.

(222)

Sharaf (*Honour*). شرف

A weekly paper printed (not lithographed) in Ṭihrán in A.H. 1326 (=A.D. 1908) under the editorship of Ghulám Ḥusayn of Ṭihrán.

See Rabino, No. 132. I possess No. 1, which is dated the 17th of Rabí' ii, A.H. 1326 (=May 19, 1908). It comprises 4 pp. of 11″ × 7″. Yearly subscription, 5 *qráns* in Ṭihrán, 6 *qráns* elsewhere in Persia, and 5 francs abroad.

(223)

Sharq (*The East*). شرق

A daily paper of large *format* printed in Ṭihrán in A.H. 1327 (=A.D. 1909) under the editorship of Sayyid Ẓiyá'u'd-Dín Ṭabá-ṭabá'í (son of Sayyid 'Alí of Yazd), who was also editor of the *Nidá-yi-Islám* ("Call of Islám") and *Barq* ("Lightning," *q.v.*). This newspaper, in consequence of its violent and revolutionary attacks on those at the head of affairs, was several times suspended, and finally changed its name and came out under the title of *Barq*. Many numbers of this paper contained one page in French. Under the title of "literary contributions" (*adabiyyát*) there appeared in this newspaper poems, criticizing in a metaphorical manner the doings of the Government, which, in point of literary value, were both important and beautiful, and, by reason of their natural simplicity and approximation in style to the colloquial language, were as distinguished in merit as they were plain in language, and, alike by virtue of their novelty and their originality, are worthy to be taken as models and exemplars. The writer of these verses was a poet of Kirmánsháh. In politics this newspaper originally represented the views of the Party of Union and Progress, but afterwards became Revolutionary.

See Rabino, No. 123. I possess a fairly complete set, including No. 1, which is dated the 14th of Ramaẓán, A.H. 1327 (=Sept. 30, 1909). Each number comprises

4 pp. of 21½"×14½", and the French supplement first appears in No. 91 (June 18, 1910). Yearly subscription, 45 *qráns* in Ṭihrán, 50 *qráns* elsewhere in Persia, and 56 *qráns* abroad.

(224)

Shafaq (*The Afterglow*). شفق

A weekly paper printed in Tabríz in A.H. 1328 (=A.D. 1910). Its owner and editor was Mírzá Ḥájji Áqá Riẓá-záda; the editorship was subsequently transferred in name to Mírzá Maḥmúd Ghaní-záda of Salmás, editor of the *Faryád*, *Bú Qalamún*, etc. This paper was remarkable for its boldness and violent writing, and especially in consequence of its patriotic articles became the object of vehement hatred on the part of the Russians, so that on the occasion of their aggressions in Muḥarram, A.H. 1330 (=January, 1912), they arrested and hanged one of its contributors, Mírzá Aḥmad, known as "Suhaylí," and suppressed the paper. It published some poetical fragments in the new style, rhymed in the European fashion. In politics it was Democrat.

See Rabino, No. 136, according to whom it was first issued on Ramaẓán 27, A.H. 1328 (=Oct. 3, 1910). I possess a good many copies, including Nos. 1 and 22 of the First Year, and Nos. 1–40 (with some gaps) of the Second Year, the last dated the 18th of Dhu'l-Ḥijja, A.H. 1329 (=Dec. 21, 1911). Each number contains 4 pp. of 15¾"×9". Yearly subscription, 7 *qráns* in Tabríz, 10 *qráns* elsewhere in Persia, and 14 *qráns* abroad.

(225)

Shafaq (*The Afterglow*). شفق

A "jelly-graphed" paper published in Khúy.

See Rabino, No. 137, on whose authority it is included here.

(226)

Shakar (*Sugar*). شكر

A weekly paper lithographed in Tabríz in A.H. 1325 (=A.D. 1907) under the editorship of Muḥammad 'Alí 'Abdu'l-Manáf-záda.

See Rabino, No. 135. I possess a copy of No. 3, which is dated the 17th of Rabí' i, A.H. 1325 (=April 30, 1907). It comprises 4 pp. of 11¾"×6¾", and is written in Ázarbáyjání Turkish, and lithographed in a poor but legible *ta'líq*. Yearly subscription, 5 *qráns* in Tabríz, 7 *qráns* elsewhere in Persia, and 2 roubles in Russia.

(227)

Shams (*The Sun*). شمس

A weekly illustrated paper printed in Constantinople in A.H. 1327 (= A.D. 1909) under the editorship of Sayyid Muḥammad Tawfíq of Baṣra, and owned by Sayyid Ḥasan of Tabríz. In politics it is Moderate.

See Rabino, No. 138. I possess a fairly complete set from the beginning. No. 1 is dated the 8th of Sha'bán, A.H. 1326 (=Sept. 5, 1908), and the paper is still appearing. Each number contains 8 pp. of 9″ × 6½″, but since the end of the Second Year the size of the paper has been considerably enlarged. Yearly subscription, 60 piastres in Constantinople, 75 piastres elsewhere in Turkey, 35 *qráns* in Persia, 6 roubles in Russia, and 17 francs in Europe.

(228)

Shams-i-Ṭáli' (*The Rising Sun*). شمس طالع

A paper printed in Ṭihrán in A.H. 1325 (= A.D. 1907).

See Rabino, No. 139. I do not possess a copy.

(229)

Shúrá-yi-Írán (*The Council of Persia*). شورای ایران

A weekly paper published in Tabríz in A.H. 1326 (= A.D. 1908). It was founded and published by the *Anjuman-i-Mashwarat* ("Society of Council"), and was jointly written by those three martyred patriots Mírzá Sa'íd of Salmás, Áqá Sayyid Ḥasan Sharíf-záda, and Ḥájji 'Alí *Dawá-furúsh* ("The Druggist"). Its politics were Conservative and Moderate Constitutional.

See Rabino, No. 140, according to whom No. 2 was dated the 19th of Rabí' ii, A.H. 1326 (=May 21, 1908). I do not possess a copy.

(230)

Shúrá-yi-Baladí (*The Municipal Council*). شورای بلدی

A weekly paper published in Ṭihrán in A.H. 1325 (=A.D. 1907).

Not in Rabino, and not seen.

(231)

Chawik (*The Little Path*). Չաւիկ

An illustrated paper in the Armenian language lithographed in Ṭihrán in A.D. 1911 (= A.H. 1310–11).

See Rabino, No. 234. Not seen by the translator.

شماره ۵   یکشنبه ۲ محرم ۱۳۳۰   سال اول

صاحب امتیاز :
... جعفرزاده

مدیر اداره
اسماعیل ...

شیدا

CHEYDA
Journal ...
Proprietair...
H. Djafarza...

ماهی دوبار
نشر میشود

روزنامه ایست فارسی و ترکی مسلک اش بیان حقیقت است

Russia presents her second ultimatum to Persia. In the background are seven others

From No. 5 of the *Shaydá*, M

(232)

Shaykh Chughundar (*The Reverend Beetroot*). شیخ چغندر

A weekly illustrated comic paper lithographed in Ṭihrán in A.H. 1329 (= A.D. 1911), of which the first number was dated the 14th of Shawwál of that year (= Oct. 8, 1911). Its proprietor, Mír Fatḥ 'Alí, and its editor, Abu'l-Ma'álí, known as Sayyid-i-Áhan-bardár ("The Iron-lifter"), were both reactionaries, but the paper was connected with the Party of Agreement and Progress (*Ittifáq u taraqqí*).

See Rabino, No. 241. I possess a copy of No. 3, dated the 28th of Shawwál, A.H. 1329 (= Oct. 22, 1911). It comprises 4 pp. (pp. 2 and 3 containing caricatures) of 12¼" × 6¾", lithographed in *ta'líq*. Yearly subscription, 12 *qráns* in Ṭihrán, 20 *qráns* in other parts of Persia, 30 *qráns* abroad.

(233)

Shaydá (*Madcap*). شیدا

A serio-comic illustrated fortnightly paper printed in Constantinople in A.H. 1329 (= A.D. 1911) under the editorship of Muḥammad Ẓiyá'u'd-Dín. It was founded by a committee of Persian students. Its proprietor and writer was Ḥájji Ḥasan Khán Ja'far-záda, its managing editor Muẓaffar Khán Isma'íl-záda, and its artist-illustrator Mírzá 'Abdu'l-Ḥusayn Khán Ṭáhir-záda. Not more than four or five numbers of it were issued. In politics it was Democrat.

Not in Rabino. I possess Nos. 1–5, the first dated the 29th of Shawwál, A.H. 1329 (= Oct. 23, 1911), and the last the 2nd of Muḥarram, A.H. 1330 (= Dec. 23, 1911), with a supplementary sheet dated the following day. Each number comprises 4 pp., and, as a rule, two caricatures (on pp. 1 and 4), of 13¾" × 8". Yearly subscription, 15 *qráns* in Persia, 30 piastres in Constantinople.

(234)

Shíráz. شیراز

A paper published in Shíráz in A.H. 1328 (= A.D. 1910).

See Rabino, No. 141. I do not possess a copy.

(235)

Ṣubḥ-i-Ṣádiq (*The True Dawn*). صبح صادق

A daily paper printed in Ṭihrán in the early part of A.H. 1325 (=Feb.–March, 1907) under the editorship of Murtaẓá-qulí Khán *Mu'ayyidu'l-Mamálik*, editor of the *Pulís-i-Írán* (*q.v.*).

See Rabino, No. 142, according to whom the paper first appeared in Ṣafar (March–April) of that year, and was subsequently edited by Mahdí-qulí Khán *Mu'ayyid-i-Díwán*. I possess 16 copies, ranging from No. 32 (May 14, 1907) to No. 149 (Oct. 8, 1907). Each number comprises 4 pp. of 11¾" × 6¾". Yearly subscription, 45 *qráns*.

(236)

Ṣubḥ-náma (*Morning Letter*). صبحنامه

A weekly "jelly-graphed" paper published in Ṭihrán in A.H. 1324 (=A.D. 1906) before the proclamation of the Constitution and for a short time after it. Its editor and writer was Áqá Sayyid Muḥammad Riẓá of Shíráz, editor of the *Musáwát* ("Equality"). This paper was circulated secretly, and not more than seventeen or eighteen numbers were published. It opposed the autocracy, and was revolutionary in politics.

See Rabino, No. 143. I do not possess a copy.

(237)

Ṣuḥbat (*Conversation*). صحبت

A paper in the Ázarbáyjání Turkish dialect lithographed in Tabríz in A.H. 1327 (=A.D. 1909), under the editorship of Mírzá Ḥusayn Khán, editor of the papers *al-Ḥadíd*, *'Adálat* and *Khabar*. In consequence of having published in No. 4, by way of a joke, an article in Turkish entitled *Kej Qáburqá* ("The Crooked Rib") on the evils of the veiling of women and the necessity of improving their condition, it drew upon itself the violent hostility of the clergy and common people, as a result of which the paper was suspended and the editor arrested and imprisoned after judgement had been given against him.

Not in Rabino, and not seen.

(238)

Ṣiḥḥat (*Health*). صحّت

A paper published in Ṭihrán in A.H. 1325 (=A.D. 1907).

Not in Rabino, and not seen.

(239)

Ṣadá-yi-Rasht (*The Rasht Echo*). صدای رشت

A paper printed in Rasht twice a week early in A.H. 1329 (= A.D. 1911) under the editorship of '*Ayn* Aḥmad-záda, Democrat in politics.

See Rabino, No. 144. The paper first appeared on the 15th (not the 29th as Rabino states) of Muḥarram (=Jan. 16, 1911) of that year. I possess Nos. 1–16. Each contains 4 pp. of 15″ × 10½″. Yearly subscription, 25 *qráns* in Rasht, 30 *qráns* elsewhere in Persia, 35 *qráns* abroad.

(240)

Ṣadáqat (*Fidelity*). صداقت

A paper lithographed in Ṭihrán in A.H. 1326 (= A.D. 1908).

Not in Rabino, and not seen.

(241)

Ṣiráṭu'ṣ-Ṣanáyi' (*The Way of Arts*). صراط الصّنایع

A paper published in Ṭihrán in A.H. 1326 (= A.D. 1908).

Not in Rabino, and not seen.

(242)

Ṣiráṭu'l-Mustaqím (*The Straight Way*). صراط المستقیم

A paper published in Tabríz in A.H. 1324 (= A.D. 1906–7).

Not in Rabino, and not seen.

(243)

Ṣiráṭu'l-Mustaqím (*The Straight Way*). صراط المستقیم

A paper published in Ṭihrán in A.H. 1325 (= A.D. 1907).

Not in Rabino, and not seen.

(244)

Ṣúr-i-Isráfíl (*The Trumpet-call of Isráfíl*). صور اسرافیل

A weekly paper printed in Ṭihrán in A.H. 1325 (= A.D. 1907). Its proprietor and editor was Mírzá Jahángír Khán of Shíráz; the second editor and publisher was Mírzá Qásim Khán of Tabríz; while its chief contributor was Mírzá 'Alí Akbar Khán of Qazwín, known as *Dihkhudá* or *Dakhaw*. It is reckoned one of the best of the Persian papers, old and new, and in particular the comic or satirical portion, entitled *Charand Parand* ("Charivari"), is the best specimen of literary satire in Persian. It became the special object of hostility on the part of the Reactionaries, and its editor Mírzá Jahángír Khán, who was captured on the occasion of the bombardment of the *Majlis* (June 23, 1908), was put to death by strangling by order of Muḥammad 'Alí Sháh. One of the most important incidents in the history of this paper was its controversy with the clergy and its critical remarks on the decline of the Islamic nations through the Doctors of Divinity, which appeared in No. 4, and gave rise to a great outcry amongst the *Mullás* and common people, and led to the suppression of the paper for about two months. In No. 7 there appeared a defence proving its innocence, which is also worthy of attention. The literary style of this paper was modelled, so far as the serious portion was concerned, on the style of Mírzá Malkom Khán, and greatly resembled his writings, while the comic or satirical portion was inspired by the Turkish *Mullá Naṣru'd-Dín*, published at Tiflis. In politics the *Ṣúr-i-Isráfíl* was Liberal and thorough-going Constitutionalist.

See Rabino, No. 145, according to whom this paper first appeared on the 17th of Rabí' ii, A.H. 1325 (=May 30, 1907), and was brought to an end on the 20th of Jumáda i, A.H. 1326 (=June 20, 1908), three days before the bombardment of the *Majlis*, and four days before the editor, Mírzá Jahángír Khán, was put to death by Muḥammad 'Alí Sháh. I possess an almost complete set. Each number comprises 8 pp. of 11¾" × 6¾". Yearly subscription, 12 *qráns* in Ṭihrán, 17 *qráns* elsewhere in Persia, and 20 *qráns* abroad.

(245)

Ṣúr-i-Isráfíl (*The Trumpet-call of Isráfíl*). صور اسرافیل

A weekly paper printed at Yverdon in Switzerland in the beginning of A.H. 1327 (= A.D. 1909) under the editorship of Mírzá 'Alí Akbar Khán *Dihkhudá*, formerly on the staff of the Ṭihrán *Ṣúr-i-Isráfíl*. Not more than four numbers of this Swiss edition were published, and the paper did not possess its former eloquence and sweetness.

See Rabino, No. 145. No. 1 was dated the first of Muḥarram, A.H. 1327 (=Jan. 23, 1909), and No. 3 the 15th of Ṣafar (=March 8) of the same year. I possess

Title of the *Ṣúr-i-Isráfíl*, or "Trumpet of Isráfíl" (the Angel of the Resurrection) with portrait of its editor, Mírzá Jahángír Khán of Shíráz, who was put to death on June 24, 1908

Nos. 1–3, which in size and appearance closely resemble the old Ṭihrán issue, save in the larger type used for the headings of articles. Yearly subscription, 15 francs in Tabríz, 20 francs elsewhere in Persia, and 25 francs abroad.

(246)

Ṭaríqatu'l-Faláḥ (*The Way of Happiness*). طريقة الفلاح

A paper published in Ṭihrán in A.H. 1325 (= A.D. 1907).

Not in Rabino, and not seen.

(247)

Ṭulú' (*The Dawn*). طلوع

A comic illustrated paper lithographed in Bushire in A.H. 1318 (= A.D. 1900–1) under the editorship of 'Abdu'l-Ḥamíd Khán *Matínu's-Salṭana*, afterwards a Member of the Second *Majlis*.

Not in Rabino, and not seen.

(248)

Ṭús. طوس

A bi-weekly paper printed in Mashhad in A.H. 1327 (= A.D. 1909) under the editorship of Mírzá Háshim Khán. The publication of the first number corresponded with the day on which the Second *Majlis* was opened in Ṭihrán.

See Rabino, No. 146, according to whom the paper began on the first of Dhu'l-Qa'da, A.H. 1327 (= Nov. 14, 1909), and ended on the 15th of Sha'bán, A.H. 1328 (= August 22, 1910), 57 numbers being published in all. I possess Nos. 2, 8, 18, 29, 33 and 34. The first two are of a smaller size (12½" × 6¼"), the later numbers are larger (16" × 11"). Yearly subscription, 30 *qráns* in Mashhad, 35 *qráns* elsewhere in Persia, and 7 roubles in Russia and the Caucasus.

(249)

Ṭihrán. طهران

A paper printed in Ṭihrán in A.H. 1326 (= A.D. 1908) under the editorship of Ḥájji Mírzá Ḥasan of Tabríz, known as *Rushdiyya*.

See Rabino, No. 147, according to whom the paper began on the 7th of Rabí' i, A.H. 1326 (= April 9, 1908), and appeared twice a week. I possess Nos. 2 and 4. Each contains 4 pp. of 11¾" × 6¾". Yearly subscription, 12 *qráns* in Ṭihrán, 17 *qráns* elsewhere in Persia, 4 roubles abroad.

(250)

'Ibrat (*Admonition*). عبرت

A weekly paper lithographed in Tabríz in A.H. 1324 (= A.D. 1906).

Not in Rabino, and not seen.

(251)

'Adálat (*Justice*). عدالت

An illustrated weekly paper lithographed in Tabríz in A.H. 1324 (= A.D. 1906) under the editorship of Mírzá Maḥmúd Khán known as *Ḥakkák-báshí* ("The Seal-engraver"), and afterwards of Mírzá Sayyid Ḥusayn Khán, editor of the newspapers *al-Ḥadíd*, *Ṣuḥbat* and *Khabar* (*q.v.*). This paper succeeded *al-Ḥadíd*, and both of them were founded by the above-mentioned Mírzá Sayyid Ḥusayn Khán.

See Rabino, No. 148, according to whom it reached the Third Year of publication. I possess a good many numbers, ranging from No. 15 of the First Year (dated the 11th of Sha'bán, A.H. 1324 = Sept. 30, 1906) to No. 4 of the Third Year, dated Jumáda i, A.H. 1325 (= June–July, 1907). Each number contains 8 pp. of 12″ × 6¾″, lithographed in fair *ta'líq*, but a few numbers are in *naskh*. Only the later numbers contain illustrations of celebrated men like Mirabeau, Cicero, etc. Yearly subscription, 22 *qráns* in Tabríz, 26 *qráns* elsewhere in Persia, 5 roubles in Russia, 13 francs elsewhere.

(252)

'Adl-i-Muẓaffar (*The Justice of Muẓaffar*). عدل مظفّر

A weekly paper "jelly-graphed" (afterwards printed) in Hamadán in A H. 1324 (= A.D. 1906) under the editorship of Dr Ḥasan Khán Ṭabíb 'Alí. It was established at the instigation and maintained by the support of *Ẓahíru'd-Dawla*, who was at that time Governor. After some twenty numbers had been published, the paper changed its name to *Ekbátán* (Ecbatana). See No. 59 *supra*.

See Rabino, No. 242. Not in my possession.

(253)

'Iráq-i-'Ajam. عراق عجم

A weekly paper printed in Ṭihrán in A.H. 1325 (= A.D. 1907) under the editorship of Mírzá Ṣádiq Khán *Adíbu'l-Mamálik*, sub-editor of the newspaper *Adab.* It was published on the part and at the charges of the political club called 'Iráq-i-'Ajam in Ṭihrán.

See Rabino, No. 149. I possess Nos. 5, 6, 8, 16–19, and 22, the first dated the 3rd of Jumáda i, A.H. 1325 (=June 14, 1907), and the last the 12th of Dhu'l-Ḥijja of the same year (=Jan. 16, 1908). Each number contains 4 or 8 pp. of 12″ × 6¾″. Yearly subscription, 12 *qráns* in Ṭihrán, 17 *qráns* elsewhere in Persia, 5 roubles in Russia, 10 francs in Europe.

(254)

'Urwatu'l-Wuthqá (*The Firm Hand-hold*). عروة الوثقى

A weekly newspaper printed in Ṭihrán in A.H. 1325 (=A.D. 1907).

See Rabino, No. 150, who gives no further particulars. I do not possess the paper.

(255)

'Aṣr (*The Age*). عصر

A weekly paper printed in Ṭihrán in A.H. 1328 (=A.D. 1910), owned and written by Mírzá Áqá of Iṣfahán, known as *Mujáhid*, and edited by Ḥájji Shaykh Ḥasan of Tabríz, formerly editor of the *Khiláfat* (*q.v.*). In politics this paper was Moderate.

See Rabino, No. 151. I possess Nos. 3–31 of this paper, the first dated the 17th of Dhu'l-Ḥijja, A.H. 1328 (=Dec. 20, 1910), and the last the 3rd of Sha'bán, A.H. 1329 (=July 30, 1911). Each number comprises 4 pp. of 14½″ × 8¼″. Yearly subscription, 10 *qráns* in Ṭihrán, 12 *qráns* elsewhere in Persia, 8 francs abroad.

(256)

'Aṣr-i-Jadíd (*The New Age*). عصر جديد

A bi-weekly paper lithographed in Mashhad early in A.H. 1328 (=Jan. 1910) under the editorship of Sayyid Ḥasan-i-Músawí.

See Rabino, No. 152. I possess Nos. 2, 4, and 18, the first dated the 23rd of Rabí' i, A.H. 1328 (=April 4, 1910), and the last the 16th of Dhu'l-Qa'da, A.H. 1328 (=Nov. 19, 1910). Each number contains 4 or 8 pp. of 13″ × 7″, lithographed in a large *naskh* hand. Yearly subscription, 16 *qráns* in Mashhad, 20 *qráns* elsewhere in Persia, and 25 *qráns* abroad.

(257)

'Ilm-ámúz (*The Teacher of Knowledge*). علم آموز

A paper published in Ṭihrán in A.H. 1325 (=A.D. 1907).

Not in Rabino, and not seen.

(258)

Ghayrat (*Zeal*). غيرت

A "jelly-graphed" newspaper secretly published in Ṭihrán in A.H. 1319 (= A.D. 1901–2) by a secret society, and chiefly directed against the *Amínu's-Sulṭán*. Something has been said about it in the Introduction (p. 21 *supra*).

Not in Rabino, and not seen.

(259)

Fárs. فارس

A weekly newspaper lithographed in Shíráz in A.H. 1289 (= A.D. 1872–3), edited and written by Mírzá Taqí Khán of Káshán, editor of the *Farhang* (mention of which has been already made on p. 12 of the Introduction), and Chief Physician (*Ḥakím-báshí*) of the *Ẓillu's-Sulṭán*. The first number of this paper appeared on Sunday, the 9th of Shahríwar, in the year 794 of the Jalálí era, corresponding to the 25th of Jumáda ii, A.H. 1289 (= August 30, 1872), and coincided with the first arrival of the *Ẓillu's-Sulṭán* at Shíráz on the occasion of his third appointment as Governor of Fárs. The first 19 numbers of this paper are preserved in the British Museum amongst the periodical publications, under the class-mark M. 2. 757. These I have seen, but they are erroneously entered in the Catalogue as published at Iṣfahán.

This paper as originally issued comprised eight pages, four in Persian and four in Arabic, the latter being an exact translation of the former. Only the first three numbers, however, appeared in this form, the Arabic part being discontinued from No. 4 onwards, an announcement in that issue declaring it to be unnecessary. No. 19 is dated the 23rd of Day-máh in the year 794 of the Jalálí era, corresponding to the 6th of Dhu'l-Qa'da, A.H. 1289 (= Jan. 5, 1873), so that the paper seems to have appeared regularly every week. Its title appears in the form of a very intricate monogram in the *thuluth* script, the deciphering of which is somewhat difficult. It appears to contain the words "printed in Fárs." At the top of the title-page stand the words "in the private printing-press in the Mirror-room of the Seat of Government of the Province: yearly subscription, 3 *túmáns*"; and at the end the signature "Director of the Fárs printing-press and writer of the paper, Mírzá Taqí *Ḥakím-báshí*." The paper is written in a fine *nasta'líq*, and contains excellent verses composed by the poets of that period and sometimes by Mírzá Taqí Khán himself. At the foot of the page are dissertations on various topics, written in the *díwání* hand, amongst these being a treatise on "the Education of Children," and another on "a Scientific Problem," dealing with the Creation of the Earth and the Science of Geology, which appeared in the eleventh and subsequent numbers. At the beginning of the latter the author says that he has written and published separately a more detailed monograph on Geology. All these treatises and articles are written by the editor himself.

Not in Rabino, and not seen.

(260)

Faraj ba'd az Shiddat (*Joy after Grief*). فرج بعد از شدّت

A weekly paper lithographed in Ṭihrán.

See Rabino, No. 154, on whose authority it is here given. He describes it as Conservative, and adds that only about seven numbers were issued. I have not seen it.

(261)

Farwardín. فروردین

A weekly newspaper printed at Urmiya (Ázarbáyján) in A.H. 1329 (=A.D. 1911) under the editorship of Mírzá Ḥabíb Áqá-záda, and written by Mírzá Maḥmúd Khán Ashraf-záda. This paper contained a comic or satirical section in Ázarbáyjání Turkish entitled "*Dághdán-Bághdán*." In politics it was Democrat.

See Rabino, No. 155, according to whom it first appeared on the 28th of Jumáda i, A.H. 1329 (=May 27, 1911). I possess No. 2, which comprises 4 pp. of 15¼" × 9¼". Yearly subscription, 12 *qráns* in Urmiya, 15 *qráns* elsewhere in Persia, 18 *qráns* abroad. The above-mentioned Mírzá Maḥmúd Khán was beaten almost to death by Russian soldiers at the command of the Russian Consul at the time of the Russian aggressions in Ázarbáyján which began on Dec. 20, 1911. A full account of this event was published in the Constantinople *Terjumán-i-Ḥaqíqat* of Feb. 11, 1912.

(262)

Farhang (*Culture*). فرهنگ

A weekly newspaper lithographed in Iṣfahán in A.H. 1296, and edited by Mírzá Taqí Khán of Káshán, editor of the newspaper *Fárs* (see above, No. 259), and after his death by Mírzá Maḥmúd Khán, father of Mírzá Muḥammad Khán, the present *Farhangu'l-Mamálik*, under the general control of the *Ẓillu's-Sulṭán*. One number of it, which lies before me (No. 364) is dated the 21st of Ramaẓán, A.H. 1303 (= June 23, 1886). The first page is numbered (in continuation of what precedes) 53, and at the end is the imprint "Manager and Editor, Mírzá Maḥmúd Khán; writer, 'Abdu'r-Raḥím." At the foot of the page is published an instalment of a book entitled "The War in the East of A.D. 1877," translated by Mírzá Káẓim, Professor of Natural Sciences in the *Dáru'l-Funún* College of Ṭihrán.

Some persons ascribe the original foundation and inception of this paper to Mírzá Ḥusayn Khán (son of the late Mírzá Yúsuf Khán *Mustashárú'd-Dawla* of Tabríz) who is at present resident in Paris and was formerly physician to the *Ẓillu's-Sulṭán*, and say that he was its founder and originator.

See Rabino, No. 156, according to whom it first appeared (under the patronage of the *Ẓillu's-Sulṭán*) on the 2nd of Jumáda i, A.H. 1296 (= April 24, 1879), and came to an end on the 12th of Muḥarram, A.H. 1308 (= August 28, 1890).

(263)

Farhang (*Culture*). فرهنگ

A weekly paper printed in Ṭihrán in A.H. 1325 (= A.D. 1907) under the editorship of the *I'tiẓádu'l-'Ulamá* Murtaẓá-yi-Sharíf.

See Rabino, No. 157. I possess No. 2, which is dated the 19th of Jumáda i, A.H. 1325 (= June 30, 1907). It comprises 4 pp. of 12" × 6¾". Yearly subscription, 12 *qráns* in Ṭihrán, postage extra in other parts of Persia, 3 roubles in Russia, 7 francs in Europe.

(264)

Faryád (*The Lament*). فریاد

A weekly paper printed in Urmiya in A.H. 1325 (= A.D. 1907) under the editorship of Mírzá Maḥmúd Ghaní-záda, editor of the *Shafaq* and *Bú Qalamún* (*q.v.*). It was written partly in Persian and partly in Turkish.

See Rabino, No. 158. I possess No. 22, which is dated the 27th of Sha'bán, A.H. 1325 (= Oct. 5, 1907). It comprises 4 pp. of 11" × 7¼". Yearly subscription, 12 *qráns* in Urmiya, 18 *qráns* elsewhere in Persia, 4 roubles in Russia, 50 piastres in Turkey, and 12 francs in Europe.

(265)

Fikr (*Thought*). فکر

A weekly paper printed in Tabríz in A.H. 1330 (= A.D. 1912). Its proprietor and chief contributor is an Armenian named Alexander Dir Wartániyáns, one of the teachers in the Armenian College. This paper was founded after the Russian aggressions and executions of the Liberal and Nationalist leaders, the suppression of all the newspapers, the entry of Ṣamad Khán *Shujá'u'd-Dawla* of Marágha into Tabríz, and the triumph of violent reaction (Muḥarram, A.H. 1330 = January, 1912), at the secret instigation of the Russians and with the encouragement of Ṣamad Khán, in order to glorify the actions of the Russians in Persia and to belittle the Constitution. It may be considered the only Persian newspaper in Persia which is an open traitor to its country. Amongst Persian newspapers it has, indeed, but one rival in this respect, namely the Transcaspian Gazette (*Majmú'a-i-Máwará-yi-Baḥr-i-Khazar*), published at 'Ishq-ábád, which will be mentioned presently.

As this paper was not started until after the publication of Rabino's Work, it is naturally not mentioned by him, nor have I seen it, though quotations from it amply sufficient to prove its detestable and unnatural tone have been published in the *Ḥablu'l-Matín* and other papers.

(266)

Fikr-i-Istiqbál (*The Thought of the Future*). فکر استقبال

A paper printed in Constantinople in A.H. 1328 (= A.D. 1910) under the editorship of 'Alí Sharíf-záda of Tabríz. The first number was dated the 21st of Sha'bán, A.H. 1328 (= Aug. 28, 1910).

See Rabino, No. 159. I possess No. 1, which comprises 8 pp. of $8\frac{3}{4}'' \times 5\frac{3}{4}''$. The subscription price is not mentioned.

(267)

Faláḥat-i-Muẓaffarí (*Muẓaffarí Agriculture*). فلاحت مظفری

A monthly scientific paper printed in Ṭihrán in A.H. 1318 (= A.D. 1900–1) under the management of the College of Agriculture, and treating of agricultural matters.

See Rabino, No. 160, according to whom the second number appeared on the first of Jumáda ii, A.H. 1318 (= Sept. 26, 1900). I possess No. 2 of the First and

No. 16 of the Second Year, the latter dated Ṣafar, A.H. 1325; but if the paper was founded in A.H. 1318, as stated above, this must be an error (easily made with Arabic figures) for A.H. 1320 (=May–June, 1902). It comprises 16 pp. of 7″ × 4¾″. Yearly subscription, 6 *qráns* in Ṭihrán, 8 *qráns* elsewhere in Persia, and 12 *qráns* abroad.

(268)

Fawá'id-i-'Ámma (*Public Benefits*). فوائد عامّه

A weekly paper printed in Ṭihrán in A.H. 1325 (=A.D. 1907). Its editor and chief contributor was the notorious Yúsuf Khán of Herát, who was also the editor of the *Kilíd-i-Siyásí* ("Political Key"), and who was responsible for the recent disturbances in Mashhad (April, 1912) and the bombardment of the Holy Shrine of the Imám Riẓá (Rabí' ii, A.H. 1330=March–April, 1912). The editor of this paper had formerly resided in Mashhad, and was suspected of being connected with the Russian Consulate there, and of being an instrument in their hands. Soon after the granting of the Constitution he came to Ṭihrán and founded this paper and the *Kilíd-i-Siyásí*. He wrote chiefly against the English. [He was captured and shot by the Persians on May 23, 1912.]

See Rabino, No. 161. Not in my possession.

(269)

Qájáriyya. قاجاريّه

A weekly paper printed in Ṭihrán in A.H. 1325 (=A.D. 1907).

Not in Rabino, and not seen.

(270)

Qálat Sharárá (*The Voice of Truth*). ܩܠܐ ܫܪܪܐ

A religious paper published in Chaldaean (Syriac) at Urmiya. It was founded and edited by a priest named Dáwúd (who has now embraced Islám, taken the name of 'Abdu'l-Aḥad, and settled in Constantinople) in 1896. The paper is now edited by French Catholic missionaries.

Not in Rabino, and not seen.

(271)

Qásimu'l-Akhbár (*The Distributor of News*). قاسم الأخبار

A weekly paper printed in Ṭihrán in A.H. 1325 (=A.D. 1907) under the editorship of Mírzá Abu'l-Qásim Khán of Hamadán.

See Rabino, No. 162, who correctly describes it as lithographed, and states that No. 2 was dated the 5th of Rabí' ii, A.H. 1325 (=May 18, 1907). I possess Nos. 2 and

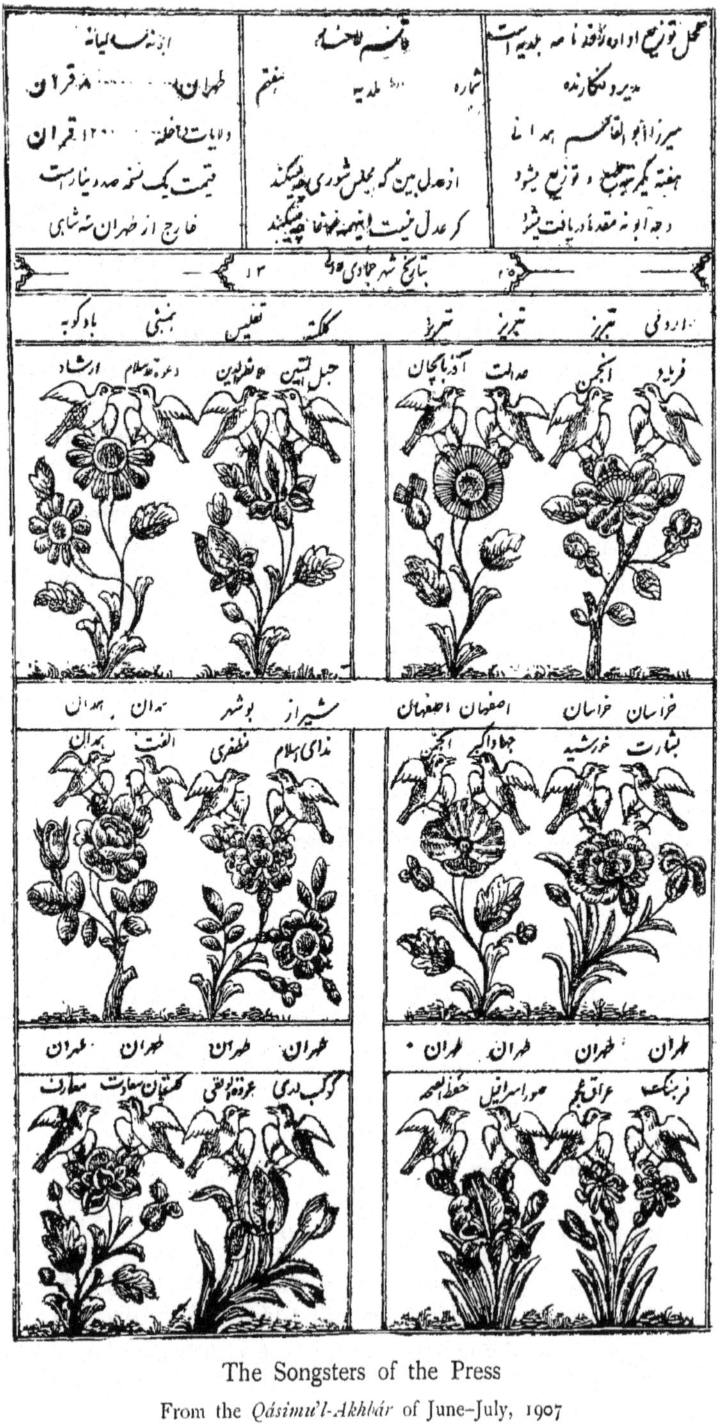

The Songsters of the Press

From the *Qásimu'l-Akhbár* of June–July, 1907

7. Each consists of a single lithographed sheet, with rude cartoons on one or both sides, measuring 12½″ × 7¾″. The writing is a large but clumsy *ta'líq*. Yearly subscription, 8 *qráns* in Ṭihrán, 12 *qráns* elsewhere in Persia.

(272)

Qánún (*The Law*). قانون

A paper printed in London in A.H. 1307 (= A.D. 1889–90), edited and written by Mírzá Malkom Khán *Náẓimu'd-Dawla.* The entry of this paper into Persia was forbidden, so that numbers of it were highly prized by such as possessed them. For the same reason, after the proclamation of the Constitution, in order to increase the number of copies it was reprinted by Háshim Áqá Rabí'-záda.

See Rabino, No. 163, who states that the reprint was made in A.H. 1326, and that he had seen 24 numbers of it. I possess a complete set of the original London edition, of which 41 numbers appeared, the first on Feb. 20, 1890. For further details, see my *History of the Persian Revolution*, pp. 35–42. Each number comprised 4 pp. of 11½″ × 8¾″.

(273)

Qazwín. قزوين

A paper printed in Qazwín twice a week in A.H. 1328 (= A.D. 1910) under the editorship of Mírzá Abu'l-Qásim. In politics it was Democrat.

See Rabino, No. 164. I possess No. 21 of the First Year, dated the 29th of Jumáda ii, A.H. 1328 (= July 8, 1910), and No. 16 of the Second Year, dated the end of Jumáda i, A.H. 1329 (= May 29, 1911). One contains 8 and the other 4 pages of 12¼″ × 7″. Yearly subscription, 10 *qráns* in Qazwín, 12 *qráns* elsewhere in Persia.

(274)

Qand-i-Pársí (*Persian Sugar*). قند پارسی

A literary magazine, published at 'Alí-gaṛh in India.

Not in Rabino, and not seen.

(275)

Káshán. کاشان

A paper published in Káshán in A.H. 1329 (= A.D. 1911).

Not in Rabino, and not seen.

(276)

Káshifu'l-Ḥaqá'iq (*The Revealer of Truths*). کاشف الحقایق

A paper printed in Ṭihrán twice a week in A.H. 1325 (= A.D. 1907–8) under the editorship of Mírzá Ḥabíbu'lláh Khán, known as "Gospodin," director of the college called *Madrasa-i-Waṭan.*

See Rabino, No. 165, who states correctly that the paper was published at Rasht, and that only one number appeared on the sixth of Dhu'l-Qa'da, A.H. 1325 (=Jan. 10, 1908). This number I possess. It comprises 4 pp. of 11¼" × 6¾". Yearly subscription, 12 *qráns* in Rasht, 18 *qráns* elsewhere in Persia, 10 francs in Europe, 4 roubles in the Caucasus, and 10 rupees in India.

(277)

Kakhwá (*The Star*). ܟܘܟܒܐ

A political paper in the Chaldaean (Syriac) language printed in Urmiya in A.H. 1326 (= A.D. 1908) under the editorship of Yúkhanná Múshá.

Not in Rabino, and not seen. I have a manuscript note in Persian in my copy of Rabino (I think by the author of this treatise, Mírzá Muḥammad 'Alí Khán "Tarbiyat"), to the effect that besides this paper, which was political and national, the Chaldaean or Syrian Christians of Urmiya had two other newspapers in their language, both religious, the one Protestant and the other Catholic.

(278)

Kirmán. کرمان

Rabino (No. 166) mentions a paper of this name (omitted by Mírzá Muḥammad 'Alí Khán) printed at Kirmán under the editorship of Mírzá Ghulám Ḥusayn of Kirmán, and adds that it was Democrat in politics and was started on the 17th of Rabí' i, A.H. 1329 (= March 18, 1911). I do not possess a copy.

(279)

Kirmánsháh. کرمانشاه

A weekly newspaper printed at Kirmánsháh in A.H. 1327 (= A.D. 1909) under the editorship of *Faṣíḥu'l-Mutakallimín.* Democrat in politics.

See Rabino, No. 167, who says that it first appeared on the 3rd of Dhu'l-Qa'da, A.H. 1327 (=Dec. 16, 1909), and was published for three months at very irregular intervals, after which it was suspended. I possess No. 11, which comprises 4 pp. of 12" × 8½", and is dated the 7th of Dhu'l-Ḥijja, A.H. 1327 (=Dec. 20, 1909), which hardly agrees with the date of inception given above. Yearly subscription, 12 *qráns* in Kirmánsháh, 15 *qráns* elsewhere in Persia, 8 francs abroad.

(280)

Kashgúl (*The Alms-gourd*). کشکول

A weekly illustrated comic paper lithographed in Ṭihrán in A.H. 1325 (= A.D. 1907–8) under the editorship of Majdu'l-Islám, also editor of the *Nidá-yi-Waṭan* and *Muḥákamát.*

See Rabino, No. 168, who gives the date of No. 2 (really No. 4) as the 22nd of Ṣafar, A.H. 1325 (= April 6, 1907). I possess Nos. 4–39 of the First Year, and Nos. 1–32 of the Second, extending from April 1907 to May 1908. Each number comprises 4 pp. of 12¼" × 6½", of which as many as three are often occupied by rude caricatures. The writing is *ta'líq*. Yearly subscription, 8 *qráns* in Ṭihrán, 10 *qráns* elsewhere in Persia, 5 francs in Europe, 3 roubles in the Caucasus and Russia, 4 rupees in India.

(281)

Kashgúl (*The Alms-gourd*). کشکول

A weekly comic paper lithographed in Iṣfahán in A.H. 1327 (= A.D. 1909) under the editorship of Majdu'l-Islám, editor of the above-mentioned Ṭihrán *Kashgúl.*

See Rabino, No. 168, according to whom 23 numbers were issued in Iṣfahán between the 12th of Rabí' i, A.H. 1327 (= April 3, 1909), and the 9th of Shawwál (= Oct. 24) of the same year. I do not possess a copy.

(282)

Kilíd-i-Siyásí (*The Political Key*). کلید سیاسی

A weekly paper printed in Ṭihrán in A.H. 1325 (= A.D. 1907) under the editorship of Yúsuf Khán of Herát, who used to sign himself "Muḥammad Yúsuf Khán, Sardár-i-Muhájir-i-Hirawí." As has been already mentioned in connection with the newspaper *Fawá'id-i-'Ámma* (No. 268 *supra*), this person recently raised the standard of Autocracy at Mashhad in the name of Muḥammad 'Alí Sháh, gathered round him a number of Reactionaries, filled Khurásán with disturbance for a long while, gave great trouble to the Government, and finally took sanctuary in the Shrine of the Imám Riẓá, until at length he afforded a pretext for the Russian aggressions against that Holy Place (in April, 1912).

See Rabino, No. 169. I possess No. 3, dated the 7th of Rábí' i, A.H. 1325 (= April 20, 1907). It comprises 32 pp. (numbered 17–48) of 7" × 3¾". Yearly subscription, 10 *qráns* in Ṭihrán, 12 *qráns* elsewhere in Persia, 3 roubles in Russia, and 4 rupees in India.

(283)

Kamál (*Perfection*). كمال

A fortnightly paper lithographed in Tabríz in A.H. 1319 (= A.D. 1901–2) under the editorship of Mírzá Ḥusayn *Ṭabíb-záda*, director of the Kamál College and editor of the newspaper *Tabríz*. See No. 100 *supra*.

See Rabino, No. 170. I do not possess a copy.

(284)

Kamál (*Perfection*). كمال

A fortnightly paper printed in Cairo in A.H. 1323 (= A.D. 1905–6) under the editorship of Mírzá Ḥusayn *Ṭabíb-záda*, formerly editor of the above-mentioned Ṭabríz *Kamál*.

Not in Rabino, and not seen.

(285)

Kingásh (*The Council*). كنگاش

A paper printed in Rasht twice a week in A.H. 1328 (= A.D. 1910) under the editorship of Muḥammad 'Alí Ḥasan-záda.

See Rabino, No. 171, who states that in politics the paper was Moderate, and that it first appeared on the 13th of Dhu'l-Qa'da, A.H. 1328 (= Nov. 16, 1910).

(286)

Kawkib-i-durrí-yi-Náṣirí کوکب دری ناصری
(*The Shining Náṣirí Star*).

A paper lithographed in Ṭihrán in A.H. 1325 (= A.D. 1907) under the editorship of Náẓimu'l-Islám of Kirmán, editor of the paper *Naw-rúz* ("New Year's Day," *q.v.*), and author of the *Ta'ríkh-i-Bídárí-yi-Íráníyán* ("History of the Persian Awakening"). Forty numbers of this paper were published yearly.

See Rabino, No. 172. I possess No. 12 of the Third Year, dated the 22nd of Rabí' ii, A.H. 1325 (= June 4, 1907). It comprises 8 pp. of 12½" × 6½", and is lithographed in a fine large *naskh*. Yearly subscription, 20 *qráns* in Ṭihrán, 25 *qráns* elsewhere in Persia, 5 roubles in Russia, 12 francs elsewhere.

(287)

Kawkib-i-Náṣirí (*The Náṣirí Star*). كوكب ناصرى

A paper lithographed in Bombay in A.H. 1309 (= A.D. 1891–2), founded and edited by Mírzá Muṣṭafá *Shaykhu'l-Islám* of Bahbahán.

Not in Rabino. I possess No. 3 of the First Year, dated Jan. 15, 1892; and Nos. 4, 5, 6 and 7 of the same year, each dated a week later than the preceding one. Each number comprises 8 pp. of 17½″ × 11½″, lithographed in *ta'líq*. Yearly subscription, 15 *qráns* in Bombay, 20 *qráns* in India, the Persian Gulf ports and 'Arabistán, and 25 *qráns* elsewhere in Persia and in Turkey and Europe. Proprietors, Mírzá Muṣṭafá and Dr Silvester (?), editor, Mírzá Muṣṭafá *Shaykhu'l-Islám* of Bahbahán.

Guftugú-yi-Ṣafá-khána-i-Iṣfahán گفتگوى صفاخانهٔ اصفهان
(*Discussions of the House of Purity of Iṣfahán*).

Another name for the paper entitled *al-Islám*. See No. 45 *supra*.

See Rabino, No. 20.

(288)

Gulistán (*The Rose-Garden*). گلستان

A weekly paper printed in Rasht in A.H. 1325 (= A.D. 1907) under the editorship of Áqá Muḥammad Ḥusayn *Ra'ísu't-Tujjár* (Chief of the Merchants).

See Rabino, No. 173, according to whom only four numbers were published, the first on the 14th of Sha'bán, A.H. 1325 (=Sept. 22, 1907), and the last on the 1st of Dhu'l-Ḥijja (=Jan. 5, 1908). I possess Nos. 1–4, which agree with the above statement. Each number comprises 4 pp. of 11″ × 6¾″. Yearly subscription, "for the present, zeal and fairness at home, justice and equality abroad." No price is mentioned.

(289)

Gulistán-i-Sa'ádat (*The Rose-Garden of Happiness*). گلستان سعادت

A newspaper lithographed twice a week in Ṭihrán in A.H. 1325 (= A.D. 1907) under the editorship of Mírzá Naṣru'lláh Khán.

See Rabino, No. 174, according to whom No. 1 appeared in Rabí' ii, A.H. 1325 (=May–June, 1907), No. 4 on the first of Dhu'l-Ḥijja of the same year (=Jan. 5, 1908), while Nos. 6 and 7 were undated. I possess Nos. 1 and 3. Each comprises 4 pp. of 12¾″ × 7¾″, lithographed in *ta'líq*. Yearly subscription, 20 *qráns* in Ṭihrán, 6 roubles in Russia, 10 rupees in India, and 15 francs in Europe.

(290)

Ganj-i-Sháyagán (*The Royal Treasure*). گنج شایگان

A paper printed in Ṭihrán in A.H. 1325 (= A.D. 1907).

Not in Rabino, and not seen.

Ganjína-i-Anṣár (*The Treasure of the Helpers*). گنجینهٔ انصار

A newspaper published at Iṣfahán. See above, No. 73, under *Anṣár* (انصار).

(291)

Ganjína-i-Funún (*The Treasury of Arts*). گنجینهٔ فنون

A fortnightly scientific magazine lithographed at Tabríz in A.H. 1320 (= A.D. 1902–3) under the management of the "Tarbiyat" Library. This periodical continued publication for just a year, and published 24 numbers, each of which comprised four parts. The first, entitled *Ganjína-i-Funún*, was a scientific and technical miscellany; the second, entitled *Hunar-ámúz* ("The Instructor in Arts") was a book compiled by the writer (Mírzá Muḥammad 'Alí Khán "Tarbiyat"); the third, entitled *Tamaddunát-i-qadíma* ("Ancient Civilizations"), was translated from the French of Gustave le Bon by Sayyid Ḥasan Taqí-záda; while the fourth, entitled *Safína-i-ghawwáṣa* ("The Diving Ship," or "The Submarine") was translated from the French of Jules Verne, the novelist, by Mírzá Yúsuf Khán *I'tiṣámu'l-Mulk.*

See Rabino, No. 175, according to whom the magazine in question began on the 1st of Dhu'l-Ḥijja, A.H. 1320 (= March 1, 1903), and ended on the same date of A.H. 1321 (= Feb. 18, 1904). I do not possess this publication.

(292)

Gílán. گیلان

A paper printed in Rasht in A.H. 1326 (= A.D. 1908–9) under the editorship of Mírzá Ḥasan Khán Asad-záda. It was connected with and managed by the *Anjuman* (Provincial Council) of Gílán.

See Rabino, No. 176, according to whom only 12 numbers were issued, the first on the 18th of Dhu'l-Ḥijja, A.H. 1326 (= Jan. 11, 1909). I do not possess a copy.

(293)

Gílán. كيلان

A paper printed in Rasht in A.H. 1328 (= A.D. 1910) and published every alternate day. It was edited by "M.Ṣ.", and in politics represented the Moderates.

See Rabino, No. 177, who gives the 26th of Sha'bán, A.H. 1328 (=Sept. 2, 1910), as the date of inauguration.

(294)

Lisánu'l-Ghayb (*The Tongue of the Unseen*). لسان الغيب

A newspaper "jelly-graphed" and clandestinely circulated in Ṭihrán about A.H. 1319 (= A.D. 1901–2) by a secret committee which used formerly to write against the *Amínu's-Sulṭán*, and concerning which something has been already said in the Introduction (p. 21).

Not in Rabino, and not seen.

(295)

Lodiana Akhbár (*Lodiana News*). لوديانه اخبار

A weekly newspaper published in Calcutta on Saturdays, which, according to Zenker's *Bibliotheca Orientalis* (No. 1834), was in circulation in A.H. 1262 (= A.D. 1846).

Not in Rabino, and not seen.

(296)

La Patrie.

A newspaper published at Ṭihrán in French in A.D. 1876 (= A.H. 1293). See above in the Introduction, pp. 16–17.

See Rabino, No. 227, who states that it began (and ended) on Feb. 5, 1876.

(297)

Mujáhid (*The National Volunteer*). مجاهد

A paper printed in Tabríz in A.H. 1325 (= A.D. 1907–8) and appearing every other day, edited by Sayyid Muḥammad Shabistarí, known as Abu'ẓ-Ẓiyá, editor of the papers *al-Ḥadíd* and *Írán-i-Naw*. In consequence of the publication in its last number, which coincided with the Abortive *Coup d'État* (of December, 1907), or Event of the Artillery Barracks (*Waq'a-i-Túpkhána*), of a letter from Baghdád containing an attack on Sayyid Káẓim of Yazd, a *mujtahid* residing at Najaf, it incurred the hatred and vengeance of certain fanatics, and its editor was subjected to a severe bastinado, and was expelled from the city. This paper was published on behalf of the Social Democrats, and served as their organ.

See Rabino, No. 178, who gives the 9th of Sha'bán, A.H. 1325 (= Sept. 17, 1907), as the date of inception, and adds that No. 22 was dated the 9th of Dhu'l-Qa'da (= Dec. 14) of the same year. I possess Nos. 1, 20, 21 and 22, which comprise 4 pp. of 10¼" × 6½". Yearly subscription, 15 *qráns* in Tabríz, 20 *qráns* elsewhere in Persia, and 25 *qráns* abroad.

(298)

Mujáhid (*The National Volunteer*). مجاهد

A paper printed in Rasht in A.H. 1325 (= A.D. 1907–8).

See Rabino, No. 179, who says that only five numbers were published, the first on the 9th of Shawwál, A.H. 1325 (= Nov. 15, 1907), and the last on the 2nd of Muḥarram, A.H. 1326 (= Feb. 5, 1908). I possess Nos. 1 and 4, which comprise 4 pp. of 12" × 6¾". Yearly subscription, 12 *qráns* in Gílán, 15 *qráns* elsewhere in Persia, 6 roubles in Russia.

(299)

Majlis (*The Assembly*). مجلس

A paper printed in Ṭihrán, which first appeared on the 8th of Shawwál, A.H. 1324 (= Nov. 25, 1906), edited by Sayyid Muḥammad Ṣádiq (son of the well-known Sayyid Muḥammad-i-Ṭabáṭabá'í), and written by the *Adíbu'l-Mamálik*, editor of the *Adab* (*q.v.*). This was the first paper in Persia which reported the debates of the National Assembly after it was opened, on which account it achieved a great celebrity, so that in the provinces it was generally supposed that it was connected with the Assembly. After the restoration of the Constitution (in July, 1909) it again began to appear under the supervision of Shaykh Yaḥyá of Káshán, a former contributor to the daily (Ṭihrán) *Ḥablu'l-Matín*, and continued publication until these latter times (end of 1911 or beginning of 1912). During the Second Constitutional Period the politics of this paper were Moderate[1].

[1] In No. 2 of this newspaper, is a very fine *qaṣída* in praise of the National Assembly by the *Adíbu'l-Mamálik*, which is one of the best poems produced during the Constitutional Period. It begins:

ش ای مجلس ملّی که بینم عنقریب' از تو آید درد ملّت را در این دوران ط

"*Hail, O National Assembly! For I see that at this epoch there will shortly issue forth from thee a healer for the Nation's ills.*"

See Rabino, No. 180. I possess a fairly complete collection of this paper. It underwent several enlargements. Thus No. 1 comprised 4 pp. of 11¾″ × 7″; No. 8 increased in size to 14½″ × 8½″; while No. 37 of the Third Year still further increased to 21″ × 14″. The yearly subscription also increased from 45 *qráns* in Ṭihrán, 55 *qráns* in the provinces, and 26 francs abroad, to 60 *qráns* in Ṭihrán, 75 *qráns* in the provinces, 40 francs abroad, and 16 roubles in Russia and the Caucasus.

(300)

مجلّهٔ انجمن اتّحادیّهٔ سعادت

Majalla-i-Anjuman-i-Ittiḥádiyya-i-Sa'ádat
(*Magazine of the Society of the Union of Happiness*).

See under *Ittiḥádiyya-i-Sa'ádat*, No. 27 *supra*.

Not in Rabino.

(301)

Majalla-i-Istibdád (*Magazine of Autocracy*). مجلّهٔ استبداد

A monthly magazine printed in Ṭihrán in A.H. 1325 (= A.D. 1907–8) and edited by [Shaykh Mahdí of Qum, entitled] *Shaykhu'l-Mamálik*.

See Rabino, No. 181, who states that 31 numbers appeared in all, the first on the 5th of Jumáda ii, A.H. 1325 (= July 16, 1907). I was acquainted with the editor when I was in Kirmán in the summer of 1888, and in memory of that old friendship he sent me this magazine month by month, so that I possess an almost complete set.

(302)

Majalla-i-Ṭabábat (*Medical Magazine*). مجلّهٔ طبابت

A scientific magazine lithographed in Ṭihrán in A.H. 1326 (= A.D. 1908–9).

Not in Rabino, and not seen.

(303)

مجلّهٔ هئیت علمیّهٔ دانشوران

Majalla-i-Hay'at-i-'Ilmiyya-i-Dánishwarán
(*Magazine of the Scientific Society of Savants*).

According to Rabino (No. 182), on whose authority this publication is here included, it appeared monthly in A.H. 1327 (= A.D. 1909).

(304)

Majalla-i-Naẓmiyya (*The Police Magazine*). مجلّهٔ نظمیّه

A paper published in Ṭihrán in A.H. 1329 (=A.D. 1911) which discussed matters concerning the Police.

Not in Rabino, and not seen.

(305)

Majmú'a-i-Akhláq (*Ethical Miscellany*). مجموعهٔ اخلاق

A magazine printed every ten days in Ṭihrán in A.H. 1323 (=A.D. 1905–6) under the editorship of Mírzá 'Alí Akbar Khán (Muṣawwir 'Alí), and under the patronage of the *Anjuman-i-Ukhuwwat* ("Society of Brotherhood") of Ẓahíru'd-Dawla, that is to say the followers of the Mystical Path of Ṣafí 'Alí Sháh. This paper discussed ethical matters and was for the most part written by Mírzá Ibráhím Khán, Deputy for Iṣfahán in the Second National Assembly.

See Rabino, No. 183. I possess Nos. 2–10, and 12–15, which are not dated. Each contains 8 pp. of $7\frac{1}{2}'' \times 4\frac{3}{4}''$, and is priced at 4 sháhís. No yearly subscription is mentioned. The magazine contains a great deal of poetry, and professedly avoids political and religious matters.

(306)

مجموعهٔ ما ورای بحر خزر

Majmú'a-i-Má-wará-yi Baḥr-i-Khazar (*The Trans-Caspian Review*).

A weekly newspaper printed at 'Ishqábád (Askabad) in A.H. 1322 (=A.D. 1904–5) under the editorship of the Russian Fedoroff. This paper was the instrument of Russian policy and the vehicle of Russian political aims in Persia. It was founded during the Russo-Japanese War to proclaim the Russian advances and victories, and was distributed gratuitously throughout Persia by the Russian Consulates.

See Rabino, No. 184, according to whom No. 4 of the Fourth Year was dated the 13th of Dhu'l-Qa'da, A.H. 1327 (=Nov. 26, 1909). I possess Nos. 3, 4 and 8 of the Third Year. Each contains 4–8 pp. of $13'' \times 8\frac{1}{2}''$. Yearly subscription, 3 roubles in Russia, $4\frac{1}{2}$ roubles abroad.

(نشر سال سوم) (۳) (عشق آباد روزنامهٔ مصوّر فارسی) (نشر سال سوم) (۳)

مجموعهٔ ماوراى بحر خزر

۱۳۲۲

قیمت ابونه در روسیه
سالیانه . . . . ۳ منات
شش ماهه . . . . ۲ منات
در بلاد خارجه
سالیانه . . . ۴ منات ۵۰ کاپیك
قیمت اعلان در صفحه اول بحساب پیتیت ۳۰ کاپیك در صفحه آخر ۲۵ کاپیك
عنوان مراسلات
عشق آباد اداره مجموعه ماوراى بحر خزر
Аскабадъ „Закаспійское Обоз"

№ 3 — شماره ۳ جمعه ۲۵ محرم سنه ۱۳۲۶ هجری مطابق ۱۵ فورال سنه ۱۹۰۸ میلادی شماره ۳ — № 3

Superscription and cover of the *Majmú'a-i-Baḥr-i-Khazar*,
or "Revue Transcaspienne"

No. 3 of the Third Year, Feb. 28, 1908

(307)

Muḥákamát (*Judgements*). محاکمات

A paper printed in Ṭihrán in A.H. 1325 (= A.D. 1907–8), at first twice and afterwards thrice a week, under the editorship of Majdu'l-Islám of Kirmán, to give publicity to the proceedings of the Law Courts.

See Rabino, No. 185, who describes it as the organ of the Ministry of Justicé, and gives the 17th (*sic*, but see below) of Jumáda i, A.H. 1325 (= June 28, 1907), as the date of its first appearance. I possess Nos. 2, 3, 22, 25, 26, 28, 29, 43, 48, and 49, the first dated the 13th of Jumáda i, A.H. 1325 (= June 24, 1907), and the last the 14th of Rabí' i, A.H. 1326 (= April 16, 1908). Each number contains 4 pp. of 11¼" × 6¾". Yearly subscription, 15 *qráns* in Ṭihrán, 18 *qráns* elsewhere in Persia, 2 mejidiyyés in Turkey and Egypt, 4 roubles in Russia and the Caucasus, and 18 francs in Europe.

(308)

Muḥákamát (*Judgements*). محاکمات

A paper published in Tabríz in A.H. 1326 (= A.D. 1908) under the editorship of Mírzá Maḥmúd Ghaní-záda of Salmás, editor of the *Faryád* and *Bú Qalamún* (*q.v.*).

Not in Rabino, and not seen.

(309)

Muḥákamat-i-Yazd (*Judgements of Yazd*). محاکمات یزد

A weekly paper lithographed in Yazd in A.H. 1327 (= A.D. 1909) under the editorship of Muḥammad Ṣádiq.

See Rabino, No. 186, who states that after the arrival at Yazd of the Bakhtiyárí Sardár-i-Jang, the newspaper *Ma'rifat* (see below, No. 328) was published under the title of *Muḥákamát*, but not more than two or three numbers were printed and circulated. I possess a copy of No. 2 of the First Year, which is dated the 17th of Dhu'l-Qa'da, A.H. 1327 (= Nov. 30, 1909). It comprises 4 pp. lithographed in large, clear *ta'líq*, of 11" × 6¼". Yearly subscription, 16 *qráns* in Yazd, 20 *qráns* elsewhere in Persia, 23 *qráns* abroad.

(310)

Mudarris-i-Fársí (*The Persian Teacher*). مدرّس فارسی

A monthly magazine published in Bombay, partly lithographed and partly printed in small (book) form, in A.D. 1883 (= A.H. 1300–1). Its contents were partly Persian and partly English, and, as its name implies, were chiefly educational and connected with the study of the Persian language. It treated of Persian grammar and literature, and contained Persian stories, anecdotes, proverbs, specimens of calligraphy, biographies, and notices of old poets and Kings of Persia, accompanied in most cases by English translations. Its first number was dated Thursday, January 1, 1883, and the following verse of poetry was printed on the top of each copy:

ز لافِ حمد و نعت اولی است بر خاكِ ادب خفتن
سجودی می توان كردن درودی می توان گفتن

A complete collection of three years (36 numbers) of this periodical is preserved in the Library of the British Museum under the class-mark 757.cc.20. The last (36th) number is dated December, 1885.

This periodical was edited by Khán Bahádur G. M. Munshí and his sons. Each number comprised 16 pp., and the yearly subscription was 4 rupees, if paid in advance, and 5 rupees if paid at the end of the year. At the beginning of each number is written in English: "to save much time, trouble and money." In the number for August, 1885, appears an advertisement of the *Farhang*, published at Iṣfahán, and an encomium on it, and in subsequent numbers news is occasionally quoted from that paper.

In the later numbers of the *Mudarris-i-Fársí* there appear advertisements of a paper entitled *Mufarriḥu'l-Qulúb*, which is highly praised, and of which it writes as follows: "This is a weekly Persian newspaper published at Karáchí in Sind, and is the best Persian newspaper in India. It has appeared regularly for thirty years, and it is now the thirtieth year of its publication. Its Persian style is very good, and entirely accords with the spoken and written idiom of Persia. It contains the latest news from every country, and is in every respect a first-class newspaper. It is chiefly maintained and published by subventions from the rulers, princes, nobility and gentry of Persia, Turkey, Afghánistán, India, Europe, etc. Its proprietors and publishers possess testimonials, guarantees and letters from most of the above-mentioned rulers, nobles and gentry which afford ample evidence as to the excellence of its style and taste. It is especially suitable for the use of students of Persian in India. It is edited and published by two learned, accomplished and well-known persons,

Mírzá Muḥammad Ja'far (the editor) and Mírzá Muḥammad Ṣádiq of Mashhad, Persian Consul at Karáchí. Yearly subscription for Indian nobles, 12 rupees, if paid in advance, and 24 rupees if post-paid: for people of the middle class, 10 and 20 rupees, respectively: and for students, 5 and 10 rupees respectively."

Not in Rabino, and not seen.

(311)

Madaniyyat (*Civilization*). مدنيّت

A fortnightly newspaper lithographed in Tabríz in A.H. 1301 (= A.D. 1883–4) under the editorship of the Secretary to the Armenian Agency, known as Ṣadrá. No. 2 was dated Wednesday the 12th of Jumáda ii, A.H. 1301 (= April 9, 1884).

Not in Rabino, and not seen.

(312)

Madí (? *Media*). مدى

A weekly paper printed in Ṭihrán in A.H. 1325 (= A.D. 1907–8), edited and written by Shaykh 'Abdu'l-'Alí, known as *Múbad*, on account of his sentiments with regard to Ancient Persia and the pure Persian language. After the *Coup d'État* of June 23, 1908, and the bombardment of the *Majlis*, he became acquainted with the celebrated M. Panoff, the correspondent of certain Liberal Russian papers in Persia, who also took part in the Gílán Rebellion in A.H. 1327 (= A.D. 1909), at the time when the Russian Legation had expelled him from Ṭihrán. He accompanied him to St Petersburg under the name of "Mírzá Shaykh 'Alí the *Mujtahid*," and endeavoured to influence public opinion in Russia in a manner favourable to Persia by means of public speeches.

Not in Rabino, and not seen.

(313)

Mirát-i-Janúb (*The Mirror of the South*). مرآت جنوب

A weekly newspaper lithographed at Kirmán in A.H. 1329 (= A.D. 1911) under the editorship of Sayyid Jalálu'd-Dín Ḥusayní *Mu'ayyidu'l-Ashráf*.

See Rabino, No. 187. I possess a copy of No. 1, which is dated the 3rd of Muḥarram, A.H. 1329 (= Jan. 4, 1911). It is lithographed in a large, clear *naskh*, and comprises 4 pp. of 11½″ × 6½″. Yearly subscription, 20 *qráns* in Kirmán. This number contains, on p. 1, a portrait of Mírzá Ḥusayn Khán *Sardár-i-Nuṣrat.*

(314)

Mirátu's-Safar wa Mishkátu'l-Ḥaḍar مرآة السّفر و مشكوة الحضر

(*The Mirror of Travel and Lamp of Sojourn*).

A newspaper published in Rabí' i, A.H. 1288 (= May–June, 1871) on the march and at the halting-places during Náṣiru'd-Dín Sháh's summer journey to Mázandarán. It gave an account of the events of the journey from start to finish, and was printed and edited by Muḥammad Ḥasan Khán *I'timádu's-Salṭana.* In all thirteen numbers were published.

This information is supplied in a letter from H.E. the *I'timádu's-Salṭana.* The paper is not mentioned by Rabino, and is not otherwise known.

(315)

Mirríkh (*Mars*). مرّيخ

A newspaper lithographed in Ṭihrán in A.H. 1296 (= A.D. 1879) under the editorship of Mírzá Ḥasan Khán *Ṣaní'u'd-Dawla.* The first number was dated Muḥarram 5 of that year (= Dec. 30, 1878) and the last number the 16th of Jumáda ii, A.H. 1297 (= May 26, 1880). In all eighteen numbers were published. This paper took the place of the *Rúznáma-i-Niẓámí* ("Military Journal") which preceded it, and would seem to have been founded by Mírzá Ḥusayn Khán *Sipahsálár*[1]. See No. 191 *supra.*

Most of the above particulars are derived from information supplied by *Zaká'u'l-Mulk.* The paper is not mentioned by Rabino, nor have I seen it.

(316)

Musáwát (*Equality*). مساوات

A weekly paper printed in Ṭihrán in A.H. 1325 (= A.D. 1907–8) under the editorship of Sayyid Muḥammad Riẓá of Shíráz, and

[1] The *I'timádu's-Salṭana* in one of his letters attributes the foundation and circulation of this newspaper to Prince Kámrán Mírzá, entitled *Ná'ibu's-Salṭana*, the son of Náṣiru'd-Dín Sháh, who published it with the assistance of the present *Sardár-i-Kull.* It came to an end, however, after only twelve or thirteen numbers had appeared. It is, however, highly probable, nay, almost certain, that the details mentioned in the text are more correct and accurate, and that the other particulars refer to some other paper of which we have no further information.

Sayyid 'Abdu'r-Raḥím of Khalkhál. This paper, by reason of its extreme boldness and steadfastness in Constitutional Principles, was one of the foremost champions in the Press of the First Constitution. It achieved great notoriety in consequence of its criticism of the Press Law, on the promulgation of which it published a number full of idle stories, fables and phantasies, saying that henceforth, in consequence of the above-mentioned Law, everything except such matters would be prohibited; and also in consequence of a celebrated article entitled "How is the Sháh?" directed against Muḥammad 'Alí Sháh. These actions led to the suppression of the paper and legal proceedings against the editor. The editor of this paper, Sayyid Muḥammad Riẓá, was one of the eight persons whose surrender Muḥammad 'Alí Sháh demanded of the First National Assembly, but after the bombardment of the *Majlis* (June 23, 1908) he escaped and could not be captured. Finally he succeeded in reaching the Caucasus, whence he made his way to Tabríz, where, during the Revolution and siege of that city, he again published the *Musáwát*. Finally he was elected by Tabríz as one of the Members of the Second National Assembly. In politics the paper was thorough-going Constitutionalist and Liberal.

See Rabino, No. 188, who says that in all 25 numbers of the Ṭihrán edition appeared, the first on the 5th of Ramaẓán, A.H. 1325 (=Oct. 12, 1907), and the last at the end of Rabí' i, A.H. 1326 (=May 2, 1908). I possess a fairly complete collection.

(317)

Musáwát (*Equality*). مساوات

A paper lithographed in Tabríz early in A.H. 1327 (= A.D. 1909) under the editorship of Sayyid Muḥammad Riẓá of Shíráz.

See Rabino, No. 188, according to whom the first issue of the Tabríz *Musáwát* appeared on Muḥarram 1, A.H. 1327 (=Jan. 23, 1909), and was numbered "26" in direct continuation of the former Ṭihrán *Musáwát*. I possess a fairly complete set of the Ṭihrán issues (Nos. 1–24, the last dated the 23rd of Rabí' ii, A.H. 1326=May 25, 1908), and No. 27 (the second) of the Tabríz issue, which is *printed*, not lithographed, and is dated the 7th of Muḥarram, A.H. 1327=Jan. 29, 1909. Each number contains 8 pp. of 12" × 6¾". Yearly subscription of Ṭihrán issue, 12 *qráns* in Ṭihrán, 17 *qráns* elsewhere in Persia, 15 francs abroad; of Tabríz issue, 12 *qráns* in Tabríz, 20 *qráns* elsewhere in Persia, and 5 roubles abroad,

(318)

Mashwarat (*Council*). مشورت

A paper published in Ṭihrán in A.H. 1325 (= A.D. 1907–8).

Not in Rabino, and not seen.

(319)

مشروطهٔ بیقانون

Mashrúṭa-i-Bí-qánún (*The Lawless Constitution*).

A paper published in Ṭihrán in A.H. 1325 (= A.D. 1907–8).

Not in Rabino, and not seen.

(320)

Miṣbáḥ (*The Lamp*). مصباح

A paper lithographed in Tabríz in A.H. 1324 (= A.D. 1906–7) under the editorship of Mírzá Abu'l-Qásim of Tabríz.

Not in Rabino, and not seen.

(321)

Muṣawwar (*The Illustrated*). مصوّر

Inserted on the authority of Rabino, No. 189, who gives no particulars. Perhaps what he had in view was the *Illustrated History of the War in the Far East*, which was published in parts in Ṭihrán.

(322)

Muẓaffarí. مظفّری

A fortnightly, and subsequently weekly, paper, first lithographed and subsequently printed in Bushire in A.H. 1319 (= A.D. 1901–2), under the editorship of 'Alí Áqá of Shíráz.

See Rabino, No. 190, who states that the paper was Democrat in politics, and that No. 2 was dated the 15th of Shawwál, A.H. 1319 (= Jan. 25, 1902). I possess a large collection of this paper from the First to the Tenth Year (A.H. 1319–1329 = Jan. 1902–April, 1911). Of these, Nos. 2–66 (Jan. 1902–Sept. 1904) are lithographed, and the remainder printed. Each number comprises 16 pp. of 9″ × 5″. Yearly subscription, 22 *qráns* in Bushire, 28 *qráns* elsewhere in Persia, 8 rupees in India, 14 francs in Europe, Turkey and Egypt, and 5 roubles in Russia and Turkistán.

(323)

Muẓaffarí. مظفّری

A paper printed in Mecca in A.H. 1326 (= A.D. 1908–9) under the editorship of 'Alí Áqá of Shíráz, editor of the homonymous Bushire paper mentioned immediately above. Only one number was published during the season of the Pilgrimage.

See Rabino, No. 190, according to whom this paper (which I have not seen) first appeared in Dhu'l-Ḥijja, A.H. 1326 (= Dec. 1908–Jan. 1909).

(324)

Maẓhar (*The Manifestation*). مظهر

Of this weekly paper, not mentioned by either Rabino or the author of this treatise, I possess one copy, No. 13, dated the 27th of Dhu'l-Qa'da, A.H. 1327 (= Dec. 10, 1909). It is printed at Tiflis, partly in Turkish, partly in Persian, and bears a superscription in Russian. It comprises 4 pp. of 16½" × 10", and contains on page 1 a portrait of Sardár-i-Humáyún, the Persian Consul-General at Tiflis. Yearly subscription, 6 roubles. It describes itself as:—

ادبی سیاسی اقتصادی و وطنه خدمت ایدر هفته‌لك ترك غزته‌سی

—"a weekly literary, political, economic and patriotic Turkish newspaper."

(325)

Ma'árif (*Instruction*). معارف

A paper lithographed in Ṭihrán in A.H. 1317 (= A.D. 1899–1900) under the supervision of the Society of Instruction (*Anjuman-i-Ma'árif*).

Not in Rabino, unless this be merely the early beginning of the next following.

(326)

Ma'árif (*Instruction*). معارف

A weekly paper printed in Ṭihrán in A.H. 1325 (= A.D. 1907–8) under the editorship of Shaykh Muḥammad 'Alí Bahjat of Dizfúl, editor of the magazine entitled *Da'watu'l-Ḥaqq*.

See Rabino, No. 191, who gives the date of No. 16 as the 12th of Ṣafar, A.H. 1325 (= March 27, 1907). I possess Nos. 13, 25, 31, and the supplement to 10. As the paper appeared weekly, it appears by reckoning backwards that it began to be published in A.H. 1324 (=A.D. 1906–7), *not* 1325, a fact also indicated on each issue, where "1324" stands immediately beneath the title. Each number comprises 8 pp. of $11\frac{1}{2}'' \times 6\frac{3}{4}''$. Yearly subscription, 17 *qráns* in Ṭihrán, 20 *qráns* in the provinces, and 12 francs abroad. In No. 36 the title is printed in *naskh* instead as heretofore in *ta'líq*.

(327)

Ma'árif (*Instruction*). معارف

A paper printed twice a week in Ṭihrán in Sha'bán, A.H. 1326 (= Sept., 1908) under the management of the Society of Learning (*Anjuman-i-Ma'árif*).

See Rabino, No. 192, and No. 326 *supra*, of which I suspect it to be a continuation. Not seen by the Translator.

(328)

Ma'rifat (*Knowledge*). معرفت

A weekly paper lithographed at Tabríz in A.H. 1319 (= A.D. 1901–2) under the editorship of Mírzá 'Abdu'lláh Khán, son of Mírzá Taqí, President of the Courts of Justice (*Ṣadr-i-'Adliyya*), one of the Jahán-sháhí Sayyids of Tabríz, and Director of the *Ma'rifat* College.

Not in Rabino, and not seen.

(329)

Ma'rifat (*Knowledge*). معرفت

A weekly paper "jelly-graphed," and subsequently lithographed, in Yazd, in A.H. 1326 (= A.D. 1908–9) under the editorship of Shaykh Abu'l-Qásim *Iftikháru'l-'Ulamá*.

See Rabino, No. 193. I possess Nos. 6 and 8. The former, dated the 15th of Muḥarram, A.H. 1326 (=Feb. 18, 1908), is "jelly-graphed"; the latter, dated the 18th of Ramaẓán, A.H. 1327 (=Oct. 3, 1909), is lithographed. From the long interval separating these two numbers, as well as from sundry differences apparent in arrangement and production, I am disposed to believe that in reality two independent papers named *Ma'rifat* were published in Yazd, one ("jelly-graphed") towards the end of A.H. 1325, and another (lithographed) about the middle of A.H. 1327. In size the two agree (4 pp. of $10\frac{1}{2}'' \times 6''$), but the yearly subscriptions differ as follows. No. 6 (the "jelly-graph"), 20 *qráns* in Yazd, 23 *qráns* elsewhere in Persia; No. 8 (the lithograph), 10 *qráns* in Yazd, 12 *qráns* elsewhere in Persia. No editor's name appears on No. 6.

(330)

Ma'rifatu'l-Akhláq (*Knowledge of Ethics*). معرفة الاخلاق

A paper published in Ṭihrán in A.H. 1326 (= A.D. 1908–9).

Not in Rabino, and not seen.

(331)

Miftáḥu'ẓ-Ẓafar (*The Key of Victory*). مفتاح الظّفر

A weekly scientific paper lithographed at Calcutta in A.H. 1315 (= A.D. 1897–8) under the editorship of Mírzá Sayyid Ḥasan of Káshán, afterwards editor of the Ṭihrán *Ḥablu'l-Matín*.

See Rabino, No. 194. I possess Nos. 13 and 4 (*sic*) of the Second Year, the former dated the 26th of Dhu'l-Qa'da, A.H. 1316 (=April 4, 1899), and the latter the 25th of Jumádá i, A.H. 1317 (=Oct. 1, 1899). The number of pages varies from 4 to 8 of $11\frac{1}{2}'' \times 6\frac{3}{4}''$, lithographed in a rather large and ungraceful *ta'líq*. Yearly subscription, 10 rupees in India and the Persian Gulf, 35 *qráns* in Persia and Afghánistán, 25 francs in China, Japan, Russia and Europe, and 5 mejidiyyés in Turkey.

(332)

Mufarriḥu'l-Qulúb (*The Rejoicer of Hearts*). مفرّح القلوب

A weekly newspaper published at Karáchí (Sind) in A.H. 1302–3 (= A.D. 1885) and edited by Mírzá Muḥammad Ja'far and Mírzá Muḥammad Ṣádiq of Mashhad, Persian Consul at Karáchí.

See above, No. 310, under the *Mudarris-i-Fársí*, through which alone it is known to us.

(333)

Mukáfát (*Recompense*). مكافات

A paper published in Khúy (Ázarbáyján) in A.H. 1327 (=A.D. 1909) under the editorship of Mírzá Áqá Khán Hirandí, director of the *Madrasa-i-Musáwát* ("College of Equality"). Most of the articles in this paper were from the pen of Abu'l-Ḥasan Khán, Muḥammad 'Alí-záda, entitled *Sa'ídu'l-Mamálik*, and Amír-i-Ḥishmat, who at that time held Khúy and Salmás on behalf of the Revolutionaries. Its proprietor was Mírzá Núru'lláh Yakání. In politics the paper was Revolutionary.

See Rabino, No. 195. I possess No. 5, dated the 24th of Ṣafar, A.H. 1327 (=March 18, 1909). It comprises 4 pp. of $11\frac{1}{2}'' \times 6\frac{1}{2}''$. Price of each copy, one 'Abbásí.

(334)

Maktab (*The School*). مكتب

A paper printed in Ṭihrán in A.H. 1323 (=A.D. 1905–6) under the editorship of Ḥájji Mírzá Ḥasan of Tabríz, known as *Rushdiyya*.

Not in Rabino, and not seen.

(335)

Mu'ayyad (*Aided*). مؤيّد

A paper "jelly-graphed" in Láhiján in A.H. 1325 (=A.D. 1907–8).

See Rabino, No. 196, on whose authority it is here inserted.

(336)

Mahdí Ḥammál (*Mahdí the Porter*[1]). مهدی حمّال

A paper printed in Rasht in A.H. 1328 (=A.D. 1910) under the editorship of Akbar-záda. Only one number of it appeared.

See Rabino, No. 197, on whose authority it is here inserted. The date of publication was the 16th of Ramaẓán, A.H. 1328 (=Sept. 21, 1910).

(337)

Mízán (*The Balance*). میزان

An illustrated comic paper lithographed in Ṭihrán in A.H. 1329 (=A.D. 1911) under the editorship of *Fakhru'l-Wá'iẓín* of Káshán. In politics it was Democrat.

Not in Rabino, and not seen.

(338)

Mitq (*Thought*). Միտք

A paper printed at Tabríz in the Armenian language in A.H. 1330 (=A.D. 1912) under the editorship of Alexander Dir Wartániyáns, also editor of the Persian *Fikr*. (See No. 265 *supra*.)

Not in Rabino, and not seen.

[1] Mahdí Ḥammál ("the Porter") was well known in Ṭihrán as a man of immense height, bulk and strength, and of voracious appetite. He would eat 1½ or 2 maunds of bread and cheese, and could carry the weight of a *kharwár* on his shoulders. His voracity has become proverbial.

(339)

Náṣirí. ناصری

A paper lithographed in Tabríz every ten days in A.H. 1311 (= A.D. 1893–4) under the editorship of Mullá Muḥammad *Nadím-báshí* ("Chief Courtier"), director of the Muẓaffarí College in Tabríz, and subsequently *Nadímu's-Sulṭán* and Minister of the Press. The paper was subsequently edited by *Iqbálu'l-Kuttáb*, and finally by Ḥájji Mírzá Mas'úd Khán *Ṣafá'u'l-Mamálik*, son of Ḥájji Sayyid Ḥasan *'Adlu'l-Mulk* of Tabríz. It was semi-official, and was even considered as one of the official newspapers, and continued to be published for nearly seven years. Its polemics against the Constantinople *Akhtar* ("Star," *q.v.* No. 34 *supra*) deserve attention.

See Rabino, No. 198. I possess No. 33 of the Third Year, dated the first of Ramaẓán, A.H. 1314 (=Feb. 3, 1897). It comprises 4 pp. of 12″ × 6¾″. Yearly subscription, 16 *qráns* in Persia, 4 roubles in Russia and the Caucasus, 40 piastres in Turkey, and 5 rupees in India.

(340)

Náqúr (*The Clarion*). ناقور

A paper lithographed twice a week in Iṣfahán in A.H. 1326 (= A.D. 1908–9) under the editorship of Mírzá Masíḥ Túysirkání. The comic or satirical portion of this paper, entitled *Zisht u Zíbá* ("Foul and Fair"), was written in a very agreeable literary style. In politics it was thorough-going Liberal and Constitutionalist.

See Rabino, No. 200, according to whom 25 numbers appeared in all, the first on the 21st of Dhu'l-Qa'da, A.H. 1326 (=Nov. 25, 1908). I possess No. 9, dated the 24th of Ṣafar, A.H. 1327 (=March 17, 1909). It comprises 4 pp. of 11¾″ × 6½″. Yearly subscription, 14 *qráns* in Iṣfahán, 17 *qráns* elsewhere in Persia. Lithographed in good *naskh*.

(341)

Nála-i-Millat (*The Nation's Cry*). نالهٔ ملّت

A paper lithographed in Tabríz in A.H. 1326 (= A.D. 1908–9) under the editorship of Mírzá Áqá, editor of the *Istiqlál*. In politics the paper was thorough-going Liberal and Constitutionalist.

See Rabino, No. 199. I possess No. 38 of the First Year, dated the 14th of Muḥarram, A.H. 1326 (=Feb. 17, 1908), which seems to show that the paper was founded in the latter part of A.H. 1325, not in 1326. It comprises 4 pp. of 12¼″ × 8¼″. Yearly subscription, 8 *qráns* in Tabríz, 10 *qráns* elsewhere in Persia, 4 roubles in Russia.

(342)

Náma-i-Ḥaqíqat (*The Letter of Truth*). نامهٔ حقیقت

A paper published in Ṭihrán in A.H. 1326 (= A.D. 1908–9).

Not in Rabino, and not seen.

(343)

Náma-i-Waṭan (*The Letter of the Fatherland*). نامهٔ وطن

A paper lithographed in Ḥaydarábád in the Deccan in A.H. 1326 (?) (= A.D. 1908–9) under the editorship of the *Ṣaḥḥáf-báshí*, a fugitive from Ṭihrán. The articles of this paper dealt with the supernatural, and it laid down sundry religious laws.

See Rabino, No. 201. I possess No. 7 of the Second Year, dated Ṣafar, A.H. 1326 (= March, 1908). It comprises 16 pp. of 10¼″ × 6½″, lithographed in poor *ta'líq*. No price is indicated.

(344)

Naját (*Salvation*). نجات

A newspaper printed at first once and subsequently twice a week in Ṭihrán in A.H. 1327 (= A.D. 1909), before the capture of Ṭihrán by the National Armies, under the editorship of Mírzá Muḥammad of Khurásán, editor of the paper *Ḥuqúq* ("Rights," *q.v.*), and afterwards Member of the Second National Assembly. In consequence of a somewhat Liberal article, this paper was suspended by Sa'du'd-Dawla's Cabinet, which suspension provided one of the causes which led to the attack of the National Volunteers (*Mujáhidín*) of Qazwín on Ṭihrán. After the capture of Ṭihrán it again resumed publication. In politics it was thorough-going Liberal and Constitutionalist, but not Democratic as Rabino asserts.

See Rabino, No. 202. I possess Nos. 1, 6, 15, 18 and 25, the first dated the 3rd of Jumáda ii, A.H. 1327 (= June 22, 1909), and the last the 4th of Shawwál (= Oct. 19) of the same year. Contains 4 or 8 pp. of 12¼″ × 6¾″. Yearly subscription, 10 *qráns* in Ṭihrán, 17 elsewhere in Persia, and 15 francs abroad.

(345)

Naját (*Salvation*). نجات

A "jelly-graphed" paper published in Rasht.

See Rabino, No. 203, on whose authority it is here inserted.

(346)

Naját (*Salvation*). نجات

A paper printed in Khúy in A.H. 1329 (=A.D. 1911). In politics it was Democratic.

See Rabino, No. 204. Not seen by the translator.

(347)

Naját-i-Waṭan (*The Country's Salvation*). نجات وطن

A paper published in Iṣfahán in A.H. 1327 (= A.D. 1909).

See Rabino, No. 205, on whose authority it is here inserted. He adds that not more than seven or eight numbers were published.

(348)

Najaf. نجف

A weekly paper printed at Najaf in A.H. 1328 (=A.D. 1910) under the editorship of Sayyid Muslim Zawín-záda and Ḥájji Muḥammad ibn Ḥájji Ḥusayn, and owned by Shaykh Ḥusayn of Ṭihrán.

See Rabino, No. 206. I possess No. 6, dated the 16th of Jumáda i, A.H. 1328 (=May 26, 1910). It comprises 8 pp. of 9½″ × 6½″. Yearly subscription, 25 piastres in Najaf, 30 piastres elsewhere in Turkey, 15 *qráns* in Persia, and 8 francs abroad.

(349)

Najm-i-Bákhtar (*The Star of the West*). نجم باختر

See above under *Payámbar-i-Bákhtar* ("The Prophet of the West"), No. 96 *supra*.

See Rabino, No. 207. It was published at Washington.

(350)

Nidá-yi-Rasht (*The Voice of Rasht*). ندای رشت

A paper printed in Rasht in A.H. 1329 (=A.D. 1911). Only two numbers of it appeared, the first, according to Rabino, on the 28th of Rabí' i, A.H. 1329 (= March 29, 1911), and the second on the 2nd of Rabí' ii (April 2) of the same year.

See Rabino, No. 208.

(351)

Nidá-yi-Islám (*The Voice of Islám*). ندای اسلام

A weekly newspaper lithographed at Shíráz in A.H. 1325 (=A.D. 1907–8) under the editorship of Sayyid Ẓiyá'u'd-Dín-i-

Ṭabáṭabá'í of Yazd, editor of the newspapers *Sharq* and *Barq* (*q.v.*).

See Rabino, No. 209. I possess Nos. 7, 14, and 25. The first is dated the 11th of Ṣafar, A.H. 1325 (=March 26, 1907). Each number consists of from 4 to 8 pp. of 10" × 7", lithographed (the earlier numbers in green ink) in a large and good *naskh*. Yearly subscription, 30 *qráns* in Shíráz, 36 *qráns* elsewhere in Persia, and 40 *qráns* abroad.

(352)

Nidá-yi-Waṭan (*The Country's Call*). ندای وطن

A weekly, subsequently bi-weekly, and finally, daily paper printed at Ṭihrán in A.H. 1324 (= A.D. 1906–7) under the editorship of Majdu'l-Islám of Kirmán, editor of the newspapers *Kashgúl* and *Muḥákamát* (*q.v.*).

See Rabino, No. 210, who gives the 11th of Dhu'l-Qa'da, A.H. 1324 (=Dec. 27, 1906) as the date of first issue. I possess a fairly complete set. Each number comprises from 4 to 8 pp. of $11\frac{1}{2}'' \times 6\frac{3}{4}''$. Yearly subscription, 30 *qráns* in Ṭihrán, 36 *qráns* elsewhere in Persia, 5 mejidiyyés in Turkey and Egypt, 17 francs in America and Europe, 10 roubles in Russia, and 15 rupees in India.

(353)

Nidá-yi-Janúb (*The Voice of the South*). ندای جنوب

Of this paper, which is not mentioned either by Mírzá Muḥammad 'Alí "Tarbiyat" or by Rabino, I possess one copy, No. 2, dated the 22nd of Dhu'l-Qa'da, A.H. 1329 (= Nov. 15, 1911). It comprises 8 pp. of $15'' \times 8\frac{1}{4}''$, and was printed in Ṭihrán. Proprietor and chief contributor, Mírzá Báqir Khán, teacher and translator, of Tabríz; responsible editor, Muḥammad Báqir Khán Tangistání. Yearly subscription, 18 *qráns* in Ṭihrán, 20 *qráns* elsewhere in Persia, and 22 *qráns* abroad. The paper is described in the title as founded in Shawwál, A.H. 1329 (= Sept.–Oct., 1911).

(354)

Nasím-i-Shimál (*The Breeze of the North*). نسیم شمال

A paper printed in Rasht in A.H. 1325 (= A.D. 1907–8) under the editorship of Sayyid-Ashraf. This was one of the best literary papers, and in particular contained many notable poems, both serious and satirical.

See Rabino, No. 211, according to whom it appeared at irregular intervals, the first issue on the 2nd of Sha'bán, A.H. 1325 (=Sept. 10, 1907), and the "Third Year" began with No. 69. I possess Nos. 9–12, 14, 16, 18, 19, 22, 23, 27, 33, 45, 48; Nos. 5 and 7 of the Third Year, No. 10 (dated the 2nd of Sha'bán, A.H. 1329 =July 29, 1911), and Nos. 12–14, 16. The numbering is somewhat erratic, and the intervals of publication were very irregular.

(355)

Naẓmiyya (*The Police*). نظميّه

A weekly illustrated newspaper lithographed in Tabríz in A.H. 1326 (=A.D. 1908–9) under the editorship of Mashhadí Maḥmúd Isgandání. The first number of it contains the portrait of *Ijlálu'l-Mulk*, Chief of the Police at Tabríz.

See Rabino, No. 212, who gives the name of the proprietor as Muḥammad 'Alí, and states that the first issue was on the 23rd of Rabí' i, A.H. 1326 (=April 25, 1908). I possess No. 1, which is lithographed in an indifferent *ta'líq*, and comprises 4 pp. of 12¾" × 6¾". Yearly subscription, 8 *qráns* in Tabríz, 10 *qráns* elsewhere in Persia.

(356)

Naqsh-i-Jahán (*The Picture of the World*). نقش جهان

An illustrated weekly paper lithographed in Iṣfahán in A.H. 1325 (=A.D. 1907–8), and published by the office of the newspaper *Iṣfahán*. (See No. 49 *supra*.)

See Rabino, No. 213, who gives the date of No. 1 as the 23rd of Shawwál, A.H. 1325 (=Nov. 29, 1907). I possess No. 1, which comprises 4 pp. of 11¾" × 6", lithographed in *ta'líq*, with two cartoons. Yearly subscription, 12 *qráns* in Iṣfahán.

(357)

Naw-Bahár (*Early Spring*). نوبهار

A paper printed in Mashhad twice a week in A.H. 1328 (= A.D. 1910), of which No. 1 was dated the 9th of Shawwál (= Oct. 14, 1910) of that year, under the editorship of the *Maliku'sh-Shu'ará* ("King of the Poets"), who signed under the *nom de guerre* of "M. Bahár." This paper had a special importance on account of its extreme boldness and fiery denunciations, especially against the Russian aggressions. Finally, in consequence of the complaints of the Russian Legation in Ṭihrán, the Ministry for Foreign Affairs ordered its suppression, but it subsequently resumed publication under the title of *Táza Bahár*. (See No. 98 *supra*.) In politics this paper was Democrat.

See Rabino, No. 214. I possess Nos. 1, 28, 39 and 48, the first dated as above, the last the 12th of Jumáda i, A.H. 1329 (=May 11, 1911). Each comprises 4 pp. of 16¼″ × 10½″. Yearly subscription, 25 *qráns* in Mashhad, 30 *qráns* elsewhere in Persia, 6 roubles abroad.

(358)

Naw-rúz (*New Year's Day*). نوروز

A weekly paper lithographed in Ṭihrán in A.H. 1320 (= A.D. 1902–3), edited by *Náẓimu'l-Islám* of Kirmán, also editor of the *Kawkib-i-durri-yi-Náṣirí* (see No. 286 *supra*), and written by Mírzá Káẓim Khán of Kirmán.

See Rabino, No. 215, who gives the date of first issue as the 22nd of Dhu'l-Ḥijja, A.H. 1320 (=March 22, 1903). I do not possess a copy.

(359)

Naw-rúz (*New Year's Day*). نوروز

A paper lithographed in Iṣfahán in A.H. 1325 (=A.D. 1907–8). See Rabino, No. 216, on whose authority it is here inserted.

(360)

Naw'-i-Bashar (*The Human Race*). نوع بشر

A paper printed in Rasht twice a week in A.H. 1329 (= A.D. 1911).

See Rabino, No. 217, who says that only six numbers appeared, the first on the 25th of Rabí' ii, A.H. 1329 (=April 25, 1911), and the last on the 23rd of Jumáda i (=May 22) of the same year. I possess Nos. 1, 3 and 6. Each comprises 4 pp. of 11¾″ × 6¾″. Yearly subscription, 15 *qráns* in Rasht, and the same elsewhere plus postage.

(361)

Nayyir-i-A'ẓam (*The Greater Luminary*). نيّر اعظم

A paper printed in Ṭihrán twice a week in A.H. 1325 (= A.D. 1907), under the editorship of the *Mu'ínu'l-'Ulamá* of Iṣfahán, who was afterwards suspected of favouring the Reaction, and, after the capture of Ṭihrán by the Nationalists (in July, 1909), was imprisoned for nearly a year with other political offenders.

See Rabino, No. 218. I possess Nos. 2 and 13, of which the former is dated the 16th of Ramaẓán, A.H. 1325 (=Oct. 23, 1907), and the latter the 6th of Dhu'l-Qa'da (=Dec. 11) of the same year. Each comprises 4 pp. of 12″ × 7″. Yearly subscription, 14 *qráns* in Ṭihrán, 17 *qráns* elsewhere in Persia, and 11 francs abroad.

(362)

Waṭan (*Fatherland*). وطن

A weekly paper printed, and afterwards lithographed, in Ṭihrán in A.H. 1324 (=A.D. 1906–7).

See Rabino, No. 219. I possess Nos. 3 and 10, dated Jan. 27 and April 22 respectively, both of which are printed; and Nos. 17, 20, 21 and 22, all of which are lithographed. The last number is dated the 12th of Ramaẓán, A.H. 1325 (=Oct. 19, 1907). Each number comprises 4 pp. of 11″ × 6¾″. Yearly subscription, 16 *qráns*.

(363)

Waṭan dili (*The Mother Tongue*). وطن دلی

This paper, mentioned only by Rabino (No. 220), was lithographed at Tabríz in the Ázarbáyjání Turkish language.

I possess one (probably incomplete) copy, consisting of a single sheet, lithographed on both sides in a good, clear *naskh*, and bearing this title at the top of p. 1, but no date, subscription price, or other particulars. The sheet measures 12″ × 6¾″. I am doubtful from its appearance whether it is a newspaper at all, in the proper sense of the word, and not rather an isolated sheet. It contains one long and complete article or appeal.

(364)

Waqt (*Time*). وقت

A full-sized daily paper printed in Ṭihrán in A.H. 1328 (= A.D. 1910) under the editorship of Mírzá Ḥusayn Khán Kasmá'í. It was a strong supporter of the Sipahdár's Cabinet, and the Moderates, and used to attack with vehemence the *Írán-i-Naw* (see No. 77 *supra*) and the Opposition (*i.e.* the Democrats), generally striving to cast suspicion on their orthodoxy in matters of Religion and Law. It had a comic or satirical section entitled *Darí-Warí*, which is almost unintelligible. In politics it was Moderate.

See Rabino, No. 221, who says that in all 66 numbers were published, the first on the 21st of Rabí' i, A.H. 1328 (=April 2, 1910), and the last on the 11th of Jumáda ii (=June 20) of the same year. I possess Nos. 1–46, the first, a single sheet printed on one side only, being dated 11 days earlier than Rabino says (March 22, 1910), and the last May 26 of the same year. Most of the numbers comprise 4 pp. of 21½″ × 14¼″. Yearly subscription, 50 *qráns* in Ṭihrán, 60 *qráns* elsewhere in Persia, and 80 *qráns* abroad.

(365)

Hidáyat (*Guidance*). هدایت

A weekly paper printed in Ṭihrán in A.H. 1325 (=A.D. 1907) under the editorship of Mírzá Muḥammad of Ṭihrán.

See Rabino, No. 222, according to whom it first appeared on the 7th of Rajab, A.H. 1325 (=Aug. 14, 1907). This is correct, but the paper seems to have been suppressed or suspended for eight months immediately afterwards, for No. 2 is dated the 5th of Rabí' i, A.H. 1326 (=April 7, 1908). I possess Nos. 1, 2 and 4. Each comprises 4 pp. of 12¼" × 7". Yearly subscription, 34 *qráns* in Ṭihrán, 40 *qráns* in the provinces, 9 roubles in Russia and the Caucasus, and 25 francs in other foreign countries.

(366)

Hidáyat (*Guidance*). هدایت

A weekly paper lithographed in Qazwín in A.H. 1326 (=A.D. 1908–9) under the editorship of Mír Hádí Shaykhu'l-Islámí.

See Rabino, No. 223. I possess Nos. 2 and 4, dated respectively the 3rd and the 20th of Rabí' i, A.H. 1326 (=April 5 and 22, 1908). Each comprises 4 pp. of 12½" × 7". Yearly subscription, 8 *qráns* in Qazwín, 10 *qráns* elsewhere in Persia, 1½ mejidiyyés in Turkey and Egypt, 2 roubles in Russia and the Caucasus, and 6 francs in Europe and America.

(367)

همه‌دان

Hama-dán (*All-knowing*—a word-play on *Hamadán*, the well-known city).

A weekly paper printed at Hamadán in A.H. 1325 (=A.D. 1907–8) under the editorship of Ḥájji Ḥusayn.

See Rabino, No. 224, who states that No. 18 was dated the 19th of Shawwál, A.H. 1325 (=Nov. 25, 1907). I do not possess a copy.

(368)

Hawá wa Hawas (*Freak and Fancy*). هوا و هوس

A paper "jelly-graphed" in Láhiján in A.H. 1325 (=A.D. 1907–8) under the editorship of Ḥájji Ḥusayn.

See Rabino, No. 225, on whose authority it is here inserted. I have not seen it.

(369)

Yádigár-i-Inqiláb (*Memorial of the Revolution*). یادگار انقلاب

A paper lithographed in Qazwín twice a week in A.H. 1327 (= A.D. 1909) under the editorship of the *Mu'tamadu'l-Islám* of

Rasht during the sojourn of the National Volunteers (*Mujáhidín*) at that place. After the Conquest of Ṭihrán, the paper was transferred thither and published there. In politics it was Revolutionary.

See Rabino, No. 226. I possess Nos. 1, 2 and 5, dated the 1st, 5th and 18th of Jumáda ii, A.H. 1327 (=June 20, June 24 and July 7, 1909). Each number comprises 4 pp. of 11¾″ × 6¾″. Price in Qazwín, 100 *dínárs* ($\frac{1}{10}$ of a *qrán*) a copy. Elsewhere in Persia, 12 *qráns* a year.

(370)

Yádigár-i-Inqiláb (*Memorial of the Revolution*). یادگار انقلاب

A paper printed in Ṭihrán in A.H. 1327 (= A.D. 1909) under the editorship of the above-mentioned *Mu'tamadu'l-Islám* of Rasht.

See Rabino, No. 226. I possess Nos. 9, 10, 12, 17, 18 and 20, the first dated the 24th of Rajab, the last the 15th of Dhu'l-Qa'da, A.H. 1327 (=Aug. 11, 1909, and Nov. 28, 1909, respectively). Each number contains 4 pp. of 11½″ × 6¾″. Yearly subscription, 12 *qráns* in Ṭihrán, 15 *qráns* elsewhere in Persia, 3 roubles in Russia, and 8 francs in Europe.

(371)

Yádigár-i-Janúb (*Memorial of the South*). یادگار جنوب

A weekly paper printed in Ṭihrán in A.H. 1329 (= A.D. 1911).

Not in Rabino, and not seen.

MODERNISING INFLUENCES IN THE PERSIAN PRESS OTHER THAN MAGAZINES AND JOURNALS.

Since the most important effect of the Press in every country is the awakening of political and literary opinion amongst the people, it is not inappropriate that we should conclude with a brief survey of the relations which exist between the early activities of the Press in Persia, and the latest movement of renascence and renovation.

That portion of this subject which is connected with periodical publications, *i.e.* newspapers and magazines, has been discussed in the preceding section, and we shall here speak only of the effects of certain books and pamphlets which were operative in bringing about this awakening of thought, most of which were either translations of European books, or were inspired by European civilization and culture, and which acted for the most part by means of a gradual and peaceful progress.

Amongst printed books of this class the first place must be assigned to the earlier scientific and technical works, whether translated or compiled, published in the early days of the foundation of the State College, or *Dáru'l-Funún*, at Ṭihrán (when a large number of European teachers were imported to give instruction there and in the Military College) to be used for teaching purposes; to which must be added a few earlier books ranging from the time of Prince 'Abbás Mírzá *Ná'ibu's-Salṭana* to that period. The greater number of these books were composed by these new European teachers or the old Persian teachers of the College, such as Lieut. Krziz, M. Buhler, M. Lemaire, M. Vauvillier, Dr Polak, Dr Albu, M. Nicolas, M. Richard, M. Andreini, and M. Gasteiger of the former[1], and Ḥájji Najmu'd-Dawla, Mírzá Zakí of Mázandarán, Mírzá Káẓim, Instructor in

[1] I am indebted to General Sir A. Houtum Schindler, K.C.I.E., for the identification of these gentlemen and for particulars concerning them. Artillery Lieut. Krziz and Dr Polak were two of the seven Austrians brought to Persia in 1851. The former returned to Europe in 1859, the latter in 1860. Capitaine Alexandre Buhler,

Natural Sciences, 'Alí Khán *Náẓimu'l-'Ulúm*, Zaká'u'l-Mulk and others of the latter./ As an appendix to this brief sketch we shall give a partial and incomplete table of the most important of these new scientific and literary works. By the special kindness of H.E. Riẓá-qulí Khán, General Superintendent of the Ministry of Sciences and of the *Dáru'l-Funún* College (son of Nayyiru'l-Mulk, and grandson of the celebrated Riẓá-qulí Khán *Lala-báshi*) I am enabled to include in this table a list of printed books composed by the older and younger writers of the Government Colleges (such as the *Dáru'l-Funún* and the Military and Political Colleges). The remaining items I have myself supplied, and the result I now put forward in the following pages so as to leave a foundation, poor and defective though it may be, which others devoted to the collecting of such information and interested in the study of the history of books and arts, may render more complete and comprehensive.

Amongst the more celebrated of the older Persian writers of this class were the late Ḥájji Najmu'd-Dawla (Mírzá 'Abdu'l-Ghaffár, son of Mírzá 'Alí Muḥammad of Iṣfahán) the Chief Astrologer (*Munajjim-báshi*), who was entitled "Professor of all the exact Sciences" in the *Dáru'l-Funún* College, and who was the author of numerous published Works on the Mathematical and Natural Sciences. He only died recently, in A.H. 1328 (= A.D. 1910), his age, according to current report, exceeding 90 years.

11 Régiment de Génie, came to Persia in 1855, captured Herát in Nov. 1856, taught military science at the College, and took part in many expeditions. He died, a General of the First Class, in 1887. M. Albert Lemaire was sent to Persia by the French Government in 1868 to teach military music. He died in 1907. M. Felix Vauvillier came to Persia in 1865 on behalf of a French Syndicate for a railway, but was afterwards employed by the Persian Government in constructing an Arsenal, and afterwards as teacher of Mineralogy at the College. He retired on a pension about 1900 and died a few years later. Dr Albu of Berlin was engaged by the Mukhbiru'd-Dawla for the College in 1882. He returned to Europe after 8 or 9 years of teaching and private practice in Persia. M. J. B. Nicolas, the translator of 'Umar Khayyám, was the father of M. Alphonse Nicolas, now French Consul at Tabríz. M. Richard came to Persia in 1844 or 1846, fell in love with a Kurdish girl, and turned Musulmán in order to marry her. M. F. Andreini was a Tuscan volunteer in the 1848 revolutionary movements, fled to Constantinople in 1849, entered the service of the Persian Government in 1852, and died in 1894. M. Gasteiger, an Austrian adventurer, came to Persia in the early sixties, was engaged on various engineering works and resigned in 1889. He died soon afterwards.

Another was Muḥammad Ḥasan Khán *I'timádu's-Salṭana* (son of Ḥájji 'Alí Khán, entitled *Ḥájibu'd-Dawla*, of Marágha), Minister of the Press, who contributed many additions to the *Sál-námas* or "Year Books." Although, according to the statements of credible authorities, he himself was devoid of any profound knowledge or scholarship, and merely caused these works to be written under his supervision and the control of the Ministry of the Press by those men of learning whom he collected from every quarter, afterwards causing their writings to be published in his own name, yet since it was under his name that these books appeared, they are commonly known as his, and must therefore necessarily be described as such.

Another was Riẓá-qulí Khán of Shíráz, known as *Lala-báshi*, and poetically named *Hidáyat* (father of the present *Nayyiru'l-Mulk*), whose literary works are some of the most important which have appeared in Persia in the last century.

Others are the late Mírzá Muḥammad Ḥusayn *Zaká'u'l-Mulk* and his son Mírzá Muḥammad 'Alí Khán, the present *Zaká'u'l-Mulk*, who co-operated in the translation and compilation of many works.

Then mention must be made of certain well-known doctors, such as Dr Muḥammad of Kirmánsháh, Dr Riẓá, Dr Abu'l-Ḥasan Khán, Dr 'Alí, and others, who have left as memorials of their learning and energy numerous works on Anatomy, Medicine, and other Natural Sciences.

After these mention may be made of the following (not in chronological order). Mírzá Yúsuf Khán *Mustasháru'd-Dawla* of Tabríz; Ḥájji Mírzá 'Abdu'r-Raḥím *Najjár-záda* of Tabríz, known as "Táliboff"; Mírzá Ḥabíb of Iṣfahán, long resident in Constantinople; Ḥájji Muḥammad Ṭáhir Mírzá (the father of the present Kafílu'd-Dawla and the grandfather of Sulaymán Mírzá, Member of the Second National Assembly); Mírzá Taqí Khán of Káshán; Mírzá Áqá Khán of Kirmán, and others. Amongst the beneficent agencies which rendered valuable services to the cause of education was the Society for the publication of books (*Shirkat-i-ṭab'-i-kutub*) in Ṭihrán, which was founded about A.H. 1320 (= A.D. 1902) or a little earlier, and published a great many important works. One of the most active members of this was Ḥájji Mírzá Yaḥyá of Dawlatábád.

Here is subjoined a brief list of the scientific, literary and historical publications of recent times, printed in Persia or abroad since the introduction of the art of printing into that country[1].

1. *List of printed books composed or compiled by the older and more recent teachers of the* Dáru'l-Funún *College.*

1. Military treatise on the science of Artillery, by Mírzá Zakí of Mázandarán.

2. Natural Philosophy and Mechanics, by the same.

3. Geography, by the same.

4. Military treatise on the science of Artillery, by M. Nicolas.

5. Ditto, by M. Buhler.

6. Mathematics, by Lieut. Krziz.

7. Algebra, by the same.

8. Surgery, by Dr Polak.

9. The Science of Artillery and Fortification, by Lieut. Krziz.

10. *Mízánu'l-Ḥisáb* (Arithmetic), by Mírzá Zakí.

11. Therapeutics, by Dr Abu'l-Ḥasan Khán.

12. Physiology, by Dr Albu.

13. The Science of Music, by M. Lemaire.

14. Principles of Chemistry, by the late Mírzá Káẓim.

15. Anatomy, by Dr 'Alí *Ra'ísu'l-Aṭibbá.*

16. Medical Dictionary, by Dr J. L. Schlimmer, published in 1874.

17. Elementary Arithmetic, by Mírzá 'Abdu'l-Ghaffár *Najmu'd-Dawla.* Its proper title is *Bidáyatu'l-Ḥisáb.*

18. *Kifáyatu'l-Ḥisáb,* a Manual of Arithmetic, by the same.

19. *Wasíṭu'l-Ḥisáb,* a more advanced Manual of the same, by the same.

[1] We shall not mention here the old books and treatises which have been printed or published during this period, but perhaps on a future occasion we may succeed in compiling a complete catalogue of all Persian printed and lithographed books, such as the American Dr Edward Van Dyck has done for Arabic printed books, under the title of *Iktifá'u'l-Qunú' bi-má huwa maṭbú'.*

20. *Niháyatu'l-Ḥisáb*, a still more advanced Manual, by the same.

21. Detailed Geometry and Abridged Geometry, by the same.

22. Geography with Atlas, by the same.

23. Algebra, by the same.

24. Natural History, by the same.

25. Translation of *Télémaque*, by the same.

✓ 26. French-Persian Dictionary, by Mírzá 'Alí Akbar Khán *Muzayyinu'd-Dawla Naqqásh-báshi.*

✓ 27. French-Persian Dialogues, by the same.

✓ 28. French Verbs, explained in Persian, by the same.

29. Elementary and secondary Geometry, by Mírzá Riẓá Khán *Muhandisu'l-Mulk.*

30. Elementary and secondary Geography, by the same.

31. Solution of Algebraical Problems, by the same.

32. Geographical projections (*Jahán-numá-yi-musaṭṭaḥa*) and Map of Persia, by the same.

33. Maps of America and Africa, by the same.

34. Chemistry, by Mírzá Maḥmúd Khán.

35. Arithmetic according to the four fundamental rules, by Mírzá Asadu'lláh Khán *Muhandisu's-Sulṭán.*

36. Elementary Geometry, by the same.

37. Elementary Geography, by the same.

38. Method of composition, by M. Richard.

39. Grammar of composition, by the same.

40. Translation of ماملیان, by the same.

41. *Uṣúl-i-'Ilm-i-Jabr*, on Algebra, by Áqá Khán *Muḥásibu'd-Dawla.*

42. Geography, by the same.

43. Geography of Muḥammad Ṣafí Khán *Náẓimu'l-'Ulúm.*

44. Pocket Atlas, by Sulaymán Khán *Iḥtisábu'l-Mulk.*

45. Elementary History of the Eastern Nations and of Greece, by Mírzá 'Alí Khán *Mutarjimu's-Salṭana.*

2. *List of Books published by the teachers of the Political College.*

46. History of Rome, by *Zaká'u'l-Mulk.*

47. Short history of Greece, translated by *Nuṣratu's-Sulṭán.*

48. History of Eastern Nations, translated by *Zaká'u'l-Mulk.*

49. Wealth, translated by the same.

50. Fundamental Rights, translated by the same.

51. *Ta'ríkh-i-mukhtaṣar-i-Írán.* History of Persia, by the same.

52. History of Greece, translated by Sayyid 'Alí Khán.

53. Fundamentàl Rights, by *Manṣúru's-Salṭana.*

54. International Rights, by *Mushíru'd-Dawla.*

3. *List of printed books composed or compiled by the older and more recent teachers of the Military College.*

55. Movement of troops, translated by M. Andreini.

56. Science of Fortification, translated by Mírzá 'Alí Akbar Khán, Engineer, of Shíráz.

57. Movement of troops, according to the English method, translated by Bahrám Khán Qájár.

58. Artillery drill with guns of 8·9 centimetres.

59. Austrian centimetry.

60. The Soldier's Whole Duty, translated by M. Gasteiger and Karím Khán.

61. Drill Book, translated by the same.

62. Drill Book.

63. Infantry formations: Austrian method, translated by Karím Khán.

64. Military Drill Book, translated by M. Gasteiger and Karím Khán.

65. General Regulations and Duties of the Barracks (translator unknown).

4. *Miscellaneous Works, translated and original.*

66. *History of Peter the Great of Russia*
67. ,, ,, *Charles XII of Sweden*
68. ,, ,, *Alexander*

} by Voltaire, translated by command of 'Abbás Mírzá *Ná'ibu's-Salṭana.*

69. *Jám-i-Jam* ("the World-showing Goblet of Jamshíd"), on Geography, translated by Farhád Mírzá *Mu'tamadu'd-Dawla,* son of 'Abbás Mírzá *Ná'ibu's-Salṭana.* [It was published about

1850, and appears to be a translation of William Pinnock's Geography.]

70. *Jahán-numá* ("the World-shower") or Geography, by Mírzá Rafá'íl.

71. *Refutation of the Materialists*, by Sayyid Jamálu'd-Dín al-Afghání.

72. *Ḥájji Bábá*, by Sir Robert Morier, translated by Shaykh Aḥmad Rúḥí of Kirmán.

73. *History of Persia*, by Sir John Malcolm, translated by Mírzá Ḥayrat.

74. *Ajmalu't-Tawáríkh*, a short history of Persia, by Riẓá-qulí Khán *Lala-báshi*, *Amíru'sh-Shu'ará*, poetically named *Hidáyat*.

75. *Safar-náma-i-Khwárazm*, by the same, being an account of his embassy to Khwárazm or Khiva. [Published by Leroux of Paris in 1879, with translation and annotations by the late M. Charles Schefer.]

76. Supplement to Mírkhwánd's Universal History, the *Rawẓatu'ṣ-Ṣafá* (composed about A.D. 1500) carrying the history down to the middle of the nineteenth century, also by the above-mentioned Riẓá-qulí Khán.

77. The *Gulistán-i-Iram* ("Rose-garden of Iram") or *Bektásh-náma*, an imaginative romance, by the same.

78. *Majma'u'l-Fuṣaḥá* ("the Assembly of the Eloquent"), a great Anthology and Biography of Persian Poets in two folio volumes, by the same.

79. *Farhang-i-Anjuman-árá-yi-Náṣirí*, a large dictionary of Persian words explained in Persian, by the same.

80. The *Khán of Lankurán*, *Musta'lí Sháh the Wizard*, and other national plays, descriptive of the condition of Persia and the Caucasus, in seven volumes, by Mírzá Fatḥ-'Alí Ákhundoff of Tiflis, translated by Mírzá Ja'far of Qarája Dágh.

81. *Yak Kalima* ("One Word"), comparing the Rights of Man and the Laws of Europe with the *Qur'án* and the Traditions, by Mírzá Yúsuf Khán *Mustasháru'd-Dawla* of Tabríz.

82. *Ganjína-i-Dánish* ("the Treasury of Knowledge"), Elementary Scientific Dialogues, for Children, by the same.

83. *The Strata of the Earth*, on Geology, translated from the Turkish, by the same.

84. *Treatise on the Potato*, how to plant it and how to raise it in a scientific manner, by the same.

85. *Ḥadá'iqu'ṭ-Ṭabí'at* ("Gardens of Nature"), on Natural Philosophy and Astronomy, by Mírzá Taqí Khán of Káshán.

86. *Education*, by the same.

87. *The Three Musketeers* of Alexandre Dumas, translated by Muḥammad Ṭáhir Mírzá.

88. *The Count of Monte Cristo* of Alexandre Dumas, translated by the same.

89. *La Reine Margot* of Alexandre Dumas, translated by the same.

90. *Louis XIV* of Alexandre Dumas, translated by the same.

91. *Louis XV* of Alexandre Dumas, translated by the same.

92. *Kitáb-i-Aḥmad; yá, Safína-i-Tálibí*, containing scientific and ethical Dialogues for children, by Mullá 'Abdu'r-Raḥím "Ṭáliboff" of Tabríz, 2 volumes.

93. *The New Astronomy* of Flammarion, translated by the above "Ṭáliboff."

94. *Natural Philosophy*, by the above "Ṭáliboff."

95. *Nukhba-i-Sipihrí* ("the Celestial Choice"), on the life of the Prophet, abridged from the *Násikhu't-Tawáríkh* (see *infra*), by "Ṭáliboff."

96. *Masáliku'l-Muḥsinín* ("Ways of Well-doers"), a romance containing scientific and political matters, by "Ṭáliboff."

97. *Masá'ilu'l-Ḥayát* ("Problems of Life"), dealing with sundry scientific and political matters, by "Ṭáliboff."

98. *Ázádí chi chíz-ast?* ("What is Freedom?"), by "Ṭáliboff."

99. *Pand-náma-i-Márkús* ("Counsels of Marcus Aurelius"), translated by "Ṭáliboff."

100. *Násikhu't-Tawáríkh* ("the Abrogator of Histories"), an immense general history, carried down to about A.D. 1857, by Mírzá Taqí, poetically named *Sipihr*, and entitled *Lisánu'l-Mulk* ("the Tongue of the Kingdom").

101. *Baráhínu'l-'Ajam* ("Proofs of the Persians"), on Literature and Prosody, by the same.

102. *Le Médecin malgré lui*, translated from the French of Molière.

103. *Le Misanthrope*, translated into verse from the French of Molière.

104. *L'Âne*, translated from the French of Molière.

105. *Mir'átu'l-'Álam* ("Mirror of the World"), a work on Geography, by *'Imádu's-Salṭana.*

106. Náṣiru'd-Dín Sháh's Journals of his Travels in Europe, in 3 volumes.

107. Muẓaffaru'd-Dín Sháh's Journals of his Travels in Europe, in 4 volumes.

108. *History of Nádir Sháh*, translated from the English by Abu'l-Qásim Khán *Náṣiru'l-Mulk* (the present Regent).

109. *Ittiḥádu'l-Islám* ("the Union of Islám"), by Ḥájji Shaykhu'r-Ra'ís.

110. *Tracts*, by Malkom Khán.

111. *Uṣúl-i-Maẓ-hab-i-Díwániyán* ("Principles of the Courtiers' Way"), by Malkom Khán.

112. Literary compositions (*Munshá'át*) of the Amír Niẓám, edited by Ḥasan 'Alí Khán of Garrús.

113. *Baththu'sh-Shakwá* ("the Preferring of our Plaint"), translated by Mírzá 'Alí *Thiqatu'l-Islám* of Tabríz.

114. "The Adventures of a Frigate," translated by *Ẓiyá'u'l-'Ulamá* of Tabríz.

115. "History of the Awakening of the Persians" (the Introduction and Vols. I and II have thus far been published), by *Náẓimu'l-Islám* of Kirmán.

116. "The Magician's Secret," translated by Mahdí Khán *Mukarramu'd-Dawla*, son of Ḥájji Mírzá Rafí' *Niẓámu'l-'Ulamá.*

117. *Bustánu's-Siyáḥat* ("Garden of Travel"), by Ḥájj Zaynu'l-'Ábidín of Shírwán.

118. *Ta'ríkh-i-Guzída* ("the Select History," a contemporary homonym of the well-known fourteenth-century work of that name, with which it must not be confounded), by Firídún Malkom, the son of Prince Malkom Khán *Náẓimu'd-Dawla.*

119. An illustrated translation of Stanley's Travels in Central Africa, the illustrations by *Kamálu'l-Mulk.*

120. *Átháru'l-'Ajam* ("Monuments of the Persians"), a

magazine containing some information about the ancient monuments of Persia, as well as about Persian literature and poetry.

121. *Pírúz nigárish-i-Párst*, an Epistolary Manual containing letters of all sorts composed in pure Persian, by Mírzá Riẓá Khán Bigishlú of Qazwín, Chargé d'Affaires and Councillor of the Persian Embassy at Constantinople.

122. *Alif-bá-yi-Bihrúzí*, on the reform of the Persian Alphabet, by the same writer as the last, also written in pure Persian.

123. *Ẓád u búm* ("Native Land"), on the historical and actual Geography of Persia, by Mírzá Muḥammad 'Alí Khán "Tarbiyat," the Author of this treatise.

124. *Náma-i-Khusrawán* ("the Book of Princes"), in 3 vols., a History of Ancient Persia, written in pure Persian, by Jalálu'd-Dín Mírzá, son of Fatḥ-'Alí Sháh.

125. *Ḥaqíqatu'l-'Álam* ("the Truth of the World"), by the above.

126. *'Anáṣiru'l-Aḥádíth* ("Elements of Events"), on the Science of the new Natural Philosophy, with something about Magic, by Mírzá Ḥasan Jawzá.

127. *Búsa-i-'Azrá* ("the Virgin's Kiss"), translated.

128. *Ghará'ib-i-'Awá'id-i-Milal* ("Strange Customs of diverse Peoples"), by Mírzá Ḥabíb of Iṣfahán.

129. *Dastúr-i-Sukhan* ("Model of Speech"), on Persian and Arabic Grammar, by the above.

130. *Dabistán-i-Pársí* ("the Persian School"), on Persian Accidence and Syntax, by the above.

131. "History of Wilhelm," a history of the last epoch in Germany, translated.

132. *Shams-i-Ṭáli'* ("the Rising Sun"), on the condition and recent developments of Japan, and its war with Russia, by Máṭá'ús Khán.

133. Treatise on Astronomy, by Mírzá Maḥmúd Khán *Musháwiru'l-Mulk*.

134. Geography.

135. Biography of the Amír 'Abdu'r-Raḥmán Khán of Afghánistán.

136. History of the Afgháns, by *I'tiẓadu's-Salṭana*, Minister of Sciences.

137. History of Napoleon the Great, translated by the above.

138. Jules Verne's *Round the World in eighty days*, translated by *Zaká'u'l-Mulk*.

139. Jules Verne's *Captain Hatteras*, translated by the same.

140. *Kulba-i-Hindí*, translated from Bernardin de Saint-Pierre's *La Chaumière Indienne* by the same.

141. *'Ishq u 'Iffat*, translated from Bernardin de Saint-Pierre's "Love and Virtue" by the same.

142. *Jám-i-Jam* ("the World-revealing Goblet of Jamshíd"), an account of travels in India, by Sayyid 'Alí Khán *Wiqáru'l-Mulk*.

143. "Conversations of an Indian traveller," a political work, published by the *Ḥablu'l-Matín* office.

144. *Siyáḥat-náma-i-Ibráhím Beg* (3 vols.), a clever satire on the methods of the old *régime* in Persia, by Ḥájji Zaynu'l-'Ábidín of Marágha. The first volume has been translated into German under the title of *Reisebuch des Ibrâhîm Beg*.

145. *Sálár-náma* ("Book of Princes"), in verse, on the model of the *Sháh-náma* of Firdawsí, by Mírzá Áqá Khán of Kirmán.

146. *History of Persia*, by the same.

147. *Gil Blas*, translated by Dr Muḥammad of Kirmánsháh.

148. *Robinson* [*Crusoe*], translated by Mírzá Muḥammad 'Alí Khán of Tabríz, son of Ḥájji Mírzá 'Abdu'lláh, the physician, of Khúy.

149. Collection of Treaties concluded between Persia and other States, by Mírzá Ḥusayn Khán *Mu'tamanu'l-Mulk*, son of Mírzá Naṣru'lláh Khán *Mushíru'd-Dawla*.

Works by Muḥammad Ḥasan Khán I'timádu's-Salṭana of Marágha.

150. *Ḥujjatu's-Sa'ádat* ("the Proof of Happiness"), a history of the events in the world in A.H. 61 (= A.D. 680–1).

151. *History of Persia*, forming an Appendix to the Year-Book (*Sál-náma*) of A.H. 1292 (= A.D. 1875–6).

152. *Mir'átu'l-Buldán* ("Mirror of the Lands"), a Geography of Persia in four volumes. Vol. I, published in A.H. 1293 (= A.D. 1876), contains a detailed account of the Persian provinces, towns and villages which fall under the first five letters of the alphabet, arranged in alphabetical order. On reaching the article *Ṭihrán* in Vol. II (published in A.H. 1294 = A.D. 1877) the author gives a complete history of modern Persia during the last century, which history also fills the greater part of Vol. III, published in A.H. 1295 (= A.D. 1878). Vol. IV, published in A.H. 1296 (= A.D. 1879), continues the geographical Index.

153. *Muntaẓam-i-Náṣirí*, in 3 volumes, published in A.H. 1298, 1299 and 1300 (= A.D. 1881–3), is a Universal History, arranged in the form of Annals, extending from A.H. 1 to A.H. 1300 (= A.D. 622–1882).

154. *Maṭla'u'sh-Shams* ("the Rising of the Sun"), in 3 volumes, published in A.H. 1301–3 (= A.D. 1884–6), a detailed history and account of the city of Mashhad.

155. *Khayrát*^un^ *Ḥisán*^un^, a biography of celebrated women and an anthology of their poems, in 3 volumes, published in A.H. 1304–7 (= A.D. 1887–90).

156. *Al-Ma'áthir wa'l-Áthár* ("Monuments and Achievements"), an account of the institutions and achievements of the reign of Náṣiru'd-Dín Sháh, containing also biographies of contemporary notables, divines and scholars.

157. *Duraru't-Tíján* ("Pearls for Crowns"), a historical work.

158. A History of the Parthians (*Bani'l-Ashkán*), in 3 volumes, dated A.H. 1308–10 (= A.D. 1891–3).

159. *At-Tadwín fí Jibáli Sharwín*, an account of the Mountains of Sharwín, published in A.H. 1311 (= A.D. 1893–4).

160. Memoirs of Mademoiselle de Montpensier, a story connected with the history of France, published in A.H. 1317 (= A.D. 1899–1900).

161. A History of the Sásánian Kings of Persia, translated from Rawlinson's well-known work by Mírzá Muḥammad Ḥusayn *Zaká'u'l-Mulk*, in two volumes, published in A.H. 1314–15 (= A.D. 1896–8).

162. *Náma-i-Dánishwarán* ("the Book of the Learned"),

compiled by a committee of scholars consisting of Mírzá Abu'l-Fazl of Sáwa, Mírzá Ḥasan of Ṭálaqán, 'Abdu'l-Wahháb of Qazwín, known as "Mullá Áqá," and Muḥammad called al-Mahdí. This work, which was not completed, is a detailed Dictionary of Biography of the notable and eminent persons, men of letters, divines, philosophers, mystics, etc., who were most celebrated in Islám, and contains accounts of their biographies, adventures, characteristics and writings. Its publication was begun in A.H. 1296 (= A.D. 1879) under the supervision of 'Alí-qulí Mírzá *I'tiẓádu's-Salṭana*. On his death in A.H. 1298 (=A.D. 1881), after the publication of two volumes, the editorial committee made over the supervision to Muḥammad Ḥasan Khán *I'timádu's-Salṭana*, so that the last five volumes (III–VII) were published as appendices to the Year Books (*Sál-náma*) of A.H. 1318, 1319, 1321, 1322 and 1323 (= A.D. 1900–5).

Here ends that which, with restricted facilities and defective materials, I have been able to collect in this brief summary, and I hope that the learned may make good its deficiencies and the discerning overlook its short-comings.

PART II

Specimens of
The Political and Patriotic Poetry
of Modern Persia.

Compiled and translated

by

EDWARD G. BROWNE.

(1)

THE first specimen given below belongs to a much earlier period than the remainder, for it was printed and published in London by Messrs W. H. Allen and Co. and R. J. Mitchell and Sons in 1882. It is taken from a *qaṣída* of 366 verses entitled "A London Sunlet" (*Shumaysa-i-Landaniyya*) composed by my old friend and first Persian teacher Mírzá Muḥammad Báqir of the district of Bawánát in Fárs, surnamed Ibráhím Ján Mu'aṭṭar. Of this remarkable and eccentric individual I have given some account in the first chapter of my *Year amongst the Persians*, published in 1893 by Messrs A. and C. Black (pp. 12–15), and I have there explained how he compelled me to read with great attention the extraordinary poem of which I subjoin a sample. Reading it again after the lapse of nearly thirty years, I cannot help being very much struck by its clear foreshadowing of the recent Anglo-Russian understanding, which at that time, midway between Plevna and Panj-dih, seemed of all things most improbable. In the rhymed translation which I have added to the original I have endeavoured to preserve as far as possible not only the sense of the latter, but its extraordinary half-prophetic half-punning style, which affords a strange mixture of rhapsody and lampoon, of grim jest and bitter earnest. The poem, which preserves the same rhyme throughout, is divided into two parts between verses 120 and 121, with which last I begin, selecting 29 verses out of the following 90 (*i.e.* between 121 and 211).

(از شُمَیْسَهٔ لندنیّهٔ میرزا محمّد باقر بواناتی)

) گوش! که بانگِ نفیر روس بر آمد، هوش! که گوش از خروش کوس کـ

) ولوله بر زن که صوتِ هلهله افزود، سلسله بفگن که فوتِ شیرِ نر

) پهنهٔ قبچاق زیر دهند قزّاق، قلزِم زخّارِ آهنین لپر

The Poet-Prophet Mírzá Muḥammad Báqir (seated on left); his son Mírzá Isma'íl (standing on right); Shaykh Muḥammad 'Abduh, afterwards Grand Muftí of Egypt (seated in middle); Ḥájji Pír-záda (seated on right); and Jemálu'd-Dín Bey (standing on left)

The photograph was taken at Beyrout about 1885

(١٢٤) پشت اندر پشت و بر ببر همه هامون، از تخمِ زشت کشتِ پا و سر آمد،

* * * * * *

(١٢٦) چندان لشکر که گر ستاره بدیدی، گفتی زین دو کدام بی شمر آمد؟،

* * * * * *

(١٢٨) از دمِ قطبِ شمال تا پُلِ کابُل، معرضِ گوپال وگُرز و یال و بر آمد،

(١٢٩) چین در ابرو گره بساعد و بازو، نز چینشان رخوه نز ختن حذر آمد،

(١٣٠) ای اسدِ خر و یا خرِ اسدین سر، خرس نگوید خر از اسد بتر آمد،

(١٣١) ترکِ چرا گوی و راه کوی وصحرا گیر، گرگ و ببر و پلنگ هم کمر آمد،

(١٣٢) سنگ بهیچت بهیچ نام نیرزید، شنگِ وهیچت بچنگِ ننگ در آمد،

* * * * * *

(١٣٨) های که رایت فزود ای شهِ قفقاس، مردی مردی از آنت این هنر آمد،

* * * * * *

(١٤٠) هیهات هیهات وعدهای دروغین، آخرمان راست تا دمِ سفر آمد،

(١٤١) افسوس افسوس لقمه در بُنِ دندان، و آوازِ حفرِ قبرِ لقمه خور آمد،

* * * * * *

(١٥٢) هندت دادم که شُکْر گوئی و حمدم، شُکْرت بس نُکْر و حمدِ تو حمر آمد،

(١٥٣) گفتم با روس چون عروس میآمیز، کاولادِ خرس وارثِ پدر آمد،

(١٥٤) از من گفتن و از تو بس نشنفتن، شِرْدِنگ و دِنگ! گفتگو هدر آمد،

(١٥٥) شرقت دادم که پی بری تو بنورم، نورم دیدی و ظلمتت خِبَر آمد،

* * * * * *

(١٦٧) خرسی پیدا شد از کنارهٔ کوهی، وز دعَرش دلبرِ سرا ذَعَر آمد،

(١٦٨) از دل و از جان بسوی خرس چمان شد، کابنم محبوب و قِرْنِ منتقر آمد،

(١٦٩) وه وه زین جنبش و خرامش و خوبی، درخوردِ حلق گُتّی نُبَر آمد،

(١٧٠) من شکرِ هند و یار شیرِ سمرقند، ترکیب این دو شیر در شکر آمد،

(١٧١) شیرِ جنوب این دلیر و خرسِ شمال آن، کیست که با خرس و شیر هم دَغَر آمد،

(١٧٢) این غرب و شرق هر دو زیرِ نگینش، آن‌را خود شرق و غرب در زُکَر آمد،

(١٧۴) هرجا خرس است جای وحشت و ترس است، هرجا شیر است لیر در فِقَر آمد،

* * * * * *

(١٧٥) انسانیّت ز روی ارض بر اُفتاد، حیوانیّت دو باره مُنْتَحَر آمد،

* * * * * *

(١٨٦) کیَرْوس که؟ که هنده عاشق روس است، گاهِ بوس و کنار و بُرّ و بر آمد،

* * * * * *

(٢٠٤) ای خرس این شیررا بگیر و بیآموز، ازآن علمی که خرس‌را هنر آمد،

* * * * * *

(٢١٠) وین خرس و شیررا برند بجائی، کانجا هر خرس و شیر چون سُغَر آمد،

(٢١١) چندی در حبس و در قنسشان دارند، تاشان طبع دَرر پی هَرَر آمد،

(*Translation*)

(121) Hark! the blare of Russian trumpets on the Northern breezes comes!
Heed ye! for the ears are deafened with the roar of Russian drums!

(122) Weep and wail! the sounds of turmoil loud and ever louder rise:
Shake thy chains and burst thy fetters, for the Lion surely dies!

(123) 'Neath the hosts of savage Cossacks all the boundless Qipcháq Plain
Seems a sea of iron billows, seems a roaring, surging main!

(124) Back to back and breast to breast throughout that spacious Plain they stand,
While an evil seed of severed heads and limbs fulfils the land.

* * * *

(126) Boundless, countless is their army, so that if the stars should see,
They would ask, "Of these two armies which may claim infinity?"

* * * *

(128) Even from the Bridge of Kábul to the regions of the Pole,
Clubs and maces, chests and shoulders, in one seething eddy roll.

(129) Frowning brows and knotted muscles doth each warrior display;
Little do they care for China, little reck they of Cathay!

(130) Think ye, Lion-Ass, or Ass with Lion's head, that yonder Bear
Doth not know the Ass will better yield to him the Lion's share?

(131) Quit the grounds wherein you hunted; turn your steps to house and town,
For the Tiger, Wolf and Leopard forces join to hunt you down!

(132) Call the *Stone* whereon you stumble "*glad*": 'tis but an empty name!
And thy Beauty *Bright* is surely caught within the claws of shame[1]!

* * * *

(138) Hail, thou great Caucasian Monarch! Full success attends thy plan!
Such success is thine by virtue of the strength which makes a man!

* * * *

(140) Welladay! Each lying promise, which, it seemed, would serve so well,
Now hath caught us, and hath brought us even to the gates of Hell!

(141) Welladay! The toothsome morsel still within thy molars lies,
While the sounds of spades which dig the morsel-eater's grave arise.

* * * *

(152) Graceless one! I gave thee India, seeking from thee prayer and laud,
But for praying heard but braying, and for laud got naught but bawd!

(153) Did I not command thee, saying, "Mate not with the Russian Bear,
For the Russian parent's offspring is the Russian parent's heir"?

(154) Mine it was to speak, and thine to lend an inattentive ear:
Mine to warn thee, thine to scorn me: mine to counsel, thine to jeer!

[1] Gladstone and Bright, the prototypes of our modern Russophil Ministers, were, however, at once more magnanimous and more moderate than these, and Gladstone on occasion showed a firmness for which we look in vain in Sir Edward Grey.

(155) I bestowed the East upon thee that thou might'st behold my Light:
Thou didst see the Light, and turning didst prefer the mirk of night.

* * * *

(167) Sudden from a mountain fastness doth the grizzly Bear appear,
And my Darling sees it, loves it, swoons away with passion sheer.

(168) Heart and soul fulfilled with longing, to the Bear she draweth nigh,
Saying, "This is my beloved, this the Apple of mine Eye!"

(169) See her form so sleek and comely! See the beauty of her gait!
Worthy such a dainty morsel for the jaws which it await!

(170) "I," said she, "am India's sugar, he the milk of Samarqand:
"We shall mix like milk and sugar, we shall travel hand in hand!

(171) "I the Lion of the South, and he the valiant Northern Bear:
"Who shall venture to oppose us when together forth we fare?"

(172) Subject to the former's sceptre are the realms of West and East:
East and West lie in the pouch and pocket of the second Beast.

(173) Where the Bear is, there is terror, there are cruelty and fear:
Where the Lion is the powers of nerve and muscle disappear.

* * * *

(175) From the face of earth all human kindliness hath passed away:
Brutish cruelty becomes once more the order of the day.

* * * *

(186) Where is Cyrus, now that India's sick with love for Russia's sake?
Let them kiss and hug each other, ere they share the stolen cake[1]!

* * * *

(204) Come, O Bear, and take this Lion: lead her to thy dismal lair,
There to teach her all the arts which make the cunning of the Bear.

* * * *

(210) Till at length there cometh one to take them both unto a place
Where like conies they shall shiver, threatened by a stronger race.

(211) There shall they be held in bondage in a prison and a cage,
Till unto a milk-like mildness turns their roughness and their rage!

(2)

The second specimen, published in No. 4 of the *Ṣúr-i-Isráfíl* ("Trumpet-call of Isráfíl") of June 20, 1907, refers to an event which happened at Qúchán in Khurásán on the Russo-Persian frontier a year or two previously[2], when a number of the inhabitants, including several young girls, were carried off by Turkmáns subject to Russia, with the connivance, it was asserted, of *Áṣafu'd-Dawla* and the governor of Burújird, who was subsequently tried for this offence.

[1] "Cyrus" typifies Persia, which, I take it, is also intended by "the stolen cake."
[2] I think in November, 1905. See my *Persian Revolution*, p. 111.

This ballad bears the following superscription:
Persian Concert, which the girls of Qúchán, at the request of the Russians and Turkmáns, give in a Café chantant *at Tiflís.*

Girls, in chorus, to the tune of the taṣníf (*ballad*)
"Ay Khudá, Laylá yár-i-má níst!"
("*O God, Laylá is not our friend!*")

(۱)

بزرگان جملگی مستِ غرورند، (خدا کسی فکر ما نیست)
ز انصاف و مروّت سخت دورند، (خدا کسی فکر ما نیست)
رعیّت بی سواد و گنگ و کورند، (خدا کسی فکر ما نیست)
هنده و هژده و نوزده و بیست
ای خدا کسی فکر ما نیست،

(۲)

فلك دیدی بما آخر چها کرد، (خدا کسی فکر ما نیست)
ز خویش و اقربا مارا جدا کرد، (خدا کسی فکر ما نیست)
جنا بیند که با ما این جفا کرد، (خدا کسی فکر ما نیست)
هفده و هژده و نوزده و بیست
ای خدا کسی فکر ما نیست،

(۳)

گر از کوی وطن مهجور ماندیم، (خدا کسی فکر ما نیست)
و گر از هجرِ او رنجور ماندیم، (خدا کسی فکر ما نیست)
نه پنداری ز عشقش دور ماندیم، (خدا کسی فکر ما نیست)
هفده و هژده و نوزده و بیست
ای خدا کسی فکر ما نیست،

(٤)

(یك دختر دوازده ساله تنها)

نفس در سینه ساکت شو که گوئی، (خدا کسی فکر ما نیست)
نسیم از کوی ما آورده بوئی، (خدا کسی فکر ما نیست)
چه بوئی دلکش آن هم از چه کوئی، (خدا کسی فکر ما نیست)

هفده و هژده و نوزده و بیست
ای خدا کسی فکر ما نیست،

(٥)

(دخترها هم آواز)

نسیم بوم ما بس جانفزا بود، (خدا کسی فکر ما نیست)
هوایش روح بخش و غم زدا بود، (خدا کسی فکر ما نیست)
ولی دردا که هجرش در قفا بود، (خدا کسی فکر ما نیست)

هفده و هژده و نوزده و بیست
ای خدا کسی فکر ما نیست،

(٦)

مگر مردانِ مارا خواب برده، (خدا کسی فکرِ ما نیست)
غیورانِ وطن را آب برده، (خدا کسی فکرِ ما نیست)
که اغیار آب از احباب برده، (خدا کسی فکرِ ما نیست)

هفده و هژده و نوزده و بیست
ای خدا کسی فکر ما نیست،

(۷)

(دختر دوازده ساله تنها)

که خواهد برد تا مجلس پیامم، (خدا کسی فکرِ ما نیست)
که ای دل بردهٔ نا داده کامم، (خدا کسی فکرِ ما نیست)
چرا شد محو از یادِ تو نامم، (خدا کسی فکرِ ما نیست)
هفده و هژده و نوزده و بیست
ای خدا کسی فکر ما نیست،

(جغد)

(تماشاچیان بهیئت اجتماع)

هورا هورا هورا! اسلاوا گراتسی وزنیم دویت سام پرسی!
اسلاوا آصف الدوله! اسلاوا مینسترست وو پرسی!
یاشاسون ایرانن گوزل قزلری! یاشاسون آصف الدوله!
یاشاسون ملّت وزیرلری،

(*Translation*)

(1)

(*The girls, in chorus*)

"Our nobles all are drunk with pride,
(*O God, nobody cares for us!*)
From justice and virtue they stand aside, (*O God, etc.*)
Dumb, blind, untaught the people abide, (*O God, etc.*)
One seven, one eight, one nine, two naught:
No one of us taketh heed or thought!

(2)

"Thou seest how Heaven with us doth play,
 (*O God, nobody cares for us!*)
From kith and kin we are torn away; (*O God, etc.*)
The ill that is wrought us shall ill repay! (*O God, etc.*)
 One seven, one eight, etc.

(3)

"Though exiled far from our home so dear,
 (*O God, nobody cares for us!*)
And plunged by exile in sorrow and fear, (*O God, etc.*)
We love it and dream of it ever here! (*O God, etc.*)
 One seven, one eight, etc.

(4)

(*A girl of twelve, solo*)

"Pause, O breath in my breast: meseems
 (*O God, nobody cares for us!*)
That the breeze with the scents of the home-land teems:
 (*O God, etc.*)
What delicate scent from what land of dreams! (*O God, etc.*)
 One seven, one eight, etc.

(5)

(*The girls, in chorus*)

"Sweet doth the breeze from the home-land smell!
 (*O God, nobody cares for us!*)
Life doth it give and grief dispel! (*O God, etc.*)
But alas, for of exile it speaks as well! (*O God, etc.*)
 One seven, one eight, etc.

(6)

"Sleep hath o'ercome our men, I ween,
 (*O God, nobody cares for us!*)
And blunted our townsmen's honour keen, (*O God, etc.*)
And our friends dishonoured by foes have been! (*O God, etc.*)
 One seven, one eight, etc.

(7)

(*The girl of twelve, solo*)

"Who to the *Majlis* a message will bear
(*O God, nobody cares for us!*)
Of heart's surrender and hope's despair?
(*O God, nobody cares for us!*)
Is our name remembered no longer there?
(*O God, nobody cares for us!*)
One seven, one eight, one nine, two naught:
No one of us taketh heed or thought!"

The spectators in unison:

"*Hurrah, hurrah, hurrah!*

Slava gratzioznim dyevitsám Persii!	*Yáshásún Íránin gyuzel qizlari!*
Slava Áṣafu'd-Dawla!	*Yáshásún Áṣafu'd-Dawla!*
Slava Ministyerstvú Persii!"	*Yáshásún millet vezírleri!*

(In Russian and Turkish.)

"Long live the pretty girls of Persia! Long live Áṣafu'd-Dawla!
Long live the Persian Ministry!"

(3)

The following poem, like the last, is taken from the *Ṣúr-i-Isráfíl* for November 20, 1907. The "Kablá'í" to whom it is addressed is taken by some to refer to the poet himself, but by others to the ex-Shah, Muḥammad 'Alí, who was at that time the ruler of Persia. The word "*Kablá'í*" or "*Kabláy*" is a popular abbreviation of *Karbalá'í*, a title given to those who have visited the holy tombs of Karbalá in Turkish Arabia; just as one who has visited Mashhad is entitled "*Mashhadí*," and one who has performed the pilgrimage to Mecca, "Ḥájji." The two former titles, however, are seldom used except by muleteers, tradespeople, and others of humble condition, and "*Kabláy*" especially has come to be used colloquially in a somewhat familiar or even contemptuous way, as though we should call a man whose name was unknown to us "Johnnie." The original poem is slangy, and this feature I have endeavoured to preserve in the translation, which is somewhat freer than the preceding ones.

(۱)

مردود خدا راندهٔ هر بنده آکبلای، از دلقك معروف نماینده آکبلای،
با شوخی و با مسخره و خنده آکبلای، نز مرده گذشتی و نه از زنده آکبلای،
هستی تو چه یکپهلو و یك دنده آکبلای،

(۲)

نه بیم زکت بین و نه جن گیر و نه رمّال، نه خوف ز درویش و نه از جذبه نه از حال،
نه ترس ز تکفیر و نه از پیشتو شپشال، مشکل ببری گور سر زنده آکبلای،
هستی تو چه یکپهلو و یك دنده آکبلای،

(۳)

صد بار نگفتم که خیال تو محالست، تا نیمی ازین طائفه محبوس جوالست،
ظاهر شود اسلام درین قوم خیالست، هی باز بزن حرف پراگنده آکبلای،
هستی تو چه یکپهلو و یك دنده آکبلای،

(٤)

گاهی به پر و پاچهٔ درویش پریدی، گه پردهٔ کاغذلوق آخوند دریدی،
اسرار نهان را همه در صور دمیدی، رُو در بایسی یعنی چه؟ پوست کنده آکبلای،
هستی تو چه یکپهلو و یك دنده آکبلای،

(٥)

گرسنگی مرد رعیّت بجهنّم، ور نیست درین قوم معیّت بجه
ك بُرید عِرْقِ حمیّت بجهنّم، خوش باش تو با مطرب و سازنده آکبلا
هستی تو چه یکپهلو و یك دنده آکبلای،

(٦)

تظری رشوه در ایران رود از یاد، آخوند ز قانون و ز عدلیّه شود ش
م ز رمّال و ز مرشد شود آزاد، یك دفعه بگو مرده شود زنده آکبلا
هستی تو چه یکپهلو و یك دنده آکبلای،

(*Translation*)

(1)

"Rejected by men and by God the Forgiving, O Kabláy!
You're a wonderful sample of riotous living, O Kabláy!
You're a wag, you're a joker, no end to your fun,
Of living and dead you are sparing of none,
Such a limb of the Devil and son of a gun, O Kabláy!

(2)

"Neither wizard, diviner nor warlock you fear, O Kabláy!
Nor the dervish's prayer, nor the dreams of the Seer, O Kabláy!
Nor Shapshál's[1] revolver, nor *mujtahid's* rage:
'Tis hard to believe you will die of old age,
You limb of the Devil and son of a gun, O Kabláy!

(3)

"Times a hundred I've told you your project will fail, O Kabláy!
While half of the nation are wrapped in a veil[2], O Kabláy!
Can Islám in you and your circle prevail?
With fresh words of folly your friends you'll regale,
You limb of the Devil and son of a gun, O Kabláy!

[1] Concerning Shapshál Khán, the Russian *agent provocateur*, see my *Persian Revolution*, pp. 105, 130, 170–1, 198–202, 207, 279, 324 and 418–420.

[2] *i.e.* the women.

(4)

"At the heels of the dervish you bark and you bite, O Kabláy!
Break the Dominie's windows[1] and let in the light, O Kabláy!
While this trumpet[2] of yours doth all secrets proclaim;
Yes, blazon them forth, for what know you of shame?
    You limb of the Devil and son of a gun, O Kabláy!

(5)

"To hell with the folk, if with hunger they pine, O Kabláy!
Devil take them, the brutes, since they cannot combine,
    O Kabláy!
Since opium hath stolen their courage away,
With your minstrels and singers be merry and gay,
    You limb of the Devil and son of a gun, O Kabláy!

(6)

"In Persia will bribes ever go out of fashion, O Kabláy?
Will the *mullás* for justice develop a passion, O, Kabláy?
From magic and *murshids*[3] can Islám win free?
Bid the dead come to life, for 'twill easier be,
    You limb of the Devil and son of a gun, O Kabláy!"

(4)

The following poem, by Ashraf of Gílán, is of a much more classical type than the last, and is what is called a *mustazád.* It appeared in No. 9 of the *Nasím-i-Shimál* ("Breeze of the North"), published at Rasht on January 2, 1908. Part of it only is translated as a specimen.

[1] The Turkish word *kághizlúq* means a window covered with paper instead of glass.

[2] This is an allusion to the paper *Ṣur-i-Isráfíl* or "Trumpet of Isráfíl," in which this poem appeared.

[3] Spiritual guides.

The Poet Sayyid Ashrafu'd-Dín of Gílán

۱	گردید وطن غرقهٔ اندوه و محن وای	ایوای وطن وای
	خیزید روید از پی تابوت و کفن وای	ایوای وطن وای
۲	از خون جوانان که شده کُشته درین راه	رنگین طبق ماه
	خونین‌شده صحرا و تل و دشت و دمن وای	ایوای وطن وای
۳	کو همّت و کو غیرت و کو جوش فتوّت	کو جنبش ملّت
	دردا که رسید از دو طرف سیل فتن وای	ایوای وطن وای
٤	افسوس که اسلام شده از همه جانب	پامال اجانب
	مشروطهٔ ایران شده تاریخ زمن وای	ایوای وطن وای
٥	تنها نه همین گشت وطن ضایع و بدنام	گمنام شد اسلام
	پژمرده شد این باغ و گل و سرو و سمن وای	ایوای وطن وای
٦	بلبل نبرد نام گل از واهمه هرگز	نرگس شده قرمز
	سُرْخند ازین غُصّه سفیدان چمن وای	ایوای وطن وای
۷	بعضی وزرا مسلکشان راهزنی شد	سرّی علنی شد
	گشته علما غرقه درین لای و لجن وای	ایوای وطن وای
۸	سوزد جگر از ماتم خلخال خدایا	محشر شده آیا
	یك جامه ندارند رعیّت ببدن وای	ایوای وطن وای
۹	گاهی خبر آرند که سرعسکر رومی	آمد بأُرومی
	گه آستره ویران شده از شاهسون وای	ایوای وطن وای
۱۰	افسوس ازین خاك گهرخیز گهرزا	گردید مُجزّا
	از چار طرف خاك به از مشك ختن وای	ایوای وطن وای
۱۱	کو بلخ و بخارا و چه شد خیوه و کابل	کو بابل و زابل
	شام و حلب و ارمن و عمّان و عدن وای	ایوای وطن وای

۱۲ بر منظرهٔ قصر زر اندود و سطرّا — جغد است صف آرا
بنشسته درین بوم و دمن زاغ و زغن وای — ایوای وطن وای
۱۳ یك ذرّه ز ارباب ندیده‌است معیّت — بیچاره رعیّت
کارش همه فریاد حسین وای حسن وای — ایوای وطن وای
۱٤ اشرف بجز از لالهٔ غم هیچ نبوید — هر لحظه بگوید
ایوای وطن وای وطن وای وطن وای — ایوای وطن وای

(فقیر)

(*Translation*)

1 Our country is flooded with sorrow and woe, — O, for our land woe!
Arise, and for coffin and cerements go! — O, for our land woe!
2 With the blood of our sons for the fatherland shed — The moon shines red;
Hill, plain and garden blood-red glow: — O, for our land woe!
3 Where are zeal and courage and strife, — A Nation's life?
The floods of trouble around us flow! — O, for our land woe!
4 Foreigners trample on every side — On Islám's pride;
Of our Freedom naught but the name they know: — O, for our land woe!
5 Not only our land is lost and misnamed; — Our faith's defamed:
E'en the flowers in the garden stunted grow: — O, for our land woe!
6 The nightingale dares not to sing of the rose: — Red the daffodil grows,
And red the lily-white flowrets blow, — O, for our land woe!
7 Some of our statesmen are brigands sheer; — No mystery here!
And the priests to follow them are not slow: — O, for our land woe!

8 For Khalkhál's sake are our hearts in gloom: 'tis the Day of Doom!
Not even a shirt hath the peasant to show: O, for our land woe!
9 To Urmi the Turkish commander, we hear, Swift draws near,
While at Astara Shahsevens strike a blow! O, for our land woe!
10 Alas for our pearl-bearing, pearl-raising land Partition is planned,
Though its dust be more fragrant than musk, I trow; O, for our land woe!

* * * *

(5)

The following poem, also by Ashraf, and also published in the *Nasím-i-Shimál* (No. 10, dated January 20, 1908), is similar to the last, and is also a *mustazád*. The allusions in verse 5 are to some of the chief newspapers published at that time, and those in verses 9 to 12 to events connected with what I have called "the abortive *Coup d'État*" of December, 1907. (See my *Persian Revolution*, pp. 162 *et seqq.*) The pessimistic strain which characterizes the last poem is also apparent in this.

١ دوش می گفت این سخن دیوانهٔ بی باز خواست   دردِ ایران بیدواست
عاقلی گفتا که از دیوانه بشنو حرف راست   دردِ ایران بیدواست
٢ مملکت از چار سو در حالِ بحران و خطر   چون مریضِ محتضر
با چنین دستور این رنجور مهجور از شفاست   دردِ ایران بیدواست
٣ پادشه بر ضدِّ ملّت ملّت اندر ضدّ شاه   زین مصیبت آه آه
چون حقیقت بنگری هم این خطا هم آن خطاست   دردِ ایران بیدواست
٤ هرکسی با هرکسی خصم است و بدخواه است وضدّ   گوید اورا مستبدّ
با چنین شکل ای بسا خونها هدر جانها هباست   دردِ ایران بیدواست

٥ صورِ اسرافیل زد صبح سعادت در دمید — ملّا نصر الدّین رسید
مجلس و حبل المتین سوی عدالت رهنماست — دردِ ایران بیدواست

٦ با وجودِ این جراید خفتهٔ بیدار نیست — یك رگی هشیار نیست
این جراید همچو شیپور و نفیر و کرّناست — دردِ ایران بیدواست

٧ شکر می کردیم جمعی کارها مضبوطه شد — مملکت مشروطه شد
باز می بینیم آن کاسه است وآن آش است و ماست — دردِ ایران بیدواست

٨ با خرد گفتم که آخر چارهٔ این کار چیست — عقل قاطع هم گریست
بعد آه و ناله گفتا چاره در دستِ خداست — دردِ ایران بیدواست

٩ شیخ فضل الله یك سو آملی از یك طرف[1] — بهرِ ملّت بسته صف
چار سمتِ توپخانه حربگاه شیخ ماست — دردِ ایران بیدواست

١٠ هیچ دانی قصدِ قاطرچی درین هنگامه چیست — یاری اسلام نیست
مقصدِ او ساعت است و کیف و زنجیر طلاست — دردِ ایران بیدواست

١١ مسجدِ مَرْوی پر از اشرارِ غارتگر شده — مدرسه سنگر شده
روحِ واقف در بهشت ازین مصیبت در عزاست — دردِ ایران بیدواست

١٢ تو نپنداری قتیلِ دستهٔ قاطرچیان — خونشان رفت از میان
وعده‌گاهِ انتقامِ اشقیا روزِ جزاست — دردِ ایران بیدواست

١٣ اشرفا هرکس درین مشروطه جانبازی نمود — رفعت و قدرش فزود
در جزا استبرقِ جنّاتِ عدنش متّکاست[2] — دردِ ایران بیدواست

(فقیر)

[1] Concerning Shaykh Faẓlu'lláh of Núr, see my *Persian Revolution*, pp. 113, 148–9, 242, 262, and 444–5. By "*Ámulí*" is meant Mullá Muḥammad of Ámul, *píshnamáz* of the Masjid-i-Marwí, another noted reactionary priest.

[2] *Cf.* Qur'án, xviii. 30; lv. 54.

The great Constitutional *Mujtahid* Mullá Muḥammad Káẓim al-Khurásání in A.H. 1324 (A.D. 1906)

امروز نگهبان خلایق علما اند'

(6)

The following poem is from the same paper (No. 11, January 31, 1908) as the two last, and is, I think, also by Ashraf, since it bears the signature *Faqír*, which he elsewhere uses. He appeals to the *'ulamá* (or so-called "clergy"), the Deputies and the Sháh (Muḥammad 'Alí) to observe the Constitution, enforce the law, and guard the country from the designs of foreign foes, "the Turk, the Two-headed Bird (*i.e.* eagle), the Bear and the Old Dog," and the Shí'ite faith from its Sunní adversaries.

امروز چو ما هیچ کس انگشت نما نیست   زیرا که کسی جاهل و بیعلم چو ما نیست
درعلم و صنایع همگی عاجز و لنگیم   در مغلطه و فتنه و آشوب زرنگیم
بر جانِ هم افتاده شب و روز بجنگیم   شرمی ز کلام الله و ترسی ز خدا نیست

اینك کلماتِ عُلَمَا نصِّ صریح است   بر اینکه بنزدِ عُلَمَا ظلم قبیح است
مشروطه چو در عقل و چو در شرع صحیح است   هر کس کند انکار ز جمع عقلا نیست

افسوس که از ناله و فریاد اثر رفت   هم زحمتِ اربابِ جراید بهدر رفت
مشروطه درین ملك بجوشید و ز سر رفت   چون صحبتِ این دوره بغیر از من و ما نیست

زود ای عُلَمَا مرکبِ مشروطه برانید   دادِ دلِ مظلوم ز ظالم بستانید
هان ای وُکَلَا قدرِ چنین روز بدانید   زیرا کسی امروز باعزازِ شما نیست

مشروطه درختیست پُر از میوه و اثمار   عدلیّه و انصاف و مساوات ورا بار
قانونِ اساسی است درو ناظرِ هر کار   فرقی بمیانِ غنی و شاه و گدا نیست

امروز نگهبانِ خلایق عُلَمَا اند   بعد از عُلَمَا حافظِ ملّت وُکَلَا اند
مسئول بهر جزئی و کلّی وزرا اند   در صحّتِ مشروطه دگر چون و چرا نیست

امسال دو سالست که مشروطه شد ایران پر شد در و دیوار ز شبنامه و اعلان
کو مُجْرِیِ قانون وچه شد همّتِ مردان؟ افسوس که مارا هوسِ صلح و صفا نیست

هر عقل که فرمانبرِ افسونگر و فالست هر مغز که از جَرْس بفکرست و خیالست
هر ملك که علمش همگی قال و مقالست قانون بچنین مملکتی راهنما نیست

احوالِ ارومیه اگر مرده شنیدی در قبر ز غیرت کفنِ خویش دریدی
از دیدهٔ ارواح همه خون بچکیدی در خلد بجز زمزمهٔ وا وطنا نیست

از چار طرف سیلِ بلا گشته سرازیر عثمانی و مرغ دو سر و خرس و سگ پیر
شاها مگر از مملکتِ خود شدهٔ سیر؟ بی قیدی و اهمال باین پایه سزا نیست

ای خسرو مشروطه طلب شاه دل آگاه مپسند که از لطمهٔ عثمانی بد خواه
منسوخ شود لفظِ عَلِیًّا ولِیُ ٱللّٰه شاها بخدا صبر ازین بیش روا نیست!

(فقیر)

(7)

The following poem is also by Ashraf, but it is placed in the mouth of an imaginary reactionary, grotesquely named (as Morier named his characters "Mullá Nádán," "Mírzá Aḥmaq," etc.) "Kharáb-'Alí Mírzá," who is supposed to reproach Ashraf for his enthusiasm for the Constitution. I have appended a prose rendering.

اشرف ازین بیش جسارت مکن، در سرِ مشروطه لجاجت مکن،
با همهٔ خلق منم خصم و ضدّ، می نشوم با احدی متّحد،
مستبدم مستبدم مستبد، هیچ بمشروطه تو دعوت مکن،
مطربکا خیز بزن چنگ و رود، ساقیکا باده بده زود زود،
دولت اگر رفت بتخم رنود، صحبت عثمانی و دولت مکن،

میخورم از خون رعیّت شراب، میکنم از گوشتِ رعیّت کباب،
هیچ نترسم ز عذاب و عقاب، وعده بفردای قیامت مکن،
تکیه بر اقوالِ فرنگان مزن، دم ز مکاتیب دبستان مزن،
طعنه تو بر کهنه پرستان مزن، ذوق ز بیداری ملّت مکن،
من چه کنم خصم شده تر دماغ، رخنه نموده است درین باغ و راغ،
زیر و زبر شد همه ساوجبلاغ، گریه بر احوال رعیّت مکن،
رفت ارومیّه خراسان بس است، آن هم اگر رفت صفاهان بس است،
هیچ نباشد خود طهران بس است، اشرف ازین بیش شرارت مکن،

(امضا خرابعلی میرزا)

(*Prose Translation*)

"O Ashraf, be no longer over-bold! Be not so insistent about the Constitution!
I am an adversary and enemy to all the people; I will not unite with any one;
I am a Reactionary, a Reactionary, a Reactionary! Do not thou preach Constitutionalism!
O little minstrel, arise, strike the harp and the lute! O little cup-bearer, give wine quickly!
If the Empire is lost, to Hell with it! Prate not of the Turk and the Empire!
I drink for wine the blood of the people; I eat for roast meat the flesh of the people;
I have no fear of torment and retribution; do not put me off with threats of to-morrow's Resurrection!
Put not thy trust in the words of the Franks; talk not of the maxims of the schools;
Do not find fault with such as love the ancient ways; do not exult in the awakening of the Nation!
What can I do? the enemy is sharp-witted? He has broken into this garden and meadow:

All Sáwujbulágh is topsy-turvy. Weep not over the people's condition!
If Urúmiyya is gone, Khurásán is enough; if that too goes, Iṣfahán is enough;
If naught else be left, Ṭihrán itself is enough! O Ashraf, work no further mischief!"

(8)

Dakhaw, to whom the following poem (published in the *Nasím-i-Shimál* of March 5, 1908) is ascribed, is best known for his contributions to the *Ṣúr-i-Isráfíl*, and especially for the weekly column entitled *Charand-parand* ("Charivari"). His real name was 'Alí Akbar, and his *nom de guerre*, "*Dakhaw*," is a local form (used at Qazwín, his native town) of *Dih-khudá* ("the villager," "rustic" or "squireen").

مکتوب قزوین

۱ بعرش می رسد امروز الامانِ دخَوْ ، بسوخت از غمِ مشروطه استخوان دخو ،
۲ دراین ولایتِ قزوین ز ظلمِ استبداد ، ز یاد رفت بیکبار خانمانِ دخو ،
۳ چو گشت نیّرِ مشروطه طالع از ایران ، بگشت روشن از اشراقِ او روانِ دخو ،
٤ طلوع کرد چو خورشید (کُنْستی تو سیون) ، همیشه صحبتِ او بود بر زبانِ دخو ،
٥ بُریده باد زبانم کنون که می شنوم ، خلل فتاده بارکانِ پارلمان دخو ،
٦ نهاده پای بمجلس سفیرِ استبداد ، وزیده بادِ خزانی به بوستانِ دخو ،
۷ میانهٔ وُکَلَا اجنبی نهاده قدم ، شکسته نسترن و سرو و ارغوانِ دخو ،
۸ خدا نکرده اگر پارلمان خلل یابد ، زنند اهلِ غرض شعلهها بجانِ دخو ،
۹ فگنند آتشِ ظلم و عناد و استبداد ، امام جمعهٔ قزوین بدودمانِ دخو ،
۱۰ ز ظلم و کینهٔ این مستبدّ میش نما ، بسنگ کرده اثر ناله و فغانِ دخو ،
۱۱ یکی ز حلقه بگوشانِ اشرف الدّینم ،
اگر که درج شود شعرِ خونفشانِ دخو ،

(*Prose Translation*)

(1) "To-day the appeal of Dakhaw ascends to the Throne of God; with grief for the Constitution the bones of Dakhaw are burned.

(2) In this land of Qazwín, through the tyranny of Despotism, the household of Dakhaw is utterly forgotten.

(3) When the luminary of the Constitution arose from Persia the spirit of Dakhaw was illuminated by its dawning.

(4) When the Sun of the Constitution arose talk of it was ever on Dakhaw's tongue.

(5) May my tongue be cut out now that I hear that harm befalls the pillars of the Parliament!

(6) The ambassador of Autocracy hath set his foot in the *Majlis*; an autumnal blast hath blown over Dakhaw's garden.

(7) The foreigner hath stepped into the midst of the Deputies; Dakhaw's gelder-rose and cypress and Judas-tree are broken!

(8) If (which God forbid!) the Parliament suffers hurt, Dakhaw's enemies will set fire to his soul.

(9) The *Imám-Jum'a* (Chief Priest) of Qazwín hath cast the fire of tyranny, malice and despotism on the family of Dakhaw.

(10) On account of the tyranny and spite of this autocrat in sheep's clothing the wailing and lamentations of Dakhaw affect the very stones.

(11) I will become one of the humble servants of Ashrafu'd-Dín if this piteous poem of Dakhaw's should be inserted [in his paper]."

(9)

The following poem, which, like No. 7, is cast in the form of a letter of remonstrance emanating from an imaginary reactionary, is also by Ashraf, and appeared in No. 16 of the second year of the *Nasím-i-Shimál*, on April 14, 1908.

(مکتوب)

١ اشرفا این ناله و فریاد چیست، از برای خلق آه و داد چیست،
٢ فاش بر گو کیستی تو چیستی، یکمنی یا ده منی یا بیستی،
٣ گر که این شهر و وطن‌را آب برد، تو یقین می دان که مارا خواب برد،
٤ روزنامه چیست این هنگامه چیست، فکرِ کاری کن که صنعت قحط نیست،
٥ روس و ژاپون بهرِ ما نآید بکار، با پروس و آلمان مارا چه کار،
٦ نیّرِ مشروطه ساطع شد چه شد، آفتابِ علم طالع شد چه شد،
٧ می کنی ترغیب و تحریصِ شدید، کودکان‌را بر مکاتیبِ جدید،
٨ گاه میخواهی بهر شهر و دیار، یك معلّم خانه سازی استوار،
٩ حیف از طفلی که بر مکتب رود، طفل باید کوچه بر کوچه رود،
١٠ طفل باید بادبان سازی کند، طفل باید شیر و خط بازی کند،
١١ طفل باید پای ملّا بشکند، روز و شب با سنگ سرها بشکند،
١٢ طفل باید پهلوان سنگ زن، بدتر از گربه بصورت چنگ زن،
١٣ روز این اطفال‌را چون شب مکن، نامِ زندان خانه‌را مکتب مکن،
١٤ چون بزیر خاك بگذارندمان، انگلیسی نیست مارا ترجمان،
١٥ از برای ما همان قُرآن بس است، پای تخت شاه‌را طهران بس است،
١٦ گر هجوم آور شده سیلِ بلا، غم مخور چون اَلبَلاءُ لِلوِلا،
١٧ گر در این دنیا ذلیلم ای عمو، لیك در محشر جلیلم ای عمو،
١٨ با قلم بر گردن ما چك مزن، روی بام شیخنا تنبك مزن،
١٩ اشرفا ترغیب بر صنعت مکن، از علومِ خارجه صحبت مکن،

٢٠ ترسم آخر بشکنندت پا و دست
فال بین و مرشد و ماضی پرست

Amenities of Muslim family life
(From *Mullā Naṣru'd-Dīn*, No. 20, June 1, 1907)

(*Prose Translation*)

(1) "O Ashraf, what is this outcry and lamentation? What is this sighing and crying for the people?

(2) Speak out plainly: who and what are you? Are you [a man of] one maund, or ten maunds, or twenty?

(3) Even if the flood carries away this city and land, know for a surety that sleep overpowers us.

(4) What is the newspaper? What is this disturbance? Think of some action, for there is no dearth of talents.

(5) Russia and Japan are nothing to us! What have we to do with Prussia and Germany?

(6) If the luminary of the Constitution hath shone forth, what is that [to us]? If the Sun of Knowledge hath arisen, what is that [to us]?

(7) You vehemently urge and incite the children to [attend] the new schools;

(8) Then you desire in every town and district to establish a teachers' college.

(9) Alas for the child who goes to school! A child should run about the streets:

(10) A child should make kites: a child should play pitch and toss:

(11) A child should break the *mullá's* ankles: a child should break [people's] heads with stones.

(12) A child should be an adept at stone-throwing: a child should be worse than a cat at face-scratching.

(13) Do not make these children's days more gloomy than nights! Do not call a prison a school!

(14) When they consign us to the earth, English will not serve to interpret our thoughts[1]!

(15) This *Qur'án* is sufficient for us: Ṭihrán is sufficient for the Sháh's capital!

(16) If the floods of misfortune attack us, grieve not, for 'misfortune is love's portion!'

[1] This refers to the "Questioning of the Tomb," when the angels Munkir and Nakír come to the dead man and examine him as to his faith. Naturally he will be expected to reply to them in Arabic, or some other Musulmán language.

(17) If I am abased in this world, O uncle, yet shall I be glorified in the Resurrection, O uncle!
(18) Smite us not on the neck with thy pen! Beat not the drum on the roof of our Shaykh!
(19) O Ashraf, do not urge us to [cultivate] Art! Do not talk to us about foreign sciences!
(20) I fear that in the end the sooth-sayer, the spiritual director and the admirer of ancient fashions will break your feet and hands!"

(10)

The following poem is another of those abounding with slang. It appeared in No. 18 of the *Nasím-i-Shimál*, dated May 11, 1908.

تا کلّهٔ شیخنا ملنگ است،   تا در دلِ ما غبار و زنگ است،
تا پیرِ دلیل مست و منگ است،   تا رشته بدستِ این دبنگ است،
این قافله تا بحشر لنگ است،
تا مصدرِ کار مستبدّ است،   تا دل بنفاق مستعدّ است،
تا ملّتِ ما بشاه ضدّ است،   تا شاه بخائنین مُمدّ است،
جان کندن و سعی ما جفنگ است،
این قافله تا بحشر لنگ است،
گفتیم قلم شده است آزاد،   ایران خرابه گشته آباد،
مشروطه قوی نموده بنیاد،   بس مدرسه‌ها شدست ایجاد،
افسوس که شیشه‌مان بسنگ است،
این قافله تا بحشر لنگ است،
مشروطه نشانهٔ ترقّی است،   مجلس هم خانهٔ ترقّی است،
این شعله زبانهٔ ترقّی است،   این شعر ترانهٔ ترقّی است،
اسلام چرا دوچارِ ننگ است،
این قافله تا بحشر لنگ است،

دستور العمل دادن سیّد محمد یزدی بجماعت اجنّه که مشروطه طلبان را ظفر رسانند

Sayyid Muḥammad Yazdí teaching the *Jinnís* how to overthrow the Constitution

(From the illustrated comic weekly *Ázarbáyján*, No. 17, Oct. 11, 1907)

خر صاحبِ اختیار گشته،   سگ مصدرِ کار و بار گشته،
روبه عظمت مدار گشته،   شپشال خزینه‌دار گشته،
شه‌مات و بخلق عرصه تنگ است،
این قافله تا بحشر لنگ است،

من بعد شود جهان گلستان،   در صحنِ سرا و باغ و بستان،
مشروطه شود هزار دستان،   شاعر بمزار همچو مستان،
تیرش ز نشاط بر خدنگ است،
این قافله تا بحشر لنگ است،

The following rhymed translation of the first, second, third and fifth stanzas of the above poem may suffice to give some idea of its structure and the arrangements of the rhymes.

(*Translation*)

(1)

While addled in our reverend master's pate,
And dust and rust our spirits obfuscate,
And drunk and dizzy's he who guides our fate,
And this old humbug still directs our gait
Needs must our caravan be lame and late!

(2)

Vainly our lives to hardship we expose
While in each heart the fire of hatred glows:
For while the Nation doth the Sháh oppose,
And while the Sháh supports the Nation's foes,
And while Reaction dominates the State
Needs must our caravan be lame and late!

(3)

We say that now at last the Press is free,
That Persia shall regain prosperity,
That firmly based is now our Liberty,
That colleges abound increasingly.
    Bottle and stone best typify our state!
    Needs must our caravan be lame and late!

*   *   *   *

(5)

An ass becomes our arbiter supreme,
A dog controls each project and each scheme,
A fox the object of respect doth seem,
Shapshál[1] a trusty treasurer we deem:
    What piece can move to save the King from mate?
    Needs must our caravan be lame and late!

(11)

The following poem, with the refrain "How can hearing be like seeing?" appeared in the *Nasím-i-Shimál* for May 29, 1908 (No. 19). It also is from the pen of Ashraf.

الا تا چند راحت آرمیدن، نرفته کی توان جائی رسیدن،
ندیده کی توان صورت کشیدن، محمّد دیدن و موسی شنیدن،
شنیدن کی بود مانند دیدن،

خبر آمد که ایران‌را بهار است، بهارستان پُر از مشکِ تتار است،
فضای پارلمان هم عطر بار است، ببباید لاله از مشروطه چیدن،
شنیدن کی بود مانند دیدن،

خبر آمد جهان امن و امان شد، برغبت شه مُطیع پارلمان شد،
بدولت نیز ملّت توأمان شد، گذشت آن ظلم و قتل و سر بُریدن،
شنیدن کی بود مانند دیدن،

[1] See *supra*, p. 181, n. 1.

جهان روشن شد از انوارِ مجلس، بود روح القدس معمارِ مجلس،
باطراف و در و دیوارِ مجلس، بباید عنکبوت آسا تنیدن،
شنیدن کی بود مانند دیدن،

بحمد اللّه ز قیدِ ظلم رستیم، سرِ دیوِ جهالت‌را شکستیم،
بطوفِ پارلمان احرام بستیم، چو وحشی باید از ظالم رمیدن،
شنیدن کی بود مانند دیدن،

خبر آمد که شد دورانِ ملّت، خلاص از مستبدّ شد جانِ ملّت،
فنا گشتند سلّاخانِ ملّت، نداند گرگ بر برّه پریدن،
شنیدن کی بود مانند دیدن،

خبر آمد که ظالم از جهان رفت، از استبداد هم نام و نشان رفت،
حدیثِ داغ و شلّاق از میان رفت، نداند گربه بر دنبه جهیدن،
شنیدن کی بود مانند دیدن،

نباید زد بسر افسار واللّه، نباید رفت زیر بار واللّه،
نباید شد خرِ اغیار واللّه، چه خوش بی[1] روح انسانی دمیدن،
شنیدن کی بود مانند دیدن،

شها تریاك جای قند تا کی، بدزدان و دغل پیوند تا کی،
بقرآن بیجهت سوگند تا کی، نصیحت باید از اشرف شنیدن،
شنیدن کی بود مانند دیدن،

[1] *Bí* is a dialect form of *buwad*, familiar to all educated Persians through the popular quatrains of Bábá Ṭáhir the Lur, who may be called the "Burns of Persia."

(12)

The following poem appeared in the *Nasím-i-Shimál* for June 18, 1908 (No. 22), five days before the *Coup d'État.*

ـن ز عطرِ علم معطّر نمی شود،   در شوره‌زار لاله میسّر نمی شود
ک و کلوخ لؤلؤ و گوهر نمی شود،   صد بار گفته‌ام مکرّر نمی شود
دندانِ مار دستهٔ خنجر نمی شود

کجا و راه روِ معدلت کجا،   سلطان کجا و با ضعفا مرحمت کجا
لِ محلّه گرد کجا تربیت کجا،   با زورِ زر گزر چو چقندر نمی شود
دندانِ مار دستهٔ خنجر نمی شود

ـم علم و صنعت و ثروت زیاده شد،   از فیلِ ظلم شاه بکلّی پیاده شد
ـوت و فنّ کاسه گری قلع ماده شد،   دیدیم مشکل است حجر زر نمی شود
دندانِ مار دستهٔ خنجر نمی شود

قولمان درست نه افعالمان صحیح،   نه عقلمان رسا و نه اعمالمان صحیح
المان معیّن و نه خانمان صحیح،   و الله این فقیر توانگر نمی شود
دندانِ مار دستهٔ خنجر نمی شود

دو ساله رفت هدر وا مصیبتا،   شد کار و بارِ خلق بتر وا مصیبتا
ـیم زهر جای شکر وا مصیبتا،   دیدیم هر سیاه چو قنبر[1] نمی شود
دندانِ مار دستهٔ خنجر نمی شود

نهالِ نورس مشروطه رخ گشود،   در پای او جداولِ خون جای آب بود
بپای نخلِ وطن خون روان نمود،   بی آب هیچ نخله تناور نمی شود
دندانِ مار دستهٔ خنجر نمی شود

[1] Qanbar was the faithful negro servant of the Imám 'Alí. To say "every negro is not a Qanbar" is equivalent to saying "every sailor is not a Nelson."

پیله‌سوار[1] گشته قدمگاه دشمنان، خلخال[2] خالخال شد از ظلمِ رهزنان،
تبریز مال مال شد از نالهٔ زنان، در حیرتم که گوشِ فلك کر نمی شود،
دندان مار دستهٔ خنجر نمی شود،

دردا و حسرتا که فزون شد جنونِ ما، ای مستبد مگو سخن از چند و چونِ ما،
قاضی برشوهٔ شده راضی بخونِ ما، این ماده بُز بحقِّ خدا نر نمی شود،
دندان مار دستهٔ خنجر نمی شود،

ای ملّتِ غیور کنون وقتِ غیرت است، ای ملّتِ نجیب کنون وقتِ غیرت است،
مذهب ز دست رفت وطن در مذلّت است، دندان مار دستهٔ خنجر نمی شود،

(13)

The following *taṣníf*, or ballad, appeared in the same issue of the *Nasím-i-Shimál* (No. 22) as the last. It is written in a very simple and somewhat colloquial style. *Mí-shé* and *na-mí-shé* ("will it be?" "it cannot be!") are common colloquial contractions for *mí-shawad* and *namí-shawad*; *siyá* (black) = *siyáh*; *shahwat-charání* means "self-indulgence," "pampering the passions"; *ján-i-Mawlá* (analogous to *ján-i-pidar*) means literally "Soul of the Lord," *i.e.* "God's beloved," and is equivalent to "my good friend"; and *yárú* ("that friend" of ours) refers to some person, known to the speaker and the hearer only, whom it is not desired to name. It is often used contemptuously, and here, presumably, refers to Muḥammad 'Alí Sháh.

میشه دولت بملّت یار گردد، نگو هرگز نمیشه های های،
باهلِ مملکت غمخوار گردد، نگو هرگز نمیشه های های،
شبیهِ نادر افشار گردد، نگو هرگز نمیشه های های،
نگو هرگز نمیشه های های
سیا قرمز نمیشه های های

[1] *Pílasuwár* (Balasowar of the maps) is situated near the western shore of the Caspian, in the northern part of the province of Tálish, close to the Russo-Persian frontier, and was the scene of one of the earliest acts of Russian aggression.

[2] *Khalkhál* is a district between Ázarbáyján and Tálish, between Ardabíl and Miyána.

میشه گرگی بگلّه آشنا شه، نگو هرگز نمیشه های های،
میشه شیطان بشکل اولیا شه، نگو هرگز نمیشه های های،
میشه شهوت چرانی پادشا شه، نگو هرگز نمیشه های های،
نگو هرگز نمیشه های های
سیا قرمز نمیشه های های

بیا شاها صفا کن جان مولا، نگو هرگز نمیشه های های،
رعیّت را رها کن جان مولا، نگو هرگز نمیشه های های،
بملّت خوب تا کن جان مولا، نگو هرگز نمیشه های های،
نمد شولا نمیشه های های
جان مولا نمیشه های های

میشه ایران ویران گردد آباد، نگو هرگز نمیشه های های،
شود ظالم از این مشروطه دلشاد، نگو هرگز نمیشه های های،
یارو راضی نمیشه های های،
پشّه قاضی نمیشه های های،

(14)

After the *Coup d'État* of June 23, 1908, and the destruction of the First National Assembly, the free press of the first Constitutional Period entirely disappeared for some months, and Mírzá Jahángír Khán of Shíráz, the editor of the *Ṣúr-i-Isráfíl* ("Trumpet-call of Isráfíl"), one of the most notable publications of that period, was put to death by the ex-Sháh Muḥammad 'Alí in the Bágh-i-Sháh. "Dakhaw[1]," one of the most talented contributors to that paper, escaped to Europe, and again began to publish the paper at Yverdon in Switzerland on Muḥarram 1, A.H. 1327 (January 23, 1909). Only three numbers, so far as I

[1] See p. 190 *supra*.

این عکس در سال ۱۹۱۰ مسیحی در استانبول انداخته شد

Mírzá 'Alí Akbar "Dakhaw" (right) and Mírzá Ḥusayn Dánish Khán (left), both notable Persian poets

know, appeared; the third, published on March 8, 1909, contained the following elegy on Mírzá Jahángír Khán, "that Martyr of the Path of Liberty and most faithful defender of the rights of his country," by his associate and friend, the above-mentioned Mírzá 'Alí Akbar Dih-khudá, better known as "*Dakhaw*." It will be noticed that this poem, in the arrangement of its rhymes, shows strong traces of European influence. It runs as follows:

وصیّت نامهٔ دوست یگانهٔ من هدیّهٔ برادری بیوفا به پیشگاهِ
آن روح اقدس و اعلی،

(۱)

ای مرغِ سحر چو این شبِ تار، بگذاشت ز سر سیاه کاری،
وز نفحهٔ روح بخش اسحار، رفت از سرِ خفتگان خماری،
بگشود گره ز زلفِ زر تار، محبوبهٔ نیلگون عماری،
یزدان بکمال شد نمودار، واهریمنِ زشت خو حصاری،
یاد آر ز شمعِ مرده یاد آر،

(۲)

ای مؤنس یوسف اندرین بند، تعبیر عیان چو شد ترا خواب،
دل پُر ز شعف لب از شکر خند، محسودِ عدو بکام اصحاب،
رفتی برِ یار خویش و پیوند، آزادتر از نسیم و مهتاب،
زان کو همه شام با تو یك چند، در آرزوی وصالِ احباب،
اختر بسحر شمرده یاد آر،

(۳)

چون باغ شود دو باره خرّم، ای بلبل مستمند مسکین،
وز سنبل و سوری و سپرغم، آفاق نگارخانهٔ چین،
گل سرخ و برخ عرق ز شبنم، تو داده ز کف قرار و تمکین،
ز آن نو گل پیش رس که در غم، نا داده بنارِ شوق تسکین،
از سردی دی فسرده یاد آر،

(٤)

ای همرهِ تیهِ پور عمران، بگذشت چو این سنین معدود،
و آن شاهدِ نغزِ بزمِ عرفان، بنمود چو وعدِ خویش مشهود،
وز مذبح زر چو شد بکیوان، هر صبح شمیمِ عنبر و عود،
ز آن کو بگناه قوم نادان، در حسرتِ روی ارضِ موعود،
بر بادیه جان سپرده یاد آر،

(٥)

چون گشت ز نو زمانه آباد، ای کودك دورهٔ طلائی،
وز طاعت بندگان خود شاد، بگرفت ز سر خدا خدائی،
نه رسمِ ارم نه اسم شدّاد، گِل بست دهانِ ژاژ خائی،
ز آن کس که ز نوكِ تیغ جلّاد، مأخوذ بجرمِ حقّ ستائی،
پیمانهٔ وصل خورده یاد آر،

(*Prose Translation*)

"*In Memory of my incomparable Friend: the offering of an unworthy brother at the shrine of that most high and holy Spirit.*

(1)

"O bird of the morning, when this gloomy night puts aside its dark deeds,
And, at the life-giving breath of the Dawn, besotted slumber departs from the heads of those who sleep,
And the Loved One enthroned on the dark blue litter loosens the knots from her golden-threaded locks[1],
And God is manifested in perfection, while Ahriman of evil nature withdraws to his citadel,
Remember, O remember, that extinguished Lamp[2]!

(2)

"O companion of Joseph in this bondage, when the interpretation of the Dream becomes plain to thee,
And thy heart is full of joy, and thy lips with sweet laughter, and thou art as thy friends would have thee, and envied by thy foes,
And thou hast gone back to thy friends and kin, freer than the zephyr or the moonlight,
Remember him who, for a while throughout the night, in the desire to meet the friends, with thee counted the stars until the morning.

(3)

"When the garden smiles again, O poor, longing nightingale,
And when the horizons become like the picture-gallery of China with hyacinths, red roses and marjoram,
And when the rose is red, and the dew stands like sweat on its cheek, while thou hast relinquished rest and consideration,

[1] The golden rays of the sun in the dark blue pavilion of the sky are intended. In Persian there is no gender, but it is worth noting that in Arabic the sun is feminine, while the moon is masculine.

[2] *i.e.* Mírzá Jahángír Khán, who lighted us on our way ere the Dawn broke, until his light was quenched in death.

Remember that budding rose which bloomed before its time, and which withered in sorrow in the chill of December ere it had assuaged the fires of its cravings!

(4)

"O thou who wert the companion in the Desert of 'Imrán's son! When these few years have elapsed,
And that sweet comrade at the Banquet of Wisdom hath made manifest his promise,
And when each morning the fragrance of ambergris and aloes ascends to Saturn from the Golden Altar,
Remember him who, for the sins of an ignorant people, yielded up his life in the Desert, hoping for a sight of the Promised Land!

(5)

"When the times are once more propitious, O Child of the Golden Age,
And God, gladdened by the obedience of His Servants, once again assumes Divinity,
And there endures neither the fashion of Iram nor the name of Shaddád[1], but earth stops the mouth of him whose food was filth (*i.e.* whose words were folly),
Remember him who, punished for the crime of glorifying the truth, drained the draught of Union from the point of the headsman's sword!"

(15)

This and the two following poems are of some historical interest in connection with the incipient rising in Rasht, which, in conjunction with the gathering of the Bakhtiyárí clans at Iṣfahán, culminated in the capture of Ṭihrán and deposition of Muḥammad 'Alí Sháh in July, 1909. The first of these three poems appeared in the *Nasím-i-Shimál* (No. 23) of February 15, 1909, and recommends "deeds not words" to the people of Gílán.

[1] For the ancient Arabian tyrant Shaddád and his wonderful Garden of Iram, see *surá* lxxxix of the *Qur'án*, verses 5—7, and the commentaries on it. Here Muḥammad 'Alí, the ex-Sháh, and his garden, the *Bágh-i-Sháh*, are meant.

سلطنت بهرِ شهان با ستم وظلم نپاید، جان نثاری پی اصلاحِ وطن باید و شاید،
تا که همّت نکنی کس برُخت در نگشاید، مرد آن است که لب بندد و بازو بگشاید،
انبیا درج نمودند مقالات عدالت، اولیا جمله سرودند عبارات عدالت،
علما جمله نوشتند روایات عدالت، گفتگو بیهُده از مظلمه امروز نشاید،
مرد آن است که لب بندد و بازو بگشاید،
جاهدوا گفت خداوند بانجیل و بقرآن، خیز از بهر وطن همچو مجاهد بفشان جان،
خنجر و تیر و خدنگ است گل و نرگس و ریحان، نغمهٔ توپ وتفنگ است که غمها بزداید،
مرد آن است که لب بندد و بازو بگشاید،

(*Prose Translation*)

Sovereignty endureth not for cruel and tyrannical kings: to lay down life for the amelioration of one's country is meet and proper.
So long as thou makest no effort, no one will open the door before thee: he is a man who shuts his lips and stretches out his arm!

The Prophets have included in their utterances discourses on Justice: all the Saints have celebrated the praises of Justice:
All the learned have enshrined in their writings traditions of Justice: unseemly to-day is vain talk about Injustice:
He is a man who shuts his lips and stretches out his arm!

"Strive" (*jáhidú*) saith God both in the Gospels and in the *Qur'án*: arise, then, and like a "striver" (*mujáhid*) lay down thy life for thy country's sake[1]!

[1] See *Qur'án*, v, 39; ix, 41, 87; xxii, 77. *Mujáhid* (the title given during the Persian Revolution to the National Volunteers) is the participle corresponding to the noun *Jihád*, which means a "striving" "in God's way" (*fí sabíli'lláh*), and in the *Qur'án* especially fighting for the Faith, but in these days for the Fatherland. The appeal to the *Gospels* as well as the *Qur'án* is interesting and characteristic, for it must be remembered that many of those *Mujáhidín* were Armenian Christians.

Dagger, arrow and javelin are as the rose, the narcissus and the basil: it is the roar of cannons and guns which will dissipate our sorrows!
He is a man who shuts his lips and stretches out his arm!

(16)

The following verses appeared in the same issue of the *Nasím-i-Shimál* as the last, and celebrate the adhesion (or apparent adhesion) of the *Sipahdár*, who had previously been employed by the Sháh in the siege of Tabríz, to the Nationalist Cause. The quatrain immediately following these verses appeared in the issue of the same paper dated March 5, 1909, and like them celebrates the praises of the *Sipahdár*.

شده گیلان دگر باره پر انوار،   ز یُمْنِ مقدم سعد سپهدار،
سزد گیلانیان یکسر نمایند،   غُبارِ مقدمش‌را کحلِ ابصار،
جهانگیرا امیرِ دستگیرا،   که نامت منتشر گشته در اقطار،
بعمرِ خود ندیدست و نبینند،   چو تو ملّت پرستی هیچ دیّار،
ز دیلم گر عیان شد آلِ بُوَیَه،   ز تنکابُن چو تو گشته پدیدار،
میانِ صد هزاران خلق چون دید،   خدایت لایقِ هر شغل و هر کار،
ز لطفِ خویش بر گوشِ دلت گفت،   که هان بشتاب و گیلان‌را نگهدار،
نگهدارش که نامت باد باقی،   نگهدارش که عمرت باد بسیار
الا تا رایتِ مشروطه بر پاست،   هلا تا جام مشروطه است سرشار
همیشه باد مدّاحِ تو اشرف
نگهدارت خداوند جهاندار،

روشن و تابنده باد نام سپهدار،   باقی و پاینده باد نام سپهدار
هم بفلك ثبت در جراید عرشی،   هم بزمین زنده باد نام سپهدار

(*Translation*)

Once again Gílán is filled with radiance by the blessing of the auspicious advance of the *Sipahdár*.
It were meet that all the people of Gílán should make the dust of his advance collyrium for their eyesight!
O Conqueror of the world, O Saviour-Chief, whose fame hath become spread abroad throughout the lands,
No inhabitant [of this land] hath ever in his life beheld or will behold a patriot like thee!
If the House of Buwayh appeared from Daylam, from Tankábun hath appeared one like thee[1]!
Since, amongst hundreds of thousands of the people, God saw thee worthy of every work and deed,
In His Mercy He whispered into the ear of thy heart, "O make haste, and take charge of Gílán!
"Take charge of it, that thy name may endure for ever! Take charge of it, and may thy life be long!"
O, so long as the Standard of the Constitution stands, and so long as the cup of the Constitution brims over,
May Ashraf ever be thy panegyrist! May God the Ruler of the world keep thee in safety!

May the name of the *Sipahdár* be bright and resplendent,
May the name of the *Sipahdár* continue and endure!
May the name of the *Sipahdár* live on earth,
And may it be inscribed in the register of Heaven!

(17)

The following poem also appeared in the *Nasím-i-Shimál*, in No. 27, issued on March 5, 1909. It is supposed to express the despair of the Devil at the downfall of Despotism, and is not lacking in merit and originality.

[1] The House of Buwayh ruled over the greater part of Southern Persia from A.D. 932 to 1055, and came originally from the shores of the Caspian Sea. Though their immediate ancestor was of humble station, they claimed noble Persian descent, and the learned al-Bírúní supports this claim.

(١)

گفت شیطانِ دغا آخ چکنم واخ چکنم، گشت مشروطه بپا آخ چکنم واخ چکنم،
مرغِ مشروطه بگلزارِ وطن شهپر زد، معدلت بر رگِ شریانِ ستم خنجر زد،
نام مشروطه بچشمِ ظلمه خنجر زد، مستبد گشت فنا آخ چکنم واخ چکنم،

(٢)

من که شیطانم از این غصّه زمین گیر شدم، مستبدّین همه مردند ز غم پیر شدم،
راستی منکه ز اوضاعِ جهان سیر شدم، گشتم انگشت نما آخ چکنم واخ چکنم،
گفت شیطانِ دغا آخ چکنم واخ چکنم،

(٣)

منکه دیوانه شدم ای عقلا دور شوید، می زنم سنگ بسرهای شما دور شوید،
مستبدّین همه گشتند فنا دور شوید، زده مشروطه لوا آخ چکنم واخ چکنم،
گفت شیطانِ دغا آخ چکنم واخ چکنم،

(٤)

سالها بود که خونِ همه‌را می خوردیم، پولها از طرف بیوه زنان می بردیم،
دلِ ملّت را بسیصد جور می آزردیم، همه گشتیم گدا آخ چکنم واخ چکنم،
گفت شیطانِ دغا آخ چکنم واخ چکنم،

(٥)

نیست شد ظلم و جفا حیله و تزویر بمرد، محو شد رنگ و ریا رشوهٔ بی پیر بمرد،
ظالم از رنج و عنا گشت زمین گیر بمرد، رفت آهش بسما آخ چکنم واخ چکنم،
گفت شیطانِ دغا آخ چکنم واخ چکنم،

(٦)

هفت مه بود که مشروطه درین ملك نبود، زارعین‌را بدن از قمچی ما بود کبود،
جوجه و مرغ و فسنجان ز سرِ خوانِ ربود، پر زد و رفت هوا آخ چکنم واخ چکنم،
مستبد گشت فنا آخ چکنم واخ چکنم،

(٧)

ای فلك آن همه بد حرفی و شلتاق چه شد، چادر و دستگه و تخته و تخماق چه شد،
نقلِ چوب و فلك و ضربتِ شلّاق چه شد، چه شد آن نشو و نما آخ چکنم واخ چکنم،
گفت شیطانِ دغا آخ چکنم واخ چکنم،

(٨)

چه شد آن قتلِ رعیّت چه شد آن ظلم و عذاب، چه شد آن برّهٔ بریان چه شد آن جام شراب،
چه شد آن شربتِ قند و چه شد آن مرغِ کباب، چه شد آن برگ و نوا آخ چکنم واخ چکنم،
گفت شیطانِ دغا آخ چکنم واخ چکنم،

(٩)

مرشدا نسخهٔ تسخیر تُه بر چین و برو، زاهدا سفرهٔ بی پیر تُه بر چین و برو،
شیخنا مسند تزویر تُه بر چین و برو، گشته دَوْرِ عقلا آخ چکنم واخ چکنم،
مستبدّ گشت فنا آخ چکنم واخ چکنم،

(١٠)

اهلِ گیلان همه یکمرتبه هشیار شدند، از حقوق وطنِ خویش خبردار شدند،
دزدی امشب نتوان کرد که بیدار شدند، شحنه در داد ندا آخ چکنم واخ چکنم،
مستبد گشت فنا آخ چکنم واخ چکنم،

(۱۱)

اصفهان در کنفِ حضرت صمصام آمد، کارِ تبریز ز سردار بانجام آمد،
خاكِ گیلان ز سپهدار نکو نام آمد، رشت بگرفت صفا آخ چکنم واخ چکنم،
مستبد گشت فنا آخ چکنم واخ چکنم،

(*Translation*)

(1)

The wily old Devil did groan and greet,
"What'll I do? O what'll I do?
"For the Constitution has found its feet:
"What'll I do? O what'll I do?
"The Bird of Liberty preens its wings in a rose-girt land,
"And Tyranny's vein is severed at last by Justice's hand,
"And the Despot's eyes are blinded by Freedom's gleaming brand,
"And the autocrats are, it would seem, dead beat,
"What'll I do? O what'll I do?"
The wily old Devil did groan and greet,
"What'll I do? O what'll I do?"

(2)

"I, the Devil, with this vexation am now laid low;
"All the despots are dead, and I am grown old with woe;
"In very truth I am sorry and sick at the way things go.
"I'm exposed to the finger of scorn in the street:
"What'll I do? O what'll I do?"
The wily old Devil did groan and greet,
"What'll I do? O what'll I do?"

(3)

"Men of sense! I am mad: 'Twere best you should let me alone!
"Lest I arise and break your heads with stick or with stone!
"For the autocrats all are uprooted and scattered and overthrown,

"And the Flag of Freedom the people greet:
"What'll I do? O what'll I do?"
The wily old Devil did groan and greet,
"What'll I do? O what'll I do?"

(4)

"For many a year from all and sundry I sucked the gore,
"And stole the hard-won moneys I found in the widow's store,
"And afflicted the heart of the people with sorrows and griefs galore:
"But now we're beggars who roam the street,
"What'll I do? O what'll I do?"
The wily old Devil did groan and greet,
"What'll I do? O what'll I do?"

(5)

"Deceit is dead, and cruel oppression hath passed away:
"Hypocrisy's crushed and godless bribery's lost its sway:
"Fallen and dead is the despot, his head with grief grown grey:
"His sighs to heaven rise swift and fleet,
"What'll I do? O what'll I do?"
The wily old Devil did groan and greet,
"What'll I do? O what'll I do?"

(6)

"For seven months this country no Constitution knew:
"With our whips and our scourges the backs of the peasants were black and blue.
"But now from the libertine's tables the chickens and game and stew
"Have taken their flight with hurrying feet:
"What'll I do? O what'll I do?"
The wily old Devil did groan and greet,
"What'll I do? O what'll I do?"

(7)

"Heavens! What hath become of our curses and oaths and
blows?
"Our pavilions and pomps, and the thrones and truncheons
which we dispose?
"The sticks and scourges and rods that were ready in ranks
and rows?
"What hath arrested our nimble feet?
"What'll I do? O what'll I do?"
The wily old Devil did groan and greet,
"What'll I do? O what'll I do?"

(8)

"What hath become of our slaughter of peasants and torments
grim?
"What of our roasted lambs and our goblets filled to the brim?
"What of our sherbets sweet and the succulent capon's limb?
"Whither is gone our delectable meat?
"What'll I do? O what'll I do?"
The wily old Devil did groan and greet,
"What'll I do? O what'll I do?"

* * * *

(18)

The following poem appeared in No. 45 of the *Nasím-i-Shimál* on July 12, 1909, the very day on which the first detachment of the Nationalist Volunteers under the command of the *Sipahdár* entered Ṭihrán[1]. It depicts Shaykh Faẓlu'lláh, the reactionary *mujtahid*, hastening to betray Persian independence and ready to sell the country by auction to the highest bidder. A rhymed paraphrase of the first half of this poem is appended.

[1] See my *Persian Revolution*, p. 315.

نه یه لازم بوخارا مسجدلر، بوخیرسز داشلار، دیره‌ک آخماق
انگلیس‌لره قویسون گیتسون .

English tourist collecting antiques

(From *Mullá Naṣru'd-Dín*, Year iii, No. 5, Feb. 16, 1908)

(۱)

حاجی بازار رواج است رواج، کو خریدار هراج است هراج،
می فروشم همهٔ ایران را، عرض و ناموسِ مسلمانان را
رشت و قزوین و قُم و کاشان را، بخرید این وطنِ ارزان را،
یزد و خوانسار هراج است هراج، کو خریدار هراج است هراج،

(۲)

دشمنِ فرقهٔ احرار منم، قاتلِ زمرهٔ احرار منم،
شیخ فضل‌اللّهِ سمسار منم، دین فروشنده ببازار منم،
مالِ مُرْدار هراج است هراج، کو خریدار هراج است هراج،

(۳)

با همه خلق عداوت دارم، دشمنی با همه ملّت دارم،
از خودِ شاه وکالت دارم، بهراج از همه دعوت دارم،
وقتِ افطار هراج است هراج، کو خریدار هراج است هراج

(٤)

شهرِ نو اردوی ملّی زده رج، متفرّق شده قزّاقِ کرج،
گر که دیوانه شوم نیست حرج، جز هراجم نبود راه فرج،
رختِ زر تار هراج است هراج، کو خریدار هراج است هراج

(٥)

طبل و شیپور علم‌را کی میخاد، شیر و خورشید رقم‌را کی میخاد،
تختِ جمشیدِ عجم‌را کی میخاد، تاجِ کی مسندِ جم‌را کی میخاد،
اسپ و افسار هراج است هراج، کو خریدار هراج است هراج

(٦)

می دهم تختِ کیان‌را بگرو، می زنم مسندِ جم‌را به علو،
می کشم قابِ خورش‌را به جلو، می خورم قیمه پلو قرمه چلو،
رشتهٔ خوشکار هراج است هراج، کو خریدار هراج است هراج،

(٧)

آن شنیدم که حجج در عتبات، زده چادر بلب شطِ فرات،
شده عازم بعجم با صلوات، جز هراجم نبود راه نجات،
دین بناچار هراج است هراج، کو خریدار هراج است هراج،

(٨)

گر ز اسلام بشد قطع اثر، ور بپا گشت بگیلان محشر،
ور بتبریز اُرُس کرد سفر، هرچه شد شد بجهنّم بسقر،
فوجِ افشار هراج است هراج، کو خریدار هراج است هراج،

(٩)

جدِّ مرحوم شه از مهر و داد، هفده شهر ز قفقازیه داد،
آنچه از مالِ پدر مانده ز یاد، می فروشد همه‌را بادا باد،
همه یکبار هراج است هراج، کو خریدار هراج است هراج،

(١٠)

می کشد صیحه سروش از طرفی، بختیاری بخروش از طرفی،
ملّتِ رشت بجوش از طرفی، شیخ‌را عزم فروش از طرفی،
فرشِ دربار هراج است هراج، کو خریدار هراج است هراج،

(۱۱)

در همه مکر و فن استادم من، مفتیِ بصره و بغدادم من،
قاضِ سلطنت آبادم من، آی عجب در تله افتادم من،
گرگ و کنتار هراج است هراج، کو خریدار هراج است هراج،

(*Translation*)

(1)

Ḥájji, the market's brisk, the bidding high;
Here comes the auctioneer! Who'll buy? Who'll buy'
I'm here the Persian land to sell or pawn,
The pride and honour of each Musulmán,
Both Qum and Rasht, both Qazwín and Káshán,
Yazd, Khwánsár, every city of Írán.
All's up for auction at a figure fair:
Come, gentlemen, where is a bidder, where?

(2)

Of Liberals I am the stalwart foe:
I'd like to kill them all, as well you know!
I represent Shaykh Faẓlu'lláh and Co.,
Brokers, who hawk Religion to and fro,
Here is the carcase. Gentlemen, draw near!
Who'll buy? Who'll buy? Here comes the auctioneer!

(3)

My countrymen I loathe and execrate;
My country is the object of my hate!
I represent our Monarch wise and great,
Who to my hands commits the Nation's fate!
'Tis time for breakfast. Put this business through!
Who bids? Who bids? Come Sir, a bid from you!

(4)

At Shahr-i-Naw behold the patriots' post!
Scattered at Karach is the Cossack host!
Well may I rave, or e'en give up the ghost!
Let's sell the land to him who offers most!
    What offer for this richly-wrought brocade
    With gold enwoven? Is no offer made?

(5)

Who wants these trumpets, drums and flags to own?
Who'd make the Lion and the Sun his own?
Who'll make a bid for Persian Jamshíd's throne?
Kay's crown, Jam's sceptre in with these are thrown!
    For this fine horse and for this bridle rare
    Who'll make a bid? Where is an offer, where?

* * * *

(19)

The following poem, which celebrates the Nationalist victory and capture of Ṭihrán, the deposition of Muḥammad 'Alí, and the accession of his young son Sulṭán Aḥmad Sháh, appeared in No. 48 of the *Nasím-i-Shimál* on August 1, 1909, only a fortnight after these stirring events. It and the poem next succeeding are remarkable not only for their spirited words and metre and the wonderful lilt of the lines, but for a note of triumph and optimism which too rarely reveals itself in these poems. The beauty of both poems lies largely in the euphony of the phrases and the splendour of the rhythm and rhymes, which I have despaired of rendering adequately into English, even in the freest paraphrase. As the poems present no particular difficulty I have not given a prose translation, but have contented myself with adding a few notes to explain allusions to current events.

شهنشاهِ جوان شیرانِ جنگ آور نگر' در نگر' عالمی دیگر نگر
را راحت از مشروطه سر تا سر نگر' در نگر' عالمی دیگر نگر

پادشاهی کن که دورانِ جهان برکامِ تست، رامِ تست، شاه احمد نامِ تست،
در محامد خویش‌را همنامِ پیغمبر نگر، در نگر، عالمی دیگر نگر،
دادخواهی کن درین مشروطه چون نوشیروان، درجهان، رخشِ همّت برجهان،
خویش‌را والاتر از دارا و اسکندر نگر، در نگر، عالمی دیگر نگر،
در معارف دشمنانِ علم‌را نابود کن، جود کن، جهل‌را مفقود کن،
وقتِ تنگ ورخشِ لنگ وسختیِ معبر نگر، در نگر، عالمی دیگر نگر،
آخر این ایران که بوده جای جم پایتختِ کی، اهلِ وی، غرقِ غفلت تا بکی،
باغبانا باغ‌را بی شاخ و برگ و بر نگر، در نگر، عالمی دیگر نگر،
ای سپهدارِ رشید ای روح بخشِ زنده دم، دمبدم، در ترقّی زن قدم،
نامِ خودرا تا جهان باقیست در دفتر نگر، در نگر، عالمی دیگر نگر،
پارلمان‌را از وکیلانِ صحیح آباد کن، داد کن، ملّتی‌را شاد کن،
خائنین‌را زود کن اخراج بر محضر نگر، در نگر، عالمی دیگر نگر،
شیخ نوری دستگیرِ فرقهٔ احرار شد[1] خوار شد، [2]مقتدر بر دار شد،
وآن [3]مفاخر گشت حلق آویز بر کیفر نگر، در نگر، عالمی دیگر نگر،
مدّتی با شیخ رفتی با حریفان ساختی، تاختی، دیدی آخر باختی،
حال و روزِ بعد ازینت‌را از این بدتر نگر، در نگر، عالمی دیگر نگر،
سینه کوبان شیخنا گوید بزاری در جلَو، کو چلَو، آخ چه شد خرما پلو،

[1] The execution of Shaykh Fazlu'lláh of Núr, the reactionary *mujtahid*, is announced in the latest news in this same issue.

[2] The allusion is to the *Muqtadir-i-Nizám*, who had been already punished in April, 1908, for the part he took in the Abortive *Coup d'État* of December, 1907. (See my *Persian Revolution*, p. 199.) He was not, however, hanged in August, 1909, as this poem implies.

[3] The *Mufákhiru'l-Mulk*, who had been Vice-Governor of Ṭihrán and had taken refuge at the Russian Legation, was condemned to death by the Special Court instituted to try such cases, and was shot on July 29, 1909. See my *Persian Revolution*, p. 329.

کو فسنجن کو مُتَنْجَن جای شربت تر نگر، در نگر، عالمی دیگر نگر،
کو خورشهای لذیذ و مرغهای با مزه، خوشمزه، نو کباب و خربزه،
کبك‌را در کوهسار و برّه را در بر نگر، در نگر، عالمی دیگر نگر،

(20)

The following poem by Bahár of Mashhad, of which the general character has been discussed in the last article, appeared in No. 1 of the *Írán-i-Naw* ("New Persia") on August 24, 1909.

می ده که طی شد دورانِ جان‌کاه، آسوده شد ملك الملك لله،
شد شاهِ نورا اقبال همراه، کوسِ شهی کوفت بر رغمِ بدخواه،
شد صبح طالع طی شد شبانگاه، الحمد لله الحمد لله،

یك چند مارا غم رهنمون شد، جان یارِ غم گشت دل غرقِ خون شد،
نامِ وطن‌را رخ نیلگون شد، و امروزه دشمن خوار و زبون شد،
زین جنبشِ سخت زین فتح ناگاه، الحمد لله الحمد لله،

چندی ز بیداد فرسوده گشتیم، با خاك و با خون آلوده گشتیم،
زیرِ پیِ خصم پیموده گشتیم، و امروز دیگر آسوده گشتیم،
از ظلمِ ظالم وز کیدِ بدخواه، الحمد لله الحمد لله،

آنانکه مارا کُشتند و بستند، قلبِ وطن‌را از کینه خستند،
از بد نژادی پیمان شکستند، از جنگِ ملّت آخر نجستند،
ازحضرتِ شیخ[1] تا حضرتِ شاه[1]، الحمد لله الحمد لله،

[1] *i.e.* Shaykh Fazlu'lláh of Núr and the ex-Sháh Muḥammad 'Alí.

ه با جور منصوب گشتند، در معدهٔ ملك مِکْرُوب گشتند[1]
بملّت مغضوب گشتند، از ساحتِ ملك جاروب گشتن
ِ جاهل شیخانِ گمراه، الحمد للّه الحمد للّ

کدخدا دید جورِ شبان را، از جا بر انگیخت ستّار خان‌را[2]
ستم ساخت آن مرزبان‌را، تا کرد رنگین تیغ و سنان‌ر
ونِ دشمن وز مغزِ بدخواه، الحمد للّه الحمد للّ

مستبدّین لختی جهیدند، گفتند لختی لختی شنیدن
ه ز هر سو شیران رسیدند، آن روبهان باز دم در کشیدن
طُعمهٔ شیر مکّار روباه، الحمد للّه الحمد للّ

شد یار با بختیاری، گیلانیان‌را حق کرد یار
عدو شد یکسر فراری، در کُنْجِ غم گشت دشمن حصار
کارِ ملّت بر طرزِ دلخواه، الحمد للّه الحمد للّ

سپهدار[3] شد فتنه‌را سد، یکسو یورش برد سردارِ اسعـ
امِ پردل[3] آمد زیك حد، بر کف گرفتند تیغ سهنـ
بر خصم از هر طرف راه، الحمد للّه الحمد للّ

خواهِ دین‌را سدّ متین بود، خاکش بسر شد پاداشش این ب
ن که با عیش دائم قرین بود، اکنون قرین است با ناله و
الحمد للّه الحمد للّه

1 "Became as microbes in the helly of the Commonwealth."

2 Sattár Khán, the hero of Tabríz.

3 The *Sipahdár*, who was nominally in command of the Army of Rasht, and the Bakhtiyárí chiefs *Sardár-i-As'ad* and *Ẓarghámu's-Salṭana*, were the chief heroes of the Nationalist Victory of July, 1909.

بخت سپهدار فرخنده بادا، سردار اسعد پاینده بادا،
صمصام ایمان بُرّنده بادا، ضرغام دین را دل زنده بادا،
کافتاد از ایشان بدخواه درچاه، الحمد لله الحمد لله،

ستّار خان را بادا ظفر یار، تبریزیان را یزدان نگهدار،
سالارشان را نیکو بود کار، احرار را نیز دل باد بیدار،
تا جمله گویند با جان آگاه، الحمد لله الحمد لله،

(ترقّی) (ملك الشّعرا بهار)

(21)

The following poem, entitled "the disordered dream of Muḥammad 'Alí Mírzá on the first night of his arrival at Odessa in Russia," appeared on December 16, 1909, in No. 91 of the *Írán-i-Naw*.

(خواب پریشان محمّد علی میرزا اوّلین شب زندگانی در اودیسای روسیه)

خواب می بینم که گویا شاه ایرانم هنوز، در میان باغ خود در بغی و عصیانم هنوز،
خواب می بینم بهادر جنگ با آن سنگ ننگ، می ستاید شه سنه قربان قربانم هنوز،
خواب می بینم ایاخوف بود پولکونیك روس، می دهد با تیپ قزّاقان خود سانم هنوز،
خواب می بینم مشیر السّلطنه چون گاو پیر، می مکاند خون مردم از دو پستانم هنوز،
خواب می بینم که سعد الدّوله آن خود خواه محض، مژدهها بخشد ز همراهیّ روسانم هنوز،
خواب می بینم که شیخ نوری و میرزا حسن، می دهند فتوای کسر حلف قرآنم هنوز،
خواب می بینم امام جمعه و امثال او، می کنند تحریك نقض عهد و پیمانم هنوز،
خواب می بینم که اکبر شاه و کور آملی، بر منابر می سرایند ظلّ سبحانم هنوز،
خواب می بینم مجلّل با صراحی شراب، در حضور استاده با زلف پریشانم هنوز،

، می بینم که در خلوت ندیمی ساده روی‘ می فریبد با دو چشم مست وفتّان

، می بینم که تالان می کنند تبریزرا‘ عین دوله با صمد خان ورحیم خا

، می بینم ز بهرصرف جنگ از بانك روس‘ با گروهمچون گدایان قرض خواها

(عشق آباد‘ منیر)

(*Translation*)

"I dream once more I rule o'er Persia's land,
And in my garden scoff at God's command.
Bahádur Jang before me still I see,
Who cries 'O King! May I thy ransom be!'
Liakhoff too, my Russian colonel true,
Marshals his Cossacks still before my view.
While old *Mushíru's-Salṭana*, the cow!
Drains, as of yore, the people's life-blood now,
And *Sa'du'd-Dawla*, egotist unique,
Still to my ears of Russian aid doth speak.
The Shaykh of Núr and Mírzá Ḥasan both
Sanction the breaking of my solemn oath.
The *Imám-Jum'a* and his pious peers
Urge me to break my word and have no fears.
Kúr Ámulí and Akbar Sháh withal
Me still 'God's shadow on the Earth' do call.
Mujallal, with the wine-cup in his hand,
With locks dishevelled doth before me stand;
While smooth-cheeked pages with love-wanton eyes
Bemuse my wits and make my heart their prize;
And *'Aynu'd-Dawla*, Ṣamad and Raḥím
Still loot the town of Tabríz in my dream.
Still from the Russian Bank my wars to wage
I beg for cash and offer pledge and gauge[1]."

[1] All the persons mentioned in the above poem were notorious reactionaries, and full accounts of most of them will be found in my *Persian Revolution*, viz. of *Amír-Bahádur Jang* on pp. 114, 162, 166, 199–200, 227, 261, 321, 330, 334 and 446–7; of *Liakhoff*, *passim*; of *Mushíru's-Salṭana*, pp. 334, 405, 445; of *Sa'du'd-Dawla*, pp. 52, 131, 137, 140, 154–5, 166, 306, 330, 334 and 443; of 'Ábidín Khán *Mujallalu's-Sulṭán*, pp. 198–200, 330, 432, 445 and 447–8; of *'Aynu'd-Dawla*,

(22)

The following fine poem originally appeared on July 26, 1909, in the *Nasím-i-Shimál*, No. 47; and again in the *Írán-i-Naw*, No. 93, on December 19, 1909. In the first only it bears the superscription من کلام عشور عمو. In the second it is followed by another poem signed Mírzá Taqí Khán *Darwísh*, but it is not clear whether this signature is intended to apply to both poems or only to the second.

(۱)

صد شکر حقوقِ وطن امروز ادا شد، به به چه بجا شد،
هنگامِ وفا وقت صنا دفع جفا شد، به به چه بجا شد،

(۲)

الحمد که قانونِ الهی جریان یافت، ملّت هیجان یافت، شد کشته و جان یافت،
قرآنِ محمّد همه‌را راهنما شد، مشروطه بپا شد، به به چه بجا شد،

(۳)

میخواست ستمگر بکُشد نوش لبان‌را، والا نسبان‌را قانون طلبان‌را،
حسرت بدلش ماند وخودش رفت وفنا شد، به به چه بجا شد،

(٤)

این غلغله وین جنبش و این شورشِ ملّی، این کوششِ ملّی وین جوششِ ملّی،
واللّه که از بهر حقوق فقرا شد، به به چه بجا شد،

pp. 105, 108-9, 111, 113, 117-118, 124, 256, 272, 327; of Ṣamad Khán *Shujá'u'd-Dawla*, pp. 270, 273, 442 and 446; and of Raḥím Khán, pp. 141-2, 148, 256, 269, 271, 296, 347, 349, 441 and 446. By "the Shaykh of Núr" is meant Shaykh Faẓlu'lláh, concerning whom see pp. 113, 148-9, 242, 262 and 444-5 of the same work. For Ḥájji Mírzá Ḥasan the *mujtahid* of Tabríz, see *ibid.*, pp. 107, 249 and 262; for the *Imám-Jum'a* of Ṭihrán, Mírzá Abu'l-Qásim, pp. 80-81, 89-90, 131, 281 and 444. By *Kúr-i-Ámulí* ("the Blind Man of Ámul") is meant Mullá Muḥammad of Ámul, in Mázandarán, also called *Kúr-i-Mawṣil*. Sayyid Akbar Sháh was a *rawẓa-khwán*, or religious rhapsodist.

(۵)

شد خلع محمّد علی از تخت کیانی، آن سان که تو دانی پیدا نه ...
از چنگ دو رنگان وطن امروز رها شد، جامان همه جا شد، به به چه بجا

(٦)

خلّاق جهان تازه بما شاه جوان داد، هم قوّتِ جان داد، بل روح روان د
از جهدِ سپهدار وطنِ کام روا شد، به به چه بجا شد،

(۷)

ای ملّت تبریز سعادت شدتان یار، ای حضرتِ ستّار و ای باقرِ سالار
از همّتتان مات عقولِ عقلا شد، به به چه بجا شد،

(۸)

تا شد عَلَمِ نَصْرٌ مِنَ ٱللّه نمایان، در خطّهٔ طهران ای ملّت گیلان
از سطوتتان محو همه ارض وسما شد، به به چه بجا شد،

(۹)

تا شد ز صفاهان عَلَمِ کاوه پدیدار، شد بخت بما یار از جلوهٔ سردار
اسعد که مدد بخشِ جنودِ سُعَدا شد، به به چه بجا شد،

(۱۰)

تا خواست خداوند که مخلوق نمیرند، ذلّت نپذیرند مشروطه بگیرند،
احمد شهِ والا بسرِ تختِ طلا شد، به به چه بجا شد،

(۱۱)

المنّة للّه که جوان شاهِ خجسته، چون لالهٔ رسته بر تخت نشسته
هان ای عقلا وقت گسیلِ وکلا شد، به به چه بجا شد،

(۱۲)

قاطرچی و الدنگ ودبوری بکجا رفت، نوری بکجا رفت سوری بکجا رفت،
بارو بدرك رفت ودبوری کله پا شد، به به چه بجا شد،

(۱۴)

یا شیخ نه بینی تو دگر رنگِ علورا، نه قیمه پلورا نه قرمه چلورا،
دودِ دلت از داغ فسنجان بهوا شد، به به چه بجا شد [1]

(23)

The following "Mother's Lullaby" (*Láy-láy-i-Mádarána*) appeared on February 2, 1910, in No. 123 of the *Írán-i-Naw* above the signature "Láhútí of Kirmánsháh."

آمد سحر و موسم کاراست بالام لای، خواب تو دگر باعث عار است بالام لای،
لای لای، بالا لای لای، لای لای بالا لای لای،
جنگ است که مردم همه درکارو تو درخواب، اقبال وطن بسته بکار است بالام لای،
بر خیز و سوی مدرسه بشتاب، لای لای بالا لای لای،
خاك تن آباء تو با خون شهیدان، برگرد تو زان خاك حصاری است بالام لای،
گردیده غمین مادر ایران، لای لای بالا لای لای،
تو کودك ایرانی و ایران وطنِ تست، جان‌را تن بی عیب بکار است بالام لای،
تو جانی و ایران چو تنِ تست، لای لای بالا لای لای،

[1] The two texts of this poem offer a certain number of variants which for my present purpose I have not deemed it necessary to record. I have followed in the main the *N.S.* version, which contains 3 stanzas (10, 11 and 13) omitted in *I.N.* The most important variant occurs in the third *miṣrá'* of stanza 8, where *N.S.* reads

ملیّتتان درج به الواحِ بقا شد.

بر خیز سلحشور و تو در حفظ وطن کوش، ای تازه گل ایران ز چه خوار است بالام لای،
پس جامهٔ عزّت ببدن پوش، لای لای بالا لای لای،
جای تو نه گهواره بود جای تو زین است، ای شیر پسر وقت شکار است بالام لای،
بر خیز که دشمن بکمین است، لای لای بالا لای لای،
نگذار وطن قسمت اغیار بگردد، با آنکه وطن‌را چو تو یار است بالام لای،
ناموس وطن خوار بگردد، لای لای بالا لای لای،

(لاهوتی کرمانشاهی)

(*Translation*)

(1)

Morn hath come and the time for work, with a *lám-láy, lám-láy*;
'Tis a shame any longer to sleep or to shirk, with a *lám-láy, lám-láy*!
Láy-láy, bálá láy-láy! Láy-láy, bálá láy-láy!

(2)

War's toward, and work for all; no time to waste, with a *lám-láy*;
Our country's hope on this work is based, with a *lám-láy, lám-láy*;
Rise, then, rise, and to college haste, with a *lám-láy, lám-láy*!
Láy-láy, bálá láy-láy! Láy-láy, bálá láy-láy!

(3)

From the martyrs' blood and thy forbears' dust, with a *lám-láy, lám-láy*,
A rampart rings thee which thou canst trust, with a *lám-láy, lám-láy*:
Sorrow we may, but struggle we must, with a *lám-láy, lám-láy*!
Láy-láy, bálá láy-láy! Láy-láy, bálá láy-láy!

(4)

A Persian boy art thou, and Persia thy fatherland, with a *lám-láy*;
Well in a faultless body a fearless soul doth stand, with a *lám-láy*!
That soul art thou, and this body of thine is the Persian land, with a *lám-láy*!
Láy-láy, bálá láy-láy! Láy-láy, bálá láy-láy!

(5)

Rise in arms, and to save the State thy quality show, with a *lám-láy*!
Wherefore, O tender rose-bud, is Persia brought so low, with a *lám-láy*!
With a garment of glory invest thyself, that it be not so, with a *lám-láy*!
Láy-láy, bálá láy-láy! Láy-láy, bálá láy-láy!

(6)

No longer the cot but the saddle now is thy proper place, with a *lám-láy*!
O lion-cub, 'tis time for the chase, with a *lám-láy, lám-láy*!
Arise, arise, for a foeman lurks in each sheltering space, with a *lám-láy*!
Láy-láy, bálá láy-láy! Láy-láy, bálá láy-láy!

(7)

Suffer not that thy native land be the foeman's share, with a *lám-láy*!
Since it hath like thee a hero bold and a champion rare, with a *lám-láy*!
Let not its honour decline and its hope be turned to despair, with a *lám-láy*!
Láy-láy, bálá láy-láy! Láy-láy, bálá láy-láy!

(24)

The following poem, also by Láhútí of Kirmánsháh, appeared on February 9, 1910, in No. 129 of the *Írán-i-Naw*, and is a denunciation of the notorious Raḥím Khán Chalíbánlú. The earlier career of this miscreant is recorded in my *Persian Revolution*. Immediately after the deposition of Muḥammad 'Alí, on August 8, 1909, he began to loot sundry Armenian villages in N.W. Persia and to massacre the inhabitants. Ten days later he openly revolted against the restored Constitutional Government. On August 29 he was captured by Russian troops, but was released by them on September 18 on payment of a considerable sum of money. A month later he marched on Ardabíl, which was reported to have fallen into his hands on November 2. A few days later a second body of Russian troops was sent to Ardabíl, ostensibly to effect his capture, and on November 10 it was stated on the authority of the *Times* correspondent at Ṭihrán that £25,000 had already been expended by the Persian Government on the equipment of an army to take the field against him. This army, commanded by Yeprem Khán, the Armenian, inflicted a severe defeat upon him on December 31, 1909, and four days later had driven him back on the Russian frontier and surrounded him so thoroughly that only across that frontier could he escape. The Persian Government, appealing to the explicit provisions of the Treaty of Turkmán-cháy, begged the Russian Government not to permit him to take refuge across their border; they not only allowed him to do this, however, but refused his extradition on February 4, 1910, and allowed him to proceed to Elizavetpol (the ancient Ganja), where he remained for nearly a year. He subsequently returned to Tabríz (about January 23, 1911) where he was ultimately put to death. His was one of the numerous flagrant cases of Russian patronage and protection accorded to Persian subjects in active revolt against their Government. An illustration facing p. 440 of my *Persian Revolution* shows him, surrounded by a number of his followers, with his hand affectionately clasping that of a Russian Consular official, while a Russian officer stands a little distance from him on the other side.

(خاطرهٔ مشئوم رحیم خان)

فو بغیرت آن بی حقوق بی ناموس، که بعد از ین همه زشتی پناه برد بروس،
گمانم اینکه بجز ملك روس جائی نیست، پناه گاه چنین مردمان بی ناموس،
جیم خان که جهان پُر ز صیت ظلم وی است، شد از حمایت روسیه از خطر محروس،
دانم از چه سبب دولتی باین عظمت، بخویش خواند این دیو سیرتان عبوس،
زار حیف کز این دوستی بی هنگام، نمود دشمنی خویش را بما محسوس،
غبار نفرت وگرد نفار این کردار، بشد ز بحر خزر تا کنار اقیانوس،
چه خوب بود بجای ضیافت و اکرام، چنین شریر ستمگار را کند محبوس،
دشمنان تمدّن هر آنکه دوست شود، مسلّم است ز کردار خود خورد افسوس،

(لاهوتی کرمانشاهی)

(*Translation*)

Fie on the traitor renegade, outlawed and unashamed,
Who after all these evil deeds from Russia shelter claimed!
In all the world save Russia no country do I ken
Willing protection to afford to such dishonoured men.
The villainies of Raḥím Khán are noised o'er land and sea,
And now 'neath Russia's shelt'ring care he stands, from danger free!
I know not why so great a Power should seem to take a pride
Such human fiends of scowling mien in calling to its side.
Alas! by friendship thus misplaced it maketh but too plain
How great a hate for us and ours it still doth entertain!
Profound mistrust and deep disgust grow ever more and more,
And deeds like these to the Seven Seas spread from the Caspian shore.
If such a tyrant vile were housed in prison it were best,
Not met with hospitable care, like some much-honoured guest.
Foes of the human race like these whoever shall befriend
Reason his action to regret finds surely in the end!

(25)

The following excellent poem, entitled *Ququlíqú* ("Cock-a-doodle-do!") appeared in the *Nasím-i-Shimál* of December, 1910, and is signed *Máhí-gír* ("Fisherman"), perhaps on account of the allusion in the last verse to the obnoxious Fishery Concession (*shílát*) on the Persian shore of the Caspian granted to a Russian named Lianzof or Lianozoff, of which the original scope was violently extended by the *concessionaire*, supported by his Government, to the upper waters of all the rivers of Mázandarán and Gílán discharging themselves into the Caspian.

(قوقولیقو)

(۱)

میخواند خروسی بشبستان قوقولیقو، می گفت که ای فرقهٔ مستان قوقولیقو،
کو بهمن و کو رستمِ دستان قوقولیقو، آوخ که خزان زد بگلستان قوقولیقو،
فریاد ز سرمای زمستان قوقولیقو،

(۲)

از سیلِ فتن شهر و وطن رو بخرابی، ما خفته و مدهوش چو مستان بشرابی،
می گفت به مرغانِ هوا آدمِ آبی، در شهر بود قحطیِ انسان قوقولیقو،
فریاد ز سرمای زمستان قوقولیقو،

(۳)

خون گریه کند مزرعه بر حالِ دهاتی، سوزد جگرِ سنگ به احوالِ دهاتی
عریان و برهنه همه اطفالِ دهاتی، ایوای ز بدبختیِ دهقان قوقولیقو
فریاد ز سرمای زمستان قوقولیقو،

(٤)

اُف باد باین زندگی وطالعِ منحوس، تُفْ باد باین غیرت واین دفترِ معکوس،
افسوس که تبریز شده دستخوشِ روس، قزوین شده جولانگهِ روسان قوقولیقو،
فریاد کشیدند خروسان قوقولیقو،

(٥)

کو بلخ وبخارا وچه شد خیوه وکابل، کو هند وسمرقند وچه شد بابل و زابل،
کو نقطهٔ قنقاز وچه شد آن چمنِ گل، این بحرِ خزر بود ز ایران قوقولیقو،
فریاد ز سرمای زمستان قوقولیقو،

(٦)

آوخ که ز کف، شهر ووطن میرود آسان، اطفالِ رعیّت همه ترسان وهراسان،
آوخ که بتبریز و بقزوین وخراسان، سالدات بهر صبح دهد سان قوقولیقو،
فریاد ز سرمای زمستان قوقولیقو،

(٧)

هَی هَی بخروشید که باز اوّلِ کاراست، شیرانه بجوشید که هنگام شکارست،
مردانه بکوشید که دشمن بکنار است، زیرِ لگد افتاده خروسان قوقولیقو،
کافر بکجا خاكِ مسلمان قوقولیقو،

(٨)

در انزلی امروز سخنهای مخوف است، دعوای لیانزوف بسر ماهیِ صوف است،
درخانهٔ ما مدخلِ او الف الوف است، صیّاد بدریا شده نالان قوقولیقو،
فریاد ز سرمای زمستان قوقولیقو،

(ماهی‌گیر)

(*Translation*)

(1)

A cock in the hen-house shrilly trolled, "Coocoolicoo!
"Hear, O revellers young and old, Coocoolicoo!
"Where are Bahman and Rustam bold? Coocoolicoo!
"The Autumn chill doth the rose enfold, Coocoolicoo!
"Alack and alas for the Winter's cold, Coocoolicoo!"

(2)

Floods of trouble have brought our land to a swift decline,
The while we sleep, bemused, like men who are drunk with wine.
The Water-man to the birds of the air doth loud repine,
"There's a dearth of men amongst young and old, Coocoolicoo!
"Alack and alas for the Winter's cold, Coocoolicoo!"

(3)

The very field sheds tears of blood o'er the peasant's state;
The very heart of the stone doth melt at the peasant's fate;
Hungry and naked the peasant's child and the peasant's mate!
Alas for the peasant's woes untold, Coocoolicoo!
Alack and alas for the Winter's cold, Coocoolicoo!

(4)

Fie on this life and this star sinister, banishing joy!
Out on this page reversed and the zeal without employ!
"Alas for Tabríz, doomed to become the Russians' toy!
And for Qazwín, by Muscovite troops patrolled, Coocoolicoo!"
Cry the cocks and the roosters young and old, Coocoolicoo!

(5)

Where are Bukhárá, Khíva, Balkh and Kábul, where?
Babylon, India, Samarqand and Zábul, where?
Where the Caucasian lands and their blossoming gardens fair?
The Caspian Sea was ours of old, Coocoolicoo!
Alack and alas for the Winter's cold, Coocoolicoo!

(6)

Alas for lands so easily lost as these have been!
Our village-children are filled with terror and fear, I ween!
In Khurásán, alas! and in Tabríz too, and eke Qazwín
    Daily the Russians manœuvres hold, Coocoolicoo!
    Alack and alas for the Winter's cold, Coocoolicoo!

(7)

Rouse ye, Ho! for as yet 'tis but the first of the work!
Rage like lions: the hunt's toward, and who would shirk?
Quit ye as men, for in every corner a foe doth lurk!
    Spurned in the dust are the roosters bold, Coocoolicoo!
    A Muslim land shall the heathen hold? Coocoolicoo!

(8)

Terrible talk is heard to-day in Anzalí
Of Lianzoff's claims to the fish which haunt our rivers and sea;
In a million ways with our homes and lands he now makes free.
    To the sea the fisherman's woes are told, Coocoolicoo!
    Alack and alas for the Winter's cold, Coocoolicoo!

(**26**)

The next poem is a ballad, or *taṣníf* ascribed to a lady named Minára Khánim, but signed "*Húp-húp.*" It is, like so many *taṣnífs*, written in a very simple and colloquial style, and contains some forms (like *wásat*, for *wásiṭa-at*, "for thee," and *mana*, for *mará*, "me") which belong to the colloquial speech or even to dialects.

(تصنیف من کلام مناره خانم)

ننه جان خواب بودم خواب دیدم، ساه رمضان شد ننه جان،
نان و گوشت ارزان شد ننه جان،
خواب من دروغ بود ننه جان، هرچه دیدم دوغ بود ننه جان،

نه‌نه جان خواب بودم خواب دیدم،	مشروطه بپا شد نه‌نه جان،
	عیش فقرا شد نه‌نه جان،
خواب من دروغ بود ننه جان،	هرچه دیدم دوغ بود ننه جان
نه‌نه جون خواب بودم خواب دیدم،	کوچه‌ها قشنگ است نه‌نه جان،
	شهر فرنگ است نه‌نه جان،
خواب من دروغ بود نه‌نه جان،	هرچه دیدم دوغ بود نه‌نه جان،
نه‌نه جان خواب بودم خواب دیدم،	حمّام تمیز است نه‌نه جان
	بشکن بریز است نه‌نه جان
باز حمام خراب است نه‌نه جان،	بلدی بخواب است نه‌نه جان
نه‌نه جان گریه مکن غصّه مخور،	نان شکری میخرم واست
	چادر زری میخرم واست
تا تو فکر رخت میکنی نه‌نه،	منه سیا بخت میکنی نه‌نه

(امضاء هوپ هوپ)

(*Translation*)

(1)

"Mother dear, I slept, I saw a vision:
Ramaẓán was over, Mother dear;
Everyone in clover, Mother dear!
But my dream was a delusion, Mother dear!
All delusion and confusion, Mother dear!

(2)

"Mother dear, I slept, I saw a vision:
The Constitution flourished, Mother dear;
All the poor were housed and nourished, Mother dear!
But my dream was a delusion, Mother dear!
All delusion and confusion, Mother dear!

(3)

"Mother dear, I slept, I saw a vision:
Spacious street and splendid square, Mother dear;
Like some Frankish city rare, Mother dear!
  But my dream was a delusion, Mother dear!
  All delusion and confusion, Mother dear!

(4)

"Mother dear, I slept, I saw a vision:
The baths were clean and sweet, Mother dear;
'Snap your fingers, stamp your feet,' Mother dear!
  But my dream was a delusion, Mother dear!
  All delusion and confusion, Mother dear!

(5)

"Weep not, Mother dear, I pray, nor worry:
I will buy you sugar-loaves and sweets untold,
And a pretty out-door mantle stitched with gold,
  For when crushed by household care, Mother dear!
  You fill me with despair, Mother dear!"

(27)

The following poem, entitled *Khabar dár!* ("Look out!") and signed *Fikrí-yi-Barzgar*, appeared in the *Nasím-i-Shimál* of May 11, 1911 (No. 7 of the Fourth Year). Its real author is said to be Ashraf of Rasht, the editor of the paper above mentioned, and this is very probable.

(خبردار!)

(۱)

بعد از نماز با شیخ مشغولِ ذکرِ خود باش، هرکس بفکرِ خویشه تو هم بفکرِ خود باش،
در روزگار هرکس مشغولِ کارِ خویش است، بلبل بنغمه خوانی عقرب بفکرِ نیش است،
ریشو بفکرِ بی ریش کوسه بفکرِ ریش است، هرکس بفکرِ خویشه تو هم بفکرِ خود باش،

(۲)

ای نورِ دیده بابا صحرا چریده بابا، در مدرسه شب و روز زحمت کشیده بابا،
جز قیل و قالِ آخوند چیزی ندیده بابا، هرکس بفکرِ خویشه تو هم بفکرِ خود باش،

(۳)

جمعی باسم شیخی بعضی باسم بابی، یك جوقه اعتدالی یك دسته انقلابی،
یك طائفه شب و روز در فکرِ بیحسابی، هرکس بفکرِ خویشه تو هم بفکرِ خود باش،

(٤)

بعضی باسمِ اسلام بدعت پدید کردند، از بهرِ مالِ دنیا رو بر یزید کردند،
اولادِ مصطفیرا ناحقّ شهید کردند، هرکس بفکرِ خویشه تو هم بفکرِ خود باش،

(٥)

بعضی باسمِ سلطان گشتند خان و سرتیپ، القابها گرفتند بی علم و عقل و ترتیب،
انباشتند از پول صندوق و کیسه و جیب، هرکس بفکرِ خویشه تو هم بفکرِ خود باش،

(٦)

بعضی باسمِ ملّت اموالِ خلق بردند، بردند پولهارا در بانکها سپردند،
نُقْل و شراب و شمپا بالای میز خوردند، هرکس بفکرِ خویشه تو هم بفکرِ خود باش،

(۷)

بعضی شتر سواره عازم سوی حجازند، بعضی میانِ مسجد مشغول در نمازند،
یك دسته جنده بازند یك فرقه بچه بازند، هرکس بفکرِ خویشه تو هم بفکرِ خود باش،

(۸)

جمعی باسمِ جمعه بعضی باسمِ شنبه، مانند سگ دریدند از یکدگر شکنبه،
آخر زدند رندان آتش بپشم و پنبه، هرکس بفکرِ خویشه تو هم بفکرِ خود باش،

(۹)

یك دسته شارلاتانها در طبعِ روزنامه، بعضی سفید نامه بعضی سیاه جامه،
وا حسرتا که آخوند بر داشته عمامه، هرکس بفکرِ خویشه تو هم بفکرِ خود باش،
(امضاء فکری برزگر)

(*Translation*)

After your prayers, O reverend Sir, to meditation turn:
Since each one minds his own affair, you mind your own
concern!
In truth in this our age each one doth mind his own affair;
The scorpion's thinking of his sting, the *bulbul* of his air;
The bearded chin of beardless cheek, the beardless chin of hair.
Since each one minds his own affair, you mind your own
concern!

O dervish friend, my eyes' delight, at large the fields you graze,
Who once in schools and colleges did spend laborious days!
Naught know you save the lecturer's rhetorical displays;
Since each one minds his own affair, you mind your own
concern!

One calls himself a Shaykhí, one calls himself a Bábí;
One faction *I'tidálí*, one party *Inqilábí*[1],
While in "self-help" another lot unto themselves a Law be;
Since each one minds his own affair, you mind your own
concern!

[1] The rival sects of the Bábís and the Shaykhís are well known to all students of modern Persian history. The political parties named *I'tidálí* ("Moderate") and *Inqilábí* ("Revolutionary") took definite shape after the opening of the Second National Assembly in 1909.

The Boy-Colonel declines to have his bath

(From *Mullá Naṣru'd-Dín*, Year iii, No. 5, Feb. 16, 1908)

Some in the name of Islám foul innovations breed;
Through love of worldly wealth some turn their faces to Yazíd,
And by their hand at his command the Prophet's children bleed[1],
Since each one minds his own affair, you mind your own concern!

By Royal Warrant this one's a Colonel, that a Knight:
Their titles and their honours nor reason have nor right,
While purse and pouch and pocket they fill with silver bright.
Since each one minds his own affair, you mind your own concern!

Some in the Nation's name the wealth of others strive to gain,
That in the Bank their balance may ever grow amain,
That they may eat the choicest meat and drink the best champagne!
Since each one minds his own affair, you mind your own concern!

Some mount the patient camel and thus to Mecca fare;
Some in the middle of the mosque are occupied with prayer;
While some pursue the women, some seek their joys elsewhere.
Since each one minds his own affair, you mind your own concern!

One takes the name of Friday: one Saturday they call,
These fight like cats and dogs and on each other's vitals fall;
The fire these wantons kindle burns cotton, wool and all!
Since each one minds his own affair, you mind your own concern!

Some charlatans in journals long articles indite,
And though the garb they don is black, the sheets they use are white;
And now, alas! his turban casts aside each reverend wight[2]!
Since each one minds his own affair, you mind your own concern!

[1] The Umayyad Yazíd ibn Mu'áwiya, the slayer of al-Ḥusayn, the Prophet's grandson, is the Pontius Pilate of Persia. The allusion here is probably to the incident described on pp. 117–118 of my *Persian Revolution*.

[2] In consternation at the "blasphemous" innovations of the Press.

(28)

The following poem, signed Sayyid Najaf-i-*Banná* ("the Builder"), appeared on May 11, 1911, in No. 7 of the Fourth Year of the *Nasím-i-Shimál*.

(۱)

این روزنامه بر همه ایران مبارك است، بر اهلِ رشت و مردمِ دهقان مبارك است،
بر زارعِ گرسنه و عریان مبارك است، امسال از برای فقیران مبارك است،

(۲)

فرخنده باد سال به اصناف خون جگر، فرخنده باد سالِ فقیرانِ رنج بر،
فرخنده باد سالِ غریبانِ در بدر، بر ساکنانِ گوشهٔ زندان مبارك است،

(۳)

بر زارعانِ مشهد و تبریز و اصفهان، زحمت کشانِ صفحهٔ شیراز و بهبهان،
محنت برانِ طارم و قزوین و طالقان، بر مفلسانِ خمسه و زنجان مبارك است،

(٤)

بر لنگرود و لاهج و شلمان و اَشْکَوَر، ماسال و شفت و فومن و پسخان و پیشور،
از انزلی و لَشْته نشا تا به رودِ سر، آن برگِ توت و حاصلِ نوغان مبارك است،

(۵)

رستیم از کمندِ مظالم هزار شکر، جستیم از تعدّیِ ظالم هزار شکر،
گشتند جاهلان همه عالم هزار شکر، مشروطه از برای مسلمان مبارك است،

(٦)

ساقی بریز شربتِ شیرین بجامِ ما، مطرب بکوب طبلِ تبارك بنامِ ما،
بلبل بخوان که گشت مبارك غلامِ ما، با این غلام سَیْرِ خیابان مبارك است،

(٧)

باز ابتدای کشمکش و قال وقیل شد، تحویلِ سالِ تازه به تنگوز ییل شد،
هنگامِ انتخابِ جنابِ وکیل شد، این انتخابِ تازه بگیلان مبارك است،

(٨)

دعوا نمی کنیم دگر بهر هیچ و پوچ، دیگر نمی زنیم بهم کلّه مثلِ قوچ،
سالداتِ روس نیز ز قزوین نموده کوچ، این مژده از برای خراسان مبارك است،

(٩)

من بعد دختران همه صاحب هنر شوند، در مکتبِ علوم همه بهره ور شوند،
اندر حقوقِ علم شریكِ پسر شوند، این اشتراكِ عالَمِ نسوان مبارك است،

(١٠)

جاری شد آبهای عدالت ز چشمه سار، دیگر نمی دهند بما ظالمان فشار،
آورد شاه تازه ز امریك مستشار، این مستشارِ تازه بطهران مبارك است،

(١١)

مشغولِ عیش و نوش خوانینِ مالدار، قربانِ زلف سرکجِ رقّاصِ خالدار،
از یك طرف کمانچه و آوازه خوان وتار، آن ماچ وموچِ نصفِ شبِ خان مبارك است،

(۱۲)

طرف گرسنه فقیرانِ لات و لوت، محتاج روز و شب همه بر قُوتِ لا ی
ان برهنه و لاغر چو عنکبوت، آن اشکِ شور و آن دلِ بریان مبارک

(۱۳)

بود همیشه ز ایرانی ای نسیم، آید ز غیب نصرتِ رحمانی ای نـ
خوار گشته مسلمانی ای نسیم، یا هو ظهورِ حجّتِ امکان مبارک
(امضاء سیّد نجف بنّا)

The optimistic tone of this poem is partly due to the withdrawal of the Russian troops (except 80 Cossacks, retained as a "Consular Guard") from Qazwín on March 13–15, 1911, alluded to in stanza 8; and partly to the arrival at Anzalí on the very day of the poem's publication of Mr Morgan Shuster and the other American advisers, alluded to in stanza 10. This poem is quite easy, and I have not thought it necessary to add a translation, but the following observations may facilitate its comprehension. The newspaper *Nasím-i-Shimál* boasts itself the champion of the poor artisans and peasants, and then gives a long list of the places in Persia where its advent is hailed with joy. Those mentioned in stanza 3 are towns of importance in various parts of Persia, while the twelve villages enumerated in stanza 4 are all in the Caspian provinces of Gílán and Mázandarán. The *Tangúz Yíl* ("Year of the Pig") mentioned in stanza 7 is one of the cycle of twelve years, each called after some animal, brought into Persia by the Tartars (*tangúz* in Oriental Turkish is equivalent to the Ottoman Turkish *domuz*). The translation of stanza 9, which may be of interest to feminists is as follows:—

"*Henceforth all the girls shall be educated;*
All shall have their share in the Colleges of Science;
They shall be equal with the boys in their rights of learning.
Blessed is this participation of the World of Women!"

Stanzas 11 and 12 contrast the luxury and dissipation of the wealthy nobles with the misery of the poor and their half-starved children. The last stanza expresses confidence that God's help will keep Persia for the Persians, however gloomy the outlook may be.

The two following poems both appeared in the *Nasím-i-Shimál* of July 30, 1911 (No. 10 of the Third Year), and both refer to the recent attempt (July 19, 1911) of the ex-Sháh Muḥammad 'Alí (aided and abetted by the Russians) to recover his lost throne, an attempt which was ended on September 5 by what the *Times* correspondent described as "a decisive and brilliant victory of the government troops," the execution of *Arshadu'd-Dawla*, the ex-Sháh's best and most devoted general, and the flight of the ex-Sháh himself on a Russian ship on September 7.

(29)

The first of these two poems, entitled "Congratulation" (*Tabrík*), is a very short one and runs as follows.

(۱)

دیدی به استراباد آمد بلای ناگاه‘ یعنی که سر بر آورد آن مستبدّ خود خواه‘
خوب اتّفاق کردند این فرقه‌های همراه‘ زین اتّفاق ملّی به به تبارك اللّه!

(۲)

هم اتّفاق دارند هم صحبت ترقّی‘ از ارمنی مسلمان در دعوت ترقّی‘
غرقند اهلِ ایران در لذّت ترقّی‘ آخر ز غصّه دق کرد آن ریش پهنِ گمراه‘
زین اتّفاق ملّی به به تبارك اللّه‘

(۳)

هم خیل اعتدالی هم فرقه دموکرات‘ دست برادری‌را دادند از مساوات‘
ایران و مستبدّین هیهات ثمّ هیهات‘ عادل به آسمان شد ظالم فتاد در چاه‘
زین اتّفاق احزاب به به تبارك اللّه‘

(Translation)

(1)

Behold o'er Astarábád what sudden plague is spread,
For there that selfish despot once more doth rear his head.
How well divergent factions to meet this plague combine!
God bless the Nation's Union! God bless this effort fine!

(2)

All, all combine together, for Progress is their quest,
And Muslim and Armenian each strives to do his best;
Absorbed are all the Persians in this endeavour blessed.
With hope deferred is wasted this vagrant libertine!
God bless the Nation's Union! God bless this effort fine!

(3)

The Democrats and Moderates, like one fraternity,
Unite their bands and join their hands in all equality:
Persia and rule of Despots—remote may these two be!
The just are now exalted, the tyrants loud repine;
God bless the Nation's Union! God bless this effort fine!

(30)

The next poem, described as a *rajaz* (a term applied to heroic, or in this case mock-heroic verse) is supposed to express the feelings of the ex-Sháh Muḥammad 'Alí on beholding the failure of his efforts to regain the throne which for two years and a half he so unworthily filled.

(رجز)

منم مرد مشهور بی ننگ و عار، که بودم همیشه بخواب و خُمار،
اگرچه مرا گنده گشته شکم، ولی گردنم آب شد دنبه‌وار،
اگر سوی طهران نمایم گذر، کنم جمله‌را شقّه قصّاب‌وار،
همه خلق‌را از صغیر و کبیر، به توپ (شرپنل) به بندم قطار،
ببُرّم سر نائب السّلطنه، که کار مرا کرده از عقل زار،

بر آرم بچاقوی ذلّت برون، دو چشمان احمد شه نامدار
ز سردار اسعد بدرّم جگر، سپهداررا می کنم پار پار
همان پارلمان‌را ببندم بتوب، که حلوای مشروطه شد زهر مار
همه خلق‌را چون شپش می کُشم، بتحریك همسایهٔ نا بکار
وکیلان ببندم بیك ریسمان، وزیران نمایم همه تار و مار
نهادم سرم‌را بروی زمین، شدم غایب از چشم ملّت چو مار
گرفتم بعنوان باج سبیل، بسالی ز خلق اشرفی صد هزار
طلاها و یاقوت و دریای نور، بشد صرف در بزم عیش و قمار
برای تماشای (ماتشکه) من، زدم تنبك و دائره حلقه دار
چو اندر (اودس) پولها تهٔ کشید، چه قاصد به بلژیك کردم گذار
فقط اسم خودرا نمودم عوض، محمّد حسین رند کامل عیار
اگرچه بود نام من ممدلی، دلی نیستم من منم عقل دار
کنم نهر از خون ملّت روان، از این استراباد تا سبزوار
مجلّل روان شد سوی اردبیل، دریغا که با وی نشد بخت یار
یکی ارشد الدّوله چون لاك پُشت، بشد در ارومیّه مشغول کار
خودم در (گُمش تپّه) ظاهر شدم، که ویران کنم جمله شهر و دیار
بدل بُغض باشد مرا از سه جا، ز تبریز و گیلان و از بختیار
خصوصاً ز تبریز ویران شده، که ستّار زد بر وجودم شرار
مرا گریه گیرد که در جنگ پارك، چرا یك نفر زنده کرده فرار
اگر شهر طهران شود جلوه گر، برون آرم از اهل طهران دمار
ز بقّال و نانوا و سبزی فروش، ز قصّاب و عطّار و از خشکبار
ز شهری و دهقانی و رنجبر، چه از پیر مرد و چه از شیرخوار

ز نجّار و آهنگر و کفش دوز، ز بزّاز و از زرگر و خورده کار،
چنان خون بریزم که روی زمین، زند موج قرمز چو گلهای نار،
ولی بسته دستِ قضا دست من، شکسته است پُشْت مرا روزگار،
فقیرم فقیرم فقیرم فقیر، ندارم ندارم ندارم ندار،
شکم ای شکم ای شکم ای شکم، تو کردی مرا اینچنین خوار و زار،
بهادر بهادر سلامٌ علیك، کجائی بدادم برس ای هوار،
شنیدم که سردار مُحْیِی ز ری، بمازندران می شود رهسپار،
یقین دارم این دفعه با این شکم، معلّق زنان میروم روی دار،
نه در کیسه پول و نه در کلّه عقل،
نه پای گریز و نه راه فرار،

(*Translation*)

(1) "I am that famous, shameless libertine
Whose days and nights were passed twixt sleep and wine!
Although my belly daily larger grows,
My strength is waning like the melting snows.
Could I to Ṭihrán once an entrance gain
Its people butcher-like I'd cleave in twain,
And its inhabitants, both great and small,
With shot and shrapnel I would dose them all!
(5) As for the Regent[1], off his head should go,
Who caused my projects to miscarry so;
And with my pen-knife out the eyes I'd bring
Of Sultán Aḥmad Sháh, the reigning king[2];
Out the Sardár-i-As'ad's heart I'd take,
And the Sipahdár into mince-meat make;
The Parliament with cannons I would shake,
For freedom's balm to me's a poisoned snake;

[1] Mírzá Abu'l-Qásim Khán *Náṣiru'l-Mulk*, elected Regent (*Ná'ibu's-Salṭana*) on September 23, 1910, immediately after the death of his predecessor *Azudu'l-Mulk*.

[2] He succeeded to the throne on July 18, 1909, on his father's deposition.

And, by my worthless Northern Friend's advice,
I'd crush the folk, as though they were but lice;
The Deputies to one long rope I'd tie,
And topsy-turvy turn the Ministry.
Now in the dust my head is bowed, and I
Glide like a serpent from the Nation's eye.
A hundred thousand guineas in a year
I wrung as 'road-tax' from the people's fear.
The 'Sea of Light[1],' gold, rubies beyond price
I squandered on my drinking bouts and dice.
To please my Russian mistress when she's glum
I play the tambourine and beat the drum.
How in Odessa, when my funds ran low,
To Belgium sped my agents, all men know.
Only to change my name I did decide—
'Muḥammad Ḥusayn, rascal double-dyed.'
Although the vulgar call me '*Mamdalí*'
I'm not '*dalí*[2]'; in wits few equal me!
The people's blood in streams I'll cause to pour
From Astarábád unto Sabzawár!
To Ardabíl *Mujallal* swift doth hie;
Alas! Ill-fortune bears him company!
Arshadu'd-Dawla, like a tortoise slow,
At Urmiya about my work doth go.
My flag at Gyumush-tepé I display,
Hoping in ruins town and land to lay.
Thought of three foes my heart with hate doth freeze—
The Bakhtiyárís, Gílán and Tabríz.
But most of all Tabríz—that ruined land
Where Sattár Khán this conflagration planned.
I weep to think that one escaped alive
Of those my foes who in the Park did strive[3].

[1] This celebrated diamond (the *Daryá-yi-Núr*) is the companion gem to the still more celebrated *Kúh-i-núr* ("Mountain of Light").

[2] "*Mamdalí*" is the vulgar contraction of *Muḥammad 'Alí*. The meaning of the Turkish word "*dalí*" (or "*deli*") is "mad."

[3] This alludes to the conflict of August 7, 1910, in the Atábak's Park at Ṭihrán, on the occasion of the disarming of the *fidá'ís*.

Should Ṭihrán once again become my share
Not one of all its people will I spare.
Of grocer, baker and of caterer,
Of druggist, butcher and of fruiterer,
Townsman and peasant, toilers without rest,
Of aged men and children at the breast,
Of blacksmith, joiner, carpenter therewith,
Of draper and of pedlar and goldsmith,
The blood in such wise on the earth I'll shed
That it shall form a sea with waves of red!
But cruel fate has tied my hands, alack!
And fortune sinister doth break my back!
I'm poor, I'm poor, I'm poor, I'm poor indeed;
I have not, have not, have not, aught I need!
O belly, belly, belly, belly mine,
'Tis you who cause me thus to grieve and pine!
To thee, Bahádur, greetings do I send;
Where art thou? Help me, O my trusty friend!
Sardár Muhiyy, I hear, hath marched from Ray,
And wends towards Mázandarán his way.
This time, for all my bulging paunch, I feel
That on the gibbet I shall dance a reel!
With empty purse and brains of sense bereft,
I've neither foot to fly nor refuge left!"

(31)

The following poem, like the last, is supposed to express the feelings of the ex-Sháh Muḥammad 'Alí after the failure of his attempt to regain the throne in August, 1911. It appeared in the *Nasím-i-Shimál* (No. 12 of the Third Year) on September 11, 1911. It contains a certain number of slang or colloquial expressions, especially in the last *bayt* of each stanza, *e.g. namí-shé* (= *namí-shawad*), *Mamdalí* (= *Muḥammad 'Alí*), *Shá* (for *Sháh*), *mí-khád* (for *mí-khwáhad*), *mí-khám* (for *mí-khwáham*), etc. I have not thought it necessary to add a translation of this poem.

(زبان حال ممدلی)

(۱)

ای فلك این چه بساطی است که چیدستی تو، چه زبردستی تو
دلِ اعداء وطن‌را زجفا خستی تو، چقدر پستی تو
عهد با هموطنان بستی و بشکستی تو، گوئیا مستی تو
کمترین ممدلیم، داروغهٔ انزلیم، تره حلوا نمیشه، ممد

(۲)

ممدلی تکیه بقول و غزلِ روس نمود، ترك ناموس نمود
خویش‌را در نظرِ اهلِ وطن لوس نمود، کار معکوس نمود
هوس حمله بتخت جم و کاوس نمود، میل پا بوس نمود
کلّه اش تاج میخاد، باج ز لیلاج میخاد، تره حلوا نمیشه، ممد

(۳)

ممدلی اشك همی ریخت مثالِ باران، از فراقِ یار
ترکمانها همه کردند فرار از میدان، همه در خون غل
هدفِ تیرِ بلا گشت رشید السّلطان، لعنِ حقّ بر شی
گولِ شیطان خوردم، آبروی خود بردم، خرقه شولا نمیشه، ممد

(٤)

تا ز روسیه در این خاك سرازیر شدم، طعمهٔ شیر شدم
جیره‌ام قطع شد از غصّه زمین گیر شدم، همچو تصویر شدم
ارشد الدّوله چو شد کُشْته زجان سیر شدم، خود بخود پیر شدم
بشکسته کمرم، خاك دو عالم بسرم، تره حلوا نمیشه، ممد

(٥)

طرفه سردارِ ظفرمند که مُجْبی نام است، فتح بر وی رام است،
بختیاری است که در معرکه چون صمصام است، ضیغم و ضرغام است،
بفرم آمد بگریزید که قتلِ عام است، ممدلی گمنام است،
دیدی آخر چون شد، مسئله دیگر گون شد، تره حلوا نمیشه، ممدلی بگ شا نمیشه،

(٦)

هوسم بود جمیع وزرارا بکشم، وکلارا بکشم،
دستخط پاره نمایم علمارا بکشم، عقلارا بکشم،
جمله اصناف و عموم فقرارا بکشم، غربارا بکشم،
مالِ مولارا میخام، چنته و شولارا میخام، تره حلوا نمیشه، ممدلی بگ شا نمیشه،

Of the persons alluded to in this poem, *Rashídu's-Sulṭán* was defeated by the Bakhtiyárís at Fírúzkúh on August 11, 1911, and was said to have been shot or to have died of his wounds two days later. *Arshadu'd-Dawla*, the best and most capable of the ex-Sháh's generals, was taken prisoner and shot by Yeprem Khán, the great Armenian general of the Constitutionalists, on September 5, 1911. A very graphic account of this event, by Mr W. A. Moore, appeared in the *Times* a day or two later. The *Sardár-i-Muḥiy* was the real leader of the Rasht army in the summer of 1909. Photographs of both him and Yeprem Khán will be found facing p. 436 of my *Persian Revolution*. The other three persons mentioned in stanza 5 are well-known chiefs of the Bakhtiyárís.

(32)

The following poem appeared in the *Charand Parand* column of the *Ṣúr-i-Isráfíl* (No. 24) for February 27, 1908. It is entitled *Ru'asá wa Millat* ("the Leaders and the Nation"), and is difficult to understand fully, being written in the language employed by mothers in speaking to their small children. Of all the poems here cited it is the most remote from the ordinary literary language. The "leaders of the people" are, apparently, represented as an ignorant mother, and the Nation as a sickly child, who finally expires in its mother's arms in consequence of her mismanagement.

(رؤسا و ملّت)

خاك بسرم! بچه بهوش آمده،   بخواب نه‌نه: یکسر دو گوش آمده،
گریه نکن: لولو می‌آد میخوره،   گربه می‌آد بُزبُزی‌را می بره،
اهه! اهه! آخر نه‌نه چنه؟ گُشْنَمَه،   بتره‌کی! این همه خوردی: کمه؟
چخ چخ سگه! نازی پیشی پیش پیش!   لالای جونم گُلَم باشی کیش کیش!
٥ از گشنگی نه‌نه دارم جون میدم،   گریه نکن! فردا بهت نون میدم،
ای وای نه‌نه! جونم داره در میره!   گریه نکن! دیزه داره سر میره،
دستم آخش! به بین چطو یخ شده،   تُف تُف جونم به بین ممه اخ شده،
سرم چرا آنقده چرخ می زنه؟   توی سرت شی‌پیشه چا می کَنَه،
خ خ خ خ... جونم چت شد؟ هاق هاق!   وای خاله! چشماش چرا افتاد بطاق،
١٠ آخ تنش م بیا به بین سرد شده،   رنگش چرا (خاك بسرم) زرد شده،
١١ وای بچم رفت زکف رود رود،   ماند بمن آه و اسف رود رود!!

(*Translation*)

(1) Dust on my head[1]! The child has woken up! Go to sleep, my pet; the Bogey-man[2] is coming!
Don't cry! The ogre[3] will come and eat you up! The cat will come and take away your kiddy[4]!

[1] This expression is equivalent to "Botheration take me!"

[2] Literally "the two-eared one-head," an imaginary monster with which children are intimidated.

[3] *Lúlú* is another kind of bogey.

[4] *Buzbuzí* is anything, such as a pet animal or a toy, to which a child is much attached.

Oh, oh! What ails you[1], my pet? "I am hungry" [you say][2]? May you burst[3]! You have eaten all this: is it too little[4]?
Get out[5], dog! Pussy, puss, puss, come here! Hushaby, darling! You are my rose! Hush, hush!
(5) "Mamma! I am ready to die with hunger!" Don't cry! To-morrow I will give you bread!
"O dear, Mamma! My life is ready to leave me!" Don't cry! The pot is just on the boil!
"O my hand! See, it is as cold as ice!" Fie, fie, my Soul! See, the breast is dry[6]!
"Why does my head spin so?" [Because] the lice are digging holes in your head!
Akh-kh-kh!...What ails you, my Soul? *Háq, háq*[7]! O my Aunt[8]! Why are its eyes turned up to the ceiling?
(10) Come here! Alas, see, its body also has become cold! Dust on my head! Why has its colour turned so pale?
(11) Woe is me! My child is gone from my hands! Alas, alas! To me there remain but sighs and grief! Alas, alas[9]!

(33)

I do not know whether or where the following poem was published, but its title, "On the departure of Mr Shuster from Persia," sufficiently fixes its date as the latter part of the year 1911. Mr Shuster's dismissal was demanded by the Russian Government on November 29 of that year, and he handed over his charge to Mr Cairns on January 7, 1912, and left Ṭihrán four days later. The poem is by 'Árif of Qazwín.

1 *Chité?=chíst-at*, "What is to thee?" "What ails thee?"
2 *Gushnama=gurasna-am*. 3 =بطركى. 4 *Kamé=kam-ast*.
5 *Chikh* ("get out!") is probably Turkish, from the verb *chiqmaq* (*chikhmaq*).
6 Persian mothers, when they wish to wean their babies, smear the nipple with some black or bitter substance (such as opium) to make the child recoil from it. Speaking of this they say, *Memé akh shuda* ("the nipple has gone sour").
7 *Háq, háq* is an onomatopoeic word indicating sobbing.
8 This is the literal rendering of *Wáy, Khála!*—an exclamation used by Persian women in a manner similar to the corresponding English vulgarism.
9 The exclamation "*Rúd, rúd!*" is used by women in lamenting the bad conduct or the death of an only and much-loved child.

تکمه ایله وروب یقمالیز

با عصا عیشود جفتك باید انداخت

شیدا — ای واه ، استقلال وطن

England (l) and Russia (r.) endeavouring to drive out Mr W. Morgan Shuster, the American Treasurer-General of Persia

From No. 3 of the *Shaydá*, Nov. 23, 1911

در باب حرکت مسیو شُستر از ایران[1]

(۱)

ننگ آن خانه که مهمان ز سر خوان برود، جان نثارش کن و مگذار که مهمان برود،
گر رود شستر از ایران رود ایران بر باد، ای جوانان مگذارید که ایران برود (1)،

(۲)

شد مسلمانی ما بین وزیران تقسیم، هرکه تقسیمی خود کرد بدشمن تقدیم،
حزبی اندر طلبت در سر یك رأی مقیم، کافریم ار بگذاریم که ایمان برود،

(۳)

مشت دزدی شده امروز درین ملك وزیر، تو درین مملکت امروز خبیری و بصیر،
دست بر دامنت آویخته یك مشت فقیر، تو اگر رفتی ازین مملکت عنوان برود،

(٤)

شد لبالب دگر از حوصله پیمانهٔ ما، دزد خواهد بزُمختی ببرد خانهٔ ما،
ننگ تاریخی عالم شود افسانهٔ ما، بگذاریم اگر شُستر از ایران برود،

(٥)

سگِ چوپان شده با گرگ چو لیلی مجنون، پاسبانِ گله امروز شبانی است جبون،
شد بدست خود آن کعبهٔ دل کن فیکون، یار مگذار کزین خانهٔ ویران برود،

(٦)

تو مرو گر برود جان و سر و هستی ما، کور شد دیدهٔ بدخواه ز همدستی ما،
در فراقت بخماری بکشد مستی ما، نالهٔ عارف ازین درد بکیوان برود،

[1] As adapted for singing, the word **برود** is repeated at the end of each line where it occurs, and the word **حبیبم** at the end of the other lines, while the following refrain is repeated at the end of each stanza :—

بجسمِ مرده جانی، تو جانِ یك جهانی، تو گنج شایگانی، تو عمرِ جاودانی،
خدا خدا کند بمانی، خدا خدا کند بمانی،

(*Translation*)

(1)

Shame on the host whose guest unfed doth from the table rise!
Rather than this should happen, make thy life his sacrifice!
Should Shuster fare from Persia forth, Persia is lost in sooth:
O let not Persia thus be lost, if ye be men in truth!

(2)

Behold, these Ministers of ours[1] our Muslimhood divide,
And each unto our common foe his portion doth confide;
One party still[2] in unison demands that thou should'st stay;
We're naught but heathens if we let our Faith thus slip away!

(3)

To-day a gang of thieves become the guardians of our land:
In all this Kingdom thou alone dost see and understand!
Close clinging to thy skirts a band of suppliants are we,
For, should'st thou go, our Country's name, alas! will go with thee!

(4)

Our cup is full unto the brim, our measure overflows;
Our homes are meanly filched away by base and cruel foes!
And if we suffer Shuster now to leave our Persian land
Eternal infamy our name in history shall brand!

(5)

The wolf and shepherd's dog are one like Laylá and Majnún[3];
A cowardly herdsman guards the flock and will betray it soon.
O what creative energy our Hearts' Exemplar[4] showed!
Let not our faithful guardian quit our desolate abode!

(6)

O leave us not, although our life and thought are merged in night!
The eyes of those who wish us ill grow blind when we unite:
But, left by thee, the banquet's glee turns to reaction drear,
And thus it is that 'Árif's wail doth reach to Saturn's sphere[5]!

[1] *i.e.* the Cabinet who effected the dissolution of the *Majlis* in December, 1911.

[2] Presumably the so-called "Democrats," who were the patriotic party.

[3] Laylá and Majnún are the typical lovers of Eastern romance.

[4] The "*Ka'ba* of hearts" is that to which men's hearts turn as the Faithful turn towards Mecca. "*Kun fa-yakún*" ("'Be!' and it is") is God's Creative Word.

[5] *i.e.* the seventh and highest heaven, which is the "Sphere of Saturn."

The Poet ʻÁrif of Qazwín

(34)

The following *qaṣída*, entitled "A Critical Tribute to Sir Edward Grey," appeared in the Calcutta *Ḥablu'l-Matín* of November 11, 1912, and is by the poet *Bahár* of Mashhad, entitled *Maliku'sh-Shu'ará* ("the King of poets").

(بجناب سر ادوارد گری : یك هديّهٔ ناقدانه،)

سوی لندن گذر ای پاك نسيم سحری، سخنی از من بر گو به سر ادورد گری،
کای خردمند وزيری که نپرورده جهان، چون تو دستور خردمند و وزير هنری،
نقشهٔ پطر بر فکر تو نقشی بر آب، رای بزمارك بر رای تو رائی سپری،
ز تولون جيشِ ناپليون نگذشتی گر بود، بر فراز هرمان نامِ تو در جلوه گری،
داشتی پاريس اگر عهدِ تو در کف نشدی، سوی الزاس و لورن لشکر المان سفری،
انگليس ار ز تو ميخواست در امريك مدد، بسته ميشد به واشنگتن رهِ پرخاشخری،
با کُماندر چيف اگر فرّ تو بودی همراه، به بوير بسته شدی سخت رهِ حمله وری،
ور به منچوری پلتيكِ تو بُد رهبرِ روس، نشد از ژاپون جيشِ کروپاتکين کمری،
بود اگر فکرِ تو با عائلهٔ مانچو يار، انقلابيّون بر شاه نگشتند جری،
ور بُدی رای تو داير بحيات ايران، اين همه ناله نمی ماند بدون اثری،
مثل است اينکه چو بر مرد شود تيره جهان، آن کند کش نه بکار آيد ازو کارگری،
تو بدين دانش افسوس که چون بيخردان، کردی آن کار که افسوس جز ازوی نبری،
بر گشودی درِ صد ساله فرو بستهٔ هند، بر رخِ روس و نترسيدی از در بدری،
بچهٔ گرگ در آغوش بپروردی و نيست، اين مماشاة جز از بيخودی و بيخبری،
بيخودانه بتمنّای زبردست حريف، در نهادی سر تسليم زهی خيره سری،
اندران عهد که با روس ببستی زين پيش، غبن ها بود و نديدی تو ز کوته نظری،

تو خود از تبّت و ایران و ز افغانستان، ساختی پیشِ ره خصم بنای سه دری،
تو ز موصل بگشودی ره آن تا زابل، وز رهِ تبّت تسلیم شدی تا به هری،
زین سپس بهرِ نگهداری این هرسه طریق، نیم ملیار قشون باید بحری و بری،
بیش از فائدت هند اگر گردد صرف، عاقبت فائدتی نیست بجز خون جگری،
انگلیس آن ضرری‌را که ازین پیمان بُرد، تو ندانستی و داند بدویّ و حضری،
نه همین زیر پی روس شود ایران پست، بلکه افغانی ویران شود و کاشغری،
ور همی گوئی روس از سر پیمان نرود، رَوْ بتاریخ نگر تا که عجائب نگری،
در بر نفع سیاسی نکند پیمان کار، این نه من گویم کاین هست ز طبع بشری،
خاصّه چون روس که او شیفته باشد بر هند، همچو شاهین که بود شیفته بر کبك دری،
ورنه این روس ز یك توطه چرا در ایران، راند قزّاق و نهاد افسر بیدادگری،
در خراسان که مهین ره رهِ هندست چرا، کرد این مایه قشون بی سببی راهبری،
فتنه‌را از چه بپا کرد و چرا آخرِ کار، کرد نستوده چنان کار بدان مشتهری،
سپه روس ز تبریز کنون تا به سرخس، بیش از بیست هزارند چو نیکو شمری،
هله کز مشرقِ ما امن بود تا بشمال، سپه روس چرا مانده بدین بی ثمری،
گرچه خود بی ثمری نیست که این جیشِ گزین، سفری کردن خواهند بصد ناموری،
سفر ایشان هند است و تمنّاشان هند، هند خواهند بلی نرم تنان خزری،
ویژه گر پای بیفشاری تا از خطِ روس، خطّ آهن بسوی هند کند رهسپری،
بعدو خطِّ ترن رهرا نزدیك کند، تا تو دیگر نروی راه بدین پُرخطری،
سدِّ بس معتبری ایران بُد در رهِ هند، وه که بر داشته شد سدّ بدین معتبری،
باد نفرین بلجاجت که لجاجت بر داشت، پرده از کار و فرو بست رخ پر هنری،

بلجاج و بغرض کردی کاری که بدو، طعنه راند عرب دشتی و ترکِ تتری،
حیف از آن خاطرِ دانای تو و رای رزین، که درین مسئله زد بیهُده خودرا بکری،

زهی آن خاطرِ دانای رزین تو زهی،
فری آن فکرِ توانای متین تو فری،

(ملك الشعراء بهار)

(*Translation*)

To London speed, O breeze of dawning day,
Bear this my message to Sir Edward Grey.
To thee in skill, wise Councillor of State,
Ne'er did the world produce a peer or mate!
Great Peter's schemes to thine were shifting sand,
And weak by thine the plans that Bismarck planned.
Ne'er from Toulon Napoleon's hosts had gone
If on the Pyramids thy name had shone.
(5) Had Paris been in league with thee, in vain
The German hosts had swamped Alsace-Lorraine.
Had England 'gainst the States sought help from thee
No Washington had won them victory.
Had thy prestige companioned England's arms
Ne'er had the Boers caused England such alarms.
Would Kuropatkin's hosts before Japan
Had fled had he been guided by thy plan?
Had the Manchus been aided by thy thought
The rebels ne'er against their king had fought.
(10) And had thy schemes included Persia's life
Not fruitless had remained this storm and strife.
"When fortune frowns on man," the proverb goes,
"His wisest act no good resultant shows."
Alas that thou, for all thy wits, hast wrought
A deed which save regret can yield thee naught!
For India's gates, closed for a hundred years,
To Russia now you open without fears.

You nurse the wolf-cub in your arms: a deed
Which folly prompts, and which to grief will lead.
(15) To this o'erbearing partner you submit,
And bow your head, bereft of sense and wit.
Your pacts with Russia made in time gone by
Brought loss unseen by your short-sighted eye.
In Afghánistán, Persia and Tibet
Before your foe a three-doored wall you've set.
Mosul to Sístán's now an open way:
Herát, Tibet they claim, nor fear your "Nay!"
Henceforth this three-fold road to watch, indeed,
A million men on land and sea you'll need.
(20) India's advantage if you squander so
Naught will you reap except remorse and woe.
You knew not, though both town and desert knew,
What hurt to England would from this accrue.
Not Persia only feels the Russian squeeze;
'Tis felt by Afgháns and by Káshgharís!
"Russia her pact will keep," you answer me:
Her records read, and wondrous things you'll see!
Not I but human nature tells you plain
That pacts weigh naught compared with present gain;
(25) The more since Russia longs for India still
As longs the hawk for partridge on the hill;
Else why did she o'er Persian lands let loose
Her Cossack hordes to crown her long abuse?
Why in Khurásán, India's broad highway,
Do all these troops of hers unmotived stay?
Such mischief wherefore hath she wrought, and why
Done deeds redounding to her infamy?
From Tabríz to Sarakhs her soldiers dwell,
Some twenty thousand, if you count them well.
(30) From North to East our land all peaceful lay:
Why without reason do the Russians stay?
Reason, forsooth! The Russians there remain
Waiting for some more glorious campaign
With India for its goal: this goal they crave,
These pampered pirates of the Caspian Wave!

The more so should you culpably delay
Till Russian rails to India find their way.
These rails shall bring thy foeman near to thee:
Avoid such roads so fraught with jeopardy!
(35) 'Twas Persia barred the road: woe worth the day
Which swept this ancient barrier away!
O cursed obstinacy, which did raise
This veil, and set the feet in such a maze!
Headstrong and rash you wrought a deed of shame
Which stolid Turk and vagrant Arab blame.
Woe to that judgement cool, that reason bright,
Which now have put you in so dire a plight!
All hail that judgement, hail that insight rare,
Of which, men say, you hold so large a share!

(35)

The following poem, entitled "An offering of thanks and welcome to the honoured and revered guest," is a curious protest against the intrusion of Germany (real or supposed) into Persian affairs; for, by the generality of Persians, Germany was favourably regarded as friendly to Islám and hostile to Russia. It appeared in No. 17 of the illustrated comic paper *Ázarbáyján* on October 11, 1907.

(عرضِ تشکّر و خیرِ مقدم بمهمان معزّز و محتشم)

(قدمْتَ خیر مقدمٍ اهلًا و مرحبًا بك یا المانیا)

مهمان تازه واردِ ایران خوش آمدی، بالای چشم جای تو المان خوش آمدی،
ایران بخوان ماند و بیگانگان بضیف، ناخوانده میهمان سرِ این خوان خوش آمدی،
صبحِ وصال شکر خدا را نمود رخ، آمد بسر لیالی هجران خوش آمدی،
از بهرِ صید مرغِ دلِ عاشقانِ زار، در دست دام و دانه بدامان خوش آمدی،
با دعوی حمایت اسلام و مسلمین، گشتی دخیلِ حوزهٔ دزدان خوش آمدی،
لیکن چو برده‌اند حریفان هر آنچه بود، ترسم شود نصیبِ تو حرمان خوش آمدی،

اسلام بود بیکس و بی داد رس کنون، صد شکر یافت چون تو نگهبان خوش آمدی،
من نیك می شناسمت ای رندِ پُر فسون، احسنت خوانِ مکرِ تو شیطان خوش آمدی،
پیوسته شامل است باسلام لطفِ تو، ما عاجز از لوازمِ شکران خوش آمدی،
دادی ز حیله دستِ محبّت بدستِ ترك، خواندی بگوشش آیهٔ خسران خوش آمدی،
و آنگه باسم یاری سلطان ملك فاس، گشتی بسوی طنجه شتابان خوش آمدی،
از صدمهٔ که دید مراکش ز چون تو دوست، هرگز ندیده‌بود ز عدوان خوش آمدی،
فارغ ز کار آن دو بگردیده بی درنگ، گشتی بمرزِ فارس نمایان خوش آمدی،
از بهرِ سرتراشی یك مُشتِ بی گناه، در کف گرفته تیغكِ بُرّان خوش آمدی،
رندانه با بهانهٔ دار الفنون و بانك، نائل شدی بمقصد پنهان خوش آمدی،
بانگ فغان هنوز ز ما میرسد بچرخ، از دست بانكِ روس و بریطان خوش آمدی،
القصّه نیست چارهٔ ما گوئیا کنون، جز انقیادِ حکمِ فرنگان خوش آمدی،

لیکن بیك قرار نماند دوار چرخ
نومید گو مباش ز یزدان خوش آمدی،

(امضا : م . ج . خ)

(*Translation*)

("Fortunate is your advent! Greeting and Welcome to thee, O Germany!")

"O newly-arrived guest of Persia, welcome!
O Germany! Your place is on our eyes: welcome!
Persia is like a well-filled table with foreigners for guests;
O guest unbidden to this table, welcome!
Thanks be to God! The morning of union hath appeared;
The nights of separation have come to an end: welcome!
To take captive the bird-like hearts of your unhappy lovers
With the snare in your hand and the grain in your apron,
welcome!

(5) Claiming to be the protector of Islám and the Muslims
Thou hast entered the gang of thieves: welcome!
But, since your competitors have carried off all that there was,
I am afraid that disappointment may be your portion: welcome!
Islám was friendless and helpless; now
A hundred thanks, it has found a guardian like thee: welcome!
I know thee well, O libertine of many spells!
The Devil sings the praises of thy cunning: welcome!
Thy favour ever embraces Islám; we are unable to voice the thanks which are your due: welcome!
(10) Cunning prompted thee to extend the hand of friendship to the Turk;
Thou didst whisper into his ear the verse of loss: welcome!
Then, on the pretext of friendship for the Sultan of Fez,
Thou didst hasten towards Tangier: welcome!
The injury which Morocco experienced from such a friend as thee
It had never experienced from the enmity [of another]: welcome!
Having finished with the affairs of these two, without delay
Thou didst appear in the land of Persia: welcome!
To shear the heads of a handful of innocents
Thou bringest in thy hand a sharp razor: welcome!
(15) Wantonly, with pretexts of College and Bank,
Thou hast attained thy secret object: welcome!
Our cry of lamentation still rises to heaven
On account of the Russian and British Banks: welcome!
In short it seems that we have now no option
Save to submit to the orders of the Franks: welcome!
(18) Yet the circling heaven remains not in one position;
Say, 'Despair not of God!' Welcome!"

[Signed: *M. J. Kh.*]

[1] Concerning German activities in Persia at this period (1907) see my *Persian Revolution*, pp. 178 and 187.

ADDITIONAL POEMS RECEIVED WHILE THE BOOK WAS GOING THROUGH THE PRESS.

POEMS BY *BAHÁR* OF MASHHAD, ENTITLED *MALIKU'SH-SHU'ARA*, OR "THE KING OF POETS."

At the end of October, 1913, I received through one of my Persian friends a collection of fifteen poems by *Bahár* of Mashhad, transcribed by the poet's own hand, only one of which (No. 20, pp. 218–20 *supra*) had previously reached me. These poems range in date from Jumáda i, A.H. 1327, to Ramaẓan, A.H. 1329 (= May–June, 1909, to August–September, 1911), and most if not all of them appeared in the Mashhad papers *Khurásán*, *Ṭús* and *Naw Bahár*, while the most celebrated of them (referred to above as already included in this book) also appeared in the *Ḥablu'l-Matín*, *Írán-i-Naw* and *Taraqqí*. I shall give a short description of these fifteen poems and the full text of several of the most striking.

(36)

The first is a fine *mustazád* (similar in form and metre to No. 5 on pp. 185–6 *supra*) written and published in the paper *Khurásán* in Jumáda i, A.H. 1327 (= May–June, 1909), towards the end of the "Lesser Tyranny" (*Istibdád-i-ṣaghír*), some few weeks before the capture of Ṭihrán and deposition of Muḥammad 'Alí by the victorious Nationalists. It was designed to arouse in Khurásán sympathy with the efforts put forth by Ázarbáyján, Gílán and Iṣfahán, and is here given in full.

با شهِ ایران ز آزادی سخن گفتن خطاست، کارِ ایران با خداست،
مذهب شاهنشهِ ایران ز مذهبها جداست، کارِ ایران با خداست،
شاه مست و میر مست وشحنه مست وشیخ مست، مملکت رفته ز دست،
هر دم از دستان مستان فتنه و غوغا بپاست، کارِ ایران با خداست،

The poet Bahár of Mashhad, entitled
Maliku'sh-Shu'ará ("the King of Poets")

هر دم از دریای استبداد آید بر فراز،   موجهای جانگداز،
زین تلاطم کشتی ملّت بگرداب بلاست،   کارِ ایران با خداست،
مملکت کشتی حوادث بحر و استبداد خس،   ناخدا عدل است و بس،
کارِ پاس کشتی و کشتی نشین با ناخداست،   کارِ ایران با خداست،
پادشه خودرا مسلمان خواند و سازد تباه،   خونِ جمعی بیگناه،
ای مسلمانان در اسلام این ستمها کی رواست،   کارِ ایران با خداست،
شاهِ ایران گر عدالت‌را نخواهد باك نیست،   زآنکه طینت پاك نیست،
دیدهٔ خفّاش از خورشید در رنج و عناست،   کارِ ایران با خداست،
روز و شب خندد همی بر ریشِ ناچیزِ وزیر،   سبلت تیز امیر،
کی شود زین ریشخندِ زشت کارِ ملك راست،   کارِ ایران با خداست،
باش تا آگه کند شه‌را ازین نا بخردی،   انتقامِ ایزدی،
انتقامِ ایزدی برق است و نابخرد گیاست،   کارِ ایران با خداست،
سنگرِ شه چون بدوشان تپّه[1] رفت از باغ شاه،   تازه‌تر شد داغ شاه،
روزِ دیگر سنگرش در سرحدِ ملك فناست،   کارِ ایران با خداست،
باش تا بیرون ز رشت آید سپهدار سُتُرگ،   فرِّ دادارِ بُزُرگ،
آنکه گیلان ز اهتمامش رشك اقلیم بقاست،   کارِ ایران با خداست،
باش تا از اصفهان صمصام حق گردد پدید،   نام حق گردد پدید،
تا ببینیم آنکه سر ز احکامِ حق پیچد کجاست،   کارِ ایران با خداست،
خاكِ ایران بوم و برزن از تمدّن خورد آب،   جُز خراسانِ خراب،
"هرچه هست از قامت ناساز بی اندام ماست"[2]،   کارِ ایران با خداست،

(بهار)

[1] *Dawshán-tepé* ("Hare Hill") is one of the Sháh's hunting-boxes situated a few miles to the N. E. of Ṭihrán. See my *Year among the Persians*, pp. 86 and 91.

[2] This line is a quotation from Ḥáfiẓ.

(37)

The second poem in this collection is, in the words of the author, a portion of "a metrical history of Persia down to the time of Muḥammad 'Alí, mingled with moving exhortations, sent to the Sháh by means of *Mushíru's-Salṭana*, the Court Chamberlain (*Wazír-i-Darbár*), which, however, produced no effect." It also was composed in Jumáda i, A.H. 1327 (= May–June, 1909), but seems not to have been published at the time. This poem also I consider worthy of being reproduced here.

(۱)

نا تا بچند این سُستی و خوابِ گران، پاسبان‌را نیست خواب از خواب سر بردار هان،
خودرا نگر بی پاسبان و بی شُبان، یك طرف گرگِ دمان و یك طرف شیر ژیان،
چنگِ این رُباید طُعْمه این از چنگِ آن، هر یك آلوده بخونِ این گله چنگ و دهان،
پاسبان مست و گله مشغول و دشمن هوشیار،
کار با یزدان بود کز کف برون رفتست کار،

(۲)

پذیر ای ملك زین پاك گوهر رایگان، نیکی از زشتان مجوی و یاری از همسایگان،
ه از سر دور کن گفتارِ این بیمایگان، پایداری چند خواهی جُست از این بی پایگان،
ِ تو خسروا گنجی است گنجی شایگان، ترسم این گنج از کفت شاها بر آید رایگان،
طرفه گنجی در کف آوردی کنون بی هیچ رنج،
چون نبردی رنج شاها کی شناسی قدرِ گنج،

* * * * * *

این همه آثارِ شاهان خسروا افسانه نیست، شاه‌را شاها گزیر از سیرتِ شاهانه نیست
خسروی اندر خورِ هرسُست و هر دیوانه نیست، مجلس افروزی ز شمع است آری از پروانه نیست
اینك اینك کدخدائی جُز تو در این خانه نیست، خانهٔ چون خانهٔ تو خسروا ویرانه نیست
خیز و از داد و دهش آباد کن این خانه‌را،
و اندك اندك دور کن از خویشتن بیگانه‌را،

(*Translation*)

(1)

"O watchman, how long this sloth and heavy sleep?
Sleep is not for the watchman; O, raise thy head from slumber!
Behold thy flock without watchman or shepherd,
On one side the raging wolf, on the other the roaring lion;
That one snatches the morsel from the claws of this one, and this one from that one,
Each one having dyed his claws and fangs with the blood of this flock.
The watchman drunk, the flock preoccupied, the enemy watchful—
The matter rests with God, for it has passed out of our hands!

(2)

"Accept advice freely, O King, from this loyal nature:
Seek not for fairness from the foul, nor friendliness from thy neighbours;
Then put away out of thine head the words of these worthless ones:
How long wilt thou seek for constancy from these inconstant ones?
Thy kingdom, O Prince, is a treasure, a royal treasure,
And I fear, O King, lest this treasure may slip from thy hands without a struggle.

A wondrous treasure hast thou got in thy hands without trouble!
O King, since thou hast obtained it without trouble, how shouldst thou know the value of the treasure?

* * * *

"All these monuments of the Kings, O prince, are no vain tale;
A king, O King, cannot dispense with kingly qualities.
Kingship does not befit every sluggard and madman;
Yea, it is the candle, not the moth, which illuminates the banquet!
Lo and behold, in this house there is no master save thee,
Yet is there no house so desolate as thine, O Prince!
Arise, cause thy house to prosper by Justice and Bounty,
And, little by little, put away the stranger from thee!"

(38)

The third poem, written about the same time as the last (May–June, 1909), is also addressed to Muḥammad 'Alí, then Sháh. It is what is technically known as a *takhmís*, or "five-some," and a *taẓmín*, or amplification, of one of Shaykh Sa'dí's odes (*ghazals*), that is to say to each verse of Sa'dí's ode are prefixed three new half-verses, the five half-verses thus obtained constituting a *band* or stanza[1]. This poem runs as follows:

(١)

پادشاها ز ستبداد چه داری مقصود، که ازین کار جز ادبار نگردد مشهود،
جود کن در رهِ مشروطه که گردی مسجود، "شرفِ مرد بجودست و کرامت بسجود،
هر که این هر دو ندارد عدمش بهْ ز وجود،"

(٢)

مَلِکا جَوْر مکن پیشه و مشکن پیمان، که مکافاتِ خدائیت بگیرد دامان،
خاك بر سر کندت حادثهٔ دوْرِ زمان، "خاكِ مصرِ طربَ انگیز نه بینی که همان
خاكِ مصر است ولی بر سر فرعون و جنود،"

[1] Concerning the *takhmís* and *mukhammas*, see Vol. I of the late E. J. W. Gibb's *History of Ottoman Poetry*, pp. 92–3, and concerning the *taẓmín* ("quotation"), p. 113. The poem of Sa'dí on which this is based will be found on pp. 292–3 of the Calcutta printed edition of A.D. 1791.

(٣)

مَلِکا خود سری وجَوْرِ تو ایران سوز است، بمکافاتِ تو امروز وطن فیروز است،
تابشِ نورِ مکافات نه از امروز است، "این همان چشمهٔ خورشید جهان افروز است،
که همی تافت بر آرامگه عاد و ثمود،"

(٤)

بیش ازین شاها بر ریشهٔ خود تیشه مزن، خود و ملّت‌را در ورطهٔ ذلّت مفگن،
بیخ خودرا بهوا و هوسِ نفس مکَن، "قیمتِ خود بملاهی و مناهی مشکن،
گرت ایمان درست است بروز موعود،"

(٥)

کِشْتِ ملّت‌را کردی ز ستم پاك دِرو، شد کهن قصّهٔ چنگیز ز بیدادِ تو نو،
بجهان دل‌زچه بندی پس ازین گفت و شنو، "ایکه در نعمت و نازی بجهان غرّه مشو،
که مُحالست درین مرحله امکان خلود،"

(٦)

بگذر از خطّهٔ تبریز و مقام شهداش، بشنو آن قصّهٔ جانسوز و دل از غم بخراش،
اندران خطّه پس از آن کُشش وآن پرخاش، "خاكِ راهی که بران میگذری ساکن باش،
که عیون است و جفون است و خدود است و قدود،"

(٧)

شاه یکدل نشد وکار هبا گشت و هدر، ملّت خسته در این مرحله کن فکر دگر،
پای اُمّید مِنَهْ بر درِ شاهِ خود سر، "دستِ حاجت چو بری پیش خداوندی بر،
که کریم است و رحیم است و غفور است و ودود،"

(۸)

شاه خودکیست بدین کبر و انانیّتِ او، تا نکو باشد در بارهٔ ما نیّتِ او،
ما پرستندهٔ حقّیم و اُلُوهیّتِ او، "کز ثری تا بثریّا بمعبودیّتِ او،
همه در ذکر و مناجات و قیامند و قعود،"

(۹)

سرزند کوکبِ مشروطه ز گردونِ کمال، بسر آید شبِ هجران و دمد صُبْحِ وصال،
کار نیکو شود از فرِّ خدای متعال، "ایکه در شدّت و فقری و پریشانی حال،
صبر کن کین دو سه روزی بسر آید معدود،"

(۱۰)

جز خطا کاری ازین شاه نمی باید خواست، کآنچه ما در او بینیم سراسر بخطاست،
مَدِهَشْ پند که بر بد منشان پند هباست، "پند سعدی که کلیدِ درِ گنج سُعَداست،
نتواند که بجای آورد الاّ مسعود،"

(*Translation*)

(1)

"O King, at what dost thou aim by thy despotism?
From such deeds naught will be witnessed save evil fortune!
Shew generosity in the way of the Constitution, that thou may'st
be adored:
'*The honour of a man is in generosity, and his nobility in*
worship:
Whoever has not these two, his non-existence is better than his
existence!'

(2)

"O King, make not cruelty thy practice, nor break thy promises,
For, if thou dost, Divine punishment will seize thy skirt!
The happenings of the cycle of time will cast dust on thy head:
'*Dost thou not see that the gladsome dust of Egypt is the same*
Dust of Egypt, but [cast] on the heads of Pharaoh and his hosts?'

(3)

"O King, thine obstinacy and tyranny consume Persia;
To-day the Nation is successful in requiting thee!
The glow of the light of requital is not [a thing] of to-day:
'*This is the same world-enkindling disc of the Sun*
Which used to shine on the dwellings of 'Ád and Thamúd!'

(4)

"O King, strike not the axe more than this on thy root!
Cast not thyself and the Nation into the gulf of abasement!
Do not dig up thine own roots through selfish desires and whims!
'*Do not mar thy worth by frivolous and forbidden pursuits,*
If thy belief in the Promised Day[1] *be sincere!*'

(5)

"With tyranny thou didst reap clean the Nation's crop;
The old story of Chingíz Khán hath been renewed by thine injustice;
After this conversation wherefore shouldst thou set thy heart on the world?
'*O thou who art in luxury and wealth, be not deceived by the world,*
For to tarry eternally in this halting-place is an impossible contingency!'

[1] *i.e.* the Day of Judgement.

(6)

"Pass by the region of Tabríz and the place of its martyrs:
Hearken to that soul-melting story, and rend thy heart with woe!
In that region, after that slaughter and strife,
'Walk gently on the dust of that road wherever thou passest,
For it is [composed of] eyes and eyelids, cheeks and bodies!'

(7)

"The King is not single-hearted, and affairs are gone to rack and ruin:
O wearied nation, think of some fresh plan at this stage!
Set not the foot of hope at the gate of this headstrong monarch!
'If thou stretchest out thine hand in supplication, stretch it towards One
Who is generous, merciful, forgiving and kind!'

(8)

"Who, indeed, is the King, with this his pride and egotism,
That his intentions with regard to us should be good?
We are the worshippers of God and His Divinity,
'In whose service, from the dust to the Pleiades,
All are engaged in commemoration, prayers, rising up and bowing down.'

(9)

"The Constellation of the Constitution appears from the Firmament of Perfection:
The Night of Parting draws to an end, and the Morn of Union dawns:
All will be well through the Glory of God Most High.
'O thou who art in hardship, poverty and distracted circumstances,
Be patient, for these few brief days will come to an end!'

(10)

"One must not expect from this King anything but mistakes,
For what we see in him is wrong from one end to the other:
Counsel him not, for vain is counsel to those of evil nature.
'The advice of Sa'dí, which is the key to the door of the Treasure of the Blessed,
None can put into practice save the favoured!'"

(39)

The fourth poem of the collection, composed "in the latter days of the Lesser Tyranny, and the beginning of the Revolt in Khurásán (*i.e.* in the early summer of A.D. 1909) in order to excite and encourage the *Fidá'ís*," was recited in the *Bágh-i-'Anbar* at Mashhad, and afterwards published in the newspaper *Khurásán*. It is remarkable in form as being what is called *Dhú Qáfiyatayn*, or having a double rhyme. Only the first of the five stanzas which constitute the poem is here given.

دوشینه ز رنج دهرِ بد خواه، رفتم سوی بوستان نهانی،
تا وا رهم از خمارِ جانکاه، از لطف هوای بوستانی،
دیدم گُلهای نغزِ دلخواه، خندان بطراوتِ جوانی،
مرغان لطیف طبع آگاه، نالان بنوای باستانی،
بر آتش روی گُل شبانگاه، هر یك سرگرم زند خوانی،
من بیخبرانه رفتم از راه، از آن نغماتِ آسمانی،
با خود گفتم بناله و آه، کای رانده ز عالم معانی،
با بال ضعیف و برِّ کوتاه، پروازِ بلند کی توانی،
بودم در این سخن که ناگاه، مرغی بزبان بی زبانی،
این مژده بگوشِ من رسانید،
کز رحمتِ حق مباش نومید،

The fifth poem has been already given (No. 20, pp. 218–20 *supra*). It was published not only in the *Írán-i-Naw* (from which it was quoted), but also in the papers *Khurásán*, *Taraqqí*, and *Ḥablu'l-Matín*.

The sixth poem was originally declaimed in a great assembly of the notables, officials and people of Mashhad held in the Holy Shrine of the Imám Riẓá to celebrate the opening of the Second National Assembly (about November 15, 1909). It is in praise of Freedom, comprises fifteen couplets, and begins:

اقی که کرد ایزد قوی ارکانِ آزادی، نمود آباد از تو خانهٔ ویران آ
بکشود بر غمدیدگان ابوابِ آسایش، فلك بر بست با دلخستگان پیمان آ

The seventh poem was written in July, 1910, at a time of political crisis and change of Cabinet. It is a *tarkíb-band* of four strophes, and appeared in the newspaper *Ṭús*, No. 50. The last strophe is as follows:

یارانِ روشِ دگر گرفتند، وز ما دل و دیده بر گرفتند،
از مسلكِ ما شدند دلگیر، پس مسلكِ خوبتر گرفتند،
در سایهٔ طبعِ اعتدالی، پیرایهٔ مختصر گرفتند،
هر زشتی‌را نکو گزیدند، هر نفعی‌را ضرر گرفتند،
وز خارجیان ز ساده لوحی، زهر از عوضِ شکر گرفتند،
فرمانِ شکوه خویشتن‌را، از دشمنِ کینه‌ور گرفتند،
باری هر کارِ پُر خطررا، کاینان ز رهِ خطر گرفتند،
بازی بازی ز کف نهادند، شوخی شوخی ز سر گرفتند،

غافل که بخانقاهِ احرار،
سیصد گوش است پُشْت دیوار،

(40)

The eighth poem appeared in No. 31 of the newspaper *Tús* on the Persian *Nawrúz* (New Year's Day), March 22, 1910. It is a *mustazád* of fifteen stanzas, and is worthy of notice both on account of its intrinsic beauty and its allusions to recent events in Persia.

(۱)

عیدِ نوروز است هر روزی بما نوروز باد، شامِ ایران روز باد،
پنجمین سالِ حیات ما بما فیروز باد، روزِ ما بهروز باد،
برقِ تیغِ ما جهان پرداز و دشمن سوز باد، جیشِ ما کین توز باد،
سالِ استقلالِ مارا باد آغازِ بهار، با نسیمِ افتخار،

(۲)

یاد باد آن نوبهارِ رفته و آن پژمرده باغ، و آن خزان تیز چنگ،
و آن همه محنت که بر بلبل رسید از جور زاغ، در رهِ ناموس و ننگ،
و آن ز خون نو جوانان بر کران باغ و راغ، لاله‌های رنگ رنگ،
و آن ز قدِّ راد مردان در کنار جویبار، سروهای خاکسار،

(۳)

یاد باد آن باغبان کز کینه آتش در فگند، در فضای این چمن،
و آن نسیمِ مهرگانی کآمد و از بیخ کند، لاله و سرو و سمن،
آن یکی بر هرزه کرد انباز رنج سخت بند، گلبنانِ ممتحن،
و آن دگر بر خیره کرد آویزِ چوبِ خشك دار، میوه‌های خوشگوار،

(٤)

ـر کرانِ گلشنِ تبریز آتش در گرفت،   از نسیمِ جورِ شاه،
گشت از آن آتش که ناگه اندران کشور گرفت،   خونِ مسکینان تباه،
چون ز مردی و دلیری ره بر آن لشکر گرفت،   لشکرِ مشروطه خواه،
ـشکر همسایه[1] ناگه سر بر آورد از کنار،   با هزاران گیر و دار،

(٥)

کاین منم افشرده پا اندر رهِ صلح و وداد،   نیست از من خوف و بیم،
آمدستم تا به بندم ره بر آشوب و فساد،   بر طریقِ مستقیم،
اللّه اللّه زآن تطاول اللّه اللّه زآن عناد،   ای خداوندِ کریم،
این چه جَوْر است وعداوت اینچه بغض است و نقار،   زین گروه باربار،

(٦)

اندك اندك زین بهانه سوی قزوین کرد روی،   وحشیانه جیشِ روس،
در شمالِ ملكِ ما افتاد از ایشان های و هوی،   ای دریغ و ای فسوس،
در خراسان هم درآن هنگامه روسِ خیره پوی،   از ستم بنواخت کوس،
حامی اشرار شد وافگند در مشهد شرار،   نی نهان بل آشکار،

(٧)

یاد بادا آن مهِ خورداد و آن جان باختن،   در رهِ ناموس و دین
و آن بسوی قُبّة الاسلام توپ انداختن،   بر عنادِ مسلمین
قومی از بیدانشی کارِ وطن‌را ساختن،   نیز قومی در کمین
تا که میدانی بدست آرند درآن گیر و دار،   غافل از انجامِ کار

[1] *i.e.* Russia.

(۸)

غافل از این کآسمان هر روز بازیها کند، بر خلافِ رای مرد،
ملّتِ بیدار دل گردن فرازیها کند، روزِ پیکار و نبرد،
کردگارِ داد گستر کارسازیها کند، بر مرام اهلِ درد،
تا که اهلِ دردرا گردد زمانه سازگار، چرخ رام و بخت یار،

(۹)

یاد باد و شاد باد آن سروِ آزادِ وطن، حضرتِ ستّار خان،
آنکه داد از رادی و مردانگی دادِ وطن، اندر آذربایجان،
راد باقر خان کزو شد سخت بنیادِ وطن، شاد بادا جاودان،
یاد بادا ملّتِ تبریز و آن مردانِ کار، آن وطنرا افتخار،

(۱۰)

یاد باد آن جیش گیلان و آن همه غرّنده شیر، و آن یورشهای بزرگ،
و آن مهین سردارِ اسعد و آن سپهدارِ دلیر، و آن جوانانِ سترگ،
یاد باد آن در سفارتخانه از ایّام سیر، چون ز شیر آشفته گرگ،
و آن حمایت پیشگان همسایگانِ دوستار، برده اورا در جوار،

(۱۱)

یاد باد آن فتنهٔ زنجان و آن قربان علی،[1] و آن همه خون ریختن،
یاد باد آن اردبیل و آن همه سنگین دلی، و آن بحلق آویختن،
یاد بادا آن رحیمِ نا کس و آن جاهلی، و آن فساد انگیختن،
یاد باد آن آتش افروزانِ پنهانِ دیار، و آن گروه دیوسار،

[1] The revolt in Zanján, headed by Mullá Qurbán 'Alí, began about the middle of August, 1909, and culminated in the Dáráb Mírzá incident in May–June, 1910. The troubles at Ardabíl began about the same time.

(۱۲)

یاد بادا آن طبیبِ روسی عیسی نفس، و آن رحیم دردمند،
و آن دوای روح پرورکش نباشد دست رس، جز به بیماری نژند،
و آن شمای عاجل و جنگ آوریهای سپس، و آن همه رنج و گزند،
و آن بهانه جستن و آوردن اندر آن دیار، لشکرِ وحشی شعار،

(۱۳)

یاد باد آن دست دادن اندرآن عکسِ گروپ[1] در فضای اردبیل،
و آن بیارانِ رحیم از شوق دادن مشق توپ، تا شود خونها سبیل[2]
و آن بخود ره دادنِ اهریمنان نا بکار، از پسِ جنگ و فرار،

(۱۴)

اینک اینک سالِ نو شد آفرین بر سالِ نو، هم بر این اقبالِ نو،
سالِ نو هر دم زند بر ملكِ ایران فالِ نو، دل کند آمالِ نو،
ماضی ما کهنه شد بنگر در استقبالِ نو، فرّ و استقلالِ نو،
فرّ و استقلال نو باشد در استقبالِ کار، منّت از پروردگار،

(۱۵)

منّت ایزدرا که قومِ خفتهرا بیدار کرد، لطفِ حیّ لا ینام،
خیره گرگانرا ز مصرِ مملکت آوار کرد، آن عزیز ذو انتقام،
اینک اینک نوبتِ کار است باید کار کرد، در رهِ ناموس و نام،
تا که مقصودی بدست آریم بعد از انتظار، بر خلافِ همجوار،

[1] The "group" photograph of Raḥím Khán and his Russian friends to which reference is here made was published in the *Ḥablu'l-Matín*, the *Manchester Guardian*, and opposite p. 440 of my *Persian Revolution*.

[2] A line has evidently fallen out here in the original.

Raḥím Khán Qarája-Dághí,

the notorious Reactionary referred to in verse 13 of Poem No. 40, holding the hand of M. Belaieff, the Secretary of the Russian Consulate-General at Tabriz

From a photograph taken about the end of August, 1909

(١٦)

همجواران‌را بما انصاف کاری هست؟ نیست! رَوْ بکن کارِ دگر
قومِ مغرب‌را بر اهلِ شرق یاری هست؟ نیست! رَوْ بجو یار دگر
خود خریداری بر این افغان و زاری هست؟ نیست! شَوْ ببازار دگر
ز آنکه کس‌را دل بحالِ کس نمی سوزد بهار کار باید کرد کار

(41)

The ninth poem, which appeared in No. 30 of the newspaper *Ṭús* about the middle of March, 1910, is a satire on the disgraceful condition of the streets of Mashhad in rainy weather on account of the mud.

افتاده‌ایم سخت بدامِ بلای گِل یا رب چو ما مباد کسی مبتلای گِل
گِل مشکلی شده است بهر معبر و طریق گامِ روندگان شده مشکل گشای گِل
هرگه که ابر خیمه زند در فضای شهر بر بامِ هر سرای بر آید لوای گِل
گِل دل نمی کَنَد ز خراسان و اهلِ او ای جانِ اهلِ شهر فدای وفای گِل
گر صد هزار کفش بدرّد بپای خلق هرگز نمی رسند بکشف غطای گِل
با خضر اگر روند بظلماتِ کوچه خلق اسکندری خورند[1] درین چشمه‌های گِل
اوّل قدم که بوسه زند گِل بپای ما افتیم بر زمین و ببوسیم پای گِل
گِلْها ثقیل و درهم وکوچه خراب و تنگ آه از جفای کوچه و داد از جفای گِل
گِل هرچه‌را به پنجه در آورد ول نکرد صد آفرین به پنجهٔ معجز نمای گِل
از گل ز بسکه خاطر و دلها فُسُرْده[2] است گُل نیز بعد از این ندمد از فضای گِل
بر روزگارِ خویش کنم گریه بامداد چون بنگرم بخندهٔ دندان نمای گِل
از پُشْت تا بشانه واز پیش تا بریش هستند خلق یکسره غرقِ غطای گِل
امروز در قلمروِ طوس از بلند و پست آنجایگه کجاست که خالی است جای گِل

[1] *Iskandarí khurdan* is a slang expression meaning "to fall on the face," but there is a *tanásub* with *Khiẓr* in the previous line.

[2] This is a conjectural emendation for *rasída*, which gives no good sense.

آید اگر جهاز زره پوش ز انگلند، حیران شود ز لجّهٔ بی منتهای گِل،
گر لای و گِل تمام نگردد ازین بلد، اهلِ بلد تمام بمانند لای گِل،
شرم آیدم ز گفتن بسیار ورنه باز،
چندین هزار مسئله باشد ورای گِل،

(42)

The tenth poem, a *musaddas* or "six-some," appeared in No. 1 of the newspaper *Naw Bahár* in the month of Shawwál, A.H. 1328 (= October–November, 1910). Five of the twelve stanzas of this poem (Nos. 3, 6, 7, 8 and 12) are here given.

(۳)

وُزرا باز نهادند ز کف کار وطن، وُکلا مُهر نهادند بکام و بدهن،
عُلما شبهه نمودند و فتادند بظن، چیره شد کشورِ ایران‌را انبوهِ فتن،
کشورِ ایران ز انبوهِ فتن در خطر است،
ای وطنخواهان زنهار وطن در خطر است،

(٦)

پارتی انگیزند این قوم در اصلاحِ اُمور، لیك پارتی شان ز اصلاح بصد مرحله دور،
غرض و حُبِّ ریاستشان اوّل منظور، غافل از اینکه وطن مانده غریب و مهجور،
ملّتِ خسته چه از مرد و چه زن در خطر است،
ای وطنخواهان زنهار وطن در خطر است،

(۷)

خرسِ صحرا شده همدستِ نهنگِ دریا، کشتی ما را رانده است بگرداب بلا،
آه ازین رنج و محن آوخ ازین جور و جفا، هان بجز جرأت و غیرت نبود چارهٔ ما،
ز آنکه ناموسِ وطن زین دو محن در خطر است،
ای وطنخواهان زنهار وطن در خطر است،

(۸)

رقیبارا بهم امروز سرِ صلح و صفاست، آری این صلح و صفاشان برهِ ذلّت ماست،
بیخبر ز آنکه مهین رایتِ اسلام بپاست، غافل آن قوم که قفقاز و لهستان ببلاست،
غافل این فرقه که لاهور و دکن در خطر است،
ای وطنخواهان زنهار وطن در خطر است،

(۱۲)

وطنیّاتی با دیدهٔ تر میگویم، با وجودیکه در او نیست اثر میگویم،
تا رسد عمرِ گرانمایه بسر میگویم، بارها گفته‌ام و بارِ دگر میگویم،
که وطن باز وطن باز وطن در خطر است،
ای وطنخواهان زنهار وطن در خطر است،

The paper *Naw Bahár* (see No. 357, p. 149 *supra*) first appeared on the 9th of Shawwál, A.H. 1328 (= October 14, 1910), at Mashhad. The celebrated Ḥaydar Khán, called *'Amú-oghlú* ("cousin"), was its founder, and our poet *Bahár*, its editor. It was suppressed at the instance of the Russians exactly a year after its inception (on October 14, 1911).

(43)

The eleventh poem is evidently modelled on a well-known fragment by the great poet Jámí, beginning:

بدندان رخنه در پولاد کردن، بناخن راه در خارا بُریدن،

and ending:

همه بر جامی آسانتر نماید، که بارِ منّتِ دونان کشیدن،

It was published in the *Naw Bahár* in Shawwál, A.H. 1328 (= October–November, 1910), and is as follows:

دو رویه زیرِ نیشِ مار خُفْتن، سه پُشْته روی شاخِ مور رفتن،
تنِ روغن زده با زحمت و زور، میانِ لانهٔ زنبور رفتن،
بکوهِ بیستون بی رهنمائی، شبانه با دو چشمِ کور رفتن،
میانِ لرز و تب با جسمِ پُر زخم، زمستان توی آب شور رفتن،
برهنه زخمهای سخت خوردن، پیاده راههای دور رفتن،
بپیشِ من هزاران بار خوشتر،
که بکجو زیرِ بار زور رفتن،

(44)

The twelfth poem is a *taṣníf*, or ballad, in the "Afshár Mode," and appeared in the *Naw Bahár* in the month of Dhu'l-Ḥijja, A.H. 1328 (= December, 1910). It runs as follows:

(در پردهٔ افشار)

(۱)

نمی دانم چرا ویرانه گشتی—وطن، مقام لشکرِ بیگانه گشتی—وطن،
تو شمعِ جمعِ ما بودی وطن جان—چرا، بشمعِ دیگران پروانه گشتی—وطن،
پروانه گشتی وطن، (مکرّر)
تو عزیزِ منی تو گلِ گلشنی، بدین خواری چرا افسانه گشتی وطن،

(۲)

خوشا روزی که بودی شاد و خندان—وطن، شکستی خصم‌را چنگال و دندان—وطن،
تو بودی سر بلند افسوس افسوس—وطن، در اُفتادی بحالِ مستمندان—وطن،
در اُفتادی بحالِ مستمندان وطن، (مکرّر)
امان امان امان بیداد بیداد بیداد، ز جورِ دشمنان ویرانه گشتی وطن،

(۳)

جان ای وطن جان ای وطن جانِ من، شفای دل دوای قلبِ سوزانِ ،
کش مادرِ زارِ پریشانِ من، پرستارِ من و گهواره جُنْبانِ ،
پرستارِ من و گهواره جُنْبانِ من، (مکرّر)
مهربان آشنای روان، بفرزندان چرا بیگانه گشتی وه

(٤)

ں و انگلیس آید ستمها بما، هجوم آرد ز هر سو درد و غمها
ر خاك ما از کین نهادند و باز، بسی حُجّت نهند این بد قدمها
این بد قدمها بما، (مکرّر)
پیمان کنند چرا کتمان کنند، ازین پیمان تو بی پیمانه گشتی
ویرانه گشتی وطن، ویرانه گشتی وطن،

The thirteenth poem was recited at the official celebration held on the birthday of Sulṭán Aḥmad Sháh by the Provincial Council of Khurásán in August, 1911, and was afterwards published in the *Naw Bahár*. It is a *qaṣída* of twenty-seven verses, composed in the style of the old poet Farrukhí, and begins:

هِلْ ز کف ای ترك و بیکسو نِه چنگ، جامهٔ جنگ فرو پوش که شد نوبت .
روز بیفْسُرْد بنِهْ باده ز دست، چنگ‌را نوبت بگذشت بنِهْ چنگ ز .

(45)

The fourteenth poem was published in the *Naw Bahár* in Ramaẓán, A.H. 1329 (= August–September, 1911). It comprises eleven verses, and is an imitation of a poem by Minúchihrí[1]

ای خطّهٔ ایرانِ مهین ای وطنِ من، ای گشته بمهرِ تو عجین جان و تنِ من،
ای عاصمهٔ دنیی آباد که شد باز، آشفته کنارت چو دلِ پُرحزنِ من،

[1] This begins:

ں باده فدای تو همه جان و تنِ من، کز بیخ بکَنْدی ز دلِ من حزنِ مر

دور از تو گُل و لاله و سرو و سمنم نیست، ای باغ گُل و لاله و سرو و سمنِ من
بس خارِ مُصیبت که خلد مرا بر پای[1]، بی روی تو ای تازه شگفته چمنِ من
ای بار خدای من گر بی تو زِیَم باز، افرشتهٔ من گردد چون اهرمنِ من
تا هست کنارِ تو پُر از لشکرِ دشمن، هرگز نشود خالی از دل محنِ من
از رنجِ تو لاغر شده‌ام چونان کز من، تا بر نشود ناله نبینی بدنِ من[2]
دردا و دریغا که چنان گشتی بی برگ، کز بافتهٔ خویش نداری کفنِ من
بسیار سخن گفتم در تعزیتِ تو، آوخ که نگریاند کس را سخنِ من
آنگاه نیوشند سخنهای مرا خلق، کز خونِ من آغشته شود پیرهنِ من
وامروز همی گویم با محنتِ بسیار،
دردا و دریغا وطنِ من وطنِ من

(46)

The fifteenth and last poem in this collection is placed in the mouth of the ex-Sháh Muḥammad 'Alí, whose raid into Persia in August, 1911, ended, in spite of the hardly-concealed help of the Russians, in the defeat and death of his most capable General, *Arshadu'd-Dawla*, at the end of August and beginning of September, and his flight back to Russia soon afterwards. This poem also was published in the *Naw Bahár*.

(زبان حالِ شاهِ مخلوع)

(۱)

با بنده فلك چرا بجنگ است، سبحان الله این چه رنگ است،
بودم روزی بشهر تبریز، آقا و ولیّ عهد و با چیز،
شه هرمز بود و بنده پرویز، و اینك شده‌ام ز دیده خونریز،
کاین چرخ چرا چنین دو رنگ است،
سبحان الله این چه رنگ است،

[1] This hemistich does not scan, but I cannot emend it.

[2] This seems to be a reminiscence of al-Mutanabbí's verse (ed. Dieterici, p. 5):

كَفَى بِجِسْمِي نُحُولًا أَنَّنِي رَجُلٌ، لَوْلَا مُخَاطَبَتِي إِيَّاكَ لَمْ تَرَنِي،

(۲)

بودم روزی بشهرِ تهران، مولا و خدایگان و سلطان،
بستم همه‌را بتوپِ غرّان، گفتم که کسی نماند از ایشان،
دیدم روزِ دگر که جنگ است،
سبحان اللّه این چه رنگ است،

(۳)

گفتیم که خلق حرفِ سُفتند، آخر دیدیم دُم کلفتند،
خیلی گفتیم و کم شنفتند، یك جنبشِ سخت کرده گفتند،
بسم اللّه ره سوی فرنگ است،
سبحان اللّه این چه رنگ است،

(٤)

گفتیم که ما ز گُنْدگانیم، رحمت ز خدا به بندگانیم
سوی اودسا شوندگانیم، غم نیست گر از روندگانیم
بنشستنِ ما بخانه ننگ است،
سبحان اللّه این چه رنگ است،

(٥)

سوی اودسا شدیم هَی هَی، مجنون آسا شدیم هَی هَی
بی برگ و نوا شدیم هَی هَی، یکباره فنا شدیم هَی هَی
آن دل که بما نسوخت سنگ است،
سبحان اللّه این چه رنگ است،

(٦)

اندر آدسا قِزِی جمیله، آمد چون لیلی از قبیله،
مجنون شدمش بلا وسیله، بگذاشت بگوشِ من فتیله،
گفتیم که وقتِ لاس و دنگ است،
سبحان الله این چه رنگ است،

(٧)

بد بختی ما نگر که خانُم، نا داد دگر بدستِ ما دُم،
یك روز و دو روز بود و شد گُم، با خود گفتیم خسروا قُم،
کن عزم سفر که وقت تنگ است،
سبحان الله این چه رنگ است،

(٨)

بر یادِ نگار عیسوی کیش، کردیم سفر بمملكِ اطریش،
درویشانه گذشتم از خویش، کز عشق شهان شوند درویش،
دیدم ره دور و پای لنگ است،
سبحان الله این چه رنگ است،

(٩)

خانم ز نظر برفت باری، مقصودِ سفر برفت باری،
رفتم بهدر برفت باری، چون عشق ز سر برفت باری،
گفتم که نه موقعِ درنگ است،
سبحان الله این چه رنگ است،

(۱۰)

دیدیم بشهر قال و قیل است، صحبت ز نگارِ بی بدیل است،
وز ما سخنانِ بس طویل است، گفتیم که نام ما خلیل است،
گفتیم که کارِ ما شلنگ است،
سبحان اللّه این چه رنگ است،

(۱۱)

با خود گفتیم ممدلی هَی، وقتِ سفر است یا علی هَی
بر خیز و برو مگر شلی هی، خودرا آماده کن ولی هی
بپّا که زمانه تیز چنگ است،
سبحان اللّه این چه رنگ است،

(۱۲)

آن کس که تراست میهمان دار، بسیار رفیقِ تست بسیار
از توپ و تفنگ و جیشِ جرّار، همره کندت مترس زنهار
بشتاب که وقتِ نام و ننگ است،
سبحان اللّه این چه رنگ است،

(۱۳)

و آنگاه ز شهرِ مارینباد، رفتیم ببادکوبه دلشاد
صاحب خانه نوید میداد، میگفت برو باستراباد
گفتیم که ممدلی زرنگ است،
سبحان اللّه این چه رنگ است،

(١٤)

گفتم قلیوف بیا بیا زود، آماده بکن یکی پراخود،
نامرد بقیمتش بیفزود، من نیز قبول کردم از جود،
گفتم که نه وقت چنگ چنگ است،
سبحان الله این چه رنگ است،

(١٥)

و آنگاه برسم میهمانها، رفتیم بایل ترکمانها،
دادیم نویدها بآنها، گفتیم که ای عزیزِ جانها،
از غم دلِ ما بونگ ونگ است،
سبحان الله این چه رنگ است،

(١٦)

گفتم سخنان بمکر و فنها، پختم همه‌را از آن سخنها،
خوش داد نتیجه ما و منها، این نقشه نه خوب گشت تنها،
هر نقشه که می کشم قشنگ است،
سبحان الله این چه رنگ است،

(١٧)

من ممدلی گریز پایم، با دولتِ روس آشنایم،
تهران تو کجا و من کجایم، خواهم که بجانبِ تو آیم،
کز عشقِ تو کلّه‌ام دبنگ است،
سبحان الله این چه رنگ است،

(۱۸)

بِر دوره‌ده سلطنت منم دی، آسایش و عافیت منم دی،[1]
هم عزّت و منزلت منم دی، آوخ که بو مملکت منم دی،
ملّت ینه ایندی قُولْتَشَنگ است،
سبحان اللّه این چه رنگ است،

(۱۹)

ای ترکمنان نیك منظر، ریزید بشهر و قلعه یکسر،
چاپید هر آنچه اسپ و استر، ز آغوش پدر کشید دختر،
کاین مایهٔ پیشرفت جنگ است،
سبحان اللّه این چه رنگ است،

(۲۰)

قالقون گِدرز بنی له همراه، همّتله ایدون منی ینه شاه،
شاه اولسام اگر اولون سِز آگاه، غارت ایدروز بنَحْوِ دلخواه،
قالقون گدرز که وقت تنگ است،
سبحان اللّه این چه رنگ است،

(۲۱)

و آنگاه دو اسپه با دلِ شاد، رفتیم بشهرِ استراباد،
کردیم عَلَم چماقِ بیداد، گفتیم که هر که پیشکش داد،
ایمن ز گلولهٔ تفنگ است،
سبحان اللّه این چه رنگ است،

[1] This and the two following verses are in Turkish.

(۲۲)

رشد که چو ما نشد هراسان،   شد عازم شاهرود و سمنان،

ز سوی دگر رشید سلطان،   شد از ره راست سوی تهران،

گفتیم که وقتِ دنگ و فنگ است،

سبحان اللّه این چه رنگ است،

(۲۳)

خود گرچه ز شوق نیز بودیم،   در وحشت و ترس نیز بودیم،

هر دم بسرِ گریز بودیم،   هر لحظه بجست و خیز بودیم،

گفتی که براهِ ما پلنگ است،

سبحان اللّه این چه رنگ است،

(۲٤)

گفتند که کارها شلوغ است،   و این کهنه چراغ بی فروغ است،

سرمایهٔ ارتجاع دوغ است،   گفتیم که جملگی دروغ است،

گفتیم که جملگی جفنگ است،

سبحان اللّه این چه رنگ است،

(۲٥)

گفتند که کُشته شد رشیدت،   گفتند که پاره شد امیدت،

گفتند وعید شد نویدت،   گفتند سیاه شد سفیدت،

دیدم سرِ من ز غُصّه منگ است،

سبحان اللّه این چه رنگ است،

(۲۶)

گفتند که خصم کینه خواه است، بد خواه براه و نیمه راه است
قصد همگی بقتلِ شاه است، دیدیم که روزِ ما سیاه است
و آئینهٔ ما قرینِ زنگ است،
سبحان الله این چه رنگ است،

(۲۷)

گفتند که ارشدت جدو شد، و آن میرِ مکرّمت کتو شد
اردوی منظّمت چپو شد، هنگامِ بدو بدو بدو شد
بگریز که جعبه بی فشنگ است،
سبحان الله این چه رنگ است،

(۲۸)

گفتند جنابِ حکم فرما، زحمت چکسوز دگر بفرما
بر گرد کجا که بودی آنجا، دیدم زین بیش جنگ و دعوا
حقّا که برای بنده ننگ است،
سبحان الله این چه رنگ است،

(۲۹)

بنمود زمانه هرزه پوئی، وین گردون کرد تیره روئی
افگند مرا بمرده شوئی، گفتیم مگر که جنگ جوئی
چون عشقِ نگار شوخ و شنگ است،
سبحان الله این چه رنگ است،

(۴۰)

امروز ز بخت در گله استم،   در گیر شکنجه و تله استنم،
در کارِ فرار و ولوله استم،   گر بنده امیر قافله استم،
این قافله تا بحشر لنگ است،
سبحان اللّه این چه رنگ است،

(47)

The following poem, not included in the above collection, is also by Bahár, and was sent to me separately by a Persian friend. It is, I think, a parody of a well-known ode (*ghazal*) of Ḥáfiẓ or some other of the classical poets, and, though couched in the erotic strain usual in this class of poems, is full of political allusions.

دل فریبان که بروسیّهٔ دل جا دارند،   مستبدّانه چرا قصد دلِ ما دارند،
دلبران خودسر و هرجائی و روسی صفتند،   ورنه در خانهٔ غیر از چه سبب جا دارند،
گاه لطف است وخوشی گاه عتاب است وخطاب،   تا چه ازین همه پولتیك تقاضا دارند،
خوبرویان اروپا ز چه در مُرْدنِ ما،   حیله سازند اگر اعجاز مسیحا دارند،
گرچه در قاعدهٔ حسن سیاسات جمال،   مسلك آنست که خوبان اروپا دارند،
عاشقانرا سرِ آزادی و استقلالست،   کی ز پولتیكِ سرِ زلفِ تو پروا دارند،
صفِ مژگانِ ترا دستِ سیاسی است دراز،   با نفوذیکه بمعمورهٔ دلها دارند،
دلِ مسکینِ من از قرضِ یکی بوسه گذشت،   با شروطی که لبانِ تو مهیّا دارند،
بچه قانونِ سپهِ نازِ تو ای ترك پسر،   در حدودِ دلِ یاران سرِ یغما دارند،
این چه صلحی است که در داخلهٔ کشورِ دل،   خیلِ قزّاقِ اشاراتِ تو مأوا دارند،
بکمسیونِ عرایض چه کنم شکوه ز تو،   که همه حالِ منِ بیدلِ شیدا دارند،

The Poet Púr-i-Dáwúd

ما بتوضیح دو چشمانِ تو قانع نشویم، زآنکه با خارجیان الفت و نجوا دارند،
در پناهِ سرِ زلفِ تو بهارستان است، که در او هیئتِ دل مجلسِ شورا دارند،
حکم فرمای که در محکمهٔ حسن و جمال، هرچه آن حکمِ تو باشد همه مُجری دارند،
رازدارانِ تو در انجمنِ سرّی دل، نطقی از رمزِ دهانِ تو تمنّا دارند،
دل غارت شده در محضر عدلیّهٔ عشق، متظلّم شد و چشمانِ تو حاشا دارند،

سخن تازه ز طبعِ تو عجب نیست بهار،
که همه مشرقیان منطقِ گویا دارند،

POEMS BY PÚR-I-DÁWÚD

(48)

The following fine poem by Púr-i-Dáwúd has a less purely Persian vocabulary than he generally affects. It was communicated to me in November, 1913, and has, I think, never before been published.

ازآه بخُشکانم آبِ همه دریارا، وز اشك کنم دریا روی همه صحرارا،
در خَیْلِ همه یاران همراز نمی جویم، نه زاهدِ روحانی نه شاهدِ زیبارا،
در جُبّهٔ دیبا نی فضل و هنرِ مردم، با علم و شرف پوشم خود جامهٔ چوخارا،
در کلبهٔ درویشی خوش باشم ار آزادم، در بند نمی خواهم صد قصرِ معلّارا،
جمعی بدرِ مسجد خَیْلی بسوی فرخار، خلقی بکنشت اندر جمعی است کلیسارا،
گر از ستمِ گیتی آتشکده شد خاموش، در کاخ دل افروزم کانونِ اَوِسْتَارا،
از مدرسه و از درس کی چاره شود دردم، ساز و دف و نی خوشتر دلداده و شیدارا،
می گرچه حرام آمد در کیشِ مسلمانی، در باده کشی پویم آئین مسیحارا،
خواهم که ز پا اُفْتم مدهوش و خمار و مست، تا تا شنوم ز ایران این غلغل وآوارا،
از ناحیهٔ ایران هر لحظه بگوش آید، صوتی که بلرزاند این گنبدِ مینارا،

صوتی که ازو گردد خود موی همه سوزن، صوتی که ازو بینی خونین دل خارارا،
گوید بتو ای فرزند اندیش بحال خویش، در یاب ز جهد امروز آسایش فردارا،
دیبا نتوانی بافت زین پشم که می تابی، زین خار نخواهی چید هرگز گلِ حمرارا،
زنجیر ز من بر گیر آنگاه بچنگ آور، زنجیرِ سرِ زلفِ محبوب دلآرارا،
من در تب و تاب و غم تو شاد و خوش و خُرّم، ننگ است چنین غفلت مانندِ تو برنارا،
از خونِ جوانانم شد دشت همه گلگون، باز آ و دمی بنگر گلگشت و تماشارا،
شد از ستمِ دونان ملكِ جم و کی ویران، پیغولهٔ جغدان بین ایران فلکسارا،
شد شیرِ کیان پنهان جولانِ شگال آمد، خواری ز عقب آمد کرّ و فرِ دارارا،
شاهنشه انوشروان در گورِ سیه خُسپید، خرس است ابر جایش بین بازی دنیارا،
گر پور رود روزی از مهر وطن بر دار،
صد شکر و سپاس آرد مر ایزد یکتارا،

(Translation)

(1) With sighs I dry up the water of all the sea, and with tears I turn into a sea all the face of the plain.

In all the company of friends I seek no confidant, nor spiritual ascetic, nor beauteous sweetheart.

The virtue and talent of a man are not in the robe of brocade; for all my learning and nobility I wear a coat of cloth.

If I be free I can be happy in a dervish's cell, while I desire not a hundred lofty palaces [if I be] in bonds.

(5) There is a crowd at the door of the Mosque, a troop [moving] towards [the idol-temple of] Farkhár, a host entering the synagogue, a congregation [filling] the church.

If the Fire-temple has been extinguished through the tyranny of Fate, I will kindle in the chamber of the heart the altar of the Avesta.

How can my sorrow be cured by colleges and lectures? Music, cymbals and flute are more congenial to the madman who has lost his heart.

Although wine is forbidden in the Musulmán creed, in the drinking of wine I will pursue the Christian practice.

I would fain fall down dazed, drunken and overcome by wine, so that I may not hear from Persia this clamour and crying.

(10) From the direction of Persia every moment there reaches the ear a voice which causes this blue vault [of heaven] to tremble;

A voice whereat the very hair becomes like needles; a voice whereat thou seest the heart of granite filled with blood.

She cries to thee, "O son, consider thy state! Seek the ease of to-morrow by the efforts of to-day!

"Out of this wool which thou art twisting thou canst not weave brocade; from this thorn thou canst not gather the red rose!

"Loose the chains from me, and only then take in thy hand the chain-like tresses of thy charming sweetheart!

(15) "I am fevered, tormented and grieved, thou art glad, happy and cheerful; such heedlessness is a shame in a youth like thee!

"Through the blood of my young men the ground is all rosy-red; come back and gaze for a moment on my rose-walks and rose-show!

"Through the tyranny of evil men the Kingdom of Jamshíd and Kay hath been made desolate: Behold Persia, once exalted to Heaven, become a ruin haunted by owls.

"The Lion of the Kayánians is hidden; it is the time of the jackal's prowling; humiliation hath succeeded the splendour and glory of Darius.

"King Núshírwán slumbers in the dark tomb, while the Bear stands over his place. Behold the tricks of Fate!"

(20) If, through love of his native land, Púr-i-Dáwúd should one day mount the scaffold, still will he give a hundred thanks and praises to the One God!

I possess some half dozen other poems by Púr-i-Dáwúd, of which three, one in praise of the *Anjuman* or Council (in this case, to judge by the context, the National Assembly or *Majlis*) and two in praise of the old Persian tongue (*Pársí-yi-Bástán*), are written in that almost pure Persian which this poet, like Shaykh 'Abdu'l-'Alí of Ṭihrán, called *Múbad*[1], and one or two others, is wont to cultivate in his writings. One of these is here given as a specimen.

(49)

چامه دیگر در فروزهٔ پارسی

زبانِ ایرانِ ماست پارسی باستان، آنِ نیاکانِ ماست پارسی باستان،
بر زبرِ کشورِ قباد و جمشید و کَیْ، چو هورِ رخشانِ ماست پارسی باستان،
سزد گر ایرانیان ورا ستایش کنند، نولهٔ یزدانِ ماست پارسی باستان،
برایگان و بهفت مده دری‌را ز چنگ، گوهر شایانِ ماست پارسی باستان،
زنده کن از پارسی کشور و آئینِ آن، زندگی و جانِ ماست پارسی باستان،
ز تازی ار ناخوشی چاره بجو از دری، دارو و درمانِ ماست پارسی باستان،
شگفت نبود اگر پور پرستد دری،
از آنکه از آنِ ماست پارسی باستان،

(50)

In the following poem, which is entitled "a National Song" and was composed in Paris on the occasion of the European New Year (probably of 1913), the poet has not attempted, and I think wisely, to exclude Arabic words and to write in pure and undiluted Persian.

نوای بومی

از هجرت ای نگارم از کف بشد قرارم، چون زلفِ مشکبارت شد تیره روزگارم،
گشتم ز ناله چون نای گشتم ز مویه چون موی، یاد آورد ز طوفان چشمانِ اشکبارم،

[1] See p. 87 *supra*.

بر گیر پرده از رُخ برهان ز انتظارم، تا نیم جانِ خودرا در مقدمت سپارم،
واعظ سخن سراید از حور و گه ز غلمان، من مایلم وطن‌را نبود بغیر کارم،
من مرغِ خوش نوایم ایرانم آشیانه، از دَوْرِ چرخ کجرَوْ پاریس شد گذارم،
گیرم که شهرِ پاریس شد رشكِ خُلْد و فردوس، امّا چه سود نبود آرامگاهِ یارم،
جشن است و خیلِ رندان افتاده مست ومدهوش، از جامِ مهرِ ایران من مستِ هوشیارم،
چنگ است و تار و تنبور رود ونی چغانه، من نالهٔ وطن‌را از دور گوش دارم،
چون کبكِ کوهساران خوبان همه خرامان، در گشت و در تماشا من زار و دلفگارم،
تا جورِ دشمنانرا تاریخ یاد دارد، از زندگی ملولم با درد و غم دوچارم،
این آه و اشك و افغان امروز بی ثمر نیست، فرداست لاله روید از تربت و مزارم،

افروخت پورِ داود در سینه عشقِ ایران،
ز آن روست شعله خیزد ز اشعارِ آبدارم،

(51)

One more poem by Púr-i-Dáwúd may be quoted. It is entitled "On Worship" (*andar Parastish*), and describes the different objects of devotion of different classes of men, not without a certain cynicism.

اندر پرستش،

یکی گیتی یکی یزدان پرستد، یکی پیدا یکی پنهان پرستد،
یکی بودا و آن دیگر برهمن، دگر زان موسی چوپان پرستد،
یکی از روی دستور اَوِسْتَا، فروغ و خاورِ رخشان پرستد،
یکی ذاتِ مسیحِ ناصری‌را، بسانِ حضرتِ سبحان پرستد،
گروهی پیروِ وخشورِ تازی، حدیث و سُنّت و قرآن پرستد،

پرستند بابی الواح و بیان را،   بهائی اقدس و ایقان پرستند،
فقیه آزمند از حرص و شهوت،   گهی حور و گهی غلمان پرستند،
چه نیرنگ است یاران مفتیِ شرع،   مریدِ ابله و نادان پرستند،
تهی انبان زاهد از زر و مال،   قصور و کوثر و رضوان پرستند،
چگویم خود تو دانی واعظِ شهر،   انین و دیدهٔ گریان پرستند،
فرو شد عارف اندر وحدت ذات،   وجوب و جوهر و امکان پرستند،
صفاجو صوفی پشمینه پوشاك،   مُرید و مرشد و عرفان پرستند،
دل از دُنیای فانی کنده درویش،   چو جُغدی گوشهٔ ویران پرستند،
قلندر واله از سرِّ انا الحقّ،   حشیشِ وحدت و قلیان پرستند،
سیه شد روزگارِ عاشق از عشق،   سوادِ طُرّهٔ جانان پرستند،
سرشك از بس فرو بارید شد کور،   هنوز او نرگسِ چشمان پرستند،
تو خود دانی که مستِ باده خواره،   کباب و پستهٔ خندان پرستند،
نهنگِ قلزمِ اندیشه شاعر،   گزاف و یاوه و هذیان پرستند،
فغان از سر دبیرِ روزنامه،   دروغ و مهمل و بُهتان پرستند،
وکیلِ محترم‌را کیش پولست،   وز او محترم عنوان پرستند،
پزشك آمد عدوی تندرستی،   جذام و سکته و یرقان پرستند،
مُنجّم سرگرم اندر سیر افلاك،   نجوم و اختر گردان پرستند،
دلِ پُر آرزوی کیمیاگر،   زر پاکیزه و رخشان پرستند،
نهد در کوره بوته در دمد دم،   پس آنگه زیبقِ لرزان پرستند،
نماند کیشِ جادوگر نهفته،   ملول از آدم و پریان پرستند،
شنیدستی که رامشگر همه عمر،   نوا و نغمه و الحان پرستند،
چمیده چون کمان پشت کشاورز،   فشانده دانه و باران پرستند،

نبیند باغبان جز کِشتهٔ خویش، از آن رو لاله و ریحان پرستد،

ندانم ازچه رو فرزند ایران، گه اطریش وگهی المان پرستد،

شناسم جمعی از مردان آزاد، در ایران کُنْده و زندان پرستد،

حذر ز آئینِ خرسِ روسپی خو، جفا و کینه و عدوان پرستد،

چرا مشتی ز شاگردان پاریس، دل و دین داده و نسوان پرستد،

برون کرده ز دل مهرِ وطن‌را، دو زلف و قامتِ خوبان پرستد،

آگر پرسی ز کیش پور داود،

جوان پارسی ایران پرستد،

POEMS OF JA'FAR-I-KHÁMNA'Í

(52)

The following poem, which might be entitled "a Persian patriot's nightmare," is by Ja'far-i-Khámna'í of Tabríz. It was communicated to me by a friend, and I do not know that it has ever been published before.

خوابی پریشان امشبِ منحوس می بینم، قضای پُرخطر پیش نظر محسوس م

، کشتی سیّار استقلالِ خورشیدی، بگردابِ حوادث ناخُدا مأیوس م

:رباریان درخوابِ غفلت تنگ و دیگر سو، وطن پامالِ قهرِ انگلیس و روس :

ِگ آدمی خوار از پی اعدامِ یك گلّه، شده‌هم عهد وهم پیمان وهم مأنوس

سان کین دوکج پالان بما تازند از هر سو، بنزدیکی سپاهِ روس‌را در طوس ،

ـائیکه برجسمِ وطن گردیده مستولی، بجزاز چاره‌اش بقراط وجالینوس

بد بختی ما در لغت تعبیر وافی نیست، چنین لفظی نه در برهان نه در قاموس

ـ بیرون‌مان شد ثروت و ماندیم در ذلّت، ز فقر و فاقه ملّت‌را ببر ملبوس

ن طوقِ رقیّت بسر تعلیمی ذلّت، کند قیدِ اسارت از ادب پابوس

سحر شد کاروان کوچی و ما خوش خفته در غفلت، بهوش از سکر نائیم از غریو کوس می بینم،
گر از بانگِ اذان امروز بیداری نشد مارا، کند بیدارمان روزِ دگر ناقوس می بینم،
بغفلت خُفته‌ایم اندر مغاك محو واضمحلال، حرامی در کمین با خدعه و سالوس می بینم،
خدایا خود بدادِ دین پاکت رس که در زودی، صلیب اندر فراز گنبدِ قابوس می بینم،
ز تأثیرِ نفاقِ مسلمین آوخ چسان گِرْیَم، لوای دین بدستِ مشرکین معکوس می بینم،
هزار افسوس کلکم بشکند محراب و مسجدرا،
بزیرِ پای ترسازادگان مطموس می بینم،

(*Translation*)

(1) "A strangely disordered dream do I see on this ill-starred night;
I see visible before my sight a fate fraught with peril.
I see the moving ship of Persian[1] Independence fallen
Into the whirlpool of misfortunes, and the Captain in despair.
I see the King and his Courtiers sunk in the sleep of heedlessness,
While on the other hand I see my Country trampled by the wrath of the English and the Russians.
I see two man-eating wolves, with intent to compass the destruction of a flock,
Linked by treaty, allied by promises, and grown familiar with one another.
(5) In such wise do these two disingenuous allies[2] attack us on every side
That I see the Russian army at Ṭús (Mashhad) in the near future.
As for those ills which have invaded the Constitution of our Country,

[1] *Khurshídí* means "Solar," "of the Sun," and, since the Lion and the Sun are the emblem of Persia, I take it here to mean "Persian"; just as China is called "the Celestial Empire."

[2] *Kaj-pálán* means a beast of burden whose pack-saddle is crooked, and is commonly used metaphorically for a shifty, dishonest and rascally fellow, or, to use the English slang equivalent, "a bad hat."

I see even Hippocrates and Galen unable to cure them.
For these misfortunes of ours there is in the dictionary no adequate term:
No such word do I find either in the *Burhán* or the *Qámús*[1]
Wealth hath escaped from our hands, and we remain in abasement:
I see the Nation clothed in the garb of poverty and misery.
With the yoke of servitude on the neck, with the rod of abasement overhead,
I see it politely kissing the fetters of its subjection!
The Caravan starts in the morning, while we slumber in happy heedlessness:
I see that not even at the sound of the drum[2] do we awaken from our intoxication.
If we do not awake to-day at the sound of the *Azán*,
I see that the Bell will awaken us on another day[3].
We slumber heedlessly in the pit of annihilation and self-effacement,
While I see the robber, with his guile and hypocrisy, lying in ambush.
O God, come Thyself to succour Thy Holy Religion, else speedily
I see the Cross set up over the Cupola of Qábús!
Alas! How can I weep [enough] at the result of Muslim dissensions?
I see the Standard of the Faith reversed by the hands of the infidels!
A thousand times alas! May my pen break! Mosque and *Miḥráb*
I see obliterated under the feet of the Christians!"

[1] The *Qámús* of al-Fírúzábádí is one of the best-known Arabic dictionaries, and the *Burhán-i-Qáṭi'* one of the most famous Persian lexicons.

[2] The beating of a drum is employed to warn travellers that the caravan is about to start.

[3] The *azán* is the Muḥammadan as the bell is the Christian call to prayer. The meaning is, "if the appeal of Islám cannot arouse us to-day, the victorious bells of Christendom will give us a rude awakening to-morrow."

(53)

The following short poem, also by Ja'far-i-Khámna'í, is interesting on account of its form, which is a departure from the classical arrangement of rhymes, and in this respect resembles No. 14 (pp. 200–4) *supra*.

(بوطن)

هر روز بیك منظرِ خونین بدر آئی، هر دم متجلّی تو بیك جلوهٔ جانسوز
از سوزِ غمت مرغِ دلم هر شب و هر روز، با نغمهٔ نو تازه کند نوحه سرائی

ای طلعتِ افسرده و ای صورت مجروح، آماجِ سیوفِ ستم آه ای وطنِ زار
هر سو نگرم خیمه زده لشکرِ اندوه، محصورِ عدو مانده تو چون نقطهٔ پرکار

محصورِ عدو یا خود اگر راست بگویم، ای شیر زبون کرده ترا روبهِ ترسو
شمشیرِ جفا آخته روی تو ز هر سو،

تا چند بخوابی؟ بگشا چشمِ خود از هم، بر خیز یکی صولتِ شیرانه نشان ده
یا جان بستان یا که درین معرکه جان ده،

(*Translation*)

In some fresh blood-stained form at each day's dawning,
In some new garb of grief the whole night long
Thou comest, O my Country, and its song
My heart renews to celebrate thy mourning!

Unhappy Mother, with the wounded face,
And mournful mien, hemmed in by swords of foes,
And girt about by hosts of grievous woes,
Like circles which the compasses do trace.

Yes, girt by foes; for now, the truth to tell,
O Lion by the cowardly fox abased,
By cruel swords on every side thou'rt faced.

How long this sleep? Awake, unclose thine eyes!
Rouse thee for one last Lion-charge, and go
To yield thy life or else destroy thy foe!

TWO POEMS COMMUNICATED BY ASHRAF-ZÁDA

The two following poems were communicated to me on October 23, 1913, by Mírzá Maḥmúd Khán Ashraf-záda, formerly editor of the newspaper *Farwardín* (published at Urmiya in Ázarbáyján), who suffered so cruelly at the hands of the Russians in January, 1912. He quoted them from memory and cannot vouch for their verbal exactitude, while, as will be seen, lines have here and there been forgotten and their places left blank.

(54)

This short poem, dealing with what is known in Persia as *Iḥtikár* or *Anbár-dárí* (*i.e.* making a "corner" in wheat or bread —an abuse which has frequently led to popular disturbances from ancient times), is by Mírzá Ḥusayn *Ṭabíb-záda*, poetically surnamed *Kamál*, who was the principal of the *Kamál* College (*Madrasa-i-Kamál*) at Tabríz, and afterwards edited a Persian paper of the same name in Egypt, in the second number of which these verses appeared. See *supra* No. 100 (pp. 60–1) and Nos. 283–4 (p. 128).

قطعهٔ احتکاریّه

تا محتکران‌را بسرِ نان بنان است٬ آشوبِ جهان است و خرابیّ زمان ا
آن طالعِ زیبای عدالت بمحاق است٬ آن طلعتِ نیکوی مُساوات نهان ا
ای طفلِ گرسنه مکن این ناله و الّا٬ روی تو و سیلی زکفِ محتکران ا
ای والده بر خاك دِه آن زینتِ آغوش٬ زیرا بشر ارزان ز یکی لقمهٔ نان ا
فرسود قلم بسکه ز نان قصّه بپرداخت٬ خونین بشد اوراقِ کمال این چه زیان ا

(*Translation*)

So long as the fingers of the bread-cornerers are on the bread
There is unrest in the world and ruin in the age.
That fair ascendant star of Justice is eclipsed;
That beauteous face of Equality is hidden.
O hungry child, cry not thus, or else
There will be a slap on thy face from the hands of the bread-cornerers!
O mother, surrender that ornament of thy embrace to the earth,
For a human life is cheaper than a mouthful of bread!
The pen is wearied of talking so much of bread;
The pages of the *Kamál* are dyed with blood: what hurt is there in this?

À propos of this holding back of corn from the people it is not out of place to quote the following verse which appeared in a *shab-náma* secretly published at Tabríz on a similar occasion.

طره قطره باران کاید بکشت زاران، هر قطره اش خدنگی است بر چشم غلّه د

"These drops of rain which fall on the arable lands,
Each drop is an arrow in the eyes of the corn-holders!"

(55)

The following poem, also communicated from memory by Mírzá Maḥmúd Ashraf-záda, is a *musammaṭ* by Mírzá Muḥammad Ṣádiq Khán *Adíbu'l-Mamálik*, which was published in the *Adab* newspaper at Mashhad. (See Nos. 38–40, pp. 37–9 *supra*.) Some of the lines and verses which Ashraf-záda had forgotten have been supplied (also from memory) by Mírzá Káẓimzáda.

(۱)

بر خیز شتربانا بر بند کجاوه، کز چرخ عیان گشت کنون رایت کاوه،
کز طول سفر حسرتِ من گشت علاوه، * * *
* * * در دیدهٔ من بنگر دریاچهٔ ساوه،
وز سینه ام آتش کدهٔ فارس نمودار،

(۲)

مائیم که از پادشهان باج گرفتیم، از پیکرشان دیبه و دیباج گرفتیم
مائیم که از دریا امواج گرفتیم، دیهیم و سریر از گهر و عاج گرفتیم
* * * * * *
اندیشه نکردیم ز طوفان و ز تیّار،

(۳)

در مصر و عدن غلغله از شوکت ما بود، در چین وخُتن ولوله از قدرت ما بود
در اندلُس و روم عیان قوّت ما بود، غرناطه و اشبیلیه در طاعت ما بود
* * * فرمان همایونِ قضا آیت ما بود
جاری بزمین و فلك و ثابت و سیّار،

(٤)

مرغانِ بساتین‌را منقار بریدند، اوراقِ ریاحین‌را طومار دریدند
گاوانِ شکمخواره بگلزار چریدند، گرگان ز پی یوسف بسیار دویدند
تا عاقبت اورا سوی بازار کشیدند، یاران بفرختندش و اغیار خریدند
آوخ ز فروشنده دریغا ز خریدار،

(٥)

چون خانه خدا خُفْت عسس ماند ز رفتن، خادم پی خوردن شد و بانو پی خُفْتن
جاسوس پسِ پرده پی راز نهفتن، قاضی همه جا درطلب رشوه گرفتن
واعظ بفسون خواندن و افسانه شنفتن، نه وقتِ شنیدن دگر و موقِع گفتن
آمد سر همسایه برون از پس دیوار،

(٦)

چون برّهٔ بیچاره به چوپانش نپیوست، از بیم بصحرا در نه خُفت و نه بنشست،
خرسی بشکار آمد و بازوش فرو بست، شد برّهٔ ما طعمهٔ آن خرس زبردست،
افسوس بر آن برّهٔ نوزادهٔ سرمست، * * *
فریاد از آن خرس کُهن سال شکم خوار،

(٧)

افسوس که این مزرعه‌را آب گرفته، دهقانِ جگر سوخته‌را خواب گرفته،
رخسارِ هُنر گونهٔ مهتاب گرفته، چشمانِ خرد پردهٔ ز خوناب گرفته،
خونِ دلِ ما رنگِ می ناب گرفته، * * *
ثروت شده بی مایه و صحّت شده بیمار،

(٨)

ابری شده بالا و گرفتست فضارا، وز دود شرر تیره نموده است هوارا،
سوزانده بچرخ اختر و در خاك گیارا، آتش زده سُکّانِ زمین‌را و سمارا،
ای واسطهٔ رحمت حق بهر خدارا، زین خاك بگردان رهِ طوفان بلارا،
بشکاف ز هم سینهٔ این ابر شرر بار،

THE LAMENT OF THE KINE

(56)

The following very simple and even uncouth verses, wherein a Persian peasant is supposed to apostrophize his cow, appeared under the heading *Adabiyyát-i-Bábá Aḥmad* ("Bábá Aḥmad's Literary Column") in No. 11 of the *Chanta-i-Pá-barahna* ("Beggar's Wallet"), which bears no date.

"The Lament of the Kine"

From No. 11 of the *Chanta-i-Pá-barahna* or "Beggar's Wallet"

ادبیّات بابا احمد،

ای رنجبر سیاه چرده، تا چند بخواب نیم مُرده
بنمای بگاو مهربانی، باقی همه‌را خودت میدانی
ای داده بپاره سنگ پهلو، اربابِ تو خُفته در اپرقو
بر دار دو بوسهٔ تو از چهر، بر گوی بگاو از رهِ مهر
ای رنگِ پلو بخواب دیده، ای بوی کباب نا شنیده
ای گاوِ من ای شریکِ زحمت، رحمت بتو صد هزار رحمت
دایم تو بزحمتیّ و رنجی، از رنجِ تو برده اند گنجی
ای گاو اگر نبودی ایران، ایران بودی تمام ویران
از نان نگشته اشکمت سیر، نا خورده بعمرِ خویش انجیر
ایران شده زنده از وجودت، آباد زمانه هم ز بودت
ای حسرتِ نان بگور بُرده، ای رنگ پریده و فسرده
گر نسلِ تو از زمانه خیزد، بال و پرِ عالمی بسوزد
ای خفته بپهلوی مغیلان، بر خیز و بیا بسوی بستان
ای آیتِ رحمتِ خدائی، ای مونسِ من دم جدائی
بر خیز که موسمِ بهار است، هنگامهٔ کشتن و شیار است
ای گاو ضعیف لاغرِ من، معبودِ هنود و مفخرِ من
بر خیز ز لانه‌ات برون شَو، شاید بکف آوری دو من جَو
ای گاو بدان که مدّعی کیست، این لاغری ترا سبب چیست
شد فصلِ بهار و موسم دَی، گردید چو عمرِ آدمی طَی
ارباب ببرده یونجه و کاه، مائیم رعیّت او بود شاه
ارباب بسوی دِه شتابان، از بهرِ تفرّج بیابان
شاه است و دلش هر آنچه خواهد، از روزی ما و تو بکاهد
هین برّه و جوجه کن تهیّه، هم بهرِ خوراك هم هدیّه

زحمت ز من و تو است در دهر، از بهر یکی شکر دگر زهر،
ای همدم گاو و مونس وی، بر خیز گذشت موسم دی،
من با تو مدام در تکاپو، کار از خر و خوردنش ز یابو،
بر خیز بگاو کن حکایت، از زحمت و رنج بی شکایت،
ما بهر شیار و تخم کردن، یابو و آقا برای خوردن،
این گاو ترا بود پرستار، در کشت و درو معاون و یار،
این رسم زمانهٔ دو رنگ است،
یك رنج کش آن یکی زرنگ است،

From a literary point of view these verses have little value, but they are interesting as an attempt to arouse the Persian peasant to a sense of his miserable condition, and as presenting a certain analogy with the opening of the ancient Zoroastrian *Gâthâs* (probably the oldest literary monument of the Iranian people), in which, to quote the words prefixed by Dr L. H. Mills to his translation of Yasna xxix, "the Soul of the Kine, as representing the herds of the holy Iranian people, their only means of honourable livelihood, raises its voice, and, expressing the profoundest needs of an afflicted people, addresses Ahura and His Divine Order, *Asha*, in bitterness[1]." In verses 1–4 the poet addresses the peasant and bids him speak to his cow in the words of verses 5–24. In the last five verses the poet again addresses the peasant as follows:

"O companion of the cow and her friend, arise, for the season of Winter hath passed!
I am ever travailing with thee: the work is the ass's and its food the pony's.
Arise, and tell the cow about uncomplaining trouble and labour.
We are for the ploughing and the tilling, the pony and the Master for the eating.
This cow is thy servant, the friendly helper in sowing and reaping.
This is the way of inconstant Fortune: one bears the toil and another is clever [enough to enjoy the proceeds]."

[1] Max Müller's *Sacred Books of the East Series*, vol. XXXI, *the Zend Avesta*. Part III, by L. H. Mills, p. 3.

I conclude this selection with five epigrams, hitherto, I believe, unpublished. The first, of which the author desires to remain anonymous, is directed against M. Mornard, the Belgian official who replaced Mr Morgan Shuster as Treasurer-General. The low opinion which it expresses of the former may be profitably compared with the high opinion of the latter expressed in No. 33 (pp. 250–2 *supra*).

(57)

گویند مردمان اروپا که کذب و شَیْد ،   با طینت اهالیِ ایران سرشته‌اند ،
هستند اگر نفوسِ اروپا چو مورنارد ،   ایرانیان بنسبت ایشان فرشته‌اند ،

(*Translation*)

The Persian nature—so the Franks repeat—
Is fraught with falsehood, fashioned with deceit:
Yet if by Mornard we may judge the Franks
The Persian nature with the Angels ranks!

(58)

The following epigram is remarkable amongst the poems cited as being directed against the Constitutionalists, though the author, *Maliku'l-Kalám* of Kurdistán, poetically surnamed *Majdí*, whose proper name is 'Abdu'l-Majíd, the son of the late Mírzá Shukru'lláh *Fakhru'l-Kuttáb*, subsequently stated that it was only intended to apply to "those robbers who came forward in the garb of Constitutionalists."

(59)

ز بس مشروطه خواهان بر ضعیفان ،   چو استبدادیان بیداد کردند ،
ضعیفان از برای دفعِ ایشان ،   ز استبداد استمداد کردند ،

(*Translation*)

Those for Democracy who claim to speak
Like Despots so oppress the poor and weak
That these at last, their malice to escape,
E'en from the Despots now assistance seek.

The same poet, in fact, has the two following pieces of verse in favour of the Constitution and against the Autocracy.

(60)

ِ ایران بود مانند مریض محتضر، اهلِ استبداد بودند از فساد اخلاط
برای دفعِ اخلاطِ ردیّه زین مریض، مجلسِ شورای ملّی گشت انتیمونِ
یابد ره بطبعِ این مریض اخلاط باز، میکند طومارِ عمرِ این مریض اخلاط

(*Translation*)

The Kingdom of Persia was like unto a man sick unto death;
The partisans of Despotism were, in their mischief, the malignant humours.
For the expulsion of these evil humours from the sick man
The National Assembly became as an emetic of antimony.
If these humours should again find their way into the constitution of the patient,
They will roll up the scroll of the sick man's life!

(61)

ِ نظر در کار استبداد و مشروطه کنی، فرقِ استبداد با مشروطه باشد بیشم
تِ استبداد میجُستند سگ از بهرِ صید، گاهِ مشروطه بجویند آدمی از بهرِ ک

(*Translation*)

If you look at the deeds of Despotism and Constitutionalism
The differences between Despotism and Constitutionalism are countless.
In the days of Despotism they sought dogs for the chase:
In the days of the Constitution they seek men for work!

I much regret that the limits imposed on the size of this book do not permit me to add to the number of poems here cited. The mass of available material was so great that I have been obliged to limit the selection almost entirely to contemporary political and topical poetry, and of this to admit only what had hitherto remained unpublished, or had been published only in an ephemeral form in the newspapers, and which, for some reason, appeared to me of some especial interest in form or matter.

Amongst the contemporary poems separately published in the form of tracts or pamphlets I should like especially to mention a remarkable *tasdís* (or "six-some") based on a *qaṣída* of the celebrated classical poet Kháqání of Shírwán by my very accomplished friend Ḥusayn Dánish, son of Mírzá Háshim of Iṣfahán, who, long resident at Constantinople in the service of the Turkish Government, is recognized as one of the leading contemporary writers both in Persian and Turkish. This poem, entitled (in Turkish) "the Ruins of Ctesiphon" (*Medá'in Kharábalari*), is dedicated to another most learned, accomplished and single-minded friend of mine, Dr Riẓá Tevfíq, Deputy for Adrianople in the last Turkish Parliament, who contributes a critical and historical preface. It was published at Constantinople in A.H. 1330 (A.D. 1912), when Persia's fortunes were at their darkest and her foes at their cruellest, as a small tract of 37 pp. at the modest price of three piastres (about 7½*d.*). In the same year, on March 21, on the occasion of the Persian *Naw-rúz*, or New Year's Day, the same poet published (also at Constantinople) another fine poem "for Persia" (*Írán ichun*), dedicated to the eminent Turkish man of letters Tevfíq Fikret Bey, entitled "A New Year's Present" (*Hadiyya-i-Sál*), and comprising 56 couplets. From both of these works I should like to have quoted here, both on account of the beauty and pathos of the verses, and on account of my regard for the author; but both poems should be read in their entirety to be judged fairly, and, moreover, can without difficulty be obtained from Constantinople.

Mention has already been made in Part I of this book of a periodical publication, in magazine form, issued at irregular intervals, beginning on April 20, 1908, entitled *Dabíriyya*, written by Mírzá Sayyid 'Abdu'r-Raḥmán *Dabíru'l-Mamálik*, and containing an extensive selection of the verses (estimated by their author at 35,000) composed by him during the preceding thirty or forty years. Most of these poems refer to the leading Persian statesmen and courtiers of this period, and many of them are satires, which naturally had to remain in manuscript until the greater freedom of the Press inaugurated by the Constitutional Régime permitted their publication. I am indebted to Mr H. L. Rabino for a bound volume containing a good many numbers of this magazine. The poems which it contains vary a good deal in quality and merit, and, though some of them deal with events subsequent to the deposition of Muḥammad 'Alí and the enthronement of his young son Sulṭán Aḥmad, the reigning sovereign, they are on the whole of an old-fashioned type, and the satirical poems incline to that coarseness of language which is characteristic of most of the older *hajwiyyát* and *hazliyyát*.

APPENDIX

A Brief Chronology of the Persian Revolution.

From December, 1905 to April, 1912.

CHRONOLOGY OF THE PERSIAN REVOLUTION

For convenience of reference, and for the better understanding of the sequence of events illustrated by the preceding poems, a brief statement of the principal events and epochs of the Persian Revolution, or Constitutional Movement, is here appended. Details of these events down to the Nationalist victory of July, 1909, the capture of Ṭihrán, and the deposition of the ex-Sháh Muḥammad 'Alí, will be found in my *Persian Revolution*, 1905–1909 (Cambridge, 1910). The connected history of the subsequent period, which I hope to embody in another volume, has not yet been written, and must be pieced together from Blue Books and press-cuttings, supplemented by such oral and written evidence as is obtainable. The admirable Persian "History of the Awakening of the Persians" (*Ta'ríkh-i-Bídárí-yi-Íráníyán*) of the *Náẓimu'l-Islám* of Kirmán, of which up to the present time only the Introduction (pp. 272), first volume (pp. 255), and second volume (pp. 240) have been published, does not at present carry the story beyond July, 1906, and so stops short of the granting of the Constitution by Muẓaffaru'd-Dín Sháh (August 5, 1906) and the opening of the First National Assembly (October 7, 1906). For all events before these dates it is by far the richest source available, and contains the texts of many important documents and masses of detail not to be found elsewhere.

From the earliest historical times until 1906 the government of Persia was, both in theory and in practice, an absolute despotism, of which the general character is well described by Mr R. G. Watson at pp. 12–13 and 15–20 of his admirable *History of Persia from the beginning of the Nineteenth Century to the Year* 1858. Signs of a new ferment appeared in Persia, as in so many other countries, in the memorable year 1848, at the end of the reign of Muḥammad Sháh and the beginning of that of his successor, Náṣiru'd-Dín Sháh, when the Bábí insurrection threatened for three or four years the stability of the Qájár Dynasty. This movement, though essentially religious, was not, as the Comte de Gobineau has well indicated, devoid of political significance, and above all showed the Persian character in a new, unexpected and heroic light. It was contemporary with and violently opposed by one of the greatest Ministers whom Persia has produced in recent times, Mírzá Taqí Khán *Amír-i-Kabír*, whose courage, integrity and far-sighted political vision have led the recent historians of the Constitution to claim him as the fore-runner of the Constitutional Movement, or at any rate as a very wise and sincere patriot. Spiritually this may be true, but historically he belongs entirely to the "Days of Autocracy" (*Ayyám-i-Istibdád*), that long period of some 2500 years through which the history of Persia can be clearly and certainly traced, and which by analogy should be called (for I have not actually met with the expression) "the Greater Autocracy" (*Istibdád-i-Kabír*), in contradistinction to "the Lesser Autocracy" (*Istibdád-i-Ṣaghír*) which lasted from June 23, 1908 to July 16, 1909, and of which we shall shortly speak.

The history of the Constitutional struggle in Persia may be divided into the following periods:

I. The Preparatory Period, or Prodromata of the Revolution.

II. The First Constitutional Period (August 5, 1906–June 23, 1908), or Period of the First *Majlis* or National Assembly (October 7, 1906–June 23, 1908).

III. The "Lesser Autocracy" (*Istibdád-i-Ṣaghír*), during which the Constitution was suspended and the ex-Sháh, Muḥammad 'Alí, re-established despotic rule (June 23, 1908–July 16, 1909).

IV. The Second Constitutional Period (July 16, 1909–December 24, 1911), which was brought to an end by the Russian Ultimatums of November 12 and November 29, the expulsion of Mr W. Morgan Shuster, Treasurer-General, and the invasion of North Persia by the Russians, with the concomitant atrocities committed by them and their myrmidons at Tabríz, Rasht and elsewhere (December, 1911 and January, 1912 onwards).

V. The present anomalous period, which can be described neither as Autocratic nor Constitutional, the Persian Government being terrorized and paralysed by Russia, which is gradually converting all North Persia into what is called in the cant of diplomacy a "Veiled Protectorate" (January 1, 1912 to the date of writing).

Some of the principal events and dates of the first four of these periods (for the last appears to be but a death-agony or mortal lethargy) will now be given.

I. *The Preparatory Period.*

The beginning of this cannot be exactly fixed, but it may be divided into two parts, one of intellectual preparation and propaganda, and one of actual revolt against the prevailing intolerable conditions. The intellectual preparation was chiefly the work of two men, Sayyid Jamálu'd-Dín al-Afghání (born 1838, died 1897) and Prince Malkom Khán *Náẓimu'd-Dawla* (born 1833, died 1908), and their disciples. The manifold political activities of the former, which are fully discussed in the first chapter of my *Persian Revolution*, began, so far as the Near East is concerned, about 1870, when he visited Egypt and Constantinople for the first time. In Persia his direct activity was greatest during the years 1886–1890, when he was expelled ignominiously; but his indirect influence survived his death in 1897, and was the chief factor in the revolt against the Tobacco Régie (May, 1890–January, 1892) and the assassination of Náṣiru'd-Dín Sháh (May 1, 1896) by Mírzá Riẓá of Kirmán, one of the Sayyid's disciples. Prince Malkom Khán's monthly paper, the *Qánún* ("Law"), which all students of the subject agree in regarding as one of the most potent literary factors in bringing about the Constitutional Movement, first appeared on February 20, 1890, and seems to have continued publication for about three years and a half, forty-one monthly numbers having been issued in all. The successful revolt against the Tobacco Concession in 1891 was a momentous epoch in the history of Persia, and may fairly be regarded as the starting-point of the Revolution, of which, however, the immediate prodromata began in December, 1905. The chief of these events, with their dates, down to the granting of the Constitution on August 5, 1906, are as follows:

1905

Dec. 11, 1905. Merchants and Sayyids bastinadoed by *'Alá'u'd-Dawla*, with the approval of *'Aynu'd-Dawla*, on account of the rise in the price of sugar. Bazaars closed and assembly at *Masjid-i-Sháh.*

Dec. 13, 1905. Some two thousand *mullás*, students and merchants, headed by Sayyid Muḥammad Ṭabáṭabá'í and Sayyid 'Abdu'lláh Bahbahání, leave Ṭihrán as a protest and take sanctuary at the Shrine of Sháh 'Abdu'l-'Aẓím. This is known as the *Hijrat-i-Ṣughrá* or "Lesser Exodus" (هجرتِ صُغْرَى).

1906

Jan. 12, 1906. After prolonged negotiations with the Sháh and his Court and Ministers, the fugitives (*muhájirín*) return to Ṭihrán on receiving from the Sháh an autograph rescript (*dast-khaṭṭ*), which was publicly read in the Mosque on the same day, promising the establishment of a "House of Justice" (*'Adálat-khána*), the dismissal of the obnoxious Ministers *'Aynu'd-Dawla* and *'Alá'u'd-Dawla*, and other demands of the people as voiced by their spiritual leaders the *mullás*. On this day, according to the "History of the Awakening of the Persians," the cry of "Long live the Persian Nation!" (*Zinda bád Millat-i-Írán!*) was first heard. On the following day Ṭihrán was illuminated as a sign of joy.

June 17, 1906. Mírzá Ḥasan *Rushdiyya*, *Majdu'l-Islám* of Kirmán and Mírzá Áqá of Iṣfahán were exiled to Kalát.

June 21, 1906. During a successful attempt made by the people to rescue one of their leaders, who had been arrested by the soldiers, some fifteen persons, including two Sayyids named Ḥusayn and 'Abdu'l-Majíd, were shot dead. The increasing discontent of the people, who saw themselves cheated of the promised reforms, was met by increasing severity on the part of the Government.

July 6, 1906. Sayyid Muḥammad Ṭabáṭabá'í preached to a vast crowd, denouncing the existing tyranny and misgovernment and urging the absolute necessity of a "House of Justice."

July, 1906. The leading ecclesiastics, accompanied by a vast concourse of students, merchants and others, left Ṭihrán for the holy city of Qum, where they took sanctuary. This is what is known as the *Hijrat-i-Kubrá*, or "Greater Exodus" (هجرتِ كُبْرَى). About the same time a number of merchants, bankers, tradesmen and others, with the permission of the British Chargé d'Affaires, Mr Grant Duff, took refuge in the grounds of the British Legation at Ṭihrán. The numbers increased daily, until they finally reached some 13,000 or 14,000 souls.

Aug. 5, 1906. Muẓaffaru'd-Dín Sháh finally gave way, granted a Constitution and Parliament, dismissed the *'Aynu'd-Dawla*, and promised monetary compensation to the relatives of the murdered Sayyids. This event, celebrated a few days later with great rejoicings as "the National Victory" (*Fatḥ-i-Millí*), marks the beginning of the Constitutional Epoch. According to the Muḥammadan Calendar it fell on the 14th of Jumáda ii, A.H. 1324, and its first anniversary was celebrated with great splendour and enthusiasm on the same date of the following Muḥammadan year, corresponding with July 25, 1907, under the title of "the National Festival" (*Jashn-i-Millí*).

II. *The First Constitutional Period.*

(*Mashrúṭa-i-Awwal*), Aug. 5, 1906–June 23, 1908.

Aug. 19, 1906. Solemn official opening of the new House of Parliament in presence of the high ecclesiastical authorities, who were entertained as the Sháh's guests for three days.

Sept. 9, 1906. Electoral Law promulgated.

Sept. 18–27, 1906. A number of citizens of Tabríz took refuge at the British Consulate there as a protest against the tyranny of Muḥammad 'Alí Mírzá, the Crown Prince, afterwards Sháh.

Oct. 7, 1906. The first *Majlis*, or National Assembly was opened under the presidency of *Ṣaní'u'd-Dawla*.

Nov. 23, 1906. Proposed joint Anglo-Russian Loan of £400,000 rejected by the *Majlis*.

Nov. 25, 1906. The newspaper *Majlis* first appeared.

Dec. 27, 1906. The newspaper *Nidá-yi-Waṭan* first appeared.

Dec. 30, 1906. The Fundamental Laws were ratified by Muẓaffaru'd-Dín Sháh and promulgated, and the form of the Persian Constitution was thus fixed and defined.

1907

Jan. 8, 1907. Death of Muẓaffaru'd-Dín Sháh.

Jan. 19, 1907. Coronation of his son Muḥammad 'Alí, of which the *Majlis* received no official notification, and to which none of its Members were invited.

Feb. 7, 1907. Arrival at Ṭihrán of the Tabríz Deputies, including Sayyid Taqí-záda, who received a great ovation.

Feb. 10, 1907. The Sháh was compelled by the *Majlis* to dismiss M. Naus, the unpopular Belgian Chief of the Customs.

March 17, 1907. The *Mushíru'd-Dawla* resigned the Premiership.

April 26, 1907. The *Amínu's-Sulṭán*, or *Atábak-i-A'ẓam*, returned to Persia after three and a half years' exile to assume, at the invitation of the Sháh, the position of Premier.

April 29, 1907. The Ṭihrán *Ḥablu'l-Matín* newspaper founded.

May, 1907. Plot contrived by Raḥím Khán and his son to raise a disturbance in Tabríz and murder leading Constitutionalists. It was believed to have been instigated by the Sháh.

May 26, 1907. This being the eve of the Sháh's birthday, and Ṭihrán decorated and prepared for illumination, the people pulled down the decorations and would not allow them to be replaced until the Sháh handed over Raḥím Khán to the Ministry of Justice to stand his trial for conspiracy.

May 30, 1907. The weekly newspaper *Ṣúr-i-Isráfíl* first appeared.

June, 1907. Rebellion of the Sháh's brother *Sáláru'd-Dawla* at Hamadán. He was defeated on the historic field of Niháwand, and surrendered, on his safety being guaranteed, to the Sháh's representative on June 22.

July 25, 1907. Celebration of the "National Festival" (*Jashn-i-Millí*) on the first anniversary (according to the Muḥammadan Calendar) of the granting of the Constitution.

Aug. 31, 1907. The Anglo-Russian Agreement was signed. The *Amínu's-Sulṭán*, or *Atábak-i-A'ẓam*, was shot by 'Abbás Áqá, a money-changer of Tabríz, as he was leaving the National Assembly, and died half an hour later. The assassin committed suicide.

Sept. 4, 1907. Sir Cecil Spring Rice's celebrated Memorandum (*Yád-dásht*), designed to allay the anxieties of the Persians as to the scope and aim of the Anglo-Russian Agreement, was communicated to the Persian Foreign Minister, and was published ten days later in the Ṭihrán *Ḥablu'l-Matín* (No. 115).

Sept. 10, 1907. *Iḥtishámu's-Salṭana* elected President of the Assembly.

Sept. 13, 1907. Death of Naṣru'lláh Khán *Mushíru'd-Dawla*. *Sa'du'd-Dawla* made Foreign Minister.

Oct. 1, 1907. The Princes of the Blood and Nobles of the Court attended the National Assembly and swore an oath of allegiance to the Constitution.

Oct. 2, 1907. *Sa'du'd-Dawla* resigned, and a new Cabinet was formed under the presidency of the *Náṣiru'l-Mulk* (the present Regent). This Cabinet resigned on the 14th of December, 1907.

Oct. 6, 1907. The fortieth day (*chilla*) after the death of 'Abbás Áqá, who killed the *Amínu's-Sulṭán*, was celebrated with great enthusiasm and circumstance by a large number of his admirers.

Nov. 6, 1907. The newspaper *Rúḥu'l-Qudus* ("the Holy Spirit") published a violent and threatening article addressed to the Sháh, and was suppressed by the National Assembly in consequence.

Nov. 12, 1907. The Sháh visited the National Assembly in state, and again swore fidelity to the Constitution.

Dec. 15, 1907. Beginning of the "Abortive Coup d'État" (called by the Persians *Wáqi'a-i-Maydán-i-Túp-khána,* "the Event of the Artillery Square," which place served as the rallying-point of the Shah's hired ruffians). Arrest and threatened destruction by the Sháh of the *Náṣiru'l-Mulk,* who was saved by the intervention of the British Legation, and left Persia next day for Europe. Complete triumph of the Assembly and collapse of the Sháh on Dec. 22. A new Cabinet was formed under *Niẓámu's-Salṭana.* The *Ẓillu's-Sulṭán* was ordered to leave Ṭihrán.

1908

Feb. 1908. An attempt was made on the Sháh's life by means of a bomb, which killed one of his attendants and wrecked an automobile. The thrower of the bomb was never identified.

April, 1908. The *Iḥtishámu's-Salṭana* resigned the Presidency of the National Assembly, and was succeeded by *Mumtázu'd-Dawla.* Several prominent reactionaries who had taken part in the Abortive Coup d'État of the preceding December, or in the murder of the Zoroastrian Arbáb Firídún, were exiled to Kalát, or bastinadoed, or both. Amongst these were *Ṣaní'-i-Ḥaẓrat* (afterwards hanged on July 29, 1909) and *Muqtadir-i-Niẓám.*

May, 1908. Increasing tension between the Sháh and the National Assembly.

June 2, 1908. Intervention, with implied threats, of the Russian Minister M. de Hartwig and the British Chargé d'Affaires Mr Marling on behalf of the Sháh.

June 3, 1908. Flight of the Sháh, escorted by Persian Cossacks under the command of the Russian Colonel Liakhoff, from Ṭihrán to his adjacent garden, the *Bágh-i-Sháh.*

June 5, 1908. At the invitation of the Sháh, a deputation of notables waited on him at the *Bágh-i-Sháh,* but were treacherously arrested.

June 11, 1908. The Sháh proclaimed martial law and threatened to bombard the *Masjid-i-Sipahsálár* unless the people there assembled dispersed.

June 12, 1908. The Sháh demanded the expulsion of eight popular leaders, control of the Press, and disarmament of the National Volunteers.

June 23, 1908. The Bombardment of the Majlis (*Túp-bandi-yi-Majlis*), Coup d'État (*Ẓarba-i-Ḥukúmat*), or Reactionary Triumph (*Waq'a-i-Irtijá'iyya*), carried out by the instrumentality of Colonel Liakhoff and the other Russian officers of the Persian Cossack Brigade. A number of leaders of the popular party were arrested and carried captive to *Bágh-i-Sháh.* Ḥájji Mírzá Ibráhím Áqá, Deputy for Tabríz, was killed.

June 24, 1908. Mírzá Jahángír Khán of Shíráz, editor of the *Ṣúr-i-Isráfíl,* and the *Maliku'l-Mutakallimín,* a prominent orator, were strangled in the *Bágh-i-Sháh.* Some of the Nationalists whose lives were in danger took refuge in the British Legation. Many houses of persons obnoxious to the Sháh, including those of his uncle the *Ẓillu's-Sulṭán*, and his cousin Prince *Jalálu'd-Dawla*, were destroyed and looted. Colonel Liakhoff was appointed military governor of Ṭihrán.

III. "*The Lesser Tyranny*" *or* "*Autocracy*" (*Istibdád-i-Ṣaghír*).

During this period, which lasted from the Coup d'État of June 23, 1908, and the destruction of the First National Assembly until the Nationalist victory and deposition of Muḥammad 'Alí on July 16, 1909, the Constitution was suspended and Reaction was dominant in Ṭihrán. Tabríz, however, rallied gallantly to the Constitutional Cause, under the leadership of Sattár Khán and Báqir Khán, expelled the Reactionaries, and sustained a siege of nine months, which was brought to an end on April 29, 1909, by the entrance of Russian troops under General Znarsky. Meanwhile its resistance had given time and encouragement to the Nationalists, who were at first bewildered and discouraged by the Coup d'État, to rally, and two armies were gradually formed, one at Rasht under the nominal leadership of the *Sipahdár*, another consisting of the Bakhtiyárí tribesmen under the leadership of their chief *Sardár-i-As'ad*, and these two forces gradually converged until they effected a junction at Karach to the west of Ṭihrán on July 8, 1909. After indecisive skirmishes at Sháhábád and Bádámak, a body of the Nationalists, eluding the vigilance of the Royalist troops and the Cossack Brigade, slipped through the lines of their opponents and entered Ṭihrán on July 13. Fighting continued in the capital for four days, until finally, on Friday, July 16, the ex-Sháh took refuge in the Russian Legation, which act was considered as tantamount to abdication, and Colonel Liakhoff and the Cossack Brigade surrendered. The ex-Sháh's son, Sulṭán Aḥmad, aged only twelve years, was proclaimed King, and the aged '*Aẓudu'l-Mulk* Regent; the Constitution was re-established, and steps were taken as soon as possible to convene a new *Majlis* or National Assembly. The principal events of this period of thirteen months, with their dates, are as follows:

August 4, 1908. The defenders of Tabríz are greatly encouraged by news of the successful Revolution in Turkey.

August 20, 1908. '*Aynu'd-Dawla* and the *Sipahdár* arrive before Tabríz to prosecute the siege.

Sept. 16, 1908. The "Race-course Incident" at Ṭihrán, where Indian *suwárs* of the British Legation guard are attacked by Persian Cossacks. Colonel Liakhoff is compelled to apologize, and the incident is hushed up.

Oct. 1, 1908. Sir George Barclay arrives at Ṭihrán as British Minister.

Oct. 5, 1908. Defeat of Royalists at Tabríz.

Oct. 11, 1908. Four hundred Persian Cossacks under the command of the Russian Captain Ushakoff leave Ṭihrán to take part in the siege of Tabríz.

Oct. 12, 1908. Further Nationalist success at Tabríz.

Oct. 17, 1908. Russia threatens to intervene at Tabríz, but Sir Edward Grey informs her that such intervention "will create a very bad impression" in England, and she desists.

Oct. 30, 1908. Formation of the Persia Committee in London.

Nov. 7, 1908. Fictitious demonstration against the revival of the Constitution at the *Bágh-i-Sháh.*

November (middle). M. de Hartwig, the Russian Minister, leaves Ṭihrán for good.

Nov. 19, 1908. The Sháh issues a proclamation declaring that he will not restore the old or grant any new Constitution.

December (middle). Expulsion of M. Panoff, the Bulgarian revolutionary and correspondent of the Russian paper *Ryech*, from Ṭihrán by the Russian Legation.

1909

Jan. 5, 1909. *Ṣamṣámu's-Salṭana* at the head of a Bakhtiyárí force takes possession of Iṣfahán, expels the Sháh's representative, and declares for the Constitution.

January (end). Arrival of Mr W. A. Moore as correspondent of the *Manchester Guardian*, *Daily News* and *Daily Chronicle* at Tabríz.

Feb. 8, 1909. Rasht is seized by the Nationalists, the Sháh's governor killed, and the Constitution proclaimed.

Feb. 11, 1909. The last road open into Tabríz, that from Julfá, is occupied by the Royalists, and the blockade of the city completed.

Feb. 22, 1909. Sattár Khán vainly endeavours to re-open the Julfá Road.

March 7, 1909. Sattár Khán's "distinguished personal courage" praised by Mr Wratislaw, the British Consul at Tabríz.

April 20, 1909. With Sir Edward Grey's approval, it was decided to send Russian troops to raise the siege of starving Tabríz, open the roads, and bring in supplies.

April 21, 1909. A last attempt was made by the besieged to break out of Tabríz to obtain provisions. The *sortie* was led by Mr W. A. Moore and Mr Baskerville, a young American. The latter was killed.

April 29, 1909. Arrival of the Russian force under General Znarsky at Tabríz.

May 5, 1909. The Constitutionalist army of Rasht occupied Qazwín.

May 6, 1909. Persian Cossacks commanded by the Russian Captain Zapolski were sent out to guard the Karach bridge, and the Nationalists were advised by the Russian Legation, with threats, to desist from their advance.

May 17, 1909. The *Sipahdár* formulates the four demands of the Constitutionalists.

May 22, 1909. Yúsuf of Ḥukmábád (who was afterwards, in Jan. 1912, most cruelly put to death and his body cut in two and hung up in the street by *Shujá'u'd-Dawla*, the Russian *protégé*) was arrested by the Russians and his house blown up with dynamite at Tabríz.

May (latter part). Sattár Khán, Báqir Khán, Taqí-záda, and other leading Constitutionalists take refuge in the Turkish Consulate at Tabríz as a protest against the high-handed actions of the Russians.

June 17, 1909. The Bakhtiyárís begin their march on Ṭihrán.

June 23, 1909. The advance guard of the Bakhtiyárís reaches Qum.

June 27, 1909. Further attempt on the part of the British Minister and the Russian Chargé d'Affaires to check the Bakhtiyárí advance.

June 30, 1909. Russian expeditionary force assembled at Bákú.

July 4, 1909. Skirmish at Sháhábád. Eight demands formulated by the *Sipahdár*.

July 4–6, 1909. Armistice of two days.

July 8, 1909. Two or three thousand Russian troops disembarked at Anzalí.

July 11, 1909. Russian troops reach Qazwín. Skirmish at Bádámak.

July 12, 1909. Fighting renewed at Bádámak.

July 13, 1909. Ṭihrán entered by part of the Nationalist forces, headed by Bakhtiyárís. After four days' fighting (July 13–16) during which some 500 men were killed (no European being hurt) Muḥammad 'Alí took refuge in the Russian Legation and abdicated. Colonel Liakhoff and the Cossack Brigade surrendered. This event is known as *Fatḥ-i-Millí* ("the National Victory," فتح ملّى) with which the Third Period, called "the Lesser Tyranny" (*Istibdád-i-Ṣaghír*) concludes.

IV. *The Second Constitutional Period* (*Mashrúṭa-i-Thání*), beginning with the accession of Sulṭán Aḥmad Sháh, and ending with the dissolution of the Second National Assembly and the Russian aggressions of Dec. 1911 and Jan. 1912[1].

July 18, 1909. The *quondam* Crown Prince (*Walí-'ahd*), Sulṭán Aḥmad, was proclaimed Sháh, entered Ṭihrán, where he was enthusiastically received, on July 20, held his first reception (*darbár*) on July 21, and was formally recognized by Russia and England on the same or the following day.

July 26, 1909. The ex-Sháh was offered a pension of £5000 a year on condition of his leaving Persia at once. Russia threatens a punitive expedition against the Sháhseven tribesmen, and increases the number of her troops at Qazwín to 2300 men. A special Court-martial (*Díwán-i-Ḥárb*) was instituted to try political offenders at Ṭihrán.

[1] As my *Persian Revolution* of 1905–1909, though recording the opening of the Second National Assembly on Nov. 15, 1909, gives a continued narrative of events only to the Conquest of Ṭihrán in July, 1909, I have made the chronology of this period very much fuller than the previous ones, though it is covered by Mr Morgan Shuster's admirable work the *Strangling of Persia* (published in 1912). Mr Shuster's narrative, however, only becomes full and continuous from the date of his arrival in Persia (May 11, 1911).

July 29, 1909. Execution of *Mufákhiru'l-Mulk* (former Head of the Police at Ṭihrán) and *Ṣaní'-i-Ḥaẓrat.*

July 30, 1909. Colonel Liakhoff recalled to Russia. He left Ṭihrán on August 4.

July 31, 1909. Execution of the *Ajúdán-báshí*, who commanded the artillery to fire on the *Majlis* on June 23, 1908; and of Shaykh Faẓlu'lláh, on the charge of complicity in the murder of Mírzá Muṣṭafá, son of Mírzá Ḥasan Ashtiyání, and one of the students of the German College.

Aug. 4, 1909. Ex-Sháh's pension fixed at £15,000 a year.

Aug. 5, 1909. The *Ẓillu's-Sulṭán*, uncle of the ex-Sháh, reached Anzalí from Vienna, where he was detained, and not allowed to leave again for Europe until he paid a forfeit of £60,000, which he only consented to do on August 23.

Aug. 8, 1909. Raḥím Khán plunders an Armenian village in N.W. Persia and massacres the inhabitants. Taqí-záda arrives at Ṭihrán from Tabríz. The Reactionary Mír Háshim is captured.

Aug. 9, 1909. Mír Háshim and his brother are hanged.

Aug. 13, 1909. Trial of the editor of the Ṭihrán *Ḥablu'l-Matín*, Sayyid Ḥasan of Káshán (see p. 74 *supra*), for publishing an article alleged to be derogatory of Islám. He was sentenced to two years' imprisonment.

Aug. 17, 1909. The extraordinary National Council (*Majlis-i-'Álí*) consisting of some 300 or 400 members, which was formed on the capture of Ṭihrán, is supplemented by a Directory (*Hay'at-i-Mudíra*) of twenty persons, including both the *Sipahdár* and the *Sardár-i-As'ad.* The elections "in the first degree" for the new National Assembly were concluded at Ṭihrán. A box containing 60,000 gold *túmáns* was discovered at the Ministry of Finance. The debts of the ex-Sháh to the Russian Bank and other creditors were estimated at £400,000.

Aug. 18, 1909. Rebellions in N.W. Persia, headed by Raḥím Khán and the Sháhseven tribesmen, who threaten Ardabíl, *Iqbálu's-Salṭana* at Mákú, and Mullá Qurbán 'Alí at Zanján.

Aug. 19, 1909. Proposed tax on alcohol, opium and salt (known as *Dá'ira-i-thalátha*) to yield £300,000 a year. Fifteen deputies elected for Ṭihrán, including Ḥusayn-qulí Khán *Nawwáb*, *Ṣaní'u'd-Dawla*, 'Abdu'l-Ḥusayn Khán of Káshán entitled *Waḥídu'l-Mulk*, and Taqí-záda.

Aug. 22, 1909. Messrs Alan Wright and James, of the Imperial Bank of Persia, kidnapped by brigands near Kirmán, but released on Aug. 26.

Aug. 29, 1909. The notorious brigand Raḥím Khán was captured by the Russians, but released again by them on Sept. 18, *q.v.*

Aug. 31, 1909. General amnesty proclaimed by Persian Government. The ex-Sháh appeals to the Tsar for support. The Russian

Legation opposes the dismissal of M. Smirnoff, the young Sháh's tutor. Fight between Kurds and Russians at Urmiya.

Sept. 1, 1909. *Amír Bahádur Jang*, *Sa'du'd-Dawla* and *Mushíru's-Salṭana* are exiled and excluded from the amnesty. Growing distrust of the *Sipahdár*. National volunteers placed under command of Taqízáda's cousin 'Alí Muḥammad Khán (afterwards assassinated on Aug. 2, 1910, *q.v.*).

Sept. 7, 1909. Signature by Persian, Russian and British representatives of the Protocol regulating the ex-Sháh's place of banishment, future conduct and pension (finally fixed at 100,000 *túmáns* or £16,666 a year). French expert called in to value Crown Jewels.

Sept. 9, 1909. Departure of ex-Sháh Muḥammad 'Alí from Ṭihrán.

Sept. 13, 1909. The young Sháh holds a *darbár* to celebrate his twelfth birthday. The Directory (*Hay'at-i-Mudíra*) is increased from 20 to 40 members.

Sept. 15, 1909. Russo-Persian "incident" at Píla-suwár (Belyasuvarski).

Sept. 18, 1909. Raḥím Khán released by the Russians on payment of £T.20 000 and 180 camels.

Sept. 23, 1909. Motor-car service established between Julfá on the Araxes and Tabríz.

Sept. 24, 1909. Arrival of the new Russian Minister, M. Poklevski-Koziell, at Ṭihrán.

Sept. 26, 1909. The *Ẓillu's-Sulṭán* is allowed to return to Europe on payment of 100,000 *túmáns* (£16,666) and the promise to pay double this sum within four months. *'Alá'u's-Salṭana*, formerly Persian Minister in London, is made Foreign Minister.

Sept. 28, 1909. The ex-Sháh reaches Rasht. The *Sipahdár* is made Premier.

Oct. 5, 1909. The ex-Sháh reaches Odessa, his place of exile.

Oct. 16, 1909. One battery and two companies of Russian troops withdrawn from Tabríz. Three days later General Znarsky, who was in command of this force, and one thousand Russian troops were stated to have been withdrawn from Tabríz.

Oct. 19, 1909. Ardabíl threatened by Raḥím Khán.

Oct. 26, 1909. The Persian Government proposes to send an expedition of 100 Persian Cossacks, 300 infantry and 2 guns to Ardabíl.

Oct. 28, 1909. The *Náṣiru'l-Mulk* (actually the Regent) returns from Europe to Ṭihrán.

Nov. 1, 1909. Announcement that the Russian force at Qazwín will be reduced to 50 men, and that 450 more will be distributed between Rasht and Anzalí.

Nov. 2, 1909. Reported fall of Ardabíl. Fresh troops sent from Russia.

Nov. 5, 1909. A second detachment of Russian troops sent to Ardabíl.

Nov. 7, 1909. Withdrawal of Russian force from Qazwín postponed. The *Times* praises the Persian relief-force destined for Ardabíl, on which some £25,000 had been expended, and regrets that Russia will not give them the chance of restoring order there by themselves.

Nov. 9, 1909. Raḥím Khán threatens to march on Ṭihrán, destroy the Constitution, and restore the ex-Sháh.

Nov. 15, 1909. Opening of the Second National Assembly under the presidency of the *Mustasháru'd-Dawla*, with the *Mumtázu'd-Dawla* and Sayyid Naṣru'lláh as Vice-presidents.

Nov. 16, 1909. Raḥím Khán retires from Ardabíl. Two thousand more Russian troops embark at Bákú for Persia.

Nov. 23, 1909. The Persian Government protests against the high-handed action of the Russians at Ardabíl.

Nov. 24, 1909. *'Aẓudu'l-Mulk* confirmed in Regency. M. Passek, Russian Consul at Bushire, attacked by brigands near Shíráz. The Persian Government apologizes for this occurrence on Dec. 1.

Nov. 26, 1909. *Rashídu'l-Mulk* made Governor of Ardabíl.

Dec. 7, 1909. The Persian Government agrees in principle to a foreign (*i.e.* Anglo-Russian) loan and to the employment of foreign advisers, but objects to Russian officers in the Gendarmerie.

Dec. 13, 1909. The Persian Government applies to England and Russia for a loan of £500,000. (See Feb. 16, 1910, *infra.*)

Dec. 31, 1909. The Persian expedition under Yeprem Khán the Armenian obtains a victory over Raḥím Khán.

1910

Jan. 20, 1910. Three more detachments of Russian troops sent to Ahar.

Jan. 24, 1910. Raḥím Khán, hard pressed by the Persian Government troops, has no way of escape save into Russian territory. On Feb. 4 he crosses the Russian frontier unhindered, and on Feb. 6 reaches Elizavetpol. The Persian Government demands his extradition in conformity with the Treaty of Turkmáncháy, but its request is ignored by Russia.

Jan. 27, 1910. *Muwaqqaru's-Salṭana* is hanged.

Feb. 4, 1910. *'Alá'u's-Salṭana* resigns the position of Foreign Minister.

Feb. 11, 1910. The people of Varámín, incited by Shaykh Maḥmúd, a Russian *protégé*, hoist Russian flags over their houses.

Feb. 16, 1910. The Russian and British Ministers formally communicate to *Thiqatu'l-Mulk*, the Acting Minister for Foreign Affairs, the conditions demanded by them for a loan of £400,000. These include "privileged rights" in their respective "Spheres of Influence" to appoint military instructors and build railways. (See Dec. 13, 1909, *supra.*)

Feb. 20, 1910. Persian merchants beg their Government not to accept the proposed loan on the conditions indicated above.

Feb. 28, 1910. Russo-Persian dispute at Langarúd as to the fishery concession (*Shílát*) in the Caspian provinces granted to the Russian Lianosoff (or Lianazoff) in Ṣafar, A.H. 1324 (= April, 1906), for a period of twenty years. Persia has to give way on March 5.

March 1, 1910. The *Sipahdár* and *Sardár-i-As'ad* tender their resignation on account of the continued presence of Russian troops on Persian soil. (See under April 20, 1910, *infra.*)

March 16, 1910. A French expert, M. Falconburg, arrives in Ṭihrán to value the Crown Jewels, at a fee of £1000 for 8 days' work, but this period proving insufficient it was afterwards extended. Rumours of a French loan to Persia. The Persian New Year's Day (*Nawrúz*) was not observed, as a sign of mourning for the continued presence of foreign troops on Persian soil.

March 17, 1910. M. Bizot, the French financial adviser, left Ṭihrán on three months' leave of absence.

March 20, 1910. *Mu'áwinu'd-Dawla* is appointed Foreign Minister. Sattár Khán and Báqir Khán leave Tabríz under Russian pressure and come to Ṭihrán.

March 27, 1910. Some 400 fresh Russian soldiers sent to Tabríz.

March 30, 1910. Herr R. Said-Ruete, representing the *Deutsche Bank*, in Ṭihrán. He left for Berlin on May 17.

April 8, 1910. Expiry of Persia's undertaking to Russia (in the Convention of 1900) not to build railways.

April 10, 1910. Persia rejects the proposed Anglo-Russian loan on account of the dangerous political conditions attached to it. The total value of the Persian Crown Jewels was stated to be £750,000, but this was mere rumour, for the actual estimate of M. Falconburg was, I believe, only known to two representatives of Persia, one of whom, Petros Andreassian, the Armenian, was subsequently hanged by the Russians at Tabríz in Jan. 1912. The other, from whom I learned these particulars, was one of my oldest Persian friends, who held many high positions in the Government, and whose word I trust implicitly.

April 17, 1910. Mr Bill, a member of the Indian Civil Service, who had been acting as British Consul at Shíráz, and who vehemently advocated British occupation of the Southern provinces, was attacked at Yazdikhwást Three days later he reached Iṣfahán safely. It subsequently transpired that Mr Bill had taken the initiative in the conflict.

April 20, 1910. The *Sipahdár* and *Sardár-i-As'ad* consent to resume office (see under March 1, 1910, *supra*) provided the *Ṣaní'u'd-Dawla*, "who is not a *persona grata* with the Legislations," is excluded. The Cabinet crisis ends on May 1.

May 6, 1910. Death of King Edward the Seventh. Reported

confederation of tribes in South Persia to maintain Persian independence.

May 25, 1910. Rumours of a projected German loan to Persia.

May 27, 1910. Violent scene in the National Assembly on account of the suppression of the daily paper *Sharq*.

May 29, 1910. Zanján attacked by Dáráb Mírzá, a Persian prince who had become naturalized as a Russian subject and held a commission in the Labinsky Cossack regiment at this time occupying Qazwín. He obtained leave of absence to go to Russia, but instead rallied round him disaffected persons, obtained for them "letters of protection" (*ta'mín-náma*) signed by the Russian Colonel Rakuza, and with their aid endeavoured to overthrow the Constitutional Government at Zanján. The Persian Government send a small force against him commanded by 'Alí Khán; the Russians also sent a force of Cossacks, which, while returning to Qazwín with Dáráb Mírzá, fell in and fought with the Persian force and killed its leader 'Alí Khán. The incident was a typical and disgraceful example of Russian intrigue, but both in the Blue Book for this period and in the debate in the House of Commons on July 1, 1910, its real nature (clearly exposed in original documents in my possession) was concealed. Internal loan of £5,000,000 authorized by Persian Government. Persian women sell their jewels to provide money for the State.

June 4, 1910. Káshán captured by the outlaw Ná'ib Ḥusayn.

June 7, 1910. Persian Government demands full statement of its debts to Russia.

June 12, 1910. Sir Charles (now Lord) Hardinge appointed Viceroy of India, and Sir Arthur Nicholson, British Ambassador at St Petersburg, appointed to succeed him as Permanent Under-Secretary at the British Foreign Office. Both appointments warmly approved by Russia, whose approval is reported by the *Times*.

June 13, 1910. Announcement that no loan will be made by Germany to Persia. Russia objects to the exemption from taxation of silver destined for the Persian Mint.

June (middle), 1910. Aggressive actions of the Russians at Tabríz, including arrest of Persian police, invasion of *Thiqatu'l-Islám's* house in search of Russian deserter, and demand for dismissal of *Mukhbiru's-Salṭána* the Governor.—Arrival at Ṭihrán of Mr W. A. Moore in connection with the projected Seligmann loan to Persia.

July 1, 1910. Triumphal entry into Ṭihrán of Yeprem Khán and his troops after suppressing the marauding tribesmen who threatened Ardabíl.

July 3, 1910. Heated debate in the *Majlis* between Taqí-záda and his party (the Democrats) and the Ecclesiastical party. Taqí-záda is "given permission to retire" for three months. He left Ṭihrán on July 30.

July 4, 1910. *Zaká'u'l-Mulk* becomes President of the *Majlis*.

July 15, 1910. Russian bombardment of a Persian village on the Caspian shore near Gyumush-tepé.—Assassination at Ṭihrán of Sayyid 'Abdu'lláh Bahbahání.

July 16, 1910. Attempted boycott of Russian goods by Persians.

July 26, 1910. New Cabinet formed, comprising *Mustawfi'l-Mamálik* (Premier), *Farmán-farmá* (Interior), Ḥusayn-qulí Khán *Nawwáb* (Foreign Affairs), *Qiwámu's-Salṭana* (War), *Dabíru'l-Mulk* (Justice), Asadu'lláh Mírzá (Post Office and Telegraphs), and *Ḥakímu'l-Mulk* (Finance).

Aug. 2, 1910. Assassination by Nawrúzoff, Karím and Mahdí-qulí of 'Alí Muḥammad Khán, a close friend of Taqí-záda's, and Sayyid 'Abdu'r-Razzáq Khán, in retaliation, as it was alleged, for Sayyid 'Abdu'lláh Bahbahání's murder on July 15. (See Aug. 17, *infra*.)

Aug. 3, 1910. State of siege proclaimed in Ṭihrán for three months.

Aug. 4, 1910. National Volunteers (*fidá'ís*) ordered to surrender their arms within 48 hours.

Aug. 5, 1910. Manifesto issued by the *Sipahdár*, *Sardár-i-As'ad*, *Ṣamṣámu's-Salṭana*, Sattár Khán and Báqir Khán declaring that they will sink all personal aims and work together for the good of the country. *Fidá'ís* surrendering arms in return for money payments.

Aug. 7, 1910. Severe fighting took place at the Atábak's Park between *Fidá'ís* who refused to surrender their arms and the Government troops. The former were eventually overcome, with a loss of 30 killed and 300 prisoners. *Mu'izzu's-Sulṭán*, who took so prominent a part in the Rasht insurrection, escaped. Both Sattár Khán and Báqir Khán were wounded. Mediation was attempted by the German Minister, Baron Quadt, and the Turkish Ambassador, but was ineffectual.

Aug. 10, 1910. *Ẓarghámu's-Salṭana* and his Bakhtiyárí followers were disarmed at Sháh 'Abdu'l-'Aẓím.

Aug. 14, 1910. The *Istiqlál-i-Írán* ("Independence of Persia") is the only paper appearing in Ṭihrán since the Coup d'État. Two thousand *túmáns* reward (£400) is offered for such information as may lead to the arrest of Sayyid 'Abdu'lláh's murderers. Proposals for a strong army and the appointment of foreign advisers.

Aug. 17, 1910. Russia obliges the Persian Government to surrender to them Nawrúzoff of Nakhjuwán, a Russian subject suspected of having taken part in the assassination of 'Alí Muḥammad Khán. (See Aug. 2, *supra*.)

Aug. 18, 1910. Sir George Barclay returns from leave to Ṭihrán. Pensions are accorded by the Persian Government to Sattár Khán and Báqir Khán.

Aug. 19, 1910. Persian Foreign Minister (Ḥusayn-qulí Khán) makes a fresh appeal to Russia to withdraw her troops from Persia.

Aug. 21, 1910. Russia protests against "Turkish violations of Persian territory."

Aug. 25, 1910. Russia demands concessions as the price of the withdrawal of her troops from Persia. Even the *Times* (Sept. 24, 1910) protests against such a demand. (See Oct. 25, *infra.*)

Sept. 6, 1910. The *Majlis* decides to appoint American advisers in preference to French.

Sept. 12, 1910. Revolt in Mázandarán headed by *Rashídu's-Sulṭán, Amír-i-Mukarram* and Isma'íl Khán. (See Oct. 12, *infra.*)

Sept. 18, 1910. The *Farmán-farmá* resigns the Ministry of the Interior.

Sept. 22, 1910. Death of the Regent, the aged *'Aẓudu'l-Mulk.*

Sept. 23, 1910. Mírzá Abu'l-Qásim Khán *Náṣiru'l-Mulk* elected Regent by 40 votes as against 29 votes given to the rival candidate *Mustawfi'l-Mamálik.*

Sept. 25, 1910. Persian Government troops worsted in an affray with Sháhseven tribesmen.

Sept. 28, 1910. Russian Government proposes to send M. Izvolsky, who has ceased to be Minister for Foreign Affairs, as Ambassador to Paris. A violent attack on him appeared in the *Novoe Vremya* about Oct. 4.

Oct. 9, 1910. Disturbances in South Persia. Yazdikhwást raided by Kúhgaylú tribesmen. *'Aynu'd-Dawla* nominated Governor of Fárs.

Oct. 12, 1910. *Rashídu's-Sulṭán* reported as overcome by Government troops and Ardabíl tranquil. Private loans to Persian Government obstructed by Russian and British Governments.

Oct. 15, 1910. Russia prevents the Persian Crown Jewels being pawned, and announces that her troops at Qazwín shall not be withdrawn, but shall go into winter quarters. "Restiveness of English banking and commercial circles" at Russia's attitude.

Oct. 16, 1910. British Note (widely described as "Ultimatum") to Persia on the disturbed condition of South Persia and interruption of the traffic on the Southern roads.

Oct. 17, 1910. Fighting with Ná'ib Ḥusayn at Káshán. British "Ultimatum" published at Ṭihrán. M. Pokhitanoff appointed Russian Consul at Ṭihrán. (He took up his appointment on Dec. 27, 1910, the day on which Ḥusayn-qulí Khán resigned the Ministry of Foreign Affairs.)

Oct. 18–19, 1910. The British "Ultimatum" arouses so much excitement and indignation in various quarters, especially in Germany, Turkey and India, that the British Foreign Office issues a *communiqué* minimizing its importance, while the Government of India disclaims all responsibility for the measures proposed in it.

Oct. 20, 1910. Turkish alarm at British "Ultimatum," which is described in the Vienna Press as "the *début* of Sir Arthur Nicholson, an energetic and unscrupulous politician." The German papers say that "the meeting between the Tsar and the Kaiser [at Potsdam] will greatly influence the Persian situation." (See under Nov. 5, *infra.*) Concentration of Turkish troops on Persian frontier. Lord Hardinge's farewell speech on the eve of his departure for India.

Oct. 22, 1910. Persian reply to British Note presented. Persia asks for Italian military instructors. (These were refused on Dec. 29 On Jan. 3, 1911, Sweden consented to lend officers for this purpose.) Treasonable correspondence between Shaykh Maḥmúd of Varámín, in refuge at the Russian Legation, and *Rashídu's-Sulṭán*, in rebellion in Mázandarán, intercepted by the Persian Government.

Oct. 23, 1910. Great protest meeting of Turks and Persians at Constantinople, where Russia and England and their policy towards Persia are violently attacked. On Oct. 27 Mr FitzMaurice, First Dragoman of the British Embassy at Constantinople, protests to Ṭal'at Bey against the language used on this occasion.

Oct. 25, 1910. Persia offers the concessions demanded by Russia in return for the immediate withdrawal of her troops from Persian soil. (See Aug. 25, *supra.*)

Oct. 28, 1910. Protest of Peace Association in London against the British "Ultimatum." British Consols fall below 80, partly in consequence of the Persian imbroglio.

Oct. 29, 1910. The Persian Government, having intercepted correspondence between the ex-Sháh and the Turkmáns proving that he was inciting them to espouse his cause, proposes to the Legations to stop his pension in accordance with Article 11 of the Protocol of Sept. 7, 1909. The Legations forbid this (apparently without condescending to examine the evidence), and send *ghuláms* to "shadow" Ḥusayn-qulí Khán, the Persian Foreign Minister, until the ex-Sháh's allowance is paid, which is done, under protest, two days later. The Persian Minister in London formally protests against this insult to Ḥusayn-qulí Khán (which is feebly defended by Sir Edward Grey) on Nov. 4.

Nov. 5, 1910. Meeting at Potsdam between the Tsar and the Kaiser. The text of the Agreement then arrived at was published in England on Jan. 5, 1911. Great disquietude is shown by the French at Russo-German relations, especially *à propos* of Herr von Bethmann-Hollweg's speech of Dec. 11 on this subject.

Nov. 8, 1910. The ex-Sháh, having surreptitiously left Odessa, the place of his banishment, without (as it was pretended) the knowledge of the Russian Government, arrived at Vienna. M. Sazonoff, the new Russian Minister for Foreign Affairs, returned to St Petersburg from Berlin.

Nov. 10, 1910. Proposals for Trans-Persian railway mooted.

Nov. 13, 1910. Resignation of Yeprem Khán. Seligmann loan to Persia finally stopped by Russia and England about this date.

Nov. 16, 1910. M. Poklevski Koziell, the Russian Minister at Ṭihrán, demands a formal apology from Ḥusayn-qulí Khán *Nawwáb*, the Persian Minister for Foreign Affairs, for alleged insults offered to Áqá Ḥasan, the Russian Consular Agent at Káshán.

Nov. 17, 1910. British reply to Persian Note of Oct. 22. Five hundred more Russian troops reach Julfá on the Araxes *en route* for Salmás.

Nov. 22, 1910. Dignified appeal issued by *Mujtahids* of Najaf. Protest of Calcutta Persian colony against British Note.

Dec. 2, 1910. M. Sazonoff made Russian Minister for Foreign Affairs, with M. Neratoff as Assistant.

Dec. 8, 1910. Proposed loan of £1,250,000 at 5 °/₀ issued by Imperial Bank of Persia at 87½ opposed by *Majlis*.—Sir George Buchanan, the new Ambassador of Great Britain to Russia, reaches St Petersburg.

Dec. 23, 1910. The ex-Sháh at Rome.

Dec. 27, 1910. Resignation of Ḥusayn-qulí Khán *Nawwáb* of the Persian Ministry of Foreign Affairs.

Dec. 28, 1910. Persian reply to British Note of Nov. 17. The All-India Muslim League protests against British policy in Persia. The new Regent, *Náṣiru'l-Mulk*, who had been expected in Persia since Oct. 19, is still at Vienna and refuses to proceed.

Dec. 29, 1910. Italy refuses to lend officers for the training and organization of the Persian Gendarmerie. Sweden is approached.

1911

Jan. 3, 1911. *Muḥtashamu's-Salṭana* made Minister for Foreign Affairs. Sweden consents to lend officers for Gendarmerie.

Jan. 6, 1911. The ex-Sháh, with *Amír Bahádur Jang*, arrived at Berlin from Brussels, having visited Meran, Rome, Nice, Paris and Vienna, and held consultations and conversations with his exiled partisans in those places.

Jan. 12, 1911. Sir Arthur Nicholson is stated to have told the Turkish Ambassador in London that "Turkish policy in Persia was a menace to England."

Jan. 16, 1911. *Náṣiru'l-Mulk*, the Regent, left Vienna for Persia.

Jan. 17, 1911. Rumoured undertaking of Turkey to help Persia. Conciliatory attitude of Persia towards Russia, and talk of withdrawal of Russian troops from Qazwín.

Jan. 18, 1911. Manifesto of Persian *Mujtahids* at Najaf, and boycott of Russian goods advocated by them.

Jan. 23, 1911. *Náṣiru'l-Mulk*, the Regent, reaches Bákú.—Raḥím Khán returns to Tabríz from Russia.

Jan. 24, 1911. American financial experts promised to Persia.

Jan. 29, 1911. *Náṣiru'l-Mulk* reaches Rasht, but is delayed there by a snow-storm.

Feb. 1, 1911. The *Mu'tamad-i-Kháqán*, Governor of Iṣfahán, and his cousin 'Abdu'r-Raḥím Khán are shot by 'Abbás, an ex-officer of police, the former being severely wounded, the latter killed. 'Abbás takes refuge with the Russian Consul, M. Bogozhavlenski, who refuses to give him up. (See under May 19, *infra.*)

Feb. 2, 1911. Five American finance experts appointed to serve the Persian Government at salaries ranging from £600 to £2000 a year. (See under May 11, *infra.*)

Feb. 6, 1911. *Ṣaní'u'd-Dawla*, the Persian Minister of Finance, shot dead by a Georgian named Ivan and two confederates. The assassins are arrested after one of them and four of the Persian Police have been wounded in the struggle. The Russian Legation demands and obtains the surrender of the assassins, who are Russian subjects. Anti-Russian feeling strongly excited. (See under May 9, *infra.*)

Feb. 8, 1911. *Náṣiru'l-Mulk*, the Regent, arrives in Ṭihrán.

Feb. 11, 1911. M. Bogozhavlenski, the Russian Consul at Iṣfahán, is found drowned in a tank in the Consulate garden. It was supposed to be a case of suicide.

Feb. 12, 1911. Russians at Ardabíl undertake primitive expedition against Galish tribesmen.

Feb. 13, 1911. *Náṣiru'l-Mulk*, the Regent, makes a strong speech to the Deputies, demanding their loyal support, which they promise him.

Feb. 15–22, 1911. Cossacks sack the village of Varmúní near Ástárá and kill some fifty persons, including women and children. An additional Russian battalion sent from Bákú, of whom 600 had already reached Ástárá.

Feb. 20, 1911. Assassins of *Ṣaní'u'd-Dawla* condemned by Russian Government to fourteen years' banishment to Siberia.

Feb. 23, 1911. The *Sipahdár* is entrusted with the formation of a Cabinet. Brawl in Ṭihrán between two parties of armed men, believed to be Russian subjects. Two, supposed to be relations of one of *Ṣaní'u'd-Dawla's* assassins, are killed.

Feb. 28, 1911. 'Alí Beg, a young Reactionary who was notorious in connection with the Coup d'État of June 23, 1908, shot himself in the Square Montholon, Paris, in consequence of a quarrel with his mistress.

March 2, 1911. Messrs Kay and Haycock robbed near Iṣfahán.

March 4, 1911. The Regent's address to the Persian Nation on the occasion of his taking the oath.

March 8, 1911. New Cabinet formed, consisting of the *Sipahdár* (War), *Muḥtashamu's-Salṭana* (Foreign Affairs), *Mustasháru'd-Dawla* (Interior), *'Alá'u's-Sulṭana* (Education), *Mu'áwinu'd-Dawla* (Commerce), *Mumtázu'd-Dawla* (Finance), *Mushíru'd-Dawla* (Justice).—Disarmament of persons not authorized to bear arms by Yeprem Khán.

March 13–15, 1911. Qazwín is evacuated by the bulk of Russian troops stationed there, except 80 Cossacks.

April 6, 1911. British Consulate at Kirmánsháh attacked by robbers.—Debate in *Majlis* on powers demanded by Cabinet.

April 12, 1911. Improved state of Shíráz roads under *Niẓámu's-Salṭana's* government of Fárs.

April 17, 1911. Arrest of *Qiwámís* by *Niẓámu's-Salṭana* at Shíráz. (See under May 8, *infra*.)

April 24, 1911. Proposed Persian loan of £1,250,000 discussed in *Majlis*; defeated on April 27; finally passed on May 2.

April 27, 1911. Proposed British railway from the Persian Gulf to Khurramábád.

May 8, 1911. *Náṣiru'd-Dawla*, one of the *Qiwámís*, is murdered.

May 9, 1911. Alleged suicide of one of *Ṣaní'u'd-Dawla's* assassins on the Caspian steamer carrying him to Russia.

May 11, 1911. Mr W. Morgan Shuster and the other American Financial Advisers reach Anzalí.

May 15, 1911. Mr Kingston, a representative of Messrs Burroughs and Welcome, is robbed near Káshán.

May 18, 1911. Hostile demonstrations before the British Consulate at Shíráz.

May 19, 1911. 'Abbás, the assassin who attempted to kill the *Mu'tamad-i-Kháqán* and succeeded in killing his cousin at Iṣfahán on Feb. 1, is found guilty and deported to Russia.—The Russian Legation demands the deportation of Amín Rasúl-záda, the editor of the important Persian daily *Írán-i-Naw*.

May 30, 1911. It is proposed in the *Majlis* and unanimously agreed on June 13 to invest Mr W. Morgan Shuster, the new American Treasurer-General, with very extensive powers. The *Sardár-i-As'ad* leaves Ṭihrán for Europe.

June 15, 1911. The *Sipahdár* leaves Ṭihrán in a huff, bidding his coachman drive "to Firangistán"; but is induced to return on July 4.

July 9, 1911. The command of the new Treasury Gendarmerie which it is proposed to organize is offered to Captain C. B. Stokes, whose appointment as Military Attaché to the British Legation at Ṭihrán is on the point of expiring. Praise of this move by Mr W. A. Moore, who has now become *Times* correspondent in the Persian capital.

July 16, 1911. The ex-Sháh's brother *Sáláru'd-Dawla* seizes Hamadán and proclaims the ex-Sháh Muḥammad 'Alí as king.

July 19, 1911. The ex-Sháh, accompanied by some of his followers, re-appears in Persia, having passed through Russia, as it is alleged, with a false beard and under a false name, unknown to the Russian Government, carrying with him a quantity of arms and ammunition, labelled "Mineral Waters," and accompanied by a Russian officer named Khabayeff, specially attached to him.—Russia objects to Captain Stokes's appointment.

July 19–21, 1911. The Persian Government takes energetic steps to deal with the ex-Sháh's raid, and protests to the Russian and British Legations at this flagrant violation of the Protocol of Sept. 7, 1909.

The Legations reply on Aug. 2 to the effect that it is no concern of theirs, but is a matter affecting Persia only.

July 25, 1911. The *Sipahdár* is removed from the Cabinet, and retires to Zarganda, the village in which is situated the Russian Legation. Mr Morgan Shuster advises the Persian Government as to steps to be taken against the ex-Sháh.

July 27, 1911. The Russian Consul at Tabríz, accompanied by 300 Russian troops and Cossacks, forcibly releases *Rashídu'l-Mulk*, the former Governor of Ardabíl, imprisoned on suspicion of treason, from the custody of the Deputy-Governor of Tabríz, and conveys him to the Russian Consulate.—Sháhrúd is looted by the ex-Sháh's Turkmán allies.

July 28, 1911. The captain and mate of the Russian steamer *Christophoros* are dismissed from their command for communicating to the Press the fact that the ex-Sháh crossed the Caspian to Persia in their vessel.

July 29, 1911. Russia again protests against Captain Stokes's appointment, which is still warmly supported by M. Jean Herbette of *l'Action* and *le Siècle* (who had been in Persia for some months to study the situation) in a series of four telegrams, despatched on July 29–Aug. 4, intended for publication in the British Press[1], but refused by the chief agencies on grounds of political expediency.—The *Majlis* voted the acceptance of the contract with Capt. C. B. Stokes by 63 votes out of 72, and decided by 59 votes out of 70 to put a price of 100,000 *túmáns* on the ex-Sháh's head and 25,000 *túmáns* each on the heads of his brothers *Shu'á'u's-Salṭana* and *Sáláru'd-Dawla*.

July 31, 1911. Russia demands that the Customs' receipts be paid to M. Mornard and not to Mr Shuster, between whom an acute conflict arises. The French and Italian Legations support Russia, and the German Legation is also said to be opposed to Mr Shuster, who is violently and coarsely attacked by the *Novoe Vremya*, which declares (Aug. 4) that, "in the absence of a miracle, the ex-Sháh will be at Ṭihrán in five days."

Aug. 4, 1911. The *Times* says that "neither the British nor the Indian Government has any power to prevent Captain Stokes accepting the appointment" offered him by the Persian Government.—British Note advising the Persian Government not to persist in the appointment.—Alleged agreement between the Russian Government and the ex-Sháh whereby the latter consents, in case of success, to cede to Russia Ázarbáyján and the Persian shore of the Caspian Sea.

Aug. 9, 1911. The Persia Committee revived in London.

Aug. 7–12, 1911. Renewed violent attack by the *Novoe Vremya* on "Stokes and Company," accompanied by expressions of surprise at the "apparent helplessness" of the British Foreign Office.

Aug. 12, 1911. Defeat of ex-Sháh's forces by Bakhtiyárís at Fírúzkúh and death of *Rashídu'l-Mulk*.

[1] Published in the *Manchester Guardian* of Aug. 8, 1911.

Aug. 21, 1911. The British Foreign Office informs the Persian Legation that Captain Stokes's resignation from the Indian Army will not be accepted.

Aug. 22, 1911. Defeat of ex-Sháh's army at Sawád-kúh.

Aug. 31, 1911. Third victory of Persian Government troops at Damáwand.—Yeprem Khán ill.—Loyalty of *Ẓiyá'u'l-Mulk* and *Amír-i-Mufakhkham* suspected.

Sept. 5–6, 1911. *Arshadu'd-Dawla*, the ex-Sháh's best and bravest General, is captured and shot.

Sept. 7, 1911. The ex-Sháh takes refuge on a Russian vessel on the Caspian Sea.

Sept. 11, 1911. Raḥím Khán is put to death at Tabríz by order of the *Anjuman* or Provincial Assembly. An understanding is arrived at between Mr Shuster and M. Mornard.

Sept. 12, 1911. The ex-Sháh arrives, a fugitive, at Gyumush-tepé with seven of his followers.

Sept. 18, 1911. Reported destruction of 120 Turkmáns forming part of *Arshadu'd-Dawla's* army at Sháhrúd.

Sept. 20, 1911. Seven additional Swedish officers appointed to the Persian Gendarmerie. Mr New's appointment as Persian Treasury officer cancelled by the *Majlis* in consequence of the British Government's objection to the appointment of Captain Stokes, but finally ratified at Mr Shuster's request on Oct. 4.

Sept. 22, 1911. Ná'ib Ḥusayn occupies Káshán.

Sept. 25, 1911. *Sáláru'd-Dawla* defeated by Persian Government troops at Sáwa, and again two days later at Nawbarán.

Sept. 27, 1911. Italian Ultimatum to Turkey. (It was stated in the *Nation*, with a great show of probability, that Italy was acting in collusion with Russia, Russia's object being to involve the Turks in a war which would prevent them from coming to Persia's aid or opposing the projected Russian invasion of N.W. Persia.)

Oct. 3, 1911. Decision of Indian Government to send Indian troops to S. Persia.

Oct. 6, 1911. Hamadán taken by Persian Government troops and *Sáláru'd-Dawla* put to flight.

Oct. 7, 1911. Conciliatory attitude of Persian Government towards Russia.

Oct. 9, 1911. The property of the ex-Sháh's brother *Shu'á'u's-Salṭana* being confiscated by the Persian Government, and Treasury Gendarmes placed in possession by order of Mr Morgan Shuster the Treasurer-General, the Russian Consul M. Pokhitanoff sends a superior force of Cossacks to expel them. Next day a large force of Gendarmes expels the Cossacks and again takes possession. Thereupon M. Pokhitanoff comes there in person, insults the Gendarmes, and does his best to provoke an "incident."

Oct. 16, 1911. Ná'ib Ḥusayn expelled from Káshán. Miss Ross robbed near Shíráz.

Oct. 17, 1911. Russia definitely refuses to withdraw her objection to the appointment of Captain Stokes. Capture of ex-Sháh's diary.

Oct. 18, 1911. *Times* attacks Mr Shuster in a leader. The ex-Sháh reaches 'Ishqábád (Askabad) in Russian territory.

Oct. 19, 1911. Persian Government protests against the sending of Indian troops to South Persia.

Oct. 20, 1911. Mr Shuster telegraphs to the *Times* that he is sending a reply to their leader of Oct. 18.

Oct. 22, 1911. Russia objects to the appointment of 20 additional Swedish officers.

Oct. 23-27, 1911. Italian massacre of 4000 Arabs, including women and children, at Tripoli.

Oct. 24, 1911. The British Government notifies Persia of the sailing of the Indian troops, of whom the first detachment land at Bushire on Oct. 27. On the same day 200 additional Russian troops are landed at Anzalí, and it is stated that 1700 more will follow, while 1900 will advance from Julfá to Tabríz.

Oct. 29, 1911. The ex-Sháh is reported as having returned from 'Ishqábád to Gyumush-tepé.

Nov. 5, 1911. First Russian Ultimatum, demanding an apology from the Persian Government for alleged insult to the Russian Consul, M. Pokhitanoff, on Oct. 9. The *Times* of this date censures Pokhitanoff's conduct.

Nov. 7, 1911. The Swedish Government is reported to have yielded to Russia's objection of Oct. 22 to the lending of more Swedish officers to the Persian Government. (But see under Nov. 17 *infra.*)

Nov. 9, 1911. Mr Morgan Shuster's reply of Oct. 20 to the *Times* leader of Oct. 18 is published in the *Times*.

Nov. 11, 1911. Captain Stokes is ordered by the British Government to return to India. Two more squadrons of Central Indian horse arrive at Bushire.

Nov. 12, 1911. Russian Note to Persian Government repeating the demand for an apology of Nov. 5.

Nov. 13, 1911. The first two squadrons of Indian troops reach Shíráz.

Nov. 15, 1911. Lord Curzon's sympathetic and eloquent speech at the Persia Society's Dinner in London.—Russian troops are ready to enter Persia.

Nov. 16, 1911. The Viceroy of the Caucasus is instructed to send 4000 more Russian troops into Persia. At Maláyir 3000 Persian Government troops are held in readiness to act against *Sáláru'd-Dawla.*

Nov. 17, 1911. Seven more Swedish officers are selected for service in Persia.—Violence of the *Novoe Vremya* against Mr Shuster.—Violent attack by the *Outlook* (which, having been strongly pro-Russian, executed an amazing *volta face* on Nov. 11) on Sir Edward Grey, whom it describes as "the painted lath at the Foreign Office."

Nov. 19, 1911. Letter from Mr Shuster in the New York *Sun* denouncing Sir George Barclay's duplicity.—Defeat of *Sáláru'd-Dawla*, with loss of 500 men, at Burújird.—Russia breaks off diplomatic relations with Persia, who appeals to England for mediation.

Nov. 20, 1911. Persia is given to understand by the British Minister that if she submits to the Ultimatum the Russian troops will not advance.

Nov. 23, 1911. The Treasury Gendarmes are withdrawn from the house of *Shu'á'u's-Salṭana*, the Persian Foreign Minister goes to the Russian Legation and offers an apology, and Persia thus complies with the terms of the First Russian Ultimatum. According to the *Times*, "Sir George Barclay assisted the reconciliation by convincing the Persians that the Russian troops would be withdrawn if an acceptable apology was tendered." The number of Russian troops in Persia is now estimated at 12,000. Russian Note to the Powers. *Wuthúqu'd-Dawla*, Foreign Minister; *Ṣamṣámu's-Salṭana*, Premier; *Mushíru'd-Dawla*, Education; *Mu'aẓidu's-Salṭana*, Posts and Telegraphs. To these were subsequently added *Sardár-i-Muḥtasham*, War; *Mustasháru's-Salṭana*, Justice; and *Zaká'u'l-Mulk*, Finance.—Three more battalions of Russian troops disembark at Anzalí.

Nov. 25, 1911. High-handed behaviour of Russian Consul at Rasht.—Russian Legation accuses Mr Shuster of circulating Persian translation of his letter to the *Times*. Mr Shuster (Nov. 28) disclaims all responsibility for this.

Nov. 27, 1911. Debate in Commons and (Nov. 28) in Lords on Persian Question. The *Novoe Vremya* foreshadows fresh demands on Russia's part.

Nov. 29, 1911. Second Russian Ultimatum presented to Persian Government.

Nov. 30, 1911. Second Ultimatum rejected. Bazaars closed, great excitement, offers of help to Persia from Armenian *Dashnaktsiyún*. Plots against Mr Shuster's life discovered.

Dec. 1, 1911. Complaints from Tabríz that Russia is openly supporting the Reactionary Ṣamad Khán *Shujá'u'd-Dawla*.—Russian troops ordered to advance.

Dec. 2, 1911. Assassination of *'Alá'u'd-Dawla*, who is suspected of intriguing with the *Sipahdár* to effect restoration of ex-Sháh. Anti-Russian demonstrations.—*Wuthúqu'd-Dawla* resigns the Ministry for Foreign Affairs.—Bakhtiyárís said to have been "squared" by Russia.

Dec. 3, 1911. Russian troops advancing on Ṭihrán.—Yeprem Khán is said to favour armed resistance. Popular demonstrations and processions crying "*Marg yá Istiqlál*" ("Death or Independence!"). Mr Shuster releases Captain Stokes from his engagement and cancels the engagements of Messrs Lecoffre, Haycock and Schindler. The *Sardár-*

i-As'ad, returning from Europe, lands at Rasht, where the Russians disarm the local militia and seize the telegraph.

Dec. 4–6, 1911. Telegrams of protest against Russia's action from Mass Meeting at Tabríz, from the President of the *Majlis*, *Mu'tamanu'l-Mulk*, from the Persian women (addressed to the Women's Suffrage Societies), and from the Persia Defence Society, Calcutta. Popular feeling runs high against England, who is considered to have betrayed the Persians.—M. Sazonoff in Paris.—*Wuthúqu'd-Dawla* resumes office (Dec. 5) of Minister of Foreign Affairs.

Dec. 7, 1911. Lord Curzon's eloquent speech on Persia in House of Lords. Lord Morley's reply.—Russia's aggressions in Mongolia and attempts to obtain from Turkey the opening of the Dardanelles. Dispute between the United States and Russia about status of American Jews and their passports.

Dec. 11, 1911. Conference of the *Sardár-i-As'ad* with British and Russian Ministers at the British Legation.—The *Mujtahids* of Najaf and Karbalá prepare for a *jihád*.—Feeling runs high in Ṭihrán.—"Russia," according to the *Times*, "regards the existence of the *Majlis* as incompatible with her interests." 4000 Turkish troops reported at Salmás.

Dec. 12, 1911. Sudden death of Mullá Muḥammad Káẓim, the chief Constitutionalist *Mujtahid* at Najaf, on the eve of his departure for Persia.—The *Majlis* still stands firm against acceptance of the Second Russian Ultimatum, and refuses to recognize the new Cabinet (see under Nov. 23, *supra*). Russia sends 800 troops and 10 guns to Khúy.

Dec. 13, 1911. General Gabieff and 4000 Russian troops concentrate at Qazwín.

Dec. 14, 1911. Boycott of British goods at Shíráz.—Resolution of Manchester Chamber of Commerce.—Debate in House of Commons.

Dec. 17, 1911. Ṣamad Khán *Mumtázu's-Salṭana*, the Persian Minister at Paris, said to be working for "a conciliatory settlement of the Russo-Persian conflict."

Dec. 18, 1911. Sollum in Cyrenaica ceded to England (or nominally to Egypt) by Turkey.—The *Majlis* rejects the Cabinet's proposed acceptance of the Second Russian Ultimatum.

Dec. 20, 1911. The Cabinet refuses to resign.

Dec. 21, 1911. By a vote of 39 to 19 the *Majlis* agrees to appoint a Commission of five Deputies to deal, conjointly with the Cabinet, with the Russian Ultimatum.—Fighting between the Russian troops and the Persians breaks out simultaneously at Tabríz, Rasht, and Anzalí.—Telegraphic communication with Persia interrupted.

Dec. 23, 1911. Persia accepts and submits to the Russian Ultimatum. Political meetings prohibited in Ṭihrán, and most of the newspapers stopped on Dec. 26. Orders sent to the people of Tabríz, Rasht, etc., to stop fighting. Mr Shuster is notified of his dismissal. Telegraphic communication with Tabríz interrupted. Fresh Russian reinforcements ordered thither.

Dec. 24, 1911. Further severe fighting at Tabríz, which is heavily bombarded by the Russians. The Russian Consul at Rasht assumes control of the town. The *Novoe Vremya* demands "merciless retribution" and "extermination of the *fidá'ís*," and says that "true humanity requires cruelty."—The Regent, on the advice of the Cabinet, dissolves the *Majlis*. Telegraphic communication with Persia only possible by Suez, and entirely interrupted between Ṭihrán and Tabríz.

Dec. 26, 1911. The *Bahâristán*, where the National Assembly was wont to sit, is closed and guarded by troops, and the newspapers are suppressed.

Dec. 27, 1911. Attack on a body of Indian troops escorting Mr W. A. Smart to Shíráz. Mr Smart, first reported as killed, was wounded and fell into the hands of the tribesmen, who, on recognizing him, treated him with much kindness and hospitality.—The Ṭihrán-Tabríz telegraph worked for a short time to-day.

Dec. 28, 1911. Amánu'lláh Mírzá, Acting Governor of Tabríz, pursued by Russian hatred on account of telegrams sent by him denouncing Russian cruelties, takes refuge in the British Consulate.—Ṣamad Khán *Shujá'u'd-Dawla*, the notorious Reactionary and partisan of the ex-Sháh, prepares, with Russian approval, to enter Tabríz and assume governorship.—The Bakhtiyárí *Amír-i-Mujáhid* said to be a candidate for the post of Treasurer-General vacated by Mr Shuster.

Dec. 29, 1911. General clamour in Imperialist Press in Great Britain and India for British expedition to South Persia.—The Russian and British Legations support the candidature of M. Mornard for the post of Treasurer-General, to the great dissatisfaction of Persian and non-official English elements.

Dec. 30, 1911. Press Association telegram from Tabríz saying that "had the *fidá'ís* continued to fight a day longer, the Russians [*i.e.* those already in the city before the arrival of their reinforcements] would have been overpowered."—Mr Smart reached Kázarún safely.

It is unnecessary to continue this chronology here over the two years (1912 and 1913) which have since elapsed, since this book deals only with events and things belonging to the Four Periods enumerated above, and the second Constitutional Period properly ends with the forcible closure of the *Majlis* on December 24, 1911. The horrors which followed the Russian invasion of Ázarbáyján, especially at Tabríz, and inaugurated the gloomy year of 1912 are briefly described in a pamphlet entitled *The Reign of Terror in Tabríz: England's Responsibility* which I published in October, 1912, and I am preparing a larger volume containing much fuller details derived from all available sources. On January 1, 1912, which coincided with the *'Áshúrá* or 10th of Muḥarram (the most solemn day of mourning amongst the Shí'a Muḥammadans), A.H. 1330, the Russians began a whole series of executions of leading citizens and patriots by publicly hanging on a gallows gaily decorated with the Russian colours eight persons, of whom the most notable were the venerable and learned ecclesiastic *Thiqatu'l-Islám*, chief *mujtahid* of Ázarbáyján; *Ẓiyá'u'l-'Ulamá*; *Ṣádiqu'l-Mulk*, a young officer; and Shaykh Salím. Amongst other notable persons hanged by them were the philanthropist Ḥájji 'Alí *Dawá-farúsh* ("the Druggist"), the poet Mírzá Aḥmad Suhaylí, and two nephews of Sattár Khán on or about Jan. 6; and the much-respected and trusted Armenian Petros Andreassian some days later. In most cases the houses of the victims were blown up with dynamite by the Russians, who installed as Governor Ṣamad Khán *Shujá'u'd-Dawla*, with the support of Mr Shipley, the British Consul at Tabríz, and the concurrence of the British Foreign Office. This miscreant tortured, killed and extorted money by methods summarily described in the pamphlet above mentioned. The executions continued in Tabríz at any rate until August, 1912, and similar deeds were done throughout Ázarbáyján. At Rasht the printing-presses were destroyed, the newspapers (some of the best in Persia) were stopped, and a few people were hanged. The unprovoked bombardment and plunder by the Russians of the sacred shrine of the Imám Riẓá at Mashhad on March 29, 1912, on which occasion many innocent people, both inhabitants and pilgrims, were killed, was the culmination of these horrors, and produced an indescribably painful impression throughout the Muslim World.

Since the closure of the Second National Assembly at the end of 1911, that is to say for more than two years, rumours have several times arisen that fresh elections were to be held and a new *Majlis* convened. These elections are now actually taking place, except in Ázarbáyján, and it is probable that this year may witness the inauguration of a Third National Assembly, which, however, welcome as it will be to Persia and her friends, will have to face with diminished strength tasks even more arduous and problems even more difficult than those which confronted its two predecessors. For on the one hand many of the most single-minded, able and resolute patriots have been slain or are in exile or in hiding, while full advantage has been taken by Russia during this two years' interregnum (when Persian Cabinet Ministers have hardly been able to hold office, much less act, without the sanction of the Russian and British Legations) to extort concessions of the most far-reaching character as to the making of railways, the exploitation of minerals and fisheries, and other matters, and to saddle the unhappy country with fresh burdens of debt at usurious rates of interest.

Bad as the situation is, however, it is impossible to deny that it might have been worse; Ṭihrán has not been occupied by the Russians nor been the scene of horrors such as those perpetrated at Tabríz; the Royal Pretenders Muḥammad 'Alí, *Shu'á'u's-Salṭana* and *Sáláru'd-Dawla* have for the present ceased to trouble, and have disappeared, it may be hoped for ever, from the political horizon; and the work effected by the new Gendarmerie under the Swedish officers in suppressing brigandage and securing the safety of the roads deserves the fullest recognition and the highest praise. For so much salvage from the general wreck we must be thankful, and for the fact that, however dark the horizon and ominous the outlook, Persia, in name at least, still remains an independent and undivided country.

INDEX

This Index comprises names mentioned in the Translator's Preface, the Author's Introduction, and the text of the Persian poems contained in Part II, as well as those occurring in the translated portion (Part I) of the book. The prefix *Abú* ("Father of —"), when it occurs in proper names, is sometimes ignored in the alphabetical arrangement, so that, for example, *Abu'z-Ẓiyá* may be found either under *Z*, or *A*. Titles, as opposed to names, of persons, as well as titles of books and newspapers, are printed in *italics*. The abbreviation *n.* after the number of a page indicates a foot-note : thus "17 n." means "p. 17, *ad calc.*," while "17 and n." means that the name in question is mentioned on p. 17 and also in a foot-note on that page.

دقّت مستشرقین و متتبّعین ادبیّات فارسی‌را جلب نموده و ملّت ایران‌را نیز از صمیم قلب تهنیت میگویم که چنین نوعروس بکر معرفت‌را بمنصّهٔ ظهور جلوه آورده است و از خداوند خواهانم که امثال ایشان‌را بیفزاید

درینجا لازم می بینم که تأسّفات خودرا از اینکه نتوانستم همهٔ آثار و منظومات شعرای این دور اخیررا جمع آوری کنم اظهار بدارم و همچنین فریضهٔ ذمّهٔ خود میدانم که تشکّرات صمیمی خودرا بدوستان دور و نزدیك که در جمع و ارسال این اشعار معاونت و بذل همّت کرده اند تقدیم نمایم و از ادبا و شعرا و معارف خواهان و منتسبین ادبیّات فارسی تمنّی می‌نمایم که هرچه از اشعار وطنی و سیاسی و تاریخی و غزلیّات و غیرها تا کنون بنظم آورده‌اند یا شنیده اند اگر برای ایشان زحمت نیست مرحمت فرموده آنهارا بعنوان مخلص بفرستند تا شاید جلد دویمی ازین دوره ادبیّات جدیده مرتّب ساخته برسم ارمغان بنظر مطالعهٔ طالبان علم و ادب برسانم چه این کاررا برای خود افتخار و شرف بزرگ میدانم عنوان این جانب از قرار ذیل است:

ادوارد برون معلّم السنه شرقیّه در دار الفنون کیمبریج (انگلستان)

فی غرّة ربیع الاوّل سنه ۱۳۳۲

EDWARD G. BROWNE,
Pembroke College, Cambridge, England.

January 29, 1914.

از فواید کثیرهٔ این انقلاب سیاسی همین بس که چنین ادبیّات بکری بوجود آورده است که در سایه آن یك خلق جدید و یك استقبال پُر امید ظهور خواهد یافت

ثانیًا از حیث اسلوب نیز این ادبیّات جدیده یك تازگی و اهمیّت مخصوصی دارد و آن این است که در اغلب اشعاری که درین دور جدید سروده اند حقیقت‌را برای اینکه همه کس بتواند فهم نماید در باس هزل و مزاح جلوه داده اند و یا با یکی از پرده های موسیقی هم آهنگ ساخته اند تا بآسانی قبول عامّه بهم رساند

بدیهی است که شخص هر قدر دارای اخلاق حمیده و تهذیب نفس باشد باز وی‌را شنیدن عیوب خود بی پرده چندان خوش آیند نخواهد بود و حقیقت گوئی در وی تأثیری چندان نخواهد کرد ولی در شکل هزل و مزاح آنرا بمیل و رغبت خواهد خواند و البتّه بی تأثیر هم نخواهد ماند

شعرای این دوره که این اسلوب مرغوب‌را پیش گرفته اند بمنزلهٔ طبیب حاذقی می باشند که مزاج مریض خودرا بدست آورده و موافق آن ادویهٔ تلخ‌را با شیرینی آمیخته بمریض میخوراند و یا مانند واعظی که درجهٔ ادراك مستمع‌را درك کرده بقدر فهم او بسادگی تمام مقاصد خودرا ادا می نماید و عامّهٔ ملّت خوانده و بحقیقت مسائل سیاسی و وطنی و معاشی واقف شوند چنانکه غزلیّات و قصائد عارف و اشرف گیلانی و دخو (میرزا علی اکبر خان دهخدا) و ملك الشعراء بهار و غیرهم در سایهٔ این اسلوب مرغوب از قراری که می نویسند امروز در نزد خاصّ و عامّ مشهور است و در محافل میخوانند و با آلات موسیقی می نوازند

این جانب بترتیب این نمونهٔ مختصر از ادبیّات وطنی و سیاسی فارسی نظر

همانا امواجی است که از قعر دریا و از طبقات پائین آن بالا می‌آید همین طور است در انقلابات سیاسی انقلابی که ثمرهٔ خوب میدهد انقلابی است که در سایهٔ جنبش طبقهٔ عامهٔ ملّت بظهور رسد و الّا انقلابی خواهد بود نا رس و نا بهنگام و سطحی که مانند امواج سطحی دریا هرگز آن قوّت‌را نخواهد داشت که بنای استبداد و خرافات متراکمهٔ چندین قرن‌را از بیخ بر اندازد

ازین رو طبقهٔ عامّهٔ ملّت بیشتر از طبقات دیگر باید منظور نظر ارباب سخن و واعظین و مخصوصًا شعرا و ادبا باشند و من چنین تصوّر میکنم که در عالم ملّتی نیست که بقدر ملّت ایران مجذوب شعر باشد و شعر در طبیعت ایرانی جاذبهٔ مخصوصی دارد که کمتر نظیر آن در سایر اقوام دیده شده است؛ ازین نقطهٔ نظر شعرائی که اصلاح حال طبقهٔ عامّهٔ ملت‌را در نظر دارند مرجّح بر دیگران می باشند و میان ایشان و سائرین که جز مدح و اخذ صله هنری دیگر ندارند همان فرق است که میان زاهد خود پرست و عالم دانش پرور چنانکه شیخ سعدی علیه الرحمة می فرماید

گفتم میان عالم و عابد چه فرق بود؛ تا اختیار کردی از آن این فریق‌را؛
گفت آن گلیم خویش بدر می برد ز موج؛ وین جهد می کند که بگیرد غریق‌را؛

و ما می بنیم که ادبا و شعرای عصر حاضر پی بدین نکته برده‌اند یعنی ابکار معانی‌را از آن دائرهٔ محدوده بیرون آورده و خوان الوان نظم‌را پیش خاصّ و عامّ گسترده طبقهٔ عامه‌را از آن برخوردار کرده‌اند و اغلب موضوعات این ادبیّات‌را از وقایع یومیّه و راجع بمسائل معاشی و اجتماعی گرفته اند که هر یك از افراد ملّت میتواند بدون صعوبت درك نماید و اگر همین اشعاررا که از ابتدای انقلاب ایران تا امروز انشاد شده جمع آوری کنند تقریبًا تاریخ منظوم انقلاب‌را تشکیل خواهد داد

از بیخبری بیخبران معذورند، ذوقی است درین باده که مستان دانند، اینك نمونهٔ از ادبیّات وطنی و سیاسی‌را که آنرا ثمرهٔ انقلاب اخیر ایران باید شمرد برای اثبات عقیدهٔ خود بنظر ارباب تتبّع می رسانم تا همچون مشکی که بخودی خود ببوید آنچه‌را که من هنوز نگفته در دل دارم بزبان خود بگوید

این نمونهٔ ادبیّات جدیده بخوبی ثابت می کند که روح شعر و طبع سخن پروری در ایران معدوم نشده سهل است که بواسطهٔ سوق این انقلاب اخیر رونق تازهٔ یافته و تأثیر بزرگی در آتیهٔ این ملّت بظهور خواهد آورد،

اگر درست دقّت کنیم خواهیم دید که این اشعار جدیده دارای دو صفت ممتازه است که در ادبیّات قدیمه موجود نبوده و بهمان نسبت شاید تأثیراتش در طبقهٔ عامّه بیشتر باشد

اوّلاً از حیث موضوع: موضوع اشعار قدما تقریباً عبارت بود از مدایح پادشاهان و بزرگان و غزلیّات و اخلاق و فلسفه و تصوّف، و آنچه راجع باوضاع و احوال معاشیّه برشتهٔ نظم در آورده‌اند نسبةً کم است اگرچه همین ادبیّات مدار افتخار ابدی ایران بوده و زبان فارسی‌را تا امروز نگاه داشته است ولی از جهت تأثیر خارجی در اوضاع اجتماعی مردم گویا چندان ثمر نداده است زیرا که دائرهٔ انتشار آن محدود و تقریباً منحصر بطبقهٔ عالیه و عالمهٔ ملّت بوده و فوایدش تعمیم نداشته است

تجارب تاریخی و جریان اوضاع اجتماعی ملل درین قرون اخیره بخوبی نشان میدهد که موثّر حقیقی در گردانیدن چرخ حیات اجتماعی یك ملّت عامّه یعنی طبقات اواسط و ادانی آن ملّت است و چنانکه امواجی که روی دریارا متلاطم آورده و بزرگترین کشتیهارا بازیچهٔ طوفان خود میسازد

تمنّای مخصوص از قارئین ایرانی

مقصود اصلی از جمع و نشر این اشعار آن است که برای برخی از متتبعین ادبیّات ایران که اغلب منکر وجود روح ادبی در ایران کنونی بوده و وجود شعر و شاعری‌را در این قرون اخیره در آن سر زمین معدوم می پندارند ثابت نمائیم که آن طبع گهربار ایرانی که اشعار آبدار قدیمه‌را بوجود آورده نمرده است

هنوز گویندگان هستند اندر عراق   که قوّت ناطقه مدد از ایشان برد

بلکه از زیر آن همه ابرهای تاریك که صفحات این مملکت‌را فرا گرفته باز آن روح فنا ناپذیر مانند آفتابی که زیر ابر نهفته پس از چندی با یك پرتو عالمفروزی دیگر جلوه‌گر گشته است٬

اغلب مستشرقین که زحمت تتبّع ادبیّات جدیدهٔ ایران‌را بخود نداده‌اند چنین تصوّر می کنند که طوطی شکر گفتار طبع شعرا و ادبای اعصار گذشتهٔ ایران از نطق فرو مانده و چندین قرن است که درین چمن خزان دیده بلبلی بترنّم نیامده و شاید هم هیچ نخواهد آمد٬ ولی این جانب که از سی و سه سال بدین طرف عمر خودرا صرف تحصیل این زبان کرده و بواسطهٔ کثرت معاشرت با آقایان ایرانی تا اندازهٔ با اشعار و ادبیّات جدیده مربوط شده و چاشنی آنرا چشیده با این عقیده اشتراك ندارم و قبول آنرا دور از انصاف و حقیقت میدانم٬ وکسانیرا که بر حسب عدم اطّلاع چنین عقیده اظهار میدارند معذور میدارم و عدم الوجدان لیس دلیلًا علی عدم الوجودرا متذکّرم

(بیت)

Cambridge:
PRINTED BY JOHN CLAY, M.A.
AT THE UNIVERSITY PRESS

I. OTHER WORKS, INCLUDING TRANSLATIONS, BY THE AUTHOR OF THIS BOOK

A Traveller's Narrative written to illustrate the Episode of the Báb. Edited in the original Persian, and translated into English, with an Introduction and Explanatory Notes, in two volumes. Vol. I, Persian Text, pp. ٢١١ + iv. Vol. II, English Translation and Notes, pp. lv + 447. Price 15*s.* net. Vol. II, separately. 10*s.* 6*d.* net. Cambridge University Press, 1891.

A Year amongst the Persians: Impressions as to the Life, Character and Thought of the People of Persia, received during twelve months' residence in that country in the years 1887–8. Pp. x + 594. Published at 21*s.* London: A. and C. Black, 1893. (*Out of print.*)

The Ta'ríkh-i-Jadíd or New History of Mírzá 'Alí Muḥammad the Báb...translated from the Persian, with an Introduction, Illustrations and Appendices. Pp. lii + 459 + ٢٦ Price 10*s.* 6*d.* net. Cambridge University Press, 1893.

A Catalogue of the Persian Manuscripts in the Library of the University of Cambridge. Pp. xl + 472. Price 15*s.* Cambridge University Press, 1896.

A Hand-list of the Muḥammadan Manuscripts in the Library of the University of Cambridge. Pp. xviii + 440. Price 15*s.* Cambridge University Press, 1900.

A Literary History of Persia. Vol. I, from the earliest times until Firdawsí. Pp. xiv + 521. Vol. II, from Firdawsí to Sa'dí. Pp. xiv + 568. Price 12*s.* 6*d.* each. London: T. Fisher Unwin, 1902 and 1906.

An Abridged Translation of the History of Ṭabaristán...of Muḥammad ibn Ḥasan ibn Isfandiyár, being Vol. II of the "E. J. W. Gibb Memorial Series." Pp. xv + 356. Price 8*s.* London: Luzac and Co., 1905.

The Persian Revolution of 1905–1909. Pp. xxvi + 470. With 46 illustrations. Price 10*s.* net. Cambridge University Press, 1910. (*Out of print.*)

II. THE PERSIAN HISTORICAL TEXT SERIES

(Five volumes printed by Messrs E. J. Brill of Leyden, and published by them and by Messrs Luzac and Co., London. The complete set is obtainable at the reduced price of 30*s.*; single volumes 7*s.* 6*d.* each.)

(VOL. I.)

The Tadhkiratu'sh-Shu'ará ("Memoirs of the Poets") of Dawlatsháh of Samarqand, 1901, in one volume of pp. يٓ + ٦٢١ + 16. Edited by E. G. BROWNE.

(VOLS. II AND IV.)

The Lubábu'l-Albáb (the oldest biography of Persian Poets, compiled about A.D. 1221) by Muḥammad 'Awfí. Edited by E. G. BROWNE and MÍRZÁ MUḤAMMAD of Qazwín, in two volumes, published in 1903 and 1906. Pp. كه + ٤٣٣ + 11, and و + ٤٧٢ + 78.

(VOLS. III AND V.)

The Tadhkiratu'l-Awliyá ("Memoirs of the Saints") of Shaykh Farídu'd-Dín 'Aṭṭár. Edited by R. A. NICHOLSON, in two volumes, published in 1905 and 1907. Pp. ٣٥٧ + 66 and ٣٦١ + ix + 119.

III. PERSIAN TEXTS EDITED FOR THE "E. J. W. GIBB MEMORIAL" SERIES

By E. G. BROWNE and MÍRZÁ MUḤAMMAD of Qazwín conjointly or separately, and obtainable from Messrs Luzac and Co., 46, Great Russell Street, London, W.C., the Publishers to the Trust.

(VOL. VIII.)

The Marzubán-náma, a book of Fables...by SA'DU'D-DÍN WARÁWÍNÍ. Edited by MÍRZÁ MUḤAMMAD, and published in one volume in 1909. Pp. کز + ٣٠٩ + xvi. Price 8*s*.

(VOL. X.)

Al-Mu'jam fí Ma'áyíri Ash'ári'l-'Ajam, a rare and ancient treatise on the Prosody and Poetic Art of the Persians by SHAMSU'D-DÍN MUḤAMMAD IBN QAYS AR-RÁZÍ. Edited by MÍRZÁ MUḤAMMAD, and published in one volume in 1909. Pp. یط + ١٢* + ٤٦٤ + xx. Price 8*s*.

(VOL. XI.)

Chahár Maqála ("The Four Discourses") by NIẒÁMÍ AL-'ARÚḌÍ of Samarqand. Edited, with Introduction, Notes and Indices, by MÍRZÁ MUḤAMMAD, and published in one volume in 1910. Pp. که + ٣٦٠ + xxiv. Price 8*s*. (An English translation, by E. G. BROWNE was published in the *Journal of the Royal Asiatic Society* (Vol. XXXI) in 1899, and can be obtained as a separate reprint from the Secretary of the Society, 22, Albemarle Street, London, W., or from Messrs Luzac and Co., 46, Great Russell Street, London, W.C.)

(VOLS. XIV, 1 AND 2.)

The Ta'ríkh-i-Guzída ("Select History") of Ḥamdu'lláh Mustawfí-i-Qazwíní, compiled in A.D. 1330, reproduced in facsimile from a MS. written in A.D. 1453, with a Translation by E. G. BROWNE and Indices by R. A. NICHOLSON. Vol. I, containing the facsimile of the text, 1910; Vol. II, containing the Translation and Indices, 1913. Pp. یج + ٨٥٣ + xix and xxi + 237 + ٢٨٦. Price 15*s*. and 10*s*. respectively.

(VOL. XV.)

The Kitáb-i-Nuqṭatu'l-Káf, being the earliest history of the Bábís, compiled by ḤÁJJI MÍRZÁ JÁNÍ of Káshán between the years A.D. 1850 and 1852, edited from the unique Paris MS. (Suppl. Pers. 1071) by E. G. BROWNE. One volume, 1910. Pp. عج + ٢٩٧ + xcv. Price 8*s*.

(VOLS. XVI, 1.)

The Ta'ríkh-i-Jahán-gushá of 'Alá'u'd-Dín 'Aṭá Malik-i-Juwayní, composed in A.D. 1260, in three volumes. Vol. I (all as yet published) containing the history of Chingíz Khán and his successors, edited with an Introduction, Notes and Indices from several old MSS. by MÍRZÁ MUḤAMMAD and published in 1912. Vol. II is in the Press, and Vol. III in preparation. Pp. قکح + ٢٩٤ + xciv. Price 8*s*.

IV. ARTICLES CONTRIBUTED FROM 1889 TO 1908 TO THE JOURNAL OF THE ROYAL ASIATIC SOCIETY

Separate reprints of the later ones (Nos. 10–20) can in most cases be obtained from the Author, or from the Secretary of the Society, 22, Albemarle Street, London, W., or from Messrs Luzac and Co.

1. **The Bábís of Persia.** I. Sketch of their History, and Personal Experiences amongst them. II. Their Literature and Doctrines. (*J.R.A.S.*, Vol. XXI, 1889.)

2. **Some Remarks on the Bábí Texts,** edited by BARON VICTOR ROSEN... (*J.R.A.S.*, Vol. XXIV, 1892.)

3. **Catalogue and Description of 27 Bábí Manuscripts.** (*J.R.A.S.*, Vol. XXIV, 1892.)

4. **Description of an Old Persian Commentary on the Qur'án.** (*J.R.A.S.*, Vol. XXVI, 1894.)

5. **Some Notes on the Poetry of the Persian Dialects.** (*J.R.A.S.*, Vol. XXVII, 1895.)

6. **A Specimen of the Gabrí Dialect of Persia.** (*J.R.A.S.*, Vol. XXIX, 1897.)

7. **Personal Reminiscences of the Bábí Insurrection at Zanján in 1850**....translated from the Persian. (*J.R.A.S.*, Vol. XXIX, 1897.)

8. **Some Notes on the Literature and Doctrines of the Ḥurúfí Sect.** (*J.R.A.S.*, Vol. XXX, 1898.)

9. **The Sources of Dawlatsháh**; with some Remarks on the Materials available for a Literary History of Persia, and an Excursus on Bárbad and Rúdagí. (*J.R.A.S.*, Vol. XXXI, 1899.)

10. **Yet More Light on 'Umar-i-Khayyám.** (*J.R.A.S.*, Vol. XXXI, 1899.)

11. **The Chahár Maqála** ("Four Discourses") **of Nidhámí-i-'Arúḍí-i-Samarqandí**, translated into English. (*J.R.A.S.*, Vol. XXXI, 1899.) Price 3*s.* paper covers, 4*s.* cloth.

12. **Some Account of the...Niháyatu'l-irab fí akhbári'l-Furs wa'l-'Arab**, particularly of that part which treats of the Persian Kings. (*J.R.A.S.*, Vol. XXXII, 1900.)

13. **Biographies of Persian Poets** contained in Ch. V, § 6, of the *Táríkh-i-Guzída*, or "Select History" of Ḥamdu'lláh Mustawfí of Qazwín. (*J.R.A.S.*, Vols. XXXII–XXXIII, 1900–1901.)

14. **Account of a rare manuscript History of Iṣfahán**, presented to the Royal Asiatic Society on May 19, 1827, by Sir John Malcolm. (*J.R.A.S.*, Vol. XXXIII, 1901.)

15. **Account of a rare manuscript History of the Seljúqs** in the Schefer Collection of MSS. in the Bibliothèque Nationale at Paris. (*J.R.A.S.*, Vol. XXXIV, 1902.)

16. **Note on the Contents of the Ta'ríkh-i-Jahán-gushá** of 'Aṭá Malik-i-Juwayní. (*J.R.A.S.*, Vol. XXXVI, 1904.)

17. **Náṣir-i-Khusraw, Poet, Traveller, and Propagandist.** (*J.R.A.S.*, Vol. XXXVII, 1905.)

18. **Mas'úd-i-Sa'd-i-Salmán**, by MÍRZÁ MUḤAMMAD IBN 'ABDU'L-WAHHÁB of Qazwín. (*J.R.A.S.*, Vols. XXXVII–XXXVIII, 1905–1906.)

19. **Further Notes on the Literature of the Ḥurúfís and their connection with the Bektáshí Order of Dervishes.** (*J.R.A.S.*, Vol. XXXIX, 1907.)

20. **Suggestions for a complete edition of the "Jámi'u't-Tawáríkh" of Rashidu'd-Dín Faḍlu'lláh.** (*J.R.A.S.*, Vol. XL, 1908.)

V. POLITICAL PAMPHLETS ON PERSIA

A Brief Narrative of Recent Events in Persia, followed by an Appendix on the Persian Constitution. Pp. 101. Luzac and Co., London, 1909. Price 1*s*.

The Persian Crisis of December, 1911, how it arose and whither it may lead us, compiled for the use of the Persia Committee, privately printed at the University Press, Cambridge, and published on New Year's Day, 1912. Pp. 18.

The Reign of Terror at Tabríz: England's Responsibility: with Photographs and a brief Narrative of the events of December, 1911, and January, 1912, compiled for the use of the Persia Committee and published in October, 1912, by Messrs Taylor, Garnett, Evans, and Co., Blackfriars Street, Manchester, and Messrs Luzac and Co., London. Pp. 15. With the Photographs. Price 6*d*.

VI. PAPERS READ TO AND PUBLISHED FOR THE PERSIA SOCIETY,

By John Hogg, 13, Paternoster Row, London, E.C.

The Literature of Persia, a Lecture delivered to the Persia Society on April 26, 1912. Pp. 43. Price 1*s*.

The Persian Press and Persian Journalism, a Lecture delivered to the Persia Society on May 23, 1913. Pp. 28. Price 1*s*.

VII. A History of Ottoman Poetry, by the late E. J. W. GIBB, M.R.A.S., in six volumes. Vol. I, 1900; Vols. II–VI, 1902–9, edited by E. G. BROWNE. Vol. VI contains the Turkish originals of the poems translated in the previous volumes. A seventh volume, dealing with the most modern period, by Dr RIẒÁ TEVFÍQ, formerly Deputy for Adrianople in the Ottoman Parliament, is in course of preparation. Price 21*s*. net each volume except Vol. V, which is 12*s*. 6*d*. net. Luzac and Co., London.

ImTheStory.com

Personalized Classic Books in many genre's

Unique gift for kids, partners, friends, colleagues

Customize:

- **Character Names**
- **Upload your own front/back cover images (optional)**
- **Inscribe a personal message/dedication on the inside page (optional)**

Customize many titles Including

- Alice in Wonderland
- Romeo and Juliet
- The Wizard of Oz
- A Christmas Carol
- Dracula
- Dr. Jekyll & Mr. Hyde
- And more...

Lightning Source UK Ltd.
Milton Keynes UK
UKOW01f1006080817
306905UK00014B/1454/P

9 781313 498784